URBA
POLITI
AND PUBL
POLIC

URBAN POLITICS AND PUBLIC POLICY

THIRD EDITION

Robert L. Lineberry

NORTHWESTERN UNIVERSITY

Ira Sharkansky

UNIVERSITY OF WISCONSIN, MADISON,
AND HEBREW UNIVERSITY OF JERUSALEM

HARPER & ROW,
PUBLISHERS
New York
Hagerstown
San Francisco
London

Sponsoring Editor: Dale Tharp
Project Editor: David Nickol
Designer: Emily Harste
Production Supervisor: Marion A. Palen
Photo Researcher: Myra Schachne
Compositor: Ruttle, Shaw & Wetherill, Inc.
Printer and Binder: The Murray Printing Company
Art Studio: Vantage Art Inc.
Cover Photo: Herwig, Stock, Boston

Photo Credits
DeWys, 25, 284, 354; Johnson, DeWys, 345; Lavine, DeWys, 50;
World Wide, 7, 68, 93, 145, 176, 219, 227, 264, 306.

**URBAN
POLITICS
AND PUBLIC
POLICY,
Third Edition**

Copyright © 1978 by Robert L. Lineberry and Ira Sharkansky

All rights reserved. Printed in the United States of America. No
part of this book may be used or reproduced in any manner
whatsoever without written permission except in the case of brief
quotations embodied in critical articles and reviews. For information
address Harper & Row, Publishers, Inc., 10 East 53rd Street,
New York, N.Y. 10022.

Library of Congress Cataloging in Publication Data

Lineberry, Robert L
    Urban politics and public policy.

    Includes bibliographical references and indexes.
      1. Metropolitan government—United States.
2. Metropolitan areas—United States.   I. Sharkansky,
Ira, joint author. II. Title.
JS422.L54 1978   352'.008'0973   77-17809
ISBN 0-06-044029-5

CONTENTS

v

PREFACE

This new edition of *Urban Politics and Public Policy* reflects our
continuing emphasis on policy choices within the urban community as
well as those made elsewhere that shape the quality of urban life.
That one of us now shares an appointment with a non-American institution and that both of us are increasingly conscious of an interdependent
urban world have caused us to examine more seriously the American city
in an international context. We emphasize throughout that urban politics
is profoundly shaped by the city's political economy and its political
sociology. The movement of persons and production, families and firms,
alters the landscape of the city and redistributes policy problems from
rural to urban areas, from city to suburb, and from region to region.
We have also tried, in this edition, to emphasize variations from one city
to another. As often as available data and space permit, we show
comparative rankings of cities on various dimensions, including air
pollution, fiscal strain, segregation, and other quality-of-life indexes.
The inclusion of a separate "index of cities" will permit the reader to
locate the mention of his or her own locale as an example or illustration.
Our facts or interpretations may on occasion be wrong or outdated;
we can know intimately only a few cities. But the use of specific cases
and comparative rankings should, we hope, bring more concreteness
and less abstraction to the study of urban politics and policy.

It is a bit difficult to collaborate on a book when separated by an
ocean. But our efforts have been made easier by valued cooperation,
especially from our wives, but from others as well. David Caputo, Peter
Eisenger, Harlan Hahn, Albert Karnig, H. Owen Porter, and Thomas
Scott provided valuable comments on the second edition, which shaped
our thinking on this one. Dale Tharp and his colleagues at Harper & Row
exhibited virtues like patience and prodding. We hold these people
blameless for any errors, as coauthors can always blame one another.

R.L.L.
I.S.

PART ONE
Prologue

1

ON THE STATE OF THE CITY AND THE STUDY OF URBAN POLITICS

Decrying the state of the American city is nothing new. From Thomas Jefferson, one can trace a straight line of despair about the city which culminates today in the "fiscal crisis," the "crime problem," and the "problem of urban decay." In this chapter, we

- emphasize the importance of understanding the city in terms of the quality of urban life and the contribution of politics and public policy to urban life quality
- introduce a model of the urban political system to aid our understanding
- emphasize a policy approach to urban political analysis

In Philadelphia more than 100,000 citizens (the number was much disputed) signed a petition demanding the recall of their mayor, tough ex-cop Frank Rizzo. He had promised, the signers claimed, not to raise taxes but had decided to do so anyway. In Oklahoma City, San Francisco, and elsewhere the police were on strike. In Washington, D.C., the Congress and the president debated about whether to bail New York City out of its brush with bankruptcy. In Boston, a large-scale school-busing program produced violence, even though a similar one began without major conflict in Detroit. Somewhere—nowhere in particular—a crime was committed, a welfare check was cashed, a civic group protested some dereliction of local authority, and a city manager sent out budget instructions to his department heads.

All of this is urban political life. Not all of it actually occurs within the city hall or even within the municipal borders. What happens in Washington, the state capital, and other local governments shapes political activity in any particular city. In this book we are concerned with urban politics and the public policies that shape the quality of urban life. Americans since Thomas Jefferson have long despaired over the nature of urban existence. Too often, however, urban commentators simply list dozens of urban problems. Doing that can produce an infinitely long "laundry list." Instead, in this chapter we discuss the state of the American city in the context of the urban political system and offer a policy approach for understanding city politics.

THE STATE
OF THE CITY

The Urban Crisis,
Old and New

It has long been fashionable to deplore the state of the city. Thomas Jefferson pronounced European cities "rat infested," and hoped that American cities never became like them. Lord Bryce, the distinguished British observer of American Life in the 1880s, called American cities the "one conspicuous failure" of American democracy. Lincoln Steffans became famous for his muckraking book, *The Shame of the Cities.*

More recently, the 1960s was the decade of the "urban crisis." It was sandwiched in between the earlier missile crisis and the later energy crisis. Even a glance at book titles from the 1960s — *Sick Cities, Cities in a Race with Time, The Death and Life of Great American Cities, The Metropolitan Enigma, The Urban Dilemma, The Unheavenly City* — suggests that the quality of urban life was increasingly inhospitable. Any listing could be extended almost *ad nauseum.* To take but a handful of examples:

- *The Fiscal Crisis.* New York City and other communities, large and small, teeter on the brink of bankruptcy.
- *The Crime Problem.* Nearly two major crimes are committed annually for every 100 persons.
- *The Pollution Problem.* Water and air pollution have reached such levels as to make human habitation in the city unpleasant for many and nearly impossible for others.
- *The Racial Problem.* The appearance of 200 instances of collective racial disorders in the period 1963–1969 suggests the severity of the racial problem.
- *The Tax Problem.* Some cities are forced to cut back on traditional services in the face of fiscal constraints, while urban tax rates spiral ever higher.
- *The Housing Problem.* For many Americans, the poor especially, but also the middle classes, housing choices are costly and often unsatisfactory.
- *The Poverty Problem.* Despite a decade of commitment to eradicating poverty, many people remain poor amid a sea of affluence.
- *The Fiscal Inequities Problem.* Some urban citizens enjoy the finest levels of public service which money and administrative know-how can produce, while others suffer the leavings.
- *The Police Problem.* Half of all ghetto dwellers believe — rightly or wrongly — that police brutality occurs in their neighborhoods.

We could extend this list by raising issues in education, transportation, energy, and so on. But in its brief form it is long enough to illustrate the widespread feeling that things in the city have gone awry.

Not all problems, of course, are crises. One may have a problem choosing between a big car and a small one, but the choice hardly constitutes a crisis. Not all urban problems are of crisis proportions. Even a summation of all the individual urban problems may not produce an overarching crisis. A crisis exists when life itself is threatened, or when problems threaten to grow to intolerable proportions. Whether these problems constitute crisis is a matter of opinion. One can believe that *any* amount of crime, *any* level of pollution, or *any* incident of poverty is intolerable. However meritorious as goals, it is fair to ask what amount of public resources should be used to eliminate such problems entirely, and whether unacceptable side effects of such policies would be encountered. The elimination of *all* crime might require a policeman in every bar, store, and residence; the elimination of *all* pollution would require, not only vast expenditures, but maybe a dramatic reduction in our standard of living. A policy is never free of costs and can rarely be evaluated in isolation from its effects on other problems. The choices are never simple because sometimes an improvement of one problem may exacerbate another. Decision makers must make — sometimes consciously, more often unconsciously — tradeoffs between policy alternatives.

Unfortunately crisis rhetoric has a "Peter and the Wolf" ring to it. As Americans tired of hearing that cities were on the brink, and as the urban violence of the 1960s dissipated, President Richard M. Nixon announced in 1972 that the urban crisis was over. The urban condition is, however, more complex than that.

Urban Politics and the Quality of Urban Life

In this book we steer a midpassage between the crisis rhetoric about cities and a "neutral" or "value free" analysis of urban politics devoid of its impact on people's lives. Assessing the impact of politics and policy on the "quality of life" is a tricky business. Standards change over time; different people have different views of "the good life"; some "objective" assessments of life quality do not match people's "subjective" assessment of their situation.[1] There is, however, sobering evidence that quality of life concerns are becoming more significant. A Louis Harris poll in the fall of 1976 showed that 44 percent of the public believes that the quality of life has deteriorated in recent years, 35 percent feels that it has improved, and 19 percent think that it has held constant.

What makes for a good city? Often we define life quality not so much in terms of good things, as in terms of "bads" that we desire to avoid, such as pollution, crime, congestion, and poverty. One intriguing effort is Arthur Louis's attempt to identify the "worst American city."[2] He took a battery of 24 indexes of life quality in the 50 largest cities, including measures of crime rates, park space, pollution levels, educational attainments, and scored each city by its collective ranking on all 24 measures. His index is subject to criticism, and we present his findings in Table 1.1 as merely suggestive.

Newark easily scores as the worst city.[3] Ranked among the 5 worst on 19 of the 24 categories, and dead last in 9, it holds no peer among the candidates for last place.

Despite the need for caution with any such overall rankings, one may nonetheless search for patterns. There are prominent regional differences in Louis's results. No older city from the Northeast makes the top ten. Places such as New York, Chicago, St. Louis, Newark, Boston, Baltimore, Cleveland, and Philadelphia appear well below

Table 1.1   The "Worst American City": Overall Mean Scores on 24 Indicators[a]

1. Seattle (average rank: 14.0)	26. Oakland (25.9)
2. Tulsa (14.8)	27. Washington (26.5)
3. San Diego (14.9)	28. Houston (27.4)
4. San Jose (15.6)	29. Buffalo (28.2)
5. Honolulu (16.4)	29. Louisville (28.2)
6. Portland (17.8)	31. Pittsburgh (28.4)
7. Denver (18.2)	32. New York (28.5)
8. Minneapolis (18.8)	33. Memphis (29.3)
9. Oklahoma City (19.1)	34. Boston (29.6)
10. Omaha (19.3)	35. Miami (29.9)
11. San Francisco (19.46)	36. Atlanta (30.0)
12. Nashville (19.54)	37. El Paso (30.7)
13. St. Paul (19.6)	37. New Orleans (30.7)
14. Columbus (19.75)	39. Philadelphia (31.0)
15. Toledo (19.79)	40. Tampa (31.1)
16. Indianapolis (20.6)	41. San Antonio (31.7)
17. Long Beach (21.2)	42. Norfolk (31.9)
18. Milwaukee (21.9)	43. Cleveland (32.0)
19. Kansas City (22.6)	44. Jacksonville (32.2)
20. Dallas (23.25)	45. Birmingham (32.5)
21. Phoenix (23.33)	46. Baltimore (32.7)
22. Los Angeles (24.6)	47. Detroit (33.0)
23. Fort Worth (24.7)	48. Chicago (33.7)
24. Cincinnati (24.9)	49. St. Louis (35.3)
25. Rochester (25.3)	50. Newark (41.6)

[a] Cities ranked from "best" to "worst" on combined index of 24 indicators.

Source: Arthur Louis, "The Worst American City," *Harper's Magazine,* January 1975, p. 71.

the median. Less obvious, but perhaps more important, is a strong correlation between the racial composition of cities and their "quality" ranking. The rank-order correlation between percent nonwhite and Louis's estimate of a city's quality is a substantial −.68.[4] The worse the city, in other words, the greater its nonwhite concentration. Either nonwhites in the United States have quite different conceptions of urban life quality than does Louis, or they tend to be clustered in cities with the most severe social and economic problems.

The nuances in this assessment of urban quality need not detain us long. In an important sense, however, the purpose of this volume is to show how a city's social and economic environments are related, through its politics and public policy choices, to the quality of life of its citizens. Edward C. Banfield offers such goals for students of urban politics:[5]

One would like to be able to show how particular causes produce particular effects. If one could trace out several links in a causal sequence, that would be especially satisfying. Thus, one might begin by showing how certain "starting place" [environmental] characteristics of a city, such as its size, rate of growth, economic function, rate of home ownership, or the class or ethnic composition of its population exert a causal influence on the form and style of its government. (By "form and style" is meant whether the electoral system is partisan or nonpartisan, whether the office of mayor is strong or weak, whether the city council is elected on a ward basis or at large, whether the system is centralized or

Seattle has been rated by two magazines as one of the most liveable cities in the United States.

decentralized, and so on.) A second link might be established by showing the causal connections between form and style on the one hand and the content of the city government's policy on the other. . . . A third link might be established by showing a causal connection between the content of city government policy and the quality of life in the city.

Banfield would link the analysis of urban politics and policy with the quality of life in the city. We should stress, of course, that this goal is unlikely to be attained soon. There is neither wide agreement on, nor any reliable measure of, the quality of urban life. We have, at best, an idea of some of the things that are *not desirable*. Whether policy makers can design policies to rid urban society of its unwanted traits remains problematic for reasons we address throughout this book.

City and Metropolis:
Some Definitions

The city, as we conceive of it here, is a set of human beings and their institutions, interacting in a densely settled finite space, producing and distributing economic resources and other values. Geographer David Harvey emphasizes that an understanding of the city "must somehow relate the social processes in the city to the spatial form which the city assumes. . . . Any successful strategy must appreciate that spatial form and social process are different ways of thinking about the same thing."[6] The social—and more particularly, the political—processes within the city sort families and firms into different physical spaces, maximizing or reducing their access to valued commodities such as housing, jobs, markets, clean air, and open space. The city is a distributional mechanism. This is true of the city as a whole, and of the government within it. The city allocates many of its values through the policy choices of its government.

Perhaps we should use this early opportunity to define what a city *is* instead of merely what a city *does*. A classical formulation of cities and urbanism is by Louis Wirth:[7]

On the basis of three variables, number, density of settlement, and heterogeneity of the urban population, it appears possible to explain the characteristics of urban life and to account for differences between cities of various types and sizes.

Cities differ from rural areas, and from each other, on all of Wirth's dimensions of size, density, and heterogeneity. In terms of *size*, cities range from the Census Bureau's lower limit of 2,500 people up to New York's 7 million. But actually the legal entity called a municipality is hardly ever coterminous with the social and economic city. In most urban areas, the borders between municipalities are imperceptible, and only street signs separate one from another. The Census Bureau has therefore defined a *standard metropolitan statistical area* (SMSA) as a central city or contiguous twin cities consisting of at least 50,000 people together with its county and contiguous counties with a metropolitan character.[8] An SMSA thus consists of a dominant central city (CC) plus a number of suburban governments, special districts, and school districts. The governmental fragmentation within an SMSA goes hand in hand with social and economic interdependence.

Density also varies within and between cities. Older cities are almost always more densely settled per square mile, and older neighborhoods are more dense than newer ones. Suburbs are normally less dense than their central cities, for reasons related to land values and their construction in the automobile era. Density does not always imply decay, although it is often related to deterioration, crime rates, congestion, and other indications of problems. Density can also suggest a life style near the core of a city and its "bright lights," which attract many people willing to pay dearly for an urban life. The magnificent and expensive concrete, steel, and glass high-rises of the big city represent a high-density life style, replete with saunas, shops, and swimming pools.

Heterogeneity is Wirth's third dimension of urbanism. The city is a mosaic of racial, ethnic, occupational, religious, and ideological groups. Their differences generate both interdependence and conflict. The spatial proximity of high density heightens the contacts and tensions among diverse interests. One of the critical issues of urban life is how people distribute themselves — and are distributed by others — over finite space. Class, racial, and ethnic segregation are old issues that appear in new guises each generation. In this generation they provoke issues such as school busing, white flight, and "exclusionary zoning" in the suburbs. Much of urban politics is conflict among heterogeneous groups competing for dominance in a densely settled "turf."

No one doubts that the American population is now an urban one; the watershed was passed with the 1920 census, which first found a majority of the population living in urban areas. Today three-fourths of the population live in urban places. Yet such a conclusion is partly an artifact of the Census Bureau's historic definition of an "urban place" as any incorporated municipality of at least 2,500 people. If we limit our notion of "urban" only to residents of SMSAs, two-thirds of the population qualifies. Only a third live in cities with a population of 50,000 or more. If we limited our notion of urban to cities of 1 million or more, we encounter less than 10 percent of the population. Most Americans *are* urbanites, but they do not live only in big cities such as Boston, Buffalo, Los Angeles, Denver, Atlanta, Houston, Cleveland, Chicago, New York, or Seattle. To understand "urban politics" as "big city politics" is to fall wide of the mark. For a plurality of Americans, urban life is *suburban* life. The proportion of people residing in SMSAs but outside the central city now outnumbers the central-city population. Urban political life exists also in a host of medium-sized places such as Tulsa, Knoxville, Springfield, Orlando, Tacoma, and Austin. Big cities have no monopoly on political conflict or on policy problems. The issues we raise in this book would have little meaning for most of our readers if they were confined to the handful of urban giants in the country. A balanced view of American urbanization recognizes that most Americans are urbanites and that urban places come in many shapes and sizes.

Nonetheless, Americans have never been fully comfortable as urbanites. There is a long history of anti-urbanism by intellectuals and an equally long history of discomfit by city residents. Many contemporary urbanites share Jefferson's aversion to cities. Their preference is for smaller rather than larger urban communities. One survey revealed that 18 percent of the population prefers to live in a city, while 22 percent want a suburb, 19 percent prefer a town, and a plurality of 38 percent prefer a rural area.[9] One of the most remarkable bits of news to come out of the Census Bureau in recent years is that nonmetropolitan counties are increasing in population, following several decades of decline. A few Americans — a trickle should not be confused with a torrent — have actualized their anti-urban preferences by leaving urban areas.

THE IDEA OF
A POLITICAL SYSTEM

This book highlights the relationships between politics and the social and economic features of urban life. Fortunately, other political scientists have worked on this issue of uniting politics with its surroundings. David Easton describes a model of the "political system" that we can modify to suit our purposes.[10] Our model describes various political, economic, and social elements, and the linkages between them: an *environment* that includes the economic and social characteristics of a community that impinge on the local government, as well as the relevant activities of national and state governments; *inputs* that transmit stimuli from the environment; a *conversion* process made up of individuals and agencies that respond to the inputs; the *outputs*, or policies formulated by decision makers in the conversion process; the *impact* of policies on the environment; and the *feedback* of subsequent inputs to decision makers in response to policy impacts. The model itself presents abstract categories that are devoid of political, economic, and social dynamics. Yet the abstractions warrant at least brief attention. They are a guide to the details of urban politics and public policy that appear in later chapters. An overview of the urban system model appears in Figure 1.1.

Figure 1.1   A Political System

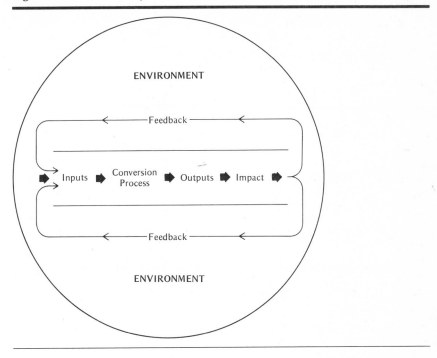

The Environment

A political system exists in an environment. "Environment" does not mean only the physical environment, although that is an important part of the environment. Rather, the term *environment* embraces all social and economic elements that shape the nature of the inputs. In this book, Part One is about the environment of the urban political system. We describe both the political sociology and the political economy of the American urban political system. The great migrations to the city, and away from the city to the suburbs, have profoundly influenced the nature of city politics. The arrival of ethnic immigrants and the migration of blacks to the city both produced service demands and demands for status, recognition, and equality. The economic decentralization of the metropolis has produced demands for policies to curb decay in the central city and to manage growth in the suburban areas.

Inputs

Inputs include demands or commitments of resources by individuals or groups that are intended to influence the choices of decision makers and thereby to alter public policies. In a very simple political system, such as a very small town, the input process is informal and in-terpersonal.[11] The only political resources needed are friendship and a little time. In larger political systems, the input process is imper-sonal and institutional. Political parties, elections, interest groups, and even mass demonstrations dominate the process. In a country such as the United States, with three layers of government that offer resources and press claims on one another, it is not possible to con-sider cities in isolation from other governments. Washington and the state capitals are prominent among the suppliers of inputs to the urban political system.

New York City's fiscal future, for example, was directly affected by inputs from the federal government in the form of loan guarantees. The conflict over busing in Boston was largely sparked by a federal judge's order to desegregate city schools.

Conversion

Decision makers convert inputs into *outputs*. Urban decision makers may be limited to elected and appointed officials and bureaucrats, or they may include members of a relatively concealed power structure of private citizens. They take the raw materials presented to them in the form of demands and resources and use them to determine public policy. Decision makers, however, are not neutral computers, auto-matically summing up resources and constraints. Rather, they are human beings who set limitations on their decisions and feel addi-tional limits from the institutions in which they operate.

Outputs and Impact

As Richard E. Dawson and James A. Robinson have pointed out, many political scientists view public policy as "the major dependent vari-able which political science seeks to explain. The task of political sci-ence, then, is to find and explain the independent and intervening variables which account for policy differences."[12] We concur in this statement of objectives, because we know that different urban politi-cal systems pursue different policies, spend more or less money, and tax more or less heavily. A major goal of this book, then, is to explain and understand such variations. But we must also understand the im-pact of policies upon urban populations.

It is tempting to view policies as the end-product of the urban polit-ical system, insofar as they are the culmination of the inputs that are processed by the decision makers. But politics does not really end with the enunciation and implementation of policies. Policies have impacts, sometimes intended, sometimes unintended. They may ac-complish precisely what decision makers desire, no more and no less, but more commonly there is slippage between the goals of a policy and its actual impact. Moreover, policies generally have side effects or unintended consequences. The impact of, and feedback from, a particular policy can be positive or negative, depending upon the goals of the policy.

Feedback

The feedback that comes to decision makers in response to the impacts of earlier policies is an imperfect guide to future policy. There are two broad kinds of feedback, one a "when-the-shoe-pinches" feedback and the other a feedback from technical research on policy impact. The when-the-shoe-pinches type most often takes the form of public complaints. Elected officials are particularly sensitive to this kind of feedback, especially if it comes from groups whose votes they need. Feedback from technical research into policy questions is relatively new. If technical analysis of policy impacts becomes more common, it may be possible to evaluate them in a systematic and continuous way, without having to wait for grievances to build to a boiling point.

MACROANALYSIS
AND MICROANALYSIS

The model of the urban political system should accommodate the distinction between macro- and microanalysis. This distinction helps to explain the behavior of whole communities (macro) as well as such subcommunity units as neighborhoods, groups, or individuals (micro).[13]

Macroanalysis deals with the behavior or properties of communities. When we explain variations in the level of public expenditures or segregation in housing, we are explaining differences between communities. When we discuss why municipalities within a metropolis have or have not coalesced into a metropolitan government, we are explaining the interactions of communities. We also use macroanalysis when we generalize about the governmental structures of a community, and refer to them as centralized or decentralized, reformed or unreformed.

Microanalysis examines the behaviors and interactions of individuals and other subcommunity units, such as groups, parties, councils, or administrative agencies. To explain who participates in riots, how budgetary decisions are reached, and what social and psychological traits affect individual participation in municipal elections is to utilize microanalysis.

The macro–micro distinction enables us to examine any particular behavior from either or both perspectives. Political participation, for example, may vary both from city to city and from individual to individual. Quite often, some additional insights can be gained by examining political participation as a function of both macro (community-level) and micro (individual-level) attributes.[14]

For example, one of the most common characteristics of participation in politics is its strong relationship to indicators of social status. Individuals with higher levels of income and education are more likely than the average to vote and otherwise to participate. Interestingly, however, when we take a macro perspective and examine the levels of turnout from community to community, we find that one measure of social status, education, is actually negatively related to the turnout rates. This finding is puzzling unless we use macroanalysis to explore how a community and its social structure an influence individual voters. Then we discover that the communities with generally high educational attainments are often culturally homogeneous – as in the prototypical dormitory suburb, for example – and have fewer bases of social conflict. Homogeneous communities generate fewer of the political issues that impel people to vote. It is the mixture of social and economic traits in a community that produces political conflict. In local elections citizens in well-educated communities may thus simply have fewer incentives to participate. Many political phenomena other than political participation can also best be understood by examining both their micro and macro dimensions.

The combined use of macro- and microanalysis also directs our attention to the *discrete* (individual) and *contextual* (environmental) factors in political behavior. Microanalysis without attention to macro-level properties may produce serious distortions by leading to a personalistic and voluntaristic view of local politics. Such a perspective, for instance, might attribute policy making to the values of the policy makers without taking account of the environmental constraints upon their behavior. We emphasize throughout this book the myriad ways in which the environment impinges on and constrains individual choices. For example, the economic base of a community is particularly important in determining the availability of resources. In deciding upon spending and taxing levels, city officials are not free to choose any level of spending they desire, because numerous community factors, not the least of which is the availability of resources, place limits on their discretion.

In 1975 New York City faced the prospect of bankruptcy as available resources appeared to be far short of current demands. Bills for salaries, supplies, pensions, and payments on past loans surpassed the receipts from taxes, service charges, established state and federal aids, and loans available from conventional sources. New York's plight and its subsequent relations with Albany and Washington variously threatened the collapse of important services and changes in the nature of federal–state–local relations. Indeed a major theme of this book (particularly in Chapters 4 and 9) is the stringent limitations imposed on urban decision makers by factors outside their control.

On the other hand, macroanalysis, without the corrective provided by microanalysis, may promote a deterministic view of local politics. To view economic forces, social structures, and other macro properties as the only explanations for social change implies that "forces" and "processes," rather than individuals, are the prime movers in such change. In sum, balanced assessment of urban politics emphasizes both macroscopic and microscopic explanations.

A MODEL OF THE URBAN POLITICAL SYSTEM

If we combine the elements in the system model with the macro–micro distinction, we can construct the more elaborate model of an urban political system shown in Figure 1.2. Each element in the political system—inputs, conversion process, outputs, impact, and feedback—can be identified at the macro (community) level, and each has an analogue at the micro (subcommunity) level.

Figure 1.2 emphasizes the environment as the source of *resources* and *constraints*. Availability of resources to individuals and groups depends in part, though not entirely, upon the magnitude of community resources. The availability of micro-level resources will enable individuals and groups to make demands on decision makers, and the availability of macro-level resources will enable decision makers to respond to these demands.[15]

Figure 1.2   Micro and Macro Elements of the Urban Political System

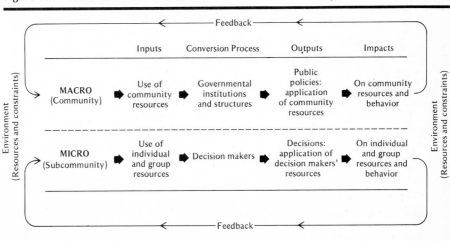

A POLICY APPROACH
TO THE CITY

Public policy making is choice taking. The critical feature of policy making is that one cannot, in policy making as in life itself, have one's cake and eat it, too. There are always tensions — economists sometimes call them tradeoffs — between maximizing one goal and another. Policy cannot encourage an automobile-based transportation system without incurring costs in pollution and energy depletion. Policy cannot encourage growth in one part of the metropolis without expecting decay somewhere else. Sometimes policies in one area may exacerbate the problems in another area. Urban policy making is a tangled web of interlocking choices. Municipal officials are rarely free to design their own policy menus, simply because the American city is deeply enmeshed in a federal system. What Washington and the state capitals do affects what urban officials can do.

Some of the policy problems of the city involve money. In Chapter 4, we show that the "irony of urban wealth" puts vast human and economic resources just beyond the reach of municipal officials. In a few areas, cities teeter on the brink of bankruptcy. In Newark, New Jersey, property taxes have risen to staggering levels — almost $2,000 on a house worth $20,000 — and further increases work mainly to drive more citizens to the suburbs, leaving behind those most in need of services and least able to pay.

One judge in New Jersey ordered Newark officials to jail because they would not comply with his court order, which would have resulted in a tax increase. Those officials were painfully aware of urban policy making as a series of tradeoffs and hard choices. A handful of cities, like New York City and Hamtramck, Michigan, for example, have investigated the possibility of municipal bankruptcy proceedings. Presently these examples are extreme and fortunately atypical. More common is the city whose financial resources are tolerable but which seems barely able to maintain traditional police, library, fire, and other services. In such places it is seldom possible to meet demands for new services. In Chapter 9, we shall investigate the urban public finance system, elucidate its problems, and describe its processes.

But even if cities were to solve their financial problems overnight, many policy dilemmas would persist. More serious than the problem of money are the problems of knowledge and information. The production and distribution of knowledge in the United States has multiplied many times in recent decades, yet policies formulated on the basis of inaccurate information still produce frustration. To adopt a policy and proclaim its virtues is one thing; to assure its success is another. Decision makers have often been more eager to proclaim and adopt policies than to evaluate and analyze their impacts. Lyndon Johnson once observed of the presidency that the problem was not to *do* what was right, but to *know* what was right. The presidency has no monopoly on such problems. Even if there were widespread consensus on eliminating the problem of poverty, for example, the number of alternative strategies is large indeed. Some would advocate giving political power to the poor, arguing that the dilemma of the poor is their lack of political clout. Some advocate a guaranteed annual income, arguing that a financial floor will enable the poor to meet minimal needs. Others advocate investments in education or skills development, others demand improvements in child-rearing or socialization patterns of poor children. Obviously if resources are limited — and the nature of politics and economics always limits resources — then one cannot do everything at once. Choices must be made, and it is the nature of these choices with which we are concerned in the remainder of this book.

Our own position on the problem of urban policy is that the problem of knowledge is in the long run more important than the problem of money. Just as money does not buy happiness, neither does it guarantee the solution of an urban problem, unless it is used wisely and well.

SUMMARY

We have outlined in this chapter some perspectives useful for understanding the rest of the book. We use the model of a political system to analyze urban politics and public policy. The political system is embedded in its environment, which is the source of both resources and constraints. The task of urban decision makers is to convert inputs from the environment into public policies designed to have an impact upon problems of the environment. Feedback from the policy impact affects future inputs and shapes new demands upon the political system.

By combining the systems model with macro and micro perspectives, we can gain a fuller understanding of the urban political process. The macro level of analysis helps to provide the big picture, and micro analysis enables us to sketch in some of the details. Any particular activity — participation, budget making, the impact of urban renewal — may be seen from either perspective.

We are concerned with the urban political system and its policy choices because of their impact on the quality of urban life. It is perhaps symbolic that people write articles about the "worst American city," reflecting a long-standing fear that cities are in trouble. Public opinion polls showing that most Americans would prefer to live somewhere *other* than in a city confirm these fears. Public policy shapes much of the life quality of urbanites. Thus the main theme of this book is that the policy choices of urban governments allocate important values and that those values ultimately determine the quality of life in the American metropolis.

Notes

1. Mark Schneider, "The Quality of Life in Large American Cities: Objective and Subjective Social Indicators," *Social Indicators Research, 1* (1975), 495–509. See also, on the issue of urban life quality in the United States, Martin Flax, *A Study in Comparative Urban Indicators: Conditions in 18 Large Metropolitan Areas* (Washington: The Urban Institute, 1972); and David M. Smith, *The Geography of Social Well-Being in the United States* (New York: McGraw Hill, 1973).

2. *Harper's Magazine,* January 1975, 67–71.

3. See also, on Newark, George Sternlieb, "The City as Sandbox," *The Public Interest, 25* (Fall 1971), 14–21.

4. We shall meet a "correlation" more than once in this book, and now is a good time to define it. Two variables (say, years of schooling and income) are said to be positively correlated when increases in the value of one, among some population (say, everyone who lives in a city), are associated with increases in the value of the other. Conversely, when one variable increases and the other decreases, the two are negatively correlated. A "perfect" correlation is +1.00, indicating that changes in the value of one predict perfectly to changes in the value of the other. Two variables whose values are entirely unrelated will thus have a correlation of 0.00.

5. *Big City Politics* (New York: Random House, 1965), p. 7.

6. *Social Justice and the City* (Baltimore: Johns Hopkins University Press, 1973), pp. 23 and 26.

7. "Urbanism as a Way of Life," *American Journal of Sociology, 44* (July 1938), 18.

8. According to the latest (1972) *Census of Governments,* there are 264 SMSAs in the United States, containing within them 22,185 units of local government. For further discussion, see Chapter 4.

9. William Watts and Lloyd A. Free, *The State of the Nation* (New York: Universe Books, 1973), p. 81.

10. David Easton, "An Approach to the Analysis of Political Systems," *World Politics, 9* (April 1957), 384.

11. Arthur Vidich and Joseph Bensman, *Small Town in Mass Society* (Princeton, N.J.: Princton University Press, 1958).

12. Richard E. Dawson and James A. Robinson, "Inter-Party Competition, Economic Variables, and Welfare Policies in the American States," *Journal of Politics, 25* (May 1963), 266.

13. An abstract, but provocative, treatment of the macro-micro distinction is contained in Amitai Etzioni, *The Active Society* (New York: Free Press, 1968), pp. 43–56.

14. See Robert L. Lineberry, "Approaches to the Study of Community Politics," in Charles M. Bonjean et al., eds., *Community Politics: A Behavioral Approach* (New York: Free Press, 1971), chap. 2.

15. The term demand is used so commonly by political scientists who follow Easton that it is worth noting that it need not imply table pounding. A demand may be articulated as forcibly as rioting in the streets or as subtly as diplomatic discourse.

PART TWO
The Environment of Urban Policy

2
THE CITY
IN COMPARATIVE
PERSPECTIVE

"Interdependence" is a word often used — perhaps even overused — to describe the world today. But nowhere is it more applicable than to the urbanized world. In this chapter we stress that American cities are tied closer and closer to international markets and international issues. The problems that American cities confront are not unique to them. Rather, they have common elements with problems in both the developed and the developing countries. Cities everywhere confront: (1) problems of migration and urbanizing populations; (2) residential segregation and racial or ethnic conflict within the city; (3) the problem of city–national relationships; (4) problems of power and control within the city; and (5) the problem of providing services in an era of scarcity. Sometimes people feel that lessons are available only from cities in developed societies like Great Britain, Canada, and France. Yet we emphasize that American cities face problems common to less-developed nations as well. Chief among these is a social and economic dualism that confronts American cities no less than those of developing urban regions.

Unquestionably urbanization is overtaking the entire world. Government officials and social scientists from New Delhi to New York, and most countries in between, worry about the continued movement of people from rural to urban places, and the problems of keeping up with demands for urban services. Table 2.1 identifies some of the great cities of the world, almost all of which share a core of common problems. However, there are important differences in urban problems from one country to the next and in the policy responses to urban demands. In most countries outside the United States, the national government takes the lead in dealing with urban problems. Local autonomy is a distinctive feature of politics in the United States and a small number of other countries.

The local nature in much of urban politics and policy making in the United States has important implications that are not often perceived by citizens familiar only with the American setting. Throughout the history of American cities, their residents have been more or less concerned with governing themselves. Early in the twentieth century a group of "muckrakers" led by Lincoln Steffans sought to take city

Table 2.1   The Great Cities of the World by Region

	Population[a]		Population[a]
North America		Moscow	7,000,000
New York	16,000,000	Leningrad	4,000,000
Los Angeles-Long Beach	8,000,000	Berlin	3,000,000
Chicago	7,000,000	Madrid	3,000,000
Philadelphia	4,000,000		
San Francisco-Oakland	3,000,000	**Asia**	
Montreal	3,000,000	Tokyo	11,000,000
		Shanghai	11,000,000
Latin America		Osaka	8,000,000
Mexico City	9,000,000	Peking	8,000,000
Buenos Aires	8,000,000	Calcutta	7,000,000
São Paulo	8,000,000	Bombay	6,000,000
Rio de Janeiro	5,000,000	Seoul	6,000,000
		Jakarta	4,000,000
Africa and the Middle East		Tientsin	4,000,000
Cairo	5,000,000	Delhi	4,000,000
Teheran	4,000,000	Karachi	4,000,000
		Madras	3,000,000
Europe		Bangkok	3,000,000
Paris	9,000,000	Manila	3,000,000
London	7,000,000		

[a] Population estimates depend on how the boundaries of a city are defined and on the accuracy of national censuses. Were New York's population confined solely to the municipality of New York City, it would contain only 7 million people. Because of these variations, the population estimates above are only approximate and are rounded off.

halls from the "bosses" and return them to popular control.[1] More recently a variety of movements carrying such labels as "neighborhood government" or "consumerism" have sought to change the priorities of urban policy makers. In the United States such movements to change urban policy-making focus mostly on local political elites. In most other countries any efforts to change decisions made in local government offices would have to concentrate on the central government elite, usually bureaucrats working in the ministry of the interior or the home ministry in the national capital.

Throughout later chapters of this book we describe the structures of American local government, the political maneuvers that take place among local politicians and public officials, and the public policies that come from councils, mayors, city managers, and municipal bureaucracies. We also deal with the financial aids and program controls that come to local officials from state and national governments. However, these state and national inputs make their contributions to what is, essentially, a local setting. If this were a book about local governments in almost any other country, it would emphasize actions concerning urban affairs taken by national politicians and offices of national governments.

It may be that the United States is becoming more like other countries in the dependence of local affairs on decisions taken by the national legislature and bureaucracy. Such a tendency, however, occurs in a historical setting that only reluctantly has put additional power into national hands. The constitutional basis of federalism helps to protect the position of the state governments against the national government and to keep the cities more within the orbits of the states than of the national government. Within the state orbit there has been considerable tension between those who would govern the cities from the state capitol and those who would govern it from city hall. In much of the United States, however, the traditions of local autonomy and the influence of local figures in state politics have assured considerable freedom for local officials. If urban affairs in the United States are moving toward the nationalization that has long been apparent in most other countries of the world, the continuation of that movement in the United States must overcome substantial opposition and is likely to occur in a slow and piecemeal fashion.

SOME VIRTUES OF
A COMPARATIVE APPROACH

The World City and the Common
Policy Problems It Poses

The United States, by comparison with most other nations, is a heavily urbanized nation. Yet urbanization poses common problems and policy issues for nations large and small, rich and poor, "developed" and "underdeveloped." In that sense the agenda of urban problems often discussed in the United States is neither unique nor unprecedented. It is not necessarily easier to resolve problems that are widely shared, but a comparative perspective may enhance our understanding by setting the problems in a global context. Parochialism in the study of urban politics is no virtue. It is, therefore, useful to set out five principal dimensions of urbanization, in a comparative context, which affect urban systems in the United States and elsewhere.

1. *The problem of migration and urbanizing populations.* The world is urbanizing, as migration depletes the hinterlands and swells the urban cores. Tribal natives move to Nairobi, rural peasants move to São Paulo, and Appalachian whites and southern blacks move to Detroit. Once in the city, new migrants create demands on already strained service facilities, expect jobs and upward mobility, and learn

new political attitudes and values.[2] The residual problems of depopulation of rural areas are the other side of that coin.

2. *The problem of residential segregation and differentiation within the city.* Nowhere do classes, races, and ethnic groups live randomly scattered about the urban landscape. Castes in Bombay and races in Boston are segregated residentially. The historic pattern in the United States has reflected a clustering of immigrant and poor groups in the core of the metropolitan area. Residential segregation has been as evident in other places, but newcomers have been clustered in *favelas* or squatter settlements on the outskirts of the cities, while middle and upper classes have occupied the cores. Whatever the pattern, the clustering phenomenon is nearly universal in the urban world.

3. *The problem of city–national relationships.* Cities are not autonomous, either economically or politically. They are deeply embedded in a national political system, and the relations between central authorities and local governments differ widely from country to country. In the United States, local governments have more autonomy than in almost any other industrialized nation. But it would be impossible to understand urban politics and policy without understanding the pattern of policy undertaken in Washington, D.C. Elsewhere (in France, for example) local governments are little more than administrative outposts of central authorities. The distribution of power between local and central authorities is an issue not only in federal systems such as ours but in all political systems.

4. *The problem of power within the city.* Who has power and what can be done with it have been major issues in the study of American cities (see pp. 172–181). The same issues are relevant in India, Latin America, and elsewhere.[3] Machines dominated the power structure of many American cities for a long time, and they can be found throughout the world. American cities, though, have become more bureaucratized, more administrative, and less dominated by the colorful politicians of a machine era. Other cities are experiencing the same transformation from a politically dominated to an administratively dominated power structure.

5. *The problem of providing services in an era of scarcity.* Scarcity — too few resources to meet citizen demands — is nothing new for most of the world's cities. Public services that Americans take for granted (clean water, fire protection, sewerage, and so on) are nonexistent elsewhere. Yet as fiscal constraints and the limits of energy reduce the flexibility of American urban systems, problems of scarcity become very real. As New York City was laying off service personnel by the thousands, Rome faced a fiscal crisis of even greater magnitude.

These and other common policy problems beset cities the world over. Growth and decay, crime and violence, poverty and inequality are not American monopolies. How cities confront and cope with such problems is a function of their urban experience in different national contexts. But the universality of the urban agendas around the urban world is striking indeed.

The American City in the World

The city is definitely not an island. It is clear enough how any city is imbedded in a national system of cities, linked by both production and consumption networks. The emergence of a bureaucratized, industrialized, "mass" society has linked the smallest places with the largest megalopolitan centers. In the twentieth century the vertical ties of cities to the national system have grown, whereas the horizontal ties within communities have weakened.[4] Yet systems of cities do not stop at national borders. Foreign relations do not take place only between official, national government actors, but also among groups, corporations, trade unions, churches, local officials, and individual citizens. Multinational corporations are usually headquartered in the primate cities of the world (e.g., New York, London, Tokyo, Frankfort, Rome, and Amsterdam) and sprinkle their complex outposts in cities around the globe. The ties between New York and Nairobi are almost as closely linked by communication and transportation networks as those between Boston and San Diego. Both the *speed* and the *volume* of communication and transportation are striking.

Migration, poverty, housing — common problems in many cities.

In an imaginative study by Chadwick Alger of Ohio State University the "foreign relations" of Columbus, Ohio, were elaborated. Columbus, although a major metropolis of 1 million people, is not New York or Chicago or Detroit, whose connections to the world economy are more obvious. Even so, in Columbus

- Local firms directly export goods worth more than $134 million annually and import products worth $88 million
- Columbus churches send about $3 million overseas annually
- Almost 30,000 plane tickets were purchased for flights from Columbus to abroad
- Columbus hosts between 5,000 and 10,000 foreign visitors a year

As Alger remarks, "Metropolitan communities provide the facilities and institutions through which international transactions take place. Here we find the airports, banks, headquarters of corporations, universities, freight forwarders, travel agencies, churches, philanthropic organizations, importers and exporters who provide the facilities and impetus for much international activity."[5]

As the world becomes more interdependent, cities are tied together more closely and transactions across national frontiers multiply. Transaction flows among cities consist of persons, money, goods, and information. The resident of an American city is ever more intimately affected by Middle East oil, whose price is fixed at a conference in Vienna or Qatar, by decisions on the price of Chilean copper made in Santiago, by multinational decisions on the state of the oceans made in New York and Moscow. The city, with its citizens, is part of a world economy; that, too, requires that we examine the American city in an international perspective.

CITIES IN POOR COUNTRIES

Politicians as well as political scientists distinguish between countries that are less and more developed. For politicians the division may fit their need to define differences between "us" and "them." For political scientists—as well as for economists, sociologists, and other social scientists—the meanings attached to "less-" and "more-developed" vary with the issues at hand. A less- or a more-developed economy does not always coincide with a less- or a more-developed political system or other traits of a society. Often efforts are made to mask the negative connotations attached to countries at the lower end of the scale. The literature offers the labels of *developing* and *modernizing*, as well as *underdeveloped* and *traditional*. What most of these terms signal is a relative lack of certain economic traits that are found in the more affluent countries. Poor countries are poor in several ways. They may not lack natural resources, but they often lack well educated and skilled people, transportation arteries and electric power, and the cash necessary to exploit profitably whatever natural resources do exist. Poor countries tend to have relatively unproductive forms of industry and agriculture. With fewer schools and clinics than are necessary to meet demands, they lack the capacity to enrich their human capital quickly and thereby add to economic productivity. Tax and banking systems in poor countries also tend to be weak, with the result that much of the cash that might be accumulated for investments is allowed to lie fallow, to be used for conspicuous consumption, or to leave the country for investment in wealthier economies. Poor countries have other disadvantages in international transactions. They tend to compete among themselves in offering crude or only semiprocessed materials in international trade. With the exception of oil-exporting countries, which have pursued a united front in pricing, poor countries generally suffer from fluctuating prices for their own commodities, while prices of goods purchased from abroad march upward.

The economic traits of poor countries have several implications for their cities. Most prominent is the great number of poor people migrating from villages to cities. Migrants seek jobs amidst their country's greatest concentrations of industry, commerce, and government, but typically without the training necessary to acquire anything more than the most menial employment. And the large numbers flowing to the city make even the lowest jobs hard to obtain. Because poor countries have no functioning welfare programs, most immigrants to the cities must live by their wits. Sidewalk vendors proliferate, as do beggars, thieves, and prostitutes. Some countries have tried to gauge the magnitude of the economic problems associated with the rural-to-urban drift. A study conducted in Kenya during the mid-1960s found 148,000 students completing primary school annually, with 92,000 having no prospect of further education, and only 3,500 being able to find urban wage employment. India is still predominantly a rural country, with 80 percent of its people living in communities of less than 5,000. However, its urban population increased by an estimated 39 percent in the 1961–1971 decade.[6] This means the absorption of some 31 million people in cities that already were ill-equipped in housing, sanitation, public transportation, public health, and employment opportunities, and without the national resources capable of meeting such urban demands. By ways of comparison, the urban population of the United States increased by only 13 percent in the 1960–1970 decade, and this in a country with infinitely greater resources for the absorption of new arrivals.

The concentration of urban populations in poor countries tends to magnify the problems of absorbing new immigrants. Scholars have adopted the term *macroephaly* to convey the image of cities that have ballooned far out of proportion to the population of the country; the term likens the problem of the dominant city to the oversized head of a dwarf. While the United States has 153 cities with more than 100,000 people each, the pattern in poor countries is to have one very large "primate" city or a very small number of them. Peru is an extreme case. The capital city of Lima has some 20 percent of the entire population, whereas while the next-largest city has but one-fifteenth of Lima's population. The Indian cities of Bombay, Calcutta, Madras, Delhi, and Bangalore have received almost 20 percent of the total increase in that country's urban population.

The shortage of housing and other critical amenities is the most visible result of too-rapid urbanization on a too-small economic base. The signs are sprawling shanty towns without proper streets or running water, open sewers, and—even in the main shopping and business streets—thousands of people who sleep and eat on the sidewalk, draw their water and bathe at the public water faucets. A study conducted for the group formulating India's Revised Fourth Plan in the late 1960s identified a housing shortage of some 15.4 million units. The situation is actually worsening, because the shortage was only 2.8 million units in the early 1950s. Another study done in 1961 estimated that 40 percent of the urban population lacked a safe water supply and that 75 percent had no underground sewage.

Public transportation is also in short supply. Antique buses carry enormous loads. They fill to the bursting point, with passengers perched and clinging to external foot- and handholds. Periodic interruptions in electric service reflect the strained capacity of the electric system. Electric clocks must be regulated daily. There are also perpetual busy signals on the telephones. More than a few visiting businessmen or scholars have learned to drive across town and ask personally for an appointment, rather than tolerate the long delays due to busy lines or wrong connections. The first shock of a foreigner is likely to be the wait required for residential telephone service. An American familiar with arranging new service in a matter of days may be told to apply now to receive service in three to five years! In some cities a special payment to the right person may speed the initial installation but does nothing to assure success once you are hooked onto the overloaded system.

Local Politics in Poor Countries:
The Case of Jalapa

The economic and social problems of poor countries leave their mark on the political traits of urban residents. General patterns show little popular participation in local politics. Indeed there is not much locally based politics to attract popular participation. Politics and policy making in poor countries occur at the national level, and there is seldom extensive popular involvement in — or control over — the national government. As a result, urban problems may receive only limited attention from the political elite.

Jalapa is a provincial capital in Mexico that reveals many of these characteristics. This is true even though Mexico scores among the most well-developed of the poor countries, and Japala is above average in income and education among Mexico's provincial cities. For these reasons the traits of Jalapa probably understate the paucity of local politics and policy making throughout the poor countries.[7]

Although Jalapa may claim to be well above average in socioeconomic traits among cities of poor countries, it scores markedly below the norms of the United States. In the mid-1960s the average family income was between $60 and $70 per month; 43 percent of the adult males had not finished primary school; and only 34 percent had some attendance at secondary school. The city saw a 38 percent growth in population between 1950 and 1966, typical of swelling urban populations in the poor countries.

When the adults of Jalapa were asked about their attitudes toward government, they expressed images of distant rulers over whom they had little control. About 90 percent said that they were powerless to deal with a serious problem in the locale, and almost that many would look to "the government" for help. Their image of the government was that of a capricious lord, to whom they must go hat in hand, asking for a favor. Only 20 percent have actually gone to an official to seek help or support, and this is the most prevalent of political activities. Even fewer belong to interest groups or political parties, have been contacted themselves by government officials seeking their cooperation, or have taken active part in a political campaign. Such figures belie the official Mexican propaganda of mass participation in the politics of a revolutionary society; they also suggest what really happens in the localities of other poor countries that describe themselves as revolutionary or popularly governed.

While the residents of Jalapa do not participate actively and do feel powerless, it would be inaccurate to view them as a seething mass waiting for an opportunity to run things in a new way. Rather, most citizens seem to have made peace with a political system that they view with cynicism. It is not surprising that the most well-to-do people are involved more than the average in local affairs and that they feel the most satisfied with the government. For the poorest and least well educated who are the least involved and the least satisfied, however, apathy and withdrawal rather than a sense of repression mark their statements.

The Centralization of Local Government

The policy-making procedures that serve Jalapa help to explain the peoples' feelings of impotence and cynicism. Government and politics are centralized in Mexico City, and managed hierarchically. Even "local" matters such as the electrification of a new area or the installation of drainage pipes may depend on administrators who are independent from—if not disdainful of—the local scene. Most officials situated in Jalapa are the regional agents of national or state ministries. Their orientations are upward to the preferences of administrative superiors and to career paths that lead out of Jalapa and to a larger city or even the national capital, rather than to the demands of local residents.

Electoral politics in Mexico provide little relief from the hierarchical nature of policy making. As in many of the poor countries, there is only one national party with legitimate standing. There is little prospect of local voters turning against the nominees of the PRI (Partido Revolucionario Institucional). Aspiring politicians must please regional and national elites who control nominations to the party slate. Again this means an orientation upward and outward from Jalapa. The path to political success for "locally elected" officials is less concerned with a demonstrated improvement in the local scene than with impressing party leaders in being able to handle assigned tasks without arousing local opposition. It is best to concentrate on projects that are quickly accomplished and highly visible, that cost relatively little, and that do not provoke controversy. In Mexico these frequently involve the refurbishing of public places and carry the label of *plazismo*. *Plazismo* results in projects that may be charming, but they seldom add up to a significant achievement. Above all, when energies are so engaged, both planning and serious attention to the key problems of public policy suffer. Symbols replace substance in developmental schemes.[8]

Centralization for Economic Growth: Brazil

Several poor countries exhibit legal forms of local autonomy but without the firm rooting in tradition to withstand changes dictated from above. In Brazil, for example, a 1964 revolution made dramatic changes that reversed earlier moves toward decentralization. The existing constitution was "municipalist" in providing for the local governments within a federal structure having defined roles for the national, state, and local authorities. However, the 1964 coup went far beyond the typical Latin American effort. It changed the constitution and many aspects of government conduct. Financial stability, economic growth, and the repression of political opposition became major themes in Brazil. This included the strengthening of the national government at the expense of states and municipalities.[9] Centralization was justified as a device to permit greater national control over economic stability and growth. When Brazil curtailed local autonomy for the sake of economic progress, it demonstrated the conflict between autonomy and economic growth. The new regime took away from the cities the control over taxes which had produced between one-half and two-thirds of the tax money they had previously controlled. Municipalities have learned not to expect state government compliance with remaining constitutional requirements to transfer certain tax collections to them. Municipal finance became dependent on nationally directed grants and shared revenues, with a host of directives and prohibitions governing their use.

What problems did local autonomy present for Brazil's economy? According to the new regime, local autonomy facilitated corruption and waste, and stood in the way of nationally directed efforts to coordinate investments for the sake of growth. The central government now prohibits municipal authorities from using certain money for "nondevelopmental" uses like decorative fountains, cars, furniture for government offices, and lighting in undeveloped areas.

Frustrated Aspirations
for Local Autonomy: India

The municipal governments of India were also built on insecure ground and are susceptible to unilateral takeovers from above. Its cities suffer from several problems that are not present in Mexico or Brazil. India must cope with a much larger population and a much poorer economy. At some 600 million, India's population is about six times greater than Brazil's and 10 times greater than Mexico's. Recent estimates for gross national product per capita show $120 for India against $750 for Brazil and $870 for Mexico. India also has more complex ethnic and linguistic problems, with regionally based populations posing what the central government considers to be threats against national unity. In addition, the country suffers from its history of opposing the authorities of the colonial British government. Only 30 years ago, prior to independence, it was considered patriotic for an Indian to avoid paying proper taxes. Now the same practice is counter to the policies of the Indian government, but many individuals perpetuate tax-avoiding behaviors that are still profitable.

Local government in India suffers endlessly from the lack of resources needed to cope with the enormity of its problems. It is short of money, skilled personnel, and efficient techniques. Local authorities seem to be the most severely affected in all of India. The more attractive careers beckon skilled persons to the state and central governments. In the words of one Indian scholar:

The meagre and inelastic resources of local bodies prevent them from competing in the employment market with [state and central] government and big business. They have thus generally to satisfy themselves with the "rejects," so to speak. Equally, their inability to provide good service conditions and incentives not only adds to the misery of their employees, but acts as a deterrent to the competent man from entering into municipal service. Second rate, or worse, personnel, generally disgruntled too, add to the current inefficiency of local government. The resultant dissatisfaction among the cities further tarnishes the image of local government and encourages the higher political and administrative levels — none to friendly anyhow — to question their utility.[10]

India acquired from Great Britain certain assumptions of local discretion but with advice, participation, and ultimately control from higher authorities. Whereas such arrangements in Britain actually bestow more authority on local personnel than the formalities suggest, similar procedures in India work in a highly centralized manner. Instead of the smooth give-and-take that marks central–local relations in Britain, relations in India feature the posturing of each side behind firm positions, with the higher authorities less inclined to advise and educate municipal officials than to assert their formal prerogatives to control policy. One year, in the important state of Uttar Pradesh, 14 of the 126 municipalities had their decisions superseded by higher governments, and one municipality was dissolved. There were sharp disputes between party factions, frequent walkouts and adjournment of meetings, and failures of officials to follow required procedures.

With severe shortages of talent in the local governments of India and shortages of the skills needed to upper levels for advising and guiding local authorities, many of the tasks expected of local government are simply not done. Especially noticeable is the lack of activity in physical planning for urban expansion. With no operational plans for new neighborhoods and no advance provision for streets, water, sewer, electric lines and market areas, newcomers set up wherever they can. They produce a jumble of huts and a maze of paths with horrendous sanitation, whose very existence serves as a barrier to subsequent orderly arrangement. Which families are to be displaced to make room for the needed streets and other facilities? And how can the task be done without creating an explosion in the political tinder of a squatter settlement that may contain tens of thousands of people?

CITIES IN WEALTHY COUNTRIES

In the cities of some wealthier countries we can find urban politics and policy making that resemble the United States in their freedom from tight central control. Local authorities are more likely to be controlled by — and responsive to — local demands and resources. In these wealthier countries it becomes possible to talk about politics and policy making that are genuinely local, as opposed to national policies for local sites.

Not every country among the economically well-to-do offers genuinely local politics and policy making. Indeed the United States is virtually unique in the extent of the autonomy enjoyed by local politicians and policy makers; and, as we see in later chapters, the autonomy of local policy makers in the United States is itself limited in important ways. A well-developed national economy may be a necessary condition for autonomous local politics and policy making, but it does not assure local autonomy. This section describes the local autonomy that starts in three countries with well-developed economies: Canada, Great Britain, and Sweden. It also describes two settings — the Soviet Union and Japan — where powerful other characteristics sharply curtail whatever degree of local autonomy might emerge from the traits of a well-developed economy.

Canada

Among all the countries of the world, Canada seems to resemble the United States most closely in its political heritage, the diversity of its population, and its general standard of living. True, it does present the contrast of a population only one-tenth that of the United States and a landmass that is 7 percent larger in area. However, the majority of Canadians are concentrated in two dozen cities that are like our own in many ways. They exist within a federal structure, and most dealings of local officials are with provincial rather than national authorities. Further, these provincial authorities enjoy genuine constitutional autonomy *vis à vis* the central government as do the American states, and the Canadian provinces have a legal superiority over their cities that resembles that developed under "Dillon's rule" in the United States (see pp. 140–141). There are additional similarities in prominent features of local policy: Canadian cities rely most heavily on locally raised real estate taxes. Their housing policies depend on government-guaranteed mortgages available to middle-class families for the construction of single-family homes; and partly as a result, Canadian cities have problems with central-city decay and sprawling metropolitan areas with poor coordination of policies between central cities and suburbs.

The most prominent event in the recent history of Canadian urban government has been the creation of a federal structure for metropolitan Toronto. This event has shown signs both of more centralization than occurs in the United States, as well as of the support given to autonomy in Canada. The enactment of reorganization depended greatly on the statutes of the provincial legislature. In most of the United States similar proposals for state-enacted metropolitian consolidation find the legislature unable to act against the demands for continued independence that come out of suburban communities. In the Toronto federation, metro authorities acquired control over public transportation, the construction of highways and schools, police, the extension of water and sewer lines, property assessment, and capital borrowing. However, municipalities retain important functions in land-use control, housing, and welfare. Also, service levels and tax rates continue to differ between municipalities. All this indicates the preservation of considerable local autonomy within the framework of metropolitan federations and maintains a place for Canada among those countries with genuinely local politics and policy making.[11]

Great Britain

Great Britain shares some features in common with the urban political systems of Canada and the United States. Despite Britain's unitary system of government and the virtually unlimited power of the national Parliament to make and alter policies that are administered locally, there is great respect for local autonomy. The combination of formal centralization but actual decentralization is not easy for outsiders to understand. In some respects it is "typically British" in its dependency on subtleties of personal interaction between officials representing central and local authorities. They seem to consult and negotiate with little dependence on formal rules of procedure. We noted above that an important theme of Indian central–local relations is the inability of this process to work, and the frequent employment by the center of extreme sanctions in actually taking over local administration. Similar powers exist in Britain, but there they are part of the background in which mutually dependent and generally agreeable relations take place between the levels of government.

Though not as fragmented as American metropolitan governments, there is a great variety of bodies involved. There are countries, boroughs, urban and rural districts, parish councils and parish meetings, metropolitan counties and metropolitan districts, plus a variety of administrative bodies having responsibility for particular services, sometimes with their territorial responsibility scattered in patchwork fashion among different urban and rural units. When there is centralization of a particular service, it is likely prompted by inequities and inefficiencies produced by the existing tangle of jurisdictions. In the case of hospitals, for example:

Hospitals had three origins — voluntary organizations, the Boards of Guardians and public health authorities. The Guardians were concerned with medical services for the poor while the health authorities were required to isolate persons suffering from infectious disease. After 1930 the medical wards of workhouses were taken over by the health committees of the counties and county boroughs and turned into general purpose hospitals. County boroughs, counties, and some other boroughs and urban districts were made responsible for maternity and child welfare from 1907 onwards and had opened clinics for this purpose. The National Health Service Act, 1946, transferred all hospitals to the new Regional Hospital Boards, but an expanded range of medical duties, including the aftercare of hospital patients, the provision of health visitors and home helps was allocated to counties and county boroughs.[12]

The organizational fractures within British government go deep within what appears to be individual local entities. Within a single jurisdiction, the civil servants of various departments may operate according to their own procedures for recruitment, promotion, salary, and control. There is no unified national civil service such as occurs in several European countries, where an officer can be posted from a local task in one community to others in the course of his career by senior officers in a national ministry. With public service becoming increasingly sophisticated and requiring the employment of highly trained technical and professional personnel, the technically proficient head of a department may informally acquire more independence from his local council than the rules suggest. His discretion may extend beyond matters of recruiting his subordinates and into details of substantive policy.

With organizational complexity and heavy reliance on extralegal conventions rather than the strict application of formal procedure, policy making in British cities does not lend itself to simple description. It is clear that there is a mixture of local and national inputs into major decisions, with mixed central–local financing and supervision of administration in many programs of great social importance: housing, health, public safety, education, and various welfare services for children, the aged, and the disabled. The British themselves describe central–local relations with terms that imply a flexible adaptation to circumstances: consultation; mutual information; research and the pooling of experience; advice; mutual persuasion; negotiation; mutual dependence.

It is because each side needs the co-operation of the other at key points that persuasion and negotiation often succeed. Despite its statutory powers the Government cannot do without local authorities, to implement national policies and collaborate as partners in adapting national objectives to local circumstances.[13]

Important in this lack of organizational coherence in British local authorities is the lack of a strong chief executive along the patterns of the American "strong mayor" or city manager. The local council—typically composed of elected officials serving part-time—is the principal authority. It usually divides itself into substantively defined committees to govern local affairs, perhaps with a central committee charged with coordination. Although more and more councils are employing chief executives, these generally lack the control over subordinates that gives considerable power to an American city manager.

One very real difference in British and American local politics is the significant role that parties play in Britain and the almost nonexistent role they play in America.[14] Either Labour or Conservative majorities control local councils, and the policy choices of councils differ depending upon who is in command. Noel Boaden's study of expenditure levels in British boroughs shows that local governments controlled by Labour councils spent disproportionately on education and on housing (the correlation between the degree of Labour control and the number of public housing units built in the city was .67), whereas Conservative councils spent more on policing.[15] In the American local system, on the other hand, nonpartisanship in most cities has effectively removed national parties from the local scene. Voters in Great Britain, therefore, have a much better idea of what they are "buying" when they go to the polls; American urbanites can often only hope for the best in picking and choosing from the not-very-informative nonpartisan ballot. But even in Great Britain, urban politics commands much less interest than national politics. British local elections attract little more than 40 percent of the eligible electorate. As we shall see in Chapter 5, American local elections attract about one-third of the eligibles. In neither system are local elections a matter of intense interest.

Sweden

Great Britain and its affluent former colonies do not have a monopoly on autonomous local governments. The local authorities in Sweden are generally well run with considerable leeway, and with some formal powers of their own which go beyond those of British local governments. And all this in a unitary system of government where the national government has an extensive reservoir of powers.

Sweden is often held up as a model of an affluent, "post-industrial"[16] society where citizens receive a wide range of public services, and policy making takes place without sharp disputes over basic principles. The country's standard of living is among the highest in Europe. Its population is relatively small with widespread education and mostly middle class in income. It lacks the ethnic or religious heterogeneity that has caused problems elsewhere. Over 90 percent of the population affiliates with the Lutheran State Church. In 1960 less than 4 percent of the people in Stockholm were foreign born, and almost 60 percent of these were from the neighboring countries of Denmark, Norway, and Finland.[17] If any cities are easy to govern and perhaps even a bit dull, it must be those of Sweden.

But there is politics in Sweden's cities. Candidates compete for election to local offices, carrying the labels of national parties and often compaigning in terms of national issues. Some 2000 interest groups in Stockholm represent labor unions, employers, merchants, white-collar and professional employees, consumer cooperatives, tenants, and landlords. However, decision making lacks sharp disputes, with participants engaging in give-and-take about details amidst a basic consensus about the outlines of policy.

An extensive range of public services is offered in Swedish cities, both by units of the municipal government and by publicly owned corporations. Stockholm offers public transportation, theaters, housing, libraries, hydroelectric plants, education, health, pensions, roads, harbors, airfields, fire protection, civil defense, and planning—either on its own initiative or in cooperation with the national government. The city has more fiscal autonomy than most cities of the world— including those of the United States. There is no control by any superior level of government over the character or rates of local taxes. Stockholm must obtain national approval for borrowing, however, and this has become an important access for the national government into city policy making. National authorities must also approve local policies in such fields as public health, education, and welfare. There is national participation in local land-use planning; and the national government's Ombudsman investigates citizen complaints against local administrators. Yet with each of these mechanisms, there seems to be a concern to use national controls loosely and with respect for local perspectives.

One problem for Swedish cities is the lack of rapid or tightly coordinated policy making. In part this feature reflects the absence of a strong executive in communal governments. Like the British cities, those of Sweden rely on elected councils, which then select a series of executive boards to administer various aspects of city services. Also in Sweden, several administrative units are likely to be involved in a particular venture—such as the communal government, quasi-public corporations, and national government authorities—without much pressure from one authority to another and with no single intergovernmental coordinator. Without large numbers of citizens feeling deprived of essentials and clamoring for services not being provided, the machinery of urban government in Sweden operates in a leisurely manner and gives to each of the official participants ample opportunity to make its own case and weigh those of the others.

In Sweden, as in Canada and Great Britain, there is much greater latitude allowed to local authorities than is evident in lesser-developed countries. In each of these countries, however, there is also the potential for involvement by high-level authorities, depending on their own view of local initiatives. This is more apparent in Britain and Sweden. There local governments exist within centralized political systems, without the protections of the federal systems in the United States or Canada. In each of these countries, as in the United States, some observers see a drift in the direction of more involvement by higher authorities in local financing, and in the guidance or approval of local planning and service policies.

Soviet Union

The Soviet Union is highly bureaucratized. In order to understand urban policy making in the Soviet Union, it is necessary to take account of the several bureaucracies that converge in the cities and of the priorities assigned to one or another of these in the Soviet system. To begin with, politics in the USSR is not the freewheeling clash of citizens, interest groups, and competitive parties that appears in the western democracies and in some lesser-developed countries. There is politics in the Soviet Union, but the politics takes place among the elites of various ministries, departments, councils and local soviets, and various state enterprises that ostensibly carry out policies of the party or the government but which also may exercise some clout of their own, especially in the local setting.

Lower-ranking officials of these different bureaucracies work in the cities, where they each depend on policies made at higher levels in their own organizations. There is no coordination of different bureaucracies at the local level. If local party or government personnel wish to change the policies being pursued by a large industry — which may affect the local scene in profound ways by the housing it provides to its employees — it is necessary to convince higher-echelon party or government officers to insert changes at the top of the industry's hierarchy. Such an action may require extensive reconsideration of priorities, consultations between party and government bureaucracies at high levels, and spillover decisions involving economic planning for other locales whose industries would be affected by the requested change in the economic plan. In such exercises, there emerge the weight of multiple bureaucracies that are both the mechanisms and the problems of Soviet policy making.

In concrete terms, such problems stand in the way of local government and party personnel altering the activities of large enterprises that create serious problems of imbalance within the community. Housing and the development of social services lag behind the creation of industry. Often, such services are under the control of factory managers, who are expected to provide amenities for their employees but who are rewarded by their superiors simply for production. The

Soviet system has struggled to change the orientation of factory managers from quantity to quality of production, and now it is struggling to develop some concern for the quality of life in the locales that surround the factories. To bring about a change on the local scene, it is not a simple matter for officials of the city soviet, the local party, and the factory manager to agree among themselves. Such local discretion and an inclination to give-and-take might be characteristic of Sweden. In the Soviet Union each local official must consult independently with his own hierarchical superiors, each of whom at various stages up their separate ladders may introduce additional considerations to complicate the local matter.

Despite all of its problems of coordination, the Soviet Union has managed to pursue a course of vigorous urbanization. Some 700 new cities appeared in the period 1926–1960, and the urban percentage of the population increased from 18 to 49. World War II came in the midst of this surge and required extensive reconstruction. The Russians recorded 1710 cities and towns destroyed, with the major cities of Stalingrad, Minsk, and Sevastopol in complete ruin and several other large cities gravely damaged. There were 20 million dead, and 25 million people homeless. Construction and reconstruction occurred rapidly, often without extensive concern for planning. Even friendly critics find much to lament in the record of Soviet urban development, at the same time that they concede the pressures on the policy makers:

New industries in new locations had to assure themselves of at least minimal housing and services in order to retain a labor force at all. If they had waited for urban planners and municipal administrators to settle on integrated development plans, then waited still more until permanent apartments, utilities and all the rest were assured, one can well imagine the fate of production targets in the early five-year plans.[18]

Thus, even when there is a strong national commitment to planning, there is no assurance of well-placed and regulated urban amenities. In the case of the Soviet Union, the planning commitment cannot assure that planning for housing, utilities, and other urban services outweighs planning for industrial production, especially in a country committed to values of production over consumption.

Japan

Japan is another well-developed country whose political traditions mitigate against autonomous urban policy making. The crucial Japanese background begins with the Meiji Restoration in the late 1860s and 1870s, which destroyed the remnants of feudalism, and prepared a strong, centralized Japan to deal with the outside world that had intruded on the nation's isolation. The central government developed a series of intermediate and local administrative structures, to be filled with centrally appointed personnel, with each fitted into a tight hierarchy. Although there were local assemblies chosen by direct elections and prefectural (intermediate-level) councils chosen by the local assemblies, the actions of these bodies were subject to review and modification by higher administrators. The pyramid for local affairs peaked in the Home Ministry of the national government. The governor of each perfecture was the principal agent of the Home Ministry in each locale and enjoyed great prestige. Kurt Steiner describes the role of the governor as follows:

The passage of a governor through a town or village was a state affair, anticipated by the mayor with trepidation and preceded by frantic preparations. The clean-swept streets, the flags, the children lined up in their school uniforms, the mayor in morning coat and white gloves, and deeply bowed heads — all gave acknowledgment to the exalted status of His Excellency, who represented the State and the Emperor, and to the lowliness of his subjects and their chosen officials.[19]

The period during World War II witnessed even greater efforts to centralize local affairs. The government disbanded political parties and established block associations to disseminate official regulations, distribute rations, collect taxes, indoctrinate citizens in current policies of the central government, and report on local compliance with national directives. These manifestations of wartime totalitarianism were not entirely out of character with the nation's heritage. Individuals traditionally had been passive in their relations with the political elite, and the role of central government officials — especially since the Meiji Restoration — had been to govern subjects rather than to lead citizens.

Against this background, the efforts of the American occupation to inculcate democracy and local home rule faced severe problems. The occupation government did impose certain changes, but the successes were more symbolic than tangible, more temporary than lasting. Japanese working along with the Americans sought to weaken the decentralization efforts, occasionally by changing subtly the meaning of constitutional terminology while translating it from English to Japanese.

At present, the central government assures itself of control over local authorities via the financial strings that run from top to bottom. The central government controls the character and rates of local taxes, which amount to 30 percent of local revenues. The remainder comes from the national government, along with detailed ministerial control over the use of funds. The local official — who lives in a hierarchical culture that reinforces patterns of subordination — must also comprehend a bureaucratic maze, including several national ministries with fingers in a bewildering assortment of pies and with tendencies to change their procedures frequently. Thus the Welfare Ministry may have crucial leverage over a matter dealing with Tokyo's water supply, and the Autonomy Ministry (rather than the National Police Agency) may control the addition of personnel to the Nara Police. If local personnel suffer deprivations under a system that is simply hierarchical, they might at least compensate for their subordination by using the rules of the hierarchy to their best advantage. When the system is both hierarchical and fluid at the top, then the problems of subordinates are even more difficult.

The Japanese voter who would use his individual leverage to affect local conditions also faces severe limits. Electoral politics focus on national issues, and those who are chosen to local offices will enjoy little autonomy in making policy. Much of what local policy makers do is to appeal to higher levels of government for the grants of power or money that are theirs alone to bestow or withhold.

In the period since the occupation, a fascinating and complex political system has emerged in Japan, against a background a wartime and prewar repression of dissidents. Japanese national politics falls somewhere on the "democratic" side of the scale between democratic and nondemocratic regimes. To this extent the workings of the occupation and the proliferation of numerous industrial and commercial interests in the economy have left their mark. However, the workings of urban policy making are still a long way from the varieties of autonomy found in such countries as the United States, Canada, Great Britain, or Sweden. Japan demonstrates that there is no assurance of local autonomy even where there is substantial indication of economic affluence and substantial progress toward democracy at the national level.

These remnants of the imperial tradition have coexisted with the new Japan, a world economic power of enormous importance. The cities of Japan house large multinational corporations that perform many social services — such as housing, recreation, and health care — often provided by governments in developed nations. For decades Japan was the most rapidly growing of the world's economies. The result was rapid urbanization of already densely settled cities. Another result was a highly industrialized economic system in a nation with few raw materials. Japan is far more dependent on importation of oil than the United States. The combination of densely settled urban populations, energy dependence, and technological sophistication produced demands for efficient transportation and communication networks, scarcely rivaled by any industrialized nation. If Columbus, Ohio, is increasingly intertwined with the larger international system of cities, then Tokyo, Osaka, and other Japanese cities are more so.

POLICY LESSONS FROM THE WORLD CITY

This chapter has been built on the assumption that comparison promotes understanding. The American city is not an island, immune from transactions with the world city. Even when transactions are missing, though, analogues are very real. American cities, like those in Mexico, India, and Brazil, must cope with urbanizing populations and with rural newcomers in an urban milieu; American cities, like those in Sweden, are expected by their citizens to produce a high level of public services and at reasonable costs in tax dollars; American cities, like those in the Soviet Union, must deal with superordinate bureaucracies whose decisions affect their economic vitality; American cities, like those in Great Britain and Canada, have complex and fragmented systems of local government, in constant tension with national authorities; and American cities, like those in Japan, operate in energy-dependent yet energy-scarce environments.

Economic and Social Origins of Local Autonomy

One principal variation among national urban systems is, as we have suggested, that of local autonomy. Despite the counterexamples of the Soviet Union and Japan, our analysis of both poor and rich countries suggests that a well-developed economy allows, if not encourages, local autonomy. (As we shall see in Chapter 6, it is in those states of the United States that are relatively wealthy that local governments tend to have the greatest control over their own affairs.) In the United States, Sweden, Canada, and Great Britain, cities are "on their own" fiscally to a larger extent than in most other nations. Perhaps the wealth itself has something to do with local autonomy. Or—to put it more bluntly—in an affluent society local elites can extract some resources out of the citizenry even after the national government has taken its bite. Where resources are abundant, central government elites can meet their own pressing needs without soaking up everything. Further, in a well-developed economy, the presence of numerous economic elites in the private sector produces an interest in protecting their own local positions; and a high incidence of well-educated citizens exhibit interest in local amenities and services.

But a well-developed economy is not, by itself, the entire explanation of local autonomy. The cases of Japan and the Soviet Union show the coexistence of centralization with affluence. Within the United States, Nebraska, Maine, and South Dakota show considerable local autonomy even with less wealth than other states. Not did Britain's recent economic reversals weaken its traditional commitment to local autonomy.

Some Lessons from Poor Countries

Instinctively Americans look to wealthier industrial democracies for guidance – to Britain especially and to western Europe generally. The United States is not a poor country, so the argument goes, and there must be few lessons to be learned from Mexico, India, Brazil, and other less-developed countries. We cannot agree. Instead we suggest that there are significant parallels between urban problems, politics, and policies in the United States and poorer countries.[20]

One striking similarity between American cities and those of the poorer nations is the massive migrations they have been required to absorb. In the United States millions of Appalachian whites, southern blacks, and Mexican immigrants have overpopulated the cities. Straining urban housing markets and urban service capacity, these groups vacillate between political quiescence and political action. They live in poverty pockets at the cores of the cities. The English word *ghetto* (originally that section of European cities set aside for enforced Jewish settlement) conjures up images similar to the Spanish word *favela*. The parallels, though they should not be exaggerated, do not end there. American cities, like those in poorer countries, are centers of wealth and privilege. Great affluence in the city lies close to great poverty. More than in the case of other countries with highly developed economies, the United States exhibits the same kind of "dualism" of affluence close to poverty found in Rio de Janeiro, Nairobi, Bangkok, and Bombay. This dualism results in tension, high crime rates, and social disorders that are much more similar to political patterns in the poor countries than to Sweden, England, or Canada.

Economic dualism reinforces a social and racial pluralism, which also is more similar to politics in less-developed nations than in Western Europe and English-speaking democracies. Multiethnic politics are common in Belgium, Canada, Switzerland, and (most painfully) Northern Ireland, but most Western nations are spared the racial and ethnic tensions *within the same city* common to both the United States and many poorer countries. Tribal tensions are reproduced in African cities; Indian–Spanish tensions are common in Latin America; and linguistic and ethnic differences unsettle Indian cities. In the United States the triethnic character of Anglo–black–Latin politics is evident from New York to Los Angeles.

In the last analysis it is the combination of the local autonomy tradition from most developed polities and the socioeconomic dualism of the less-developed polities that makes American urban politics and policy distinctive. Governmental fragmentation and local autonomy means that American city governments are expected to handle massive social convulsions and inequalities that elsewhere would be dealt with by central authorities. The fragmented system of local government in the United States exacerbates, as we shall see in Chapter 3, social and economic dualism among cities and suburbs. Local governments depend heavily on their own resources for dealing with the attendant problems of migration, racial conflict, and economic inequality. Yet the resources are very unequally distributed among local governments within a metropolis. There are usually large differences in affluence between central city governments and suburban governments. But there is also much diversity among the suburbs; working-class, black, or racially mixed suburbs adjoin upper-income white suburbs. Indeed, the problems of the poor suburbanite may be worse than those of the central-city ghetto dweller, simply because the central city has taxable commerce and industry within its borders. Harvey and Maywood outside Chicago, Compton outside Los Angeles, and Highland Park and Inkster outside Detroit are all poor suburbs where local autonomy means little more than access to skimpy tax resources.

We should not exaggerate the resemblance between cities of the United States and those of poor countries. Urban problems in the Third World are more severe than in the United States. Poor countries suffer from a higher rate of urban growth. Within the United States the increase of metropolitan population was only 2.4 percent greater than the overall national growth during 1960–1970; in much of Africa, in contrast, urban areas are growing at twice the national rate. This rapid growth in poor countries means that weak administrative structures are inundated with demands that far outstrip available resources. Moreover, the slums of Latin America, Asia, and Africa lack amenities found even in the slums of Chicago, Newark, and Atlanta. Yet the starkness of urban dualism in the United States sets this country apart from other "developed" countries. As we consider urban politics and policy in the United States, we pay considerable attention to the problems and demands resulting from social and economic dualism. In fact, we explore such questions in the next chapter.

Notes

1. See Lincoln Steffans, *The Shame of the Cities* (New York: Hill and Wang, 1957).
2. On the problems of migration in different urban systems, see Stanley Greenberg, *Poverty and Politics* (New York: Wiley, 1974), chap. 2; Joan M. Nelson, "The Urban Poor: Disruption or Political Integration in Third World Cities," *World Politics*, 22 (April 1970), 393–414; and Wayne A. Cornelius, *Politics and the Migrant Poor in Mexico City* (Stanford, Calif.: Stanford University Press, 1975).

3. On comparative power structure research, see Delbert C. Miller, *International Community Power Structure* (Bloomington, Ind.: Indiana University Press, 1970); Francine Rabinovitz, "Sound and Fury Signifying Nothing? — A Review of Community Power Research in Latin America," *Urban Affairs Quarterly, 3* (March 1968), 111–122; and Donald B. Rosenthal, *The Limited Elite: Politics and Government in Two Indian Cities* (Chicago: University of Chicago Press, 1970).

4. Roland L. Warren, *The Community in America*, 2d ed. (Chicago: Rand-Mc-Nally, 1972), chap. 3.

5. Chadwick Alger, "The International Relations of Cities: Creating Images of Alternative Presents," unpublished ms., p. 3.

6. The information about Indian cities in this chapter comes mainly from A. Avasthi, ed., *Municipal Administration in India* (Agra: Lakshmi Narain Agarwal, 1972).

7. This section relies on Richard R. Fagen and William S. Tuohy, *Politics and Privilege in a Mexican City* (Stanford, Calif.: Stanford University Press, 1972).

8. Ibid., p. 29.

9. See Ivan L. Richardson, *Urban Government for Rio de Janeiro* (New York: Praeger, 1973).

10. Girijapati Mukharji, "Problems of Urban Government," in Avasthi, op. cit., p. 6.

11. See Lionel D. Feldman and Michael D. Goldrick, eds., *Politics and Government of Urban Canada: Selected Readings* (Toronto: Methuen, 1969). On metropolitan Toronto, see Harold Kaplan, *Urban Political Systems: A Functional Analysis of Metro Toronto* (New York: Columbia University Press, 1967).

12. Peter G. Richards, *The Reformed Local Government System* (London: Allen and Unwin, 1973), pp. 30–31.

13. Lord Redcliffe-Maud and Bruce Wood, *English Local Government Reformed* (London: Oxford University Press, 1974), p. 132.

14. Douglas E. Ashford, "Parties and Participation in British Local Government and Some American Parallels," *Urban Affairs Quarterly, 11* (September 1975), pp. 58–81.

15. Noel Boaden, *Urban Policy-Making: Influences on County Boroughs in England and Wales* (London: Cambridge University Press, 1971).

16. See Daniel Bell, *The Coming of Post-Industrial Society: A Venture in Social Forecasting* (New York: Basic Books, 1973).

17. See Hans Calmfors, Francine F. Rabinovitz, and Daniel J. Alesch, *Urban Government for Greater Stockholm* (New York: Praeger, 1968).

18. Quoted in William Taubman, *Governing Soviet Cities: Bureaucratic Politics and Urban Development in the USSR* (New York: Praeger, 1973), pp. 26–27.

19. Kurt Steiner, *Local Government in Japan* (Stanford, Calif.: Stanford University Press, 1965), p. 54.

20. See Ira Sharkansky, *The United States: A Study of a Developing Country* (New York: David McKay, 1975), especially chap. 4.

3

THE POLITICAL SOCIOLOGY OF AMERICAN CITIES

The city is of people, and their ebbs and flows determine the contours of urban political life. Who lives where, and why, are principal issues of urban political sociology. The migrations which have shaped the American city include (1) the urbanization of the American population and its concentration in metropolitan areas; (2) the movement of black Americans from the rural south to the central cities of metropolitan areas; (3) the ethnic migrations to the city; (4) the massive suburbanization of the American urban population; and (5) the rise of the so-called "sunbelt" cities. In this chapter we describe these migrations and emphasize their connections with urban politics.

"Never under any circumstances would I move back into the city," remarked Steve Lemons after moving from a North Side Chicago neighborhood to the more comfortable suburbs. Crime, beer cans in his yard, and an influx of problem families were reasons why the Lemons decided to pull up stakes. Another couple, Dr. and Mrs. David Axelrod, went the other direction. After living in a large suburban house for years, Dr. Axelrod was tired of commuting 200 miles a day around Chicago hospitals. They sold their suburban home and bought a condominium in the city. Today they emphasize that "the problems of city life don't seem nearly as bad when you consider that there are more opportunities to develop your own interests and live your own life style" in the city. The Slaters, a black couple, intent on living in an integrated neighborhood, tried it for a while on Chicago's South Side. Soon the integrated neighborhood became almost entirely black and Mrs. Slater found a job at a government laboratory in the blue-collar suburb of Batavia. They, too, made a choice, and moved to Aurora, cutting her commuting time to 10 minutes yet still enjoying some interracial contacts available in their new community.[1]

These and literally millions of other choices cumulate in the pattern of urban location. The city is a mosaic of groups occupying a relatively limited spatial plane. The decisions of millions of urbanites about where to live are a product of many forces, including transportation, housing costs, discrimination, access to jobs, and choices of life styles. Not all these "choices" are really free choices. Many are fully constrained by income variables or other factors. Most are partially constrained. But the accumulated residential choices determine the city as a social organization.

In this chapter we emphasize that the American city has been shaped by a series of migrations. A migration is the aggregate of countless choices made by families like the Lemons, the Axelrods, and the Slaters. We will show that the landscape of the American city has been shaped by five great migrations, the urbanization of the American population, the "blackening" of the central city, the ethnic clustering in cities, the suburbanization of metropolitan populations, and the "southernization" of the American populations. Later, in Chapter 5, we will argue that migration represents an important mode of response to urban problems, with some citizens exercising their "exit" options when problems become intolerable. Mobility is therefore not merely a sociological phenomenon, but a very real political one as well.

THE URBANIZATION OF
THE AMERICAN POPULATION

From Farm to Metropolis

The United States Bureau of the Census was created to fulfill the constitutional stipulation of a counting of the American population each ten years. It conducted its first enumeration in 1790, adopting at that time a definition of urban place as a city with 2,500 inhabitants or more. It has stuck to this definition faithfully through the years for purposes of consistency but has added more contemporary definitions as our conception of "urban" changed. In that first census only 5 percent of the population resided in cities. By 1920, which essentially was the watershed of urbanization, more than one-half the population qualified as urbanites, and by 1970 fully three-fourths fit the urban label. *Whatever the definition of urban, Americans have become an overwhelmingly urban people.* Two-thirds of the population now resides in what the Census Bureau calls "standard metropolitan statistical areas," consisting of central cities of 50,000 people or more and their surrounding county or counties.

Not all, but a good deal, of this escalated urbanization came from a massive population redistribution from rural to urban areas. The attractions of industrialization brought millions to the city in search of employment. There they swelled the urban labor force and remained to stay, as did their children and grandchildren. Particularly in the twentieth century, the modernization of agriculture drove others, usually the marginal, "family" farmer, off the land and into the arms of the waiting city.[2] Today, as agribusiness gobbles up family farms, the process continues. One of the most remarkable facts to emerge from the 1970 census is this: Between 1960 and 1970, the *farm* population of the United States declined by more than one-third, from more than 15 to less than 10 million people. Not all of this farm decline reflected city growth. Some people simply died without being replaced by a new farm resident. But fundamental alterations of rural American life continue to add to the human swelling of urban America. Because many of these new migrants tend to enter the city expecting to find more opportunity than proves to be there — selling their worldly goods to go to the city clutching a copy of the want ads with hundreds of positions listed — they become a fundamental part of the problem of core city areas within the metropolis. Many, of course, are black, but they will fit another migration that we shall examine shortly.

The patterns of urban growth indicates the concentration of economic opportunities in urban, as opposed to rural, areas. Figure 3.1 depicts the population growth in the twentieth century of the United

Figure 3.1   The Growth of the U.S. Population, 1900–1970

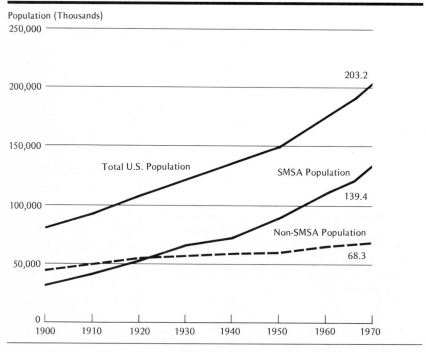

Source: U.S. Department of Commerce, *Statistical Abstract of the United States* (Washington, D.C.: Government Printing Office, 1974), p. 17.

Table 3.1   Distribution of United States Population, 1950–1970

| | 1950 | | 1960 | | 1970 | |
Area	Mil-lions	Per-cent	Mil-lions	Per-cent	Mil-lions	Per-cent
SMSAs						
Inside central cities	53.7	36	59.9	34	63.8	31
Outside central cities	40.9	27	59.6	33	75.6	38
Nonmetropolitan areas (outside SMSAs)	56.7	37	59.7	33	63.8	31
Total	151.3	100.0	179.2	100.0	203.2	100.0

Source: U.S. Department of Commerce, Bureau of the Census, Statistical Abstract of the United States, 1974 (Washington, D.C.: Government Printing Office, 1974), p. 17.

States as a whole, together with growth in standard metropolitan statistical areas (SMSAs) and non-SMSAs. In 1900 approximately 42 percent of the American population resided in the SMSAs, a proportion that has increased to an estimated 70 percent by the mid-1970s. Table 3.1 shows population growth in urban and rural areas between 1950 and 1970.

The Consequences of Urbanization

What does it mean to be "urbanized"? In one sense "urbanized" is only a statistical artifact of Census Bureau definitions. It is technically possible for a farmer on the outskirts of a city to fall into a metropolitan statistic by having a farm within an SMSA county. Surely, though, urbanization means more than this. There are several significant traits which sociologists have long associated with the urban condition:[3]

1. Urbanization is usually, though not always, associated with industrialization. The assembly line is an urban invention and production is more efficient in an urban than in a rural context.
2. Urbanization is often associated with the growth of large, secondary institutions and the lessened role of primary groups such as the family. Urban life is typically bureaucratic life, where service provision is accomplished by institutions rather than individual initiative.
3. Urbanization is sometimes said to be a cause of greater social isolation and even alienation. The city contains shallower roots and more transience than the small town, and rootlessness may result. The fact that crime rates are highest in the biggest cities gives some support to these suspicions.
4. Clearly urbanization is associated with greater interdependence. Urbanites are at the mercy of others. We emphasized in Chapter 2 that the urban world is an increasingly interdependent world economy.
5. Urbanization undoubtedly represents greater social diversity and pluralism.

Small towns and rural areas have people with more in common than urban areas, where different races, cultures, languages intermingle.

The consequences of urbanization are not confined to the American city. In Chapter 2 we explored the great migrations to the cities of the Third World. There a process that took the United States 200 years to accomplish is often telescoped into a few decades. The movement of blacks from the South to the North, the depopulation of the American farm, and the urbanization of Appalachian coal miners all have their parallels in Caracas, Mexico City, or Calcutta. The arrivals of once-rural groups adds to the political problems of governing an urban civilization.

IMMIGRATION AND THE CITY

The Old Immigration

If an American knows nothing else about the history of the American city, he or she knows about the great tidal waves of immigration to the American city. Immigration added significantly to the size of the cities, especially in the era between the Civil War and World War I. First came the northern European immigrants from England, Scotland, Ireland, and Germany, than later the southern and eastern Europeans, including Poles, Czechs, Slovaks, Greeks, and Russian Jews. At the same time, large numbers of Orientals were virtually imported

Blacks in the city—the most segregated migrants.

into the United States to the cities of the Pacific. Some of these immigrants toiled and became fantastically successful. Stephen Birmingham's *Our Crowd* tells the story of a handful of Jewish families who came first to the cities, often became peddlers, and later became financiers and bankers. Others were unsuccessful and returned to the old country. But most prospered and struggled to middle class status. Today the European ethnics no longer occupy clusters of housing in the central city. First- and second-generation European ethnics are about equally likely to live in the central city as the suburbs.[4] They remain a potent political force (as we shall see in Chapter 5, pp. 107–109), however.

This tidal wave of immigration was cut to a trickle with the passage of a restrictive immigration law of 1924. Representing a powerful outpouring of American nativism, it established quotas not to be repealed for a half century. The quotas favored certain kinds of groups — especially northern Europeans, who were actually the least likely to be immigrating — and disfavored others, particularly southern Europeans and, even more, Orientals. That legislation had the effect of virtually shutting off the traditional sources of immigrants.

The New Immigration

The "old immigration" is dead, but a "new immigration" has emerged to replace it. Today immigration to the cities continues, although its points of origin are different. The roots of the new immigration are almost entirely Latin in character, composed primarily of three groups. Cubans have come in large numbers — a half million in Miami alone — to populate southeastern cities. Puerto Ricans, who as commonwealth citizens have easy access to the United States, have come to constitute the second largest minority group in most northeastern cities, particularly New York and Newark. But the largest share of the nation's Spanish-heritage population of 9.3 million belongs to the Chicano of Mexican heritage. (Only blacks constitute a larger minority group than Chicanos.) In contrast to the stereotypes depicting these people as largely migrant laborers or *braceros*, Mexican Americans are an overwhelmingly urban people. More than four-fifths of them live in cities. The three largest concentrations are in Los Angeles (with almost a million and a half), San Antonio, and Chicago, but increasing proportions are found in cities like Houston, Phoenix, San Diego, Austin, and Denver. The immigration of Chicanos continues, and any estimates of their numbers are tentative. Vast numbers of illegal entrants cross the U.S.-Mexican border annually. The border patrol apprehends and returns no fewer than 500,000 entrants per year (an unknown number of whom, of course, are multiple entrants), a proportion that almost certainly does not reflect more than one-third to one-half of all entrants. In the cities unemployment and underemployment of these groups remains high; their housing is often the poorest in the metropolitan area; and their schooling is afflicted by the special disabilities of language.

THE URBANIZATION OF BLACK AMERICANS

Black Migration and Some Misconceptions

In 1910, 9 of every 10 blacks lived in the rural South. Today, less than half live in the South. But more important than the northward migration to Cleveland, Newark, Chicago, New York, Detroit, and elsewhere is the general urbanization of blacks, both north and south. There are now four large cities with black electoral majorities (Washington, Atlanta, Gary, and Newark) and others (Detroit, St. Louis, Baltimore, New Orleans, Wilmington, Birmingham, and Charleston) with near-majorities of 40 percent or larger. The proportion of blacks in larger cities increases with each census count. More cities will cross the line in the future. In many of these cities, blacks have accumulated sufficient electoral clout to select black mayors. Not only in Detroit, Gary, Cleveland, Newark, and Atlanta with their large black populations, but even in Los Angeles with its smaller one (17.9 percent), black chief executives have steered the rocky urban ship of state.

The movement of blacks to the city is well known. There are two myths, however, which have grown up about this migration. The first is the "grapes of wrath" impression of black migrants, that they are usually unskilled, poorly educated, and suffer severe problems adjusting to urban life. The facts, as Charles Tilly and others have shown, are otherwise.[5] Actually migrants tend to be the "cream of the crop" at their point of origin, better educated, more ambitious, and more likely to get ahead. They also tend to *raise* the educational and occupational level of the city to which they go. There is very little evidence connecting recent migrants with more serious family problems, broken homes, crime, or delinquency. Evidence about the participants in the urban ghetto revolts of the 1960s shows that recent migrants were *less* likely to have participated in violence. The problems that migrants face in the city, therefore, are structural problems associated with the city and not deficiencies they brought with them.

There is a second, and even more pervasive, myth about black migration, which could be described as the "blacks are just like the Irish" argument. Its most articulate proponent is Edward C. Banfield, who puts it this way:[6]

Today the Negro's *main* disadvantage is the same as the Puerto Rican's and the Mexican's: namely, that he is the most recent unskilled and hence relatively low-income migrant to reach the city from a backward rural area. The city is not the end of his journey but the start of it. He came to it not because he was lured by a cruel and greedy master but because he was attracted by job, housing, school, and other opportunities that, bad as they were, were nevertheless better by far than any he had known before. Like earlier immigrants, the Negro has reason to expect that his children will have increases of opportunity even greater than his.

The principal deficiency of such a perspective, however, is that blacks and "new immigrants" came to the city in a very different state of development than the "old immigrants." The "new immigrants" have arrived at the urban threshold at the wrong time — when urban dynamism has shifted almost entirely to the periphery. The core city is not what it used to be. When Irishmen, Italians, Greeks, and Slavs came to the core, there was ample economic opportunity in the city to be seized, even for relatively unskilled laborers. Today (as we shall see momentarily) the economic constrictions of the core city area make it the least productive place for migration. Partly as a consequence, unemployment rates among urban blacks are almost universally two to three times that of the national average (whether the national average is 4, 6, or 8 percent). The unemployment figures in urban areas among black teenagers are even higher, pushing 30 and 40 percent in most cities and in some places even an incredible 50 percent. This is not the stuff of which upward mobility is forged. There are three key changes in the city itself and the economic system in general that have made the city to which the "old immigrants" came and to which the "new immigrants" (including but not limited to blacks) come a very different place:

1. For the "old immigrants," the core city was the center of economic vitality, while the "new immigrants" face a core riddled with decay and movement of economic activity to the periphery.
2. The whole structure of the labor market itself has changed dramatically since the 1880s. No longer are there hundreds of thousands of openings for unskilled and marginally skilled workers, as the economic system has become increasingly capital intensive and dependent on a highly skilled urban labor force.
3. Never, not in the most overdrawn stories of "Little Italy," "Little Dublin," and other ethnic neighborhoods, did the scope of residential segregation approximate that of blacks today, where square mile after square mile of the larger cities is occupied solely by a single group.

Segregation in the Metropolis

It is that last fact — the extreme levels of segregation of black urbanites — which may be the most important single fact about black life in the city. To say this is not to perpetuate still another persistent myth, that almost all blacks are huddled into crowded tenements often called ghettos. Black Americans constitute 12 percent of the total population, and they exhibit considerable variety. There are prosperous black communities and poor ones; black suburbs as well as white ones. But two facts stand about about black life in the city:

1. First, blacks are overwhelmingly segregated into the central cities of metropolitan areas.
2. Blacks are overwhelmingly segregated into virtually all-black neighborhoods within the central cities.

Blacks tend overwhelming to live in the central city; whites tend increasingly to live in the suburbs. At least 56 percent of all American blacks now live in the central cities of metropolitan areas, North and South, whereas only 25 percent of white Americans live there. The proportion of suburban populations which are black has showed practically no change whatever since 1940, and hovers around 4–5 percent in every census. Despite numerous policies emphasizing housing desegregation, the image of a "white noose around a black neck" remains. Moreover, it is a myth to think of black suburbanization as "salt and pepper" residential patterning. Housing segregation in the suburbs is even sharper than in the central cities. Most black suburbanization has actually occurred in two kinds of places, either the all-black suburb or simply the pushing outward beyond central-city boundaries of an all-black neighborhood. Blacks are concentrated in central cities generally and even in particular central cities. Two-thirds of all northern black families live in only 7 metropolitan areas containing more than 300,000 blacks each (New York, Chicago, Detroit, Philadelphia, St. Louis, Newark, and Cleveland).[7]

Within the central city, blacks normally live in virtually all-black neighborhoods. The most careful research on race and residential segregation has been undertaken by the sociologists Karl and Alma Taueber.[8] They developed a "segregation index," which varies from 100 (complete segregation with no whites in black areas and no blacks in white areas) to 0 (random distribution by race). The Tauebers have computed segregation indexes for 109 American cities from 1940 through 1970. With the public policy commitment to open housing and the rising affluence of black families, one might think that segregation has declined significantly. The data in Table 3.2 suggest virtually no change at all through 1960 and only a very modest dip between 1960 and 1970. One intuitive way of thinking about the segregation index is this: 81.6 percent of all families in the typical city would have to move in order to have integrated housing.

What are the causes of this residential segregation? Karl Taeuber[9] has cited Gunnar Myrdal, the distinguished Swedish economist and student of the American race problem, who has offered three hypothe-

Table 3.2   Segregation Indices for 109
Cities, 1940–1970, and for Selected Cities
in 1970

A. Mean segregation indices, 1940–1970

Year	Mean
1940	85.2
1950	87.3
1960	86.1
1970	81.6

B. Selected cities, 1970

City	Segregation index
Akron	82.5
Boston	84.3
Des Moines	83.7
Fort Worth	95.4
Little Rock	90.6
Newark	76.4
New York City	77.3
Oakland	70.4
Richmond	91.4
Sacramento	71.1
Topeka	79.4
Washington	78.8

Source: Annemette Sørenson, Karl E.
Taeuber, and Leslie J. Hollingsworth, Jr.,
Sociological Focus, 8 (April 1975), 125–142

ses to explain housing segregation. First, it may result from deliberate preference for living among members of one's own race. Second, it may result from poverty. Because the income levels of whites and blacks differ markedly, blacks may simply be unable to afford homes anywhere but in the poorest neighborhoods. Housing segregation would thus be a matter of class, rather than of race. Third, it may be the result of discrimination.

There is no doubt some merit in each of these explanations. Surely deliberate choice is involved in residential location, but Myrdal and the Taeubers all have noted that choice is not altogether *free* when made in a society in which racial discrimination and prejudice are widespread. The more probable explanations for segregated housing patterns are thus the income and discrimination theories.

"Discrimination," however, covers quite literally a multitude of sins. In its blatant form it includes outright refusal to sell or rent homes to nonwhite families (now strictly illegal). It can be very blatant when newcomers are met with violence, hostility, or indifference. But we should also seek more subtle causes. The structural determinants of residential segregation are numerous. The use of exclusionary zoning, the location of public (and mostly black) housing projects, and the drying up of mortgage money in minority neighborhoods are some reasons that we examine in Chapter 14.

THE SUBURBANIZATION OF THE METROPOLIS

Suburbia

Suburbanization became a massive social phenomenon in the years after World War II. It has been a response to some of the major social tensions in urban areas and is itself responsible for several of the major issues of urban public policy. The suburbs have also spawned myths, and to understand urban problems and policies it is necessary to examine these myths to see what truth there may be in them.[10]

In suburbia, according to myth, one will find a home of one's own, a small piece of real estate on which to practice yeoman's skills, good schools, plenty of land for recreation, clean and traffic-free neighborhoods, a small-town atmosphere, a local government with whose members one is on first-name terms, low taxes, Christmas lights, a Fourth of July parade, a homogeneous community without social tension, young neighbors, and an open leadership unstratified by age or social class. In many suburban areas this myth is a reality. When compared with those of metropolitan central cities, suburban homes are far less often judged "dilapidated" or "crowded" by the Census Bureau. Many suburbs also tend to show higher levels of family income and adult education, spend proportionately more of the local budgets on education, and have younger and almost entirely white populations.

These features make the suburbs attractive to many young families, who choose to move there also because of crowding and the lack of suitable dwellings within their financial means in the central city; easy commuting from the suburbs to work or shopping; increasing availability of jobs, shopping, and service facilities in the suburbs themselves; aesthetic appeal of middle-class neighborhoods with private homes and yards; the fear of central-city crime; and reluctance to send their children to central-city schools. Increasingly, young families do not have to face the question of *moving* from the central city to the suburbs. The "war babies" of the 1940s who have now advanced into parenthood have the simpler decision to remain in the type of community they have known since birth.

Not all the elements of the suburban myth are true. Some appear to be rather gross distortions, whereas others are oversimplifications that hide significant exceptions. For one thing, the surplus land in a new suburb is characteristically taken up by private home sites and commercial developments, with the result that there is often a smaller proportion of park land in a mature suburb than in the central city. Suburbs may grow more rapidly than their leaders' taste for — or skill in — controlling land use. One frequent result is a proliferation of filling stations and tawdry driven-ins along a main road that had been tree-lined and free of litter; another may be failure to control unsanitary alignments of private wells and septic tanks. Taxes may be low when the first new families migrate to an established small town, but when the migration increases to flood proportions the demand for more schools and teachers produces a sudden bulge in the local budget that may send property taxes above their levels in the central city. The social homogeneity of many suburbs may be attractive to members of the local "tribe," but, if it is uniformly of the working class and if there is no large tax revenue from industry or shopping centers, it may be impossible to support a level of education that is better than or even as good as that in the city.

The myth also emphasizes high participation in and personal familiarity with suburban government, but studies indicate that the rates of organizational participation are no higher in the suburbs than in central-city neighborhoods of comparable class levels, and voting turnouts in suburban local elections are frequently lower.[11] Finally, although conflicts in the suburbs may not have their origins in class or ethnic tensions, there are antagonisms. Old-timers and newcomers, Main Street merchants and commuters tend to clash.

Where the Growth Is

Virtually all of the population growth in the United States is concentrated in the outside-central-city areas of the metropolis, in other words, in the "suburbs." The populations of rural areas, small towns, and central cities are virtually stagnant. The population advantage of outside-central-city areas, compared with central-city areas, is shown in Figure 3.2. The year 1960 marked near-equality of central-city and suburban population. Since that time cities have declined rapidly, and suburban areas have grown equally fast. By the 1970 census, 54.2 percent of the metropolitan population resided in the suburban areas. Even in the brief period from 1970–1974, central cities lost 1.2 million people or 2 percent of their populations, while suburban areas gained 6.2 million or 8.4 percent of their populations.[12]

Figure 3.2   The Trend in Distribution of SMSA Population Between Central Cities and Outside, 1900–1975

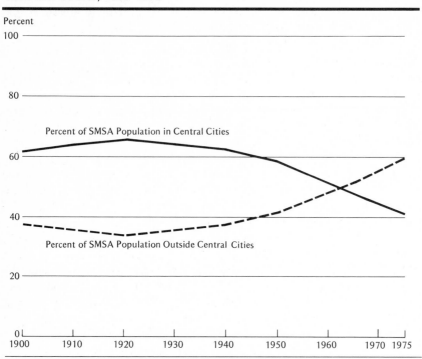

The case of St. Louis is illustrative. Once the nation's fourth largest city, the population decline in St. Louis between 1960 and 1975 was great enough to drop the city back to its 1890 population. From 850,000 people in 1950, it had shrunk to an estimated 550,000 in 1975. A RAND Corporation report declared that St. Louis was the first major city to "lose" its central city. Clayton, the seat of government of suburban St. Louis County, became the dominant "central city" of the SMSA. One observer, Professor George Wendel of St. Louis University remarked that "they used to call us 'first in shoes, first in booze, and last in the American League.' Now the shoe factories and most of the breweries are gone, and we're not even in the American League anymore."[13] While housing pressures build up in the suburbs, 2,200 vacant buildings lie prey to vandals in the city. The same pattern, though on a smaller scale, is apparent in Baltimore, Chicago, Milwaukee, New York City, and other older SMSAs. Between 1950 and 1970 the population in each of the 15 largest central cities declined as a percentage of their total metropolitan area's population. Baltimore's percentage of its SMSA population went from 68 to 44, Chicago's from 70 to 48, and Washington's from 55 to 27.

The Sociology of the Suburbs

"Suburbia" is almost a stereotype. The image includes single-family dwelling units, two cars in every garage, commuting to jobs in the central city, PTA meetings and Cub Scouts, tree-shaded streets, barbecue grills, almost all white and middle-class ("WASP"—White Anglo-Saxon Protestant—is supposedly the dominant "ethnic group") residents, and ranch-style housing. This stereotyped image of suburbia cannot be sustained, at least not for many suburbs.[14] The image evokes, however, a *cultural* or *life style* meaning of suburbia. There is, however, another meaning of suburb, a *demographic* meaning. One common confusion about suburbia stems from mixing the life style and demographic implications of the concept. *Demographically a suburb is an incorporated municipality within the metropolitan area other than the central city.* One can be a suburbanite in either a cultural sense or a demographic sense, or even both. But living in a demographic suburb may or may not overlap with living in a culturally suburban area. Demographic suburbs come in all shapes, sizes, and types. Conversely, one may live in a culturally suburban area but within a central city. Vast tracts of land within large central cities, especially newer ones such as Seattle, Portland, Tampa, Houston, and Phoenix, seem to be as suburban in their life style and appearance as are the stereotypical suburbs elsewhere. The important point is not to confuse the cultural with the demographic traits of suburbia.

The demographic suburb is far more varied than stereotypes commonly assume. Suburbs come in different colors. Some, such as Robbins, Illinois, or Compton, California, are primarily black. They come in different sizes: a few suburbs of the largest metropolitan areas could qualify as metropolitan areas themselves were they not already included in one. East Los Angeles and Pasadena within the Los Angeles metropolitan area each have populations well in excess of 100,000. Some are pristine residential greenbelts composed of very wealthy people, providing the finest public schools and public services that money can buy (Kenilworth, Illinois, is an example). Some are tourist-oriented, such as Arlington, Texas; others are primarily industrial, such as Hamtramck, Michigan; or mostly working class such as East Orange, New Jersey. In fact, suburbs are beginning to duplicate the endless variety of economic, social, and political patterns once so apparent in the large city itself. Louis Masotti has called this the "urbanization of the suburbs."[15]

Still, despite the suburban variety, one should not miss the forest for the trees. One can find poverty in cities and outside-central-city areas; one can find segregated black populations within central cities and in the periphery; one can find culturally suburban and affluent neighborhoods within both areas. All of these generalizations are "more or less" or "others things being equal" propositions. Each of them contains exceptions (the trees), but each of them also reflects a general pattern duplicated over and over again in metropolitan areas (the forest). Three generalizations accurately characterize the differences between central cities (on the average) and suburbs (on the average):

1. Virtually all the population growth in metropolitan areas is concentrated in outside-central-city areas.
2. Outside-central-city areas are overwhelmingly white, while central cities are increasingly black.
3. Outside-central-city areas are typically more affluent than central city areas.

THE NEW URBANIZATION

Go West and South

A century ago Horace Greeley advised his readers to "go west, young man, go west." Americans are still taking that advice, as the growth and decline of regional populations show. Journalist Kirkpatrick Sale describes a "power shift" to the area he calls the southern rim.[16] If one draws a line from Washington, D.C., in the East to San Francisco in the West, the area south of that line is Sales's southern rim. Much of the population growth of the nation is now concentrated there, particularly in the cities.

The massive area from Boston on the north, down through New York and Philadelphia, and to Washington, D.C., and Baltimore on the south, remains the largest agglomerate of urban population in the United States. This urbanized northeastern seaboard, often called BosWash or Megalopolis, contains nearly 50 million people. Add to it the great sweep of urban population along the Great Lakes, in Buffalo, Pittsburgh, Cleveland, Detroit, Chicago, and Milwaukee, and their environs (sometimes called "Chipitts"), and the urban swatch can be extended to cover a vast portion of the northeastern quadrant of the nation. Here the commercial, industrial, and political centers of the nation are clustered.

But the urban dominance of the old, industrialized cities is being rapidly eroded by the rise of new metropolitan centers outside the northeastern corridor. In fact, most metropolitan growth is now increasingly concentrated in the South, Southwest, and West. What is happening to urban growth regionally is depicted in Table 3.3. There we break the country into four quadrants on lines drawn from Washington, D.C., and westward and use the Mississippi as the North–South axis (incorporating St. Louis into the North where it might feel more comfortable than with the Southwest). The nation's 24 largest SMSAs all appear there, and the pattern is plain. Between 1950 and

Table 3.3 Population Change (in Percent) for Central Cities of the 24 Largest SMSAs, 1950–1970, by Region

Northwest		Northeast	
San Francisco	+ 7.7	New York	− 0.3
Seattle	+ 13.5	Chicago	− 7.0
		Philadelphia	− 3.3
		Detroit	− 19.2
		Boston	− 18.8
		Pittsburgh	− 23.1
		St. Louis	− 27.3
		Cleveland	− 17.9
		Newark	− 12.9
		Cincinnati	− 12.0
		Buffalo	− 20.2
		Milwaukee	+ 10.9
		Minneapolis	− 16.9
Southwest		**Southeast**	
Houston	+107.1	Washington	− 5.7
Dallas	+ 94.3	Baltimore	− 3.6
Los Angeles	+ 44.0	Miami	+ 34.3
Kansas City	+ 11.1	Atlanta	+ 47.0
Denver	+ 21.4		

1970, 12 of the 13 cities in the Northeast suffered population reverses. The southern cities were split, but the key to the story is in southwestern cities stretching from Houston to Los Angeles. In the Southwest, the dominant pattern is impressive growth. Houston had a 1960–1970 growth rate of 107 percent, Dallas 94 percent, and Los Angeles 44 percent. The West has now displaced the Northeast as the most urbanized section of the nation. Texas contains the largest number of SMSAs, having as many as New York and California combined. Perhaps it is no accident that the "urban fiscal crisis" was focused on places such as New York City, Pittsburgh, and Chicago. One northeastern state official remarked simply that "every time I go to Dallas I get sick."

Climatic advantages, lower taxes, the prevalence of right-to-work laws, cheap energy, and lower living costs may all play a role. Many of the reasons for this shift are economic, a subject we discuss in the next chapter. The federal government has also poured moneys into southern states while draining them from northeastern states. NASA's location in Houston and Florida and heavy defense spending in Texas, California, Florida, South Carolina, and other southern rim states have made a difference in employment opportunities. In 1974, the "sunbelt states" netted $13 billion in federal spending more than they paid in taxes, while northern states got back $20 billion less than they contributed in federal tax revenues.[17] These and other reasons have solidified the position of the "southern rim" as the growth area for the third century of American life. No one should fear that the Northeast will wither away. Key industries such as steel and automobiles are concentrated there. But the problems of northeastern cities are increasingly those of containing decay, whereas the problems of southern and western cities are increasingly those of managing growth.

CONCLUSIONS

Urban political sociology attempts to understand where people live and what difference that makes for politics. Americans have been a highly mobile people, setting out on a westward journey that still continues. The earliest westward movement was mostly to open land. Today's migration is to the cities in the West and South, creating the new urbanization. Blacks and whites alike have made an urban journey, and the urbanization of the American population is important in understanding the problems that cities present. The urbanization of the population, however, has begun to slow down. The *sub*urbanization, a movement that has now made a plurality of all Americans suburbanites, continues. Ethnics who once came to the city have now become scattered across the metropolitan landscape. Often they have been replaced by blacks newly arrived in the central city. These five migrations — urbanization, the ethnic migration, the "blackening" of the central city, suburbanization, and the new westward and southern migration — constitute an important backdrop for understanding politics in the city.

Notes

1. *U.S. News and World Report,* 5 April 1976, 57–61.
2. On agricultural modernization and urbanward movement, see Frances Fox Piven and Richard Cloward, *Regulating the Poor* (New York: Pantheon, 1971), chap. 7. See also Niles Hansen, *Rural Poverty and the Urban Crisis* (Bloomington, Ind.: Indiana University Press, 1970).
3. Some excellent sociological writing on the city includes Scott Greer, *The Emerging City* (New York: Free Press, 1962); Herbert Gans, *The Urban Villagers* (New York: Free Press, 1962); and Elliot Liebow, *Tally's Corner* (Boston: Little, Brown, 1967).
4. Stanley Lieberson, *Ethnic Patterns in American Cities* (New York: The Free Press, 1963), pp. 98–99.
5. Charles Tilly, "Race and Migration to the American City," in James Q.

Wilson, ed., *The Metropolitan Enigma* (Cambridge, Mass.: Harvard University Press, 1968).

6. *The Unheavenly City Revisited* (Boston: Little, Brown, 1974), p. 78.

7. Evidence on housing segregation within suburbs and cities is usefully summarized in Karl E. Taueber, "Racial Segregation: The Persisting Dilemma," *Annals of the American Academy of Political and Social Science, 422* (November 1975), 87–96. See also the article by William J. Siembieda in the same volume.

8. *Negroes in Cities: Residential Segregation and Neighborhood Change* (Chicago: Aldine, 1965).

9. Karl E. Taueber, "Residential Segregation," *Scientific American, 213* (August 1965), p. 19.

10. Suburban myths have been explored in a number of careful studies, including Robert C. Wood, *Suburbia* (Boston: Houghton Mifflin, 1959); Bennett Berger, *Working Class Suburb* (Berkeley: University of California Press, 1960); William Dobriner, *Class in Suburbia* (Englewood Cliffs, N.J.: Prentice-Hall, 1963); and Herbert Gans, *The Levittowners* (New York: Basic Books, 1967). Excellent recent treatments of suburbs include Frederick M. Wirt et al., *On the City's Rim: Suburban Politics and Policies* (Lexington, Mass.: Heath, 1972); Anthony Downs, *Opening Up the Suburbs* (New Haven: Yale University Press, 1973); and *Annals of the American Academy of Political and Social Science,* op. cit.

11. John C. Bollens et al., *Exploring the Metropolitan Community* (Berkeley: University of California Press, 1961), pp. 87–88.

12. Vincent P. Barabba, "Shifts and Flows of Jobs and People," paper presented at the Conference on the Aging Metropolis, Rutgers University, March 11, 1975, p. 5.

13. Ed McManus, "Is St. Louis Now 'Just Another Suburb'?" Chicago *Tribune,* January 1976, 14.

14. The distinctions among types of suburbs made here come from Robert L. Lineberry, "Suburbia and the Metropolitan Turf," *Annals,* op. cit., 2–4.

15. Louis H. Masotti and Jeffrey K. Hadden, eds., *The Urbanization of the Suburbs* (Beverly Hills, Calif.: Sage Publications, 1973).

16. Kirkpatrick Sale, *Power Shift: The Rise of the Southern Rim and Its Challenge to the Eastern Establishment* (New York: Random House, 1975).

17. "Federal Spending: The North's Loss Is the Sunbelt's Gain," *National Journal,* 26 June 1976, 878–891.

4

THE POLITICAL ECONOMY OF AMERICAN CITIES

The irony of urban wealth is that the massive concentrations of wealth and capital in the cities coexist with significant service and resource shortages in urban governments. The urban political economy is the producer of great wealth and contains enormous human capital. Yet the metropolitan political system is a complicated system of fragmented governments, limited and constrained by their own resources and tax bases. Wealth may exist in one place, but poverty in another, poorer, jurisdiction. To understand the *political* economy of metropolitan areas, we shall want to understand the fragmentation of metropolitan areas and the efforts urban officials make to cope with limited resources. Thus, in this chapter we show

- how American metropolitan areas have become the principal sources of wealth and capital in the American economy
- yet how the fragmented metropolitan government and other constraints limit the access of urban governments to this wealth
- how urban politics is typically a politics of economics, with officials constantly trying to cope with the limits of their fiscal powers

To some observers, New York City is the bellwether among American cities. As New York went, so would a nation of cities go. The worries about New York's possible default and bankruptcy were magnified into horror stories about the fiscal collapse of other cities. An article in *New York* magazine in 1975 was entitled "The Day New York Defaulted" and painted a gloomy picture of the international and domestic reverberations of the fiscal demise of the world's richest city. Appealing for federal aid, city officials got mostly deaf ears. A famous headline in the New York *Daily News* blared President Gerald Ford's position: "Ford to City: Drop Dead." (New York voters returned the compliment on election day 1976, giving a decisive margin to Jimmy Carter). It almost seemed as though all the issues of urban political economy had come to a head in the New York case. Population was declining. Every week, 2,000 New Yorkers called a moving van, and most were not replaced. The city had lost 464,000 jobs since 1970. For the first time in 33 years, the total value of taxable property declined. In 1964, taxes were 7.6 percent of personal income; in 1974, they were 10.2 percent. New office construction had come to a halt and other buildings were vacated. For years the city had met its problems with a large public sector—the most humane government in America, its defenders maintained—and well-paid, unionized municipal employees. These high expenditures necessitated high rates of borrowing, often to meet current payrolls rather than long-run capital investments. The city lived from hand to mouth. The world's richest city teetered then, as it does now, on the brink of fiscal collapse.

It is ironic that the richest place in the world should confront such problems. Consequently our theme in this chapter is "the irony of urban wealth." American cities are the principal producers of wealth in the economic system. Yet the political economy of cities produces significant problems for urban officials and citizens. Many of these problems result from the disjuncture between the political city and the economic city. The fragmentation of metropolitan government often separates wealth from need. Coping with the urban political economy is the most difficult challenge that urban policy makers face. How they try to cope is one of our interests in this chapter.

THE IRONY OF
URBAN WEALTH

The irony of urban wealth is that the tremendous human and economic capital in our cities lies tantalizingly just beyond the reach of urban policy makers. Observers differ in their estimates of our cities' future, but there is wide agreement about the current situation of urban areas—especially about the congestion, pollution, and tensions of the cities and about the inability of local politicians to alleviate these problems because they do not command enough resources to do so. We discuss in this chapter three key aspects of the policy environment of the urban political system: (1) the great economic and human resources of urban areas, (2) the distribution of those resources within the metropolitan area, and (3) the impediments to the use of those resources by urban governments.

It is difficult for urban governments to use these resources because of the uneven distribution of wealth and problems within the metropolis, and because of legal, political, and economic barriers. In Greek mythology Tantalus, from whose name the verb "tantalize" is derived, is condemned to have fruit and water recede beyond his reach whenever he tries to grasp them. The irony of urban wealth is not that simple, but the inability of cities to use what lies just beyond their reach is at the core of the American urban crisis.

The Wealth of Cities

Cities are the major producers of wealth in the contemporary United States, primarily because they have the personnel and facilities that process the raw materials of the fields and mines into finished commodities. Almost as important, cities have those specialists in medicine, law, theater, the arts, fashion, and entertainment whose work is highly prized in a culture of increasingly sophisticated tastes. Money flows to the cities to pay for the services of these specialists, and prospective specialists flow to the cities to complete their own training and to compete for employment.

According to Jane Jacobs, cities have always led the way in economic development.[1] She argues against the traditional view that cities grew on a rural base. Her evidence shows that settled agriculture began in cities, and that historic as well as contemporary cities provided the basic opportunities and technologies for rural development: for example, the markets, hybrid seeds, pesticides, and sophisticated fertilizers that have spurred production; the capital for irrigation; and the financial and commercial mechanisms that have linked growers with consumers. In such a view, human society as we know it is urban, and the large cities of today stand as the latest examples of the sources for economic growth.

The population growth of urban areas is one sign of economic power. Yet this growth is also a source of problems for urban authorities. Prosperity also attracts many untrained segments of the population who want better opportunities for themselves and their families. The cost to the city of providing some newcomers with services is substantially greater than the value of these newcomers' skills to the city's economy. Urban slums, to which many of these immigrants flock, represent a combination of the attractions of the city for poor people and the inability of many immigrants to succeed in the urban environment. Here again is an irony of the urban economy: an abundance of wealth that begets poverty even while its reproduces itself, and local authorities who do not have adequate access to the resources to satisfy the intense demands made on them.

All wealth is either in the form of human capital or physical and fiscal capital. Human capital, of course, is difficult to measure precisely, but the skills of the labor force are probably better described by educational levels than by any other single measure. The distribution of educational attainments shown in Table 4.1 mirrors the distribution of personal wealth and population growth. The urbanite is generally better educated than is his rural cousin, indicating that cities possess greater reservoirs of human skills on which to draw.

Median family incomes reflect these differences in educational attainments. They are consistently higher in metropolitan than in nonmet-

Table 4.1   Distribution of Educational Attainments in Urban and Rural Areas

Educational characteristic	SMSA	Non-SMSA
Median school years completed	12.2	11.4
Percentage completing fewer than 5 years of school	4.8	7.0
Percentage completing 4 years of college or more	12.0	7.7

Source: U.S. Bureau of the Census, *U.S. Census of Population, 1970, General Social and Economic Characteristics: Final Report* (Washington, D.C.: Government Printing Office, 1971).

Table 4.2   Median White Family Income in Metropolitan and Nonmetropolitan Areas, 1970

	SMSA	Non-SMSA
Central city	$10,385	—
Outside central city	11,701	—
Nonfarm	—	$8,871
Farm	—	6,819

Source: *Statistical Abstract of the United States, 1972* (Washington, D.C.: Government Printing Office, 1972). Data for blacks are lower, but parallel with respect to SMSA–Non-SMSA differentials.

ropolitan areas, as Table 4.2 indicates. Rural farm residents who live on the fringes of the metropolitan areas are well situated to exploit the economic appeal of the metropolis. They often commute to jobs in the city, or they profit from truck farming that serves the big-city market.

Metropolitan areas also contain the great engines of production and management needed to run the American economy. We often associate cities with their economic activities: Pittsburgh and steel, Detroit and cars, New York and Wall Street; Hartford and insurance; Seattle and aircraft production; Houston and oil. In short, the great economic and human energies of the United States are concentrated in its metropolitan areas. Metropolitan areas, containing two-thirds of the nation's population, also account for:

1. more than four-fifths of savings-and-loan deposits
2. four-fifths of all bank deposits
3. more than three-fourths of value added by manufacturing
4. three-fourths of the nation's personal income
5. more than seven-tenths of all retail sales
6. seven-tenths of assessed property value

The Migration of Urban Wealth
and the Roots of the Irony

We showed in Chapter 3 how population has been redistributed through several major migrations. Two of these in particular—the movement to the suburbs and the rise of the "sunbelt"—are parallelled by the migration of production and industrial wealth.

The movement of industries and commercial establishments has both followed and encouraged the movement of families. Most economic growth is now concentrated in outside-central-city areas. The flight of industry and commerce from central cities exacerbates the already high unemployment rates in those areas. The reasons for industrial movements resemble those for families. Hoover and Vernon mention: (1) the search for space, (2) changes in transportation technology, (3) movement of labor, (4) the availability of external economies, and (5) the flight from taxes.[2] Perhaps the paramount reason for both family and business movement is the sheer need for space. The cost of relocating a growing plant in a central city is many times more than that of moving it to a suburb. Moreover, plants now located in areas zoned for residential purposes often cannot obtain permission to expand.

As rails displace waterways and roads displace rails, there is less reason to concentrate production in small core areas. Indeed, intermet-

Economic factors in Chicago have led to a metropolitan area with a population of 7 million.

ropolitan movement is facilitated by location outside the congested downtown areas, as are a firm's chances of obtaining a labor supply. The majority of skilled personnel now live in suburbs, including three-fourths of union members under age 40.

By *external economies* Hoover and Vernon mean input factors and tertiary services necessary to produce commodities. These external economies of large firms can be maximized outside the central city. Smaller (and often less profitable) operations are left in the central city, where they benefit from close contact with suppliers and distributors. A small garment manufacturer is typical of the kind of firm that still benefits from a central city location. Equally typical, unfortunately, are the low wages and unpromising futures that the garment industry offers its employees. The pursuit of low taxes, though often exaggerated by businessmen and families seeking new locations, has been a determining force in some movement to suburbs.

Some of this industrial migration to the suburbs has been at the expense of the central cities. New York's 464,000 lost jobs have not simply disappeared but have largely gone to the suburbs of Connecticut and New Jersey. The New York Stock Exchange once seriously contemplated moving to New Jersey; hundreds of firms actually made the move. Wilbur Thompson, one of the most distinguished urban economists, observes that "in broad terms, the largest metropolitan areas have been evolving into two easily identifiable, although heavily overlapping economies. The central city is more and more a place of business and professional service – the workplace of lawyers, consultants, financiers, and officials of all kinds; the suburbs are more and more the heart of the manufacturing district."[3]

Boston: A Case in Point

Boston is the home of the freedom trail, the Old North Church from which Paul Revere warned the citizenry, and other historic sites. It was also, in 1950, the location of 101,000 manufacturing jobs.[4] By 1970 it was the location of only 63,000 manufacturing positions. Total employment had remained fairly constant, but production had moved elsewhere. A survey of Boston city manufacturing firms showed that 58.3 percent contemplated moving in the future. More than 70 percent of Boston suburban firms doubted that they would move. One reason was land costs. At most, there are probably no more than 220 acres available for industrial development in Boston, at a cost of $3.50–$4.00 a square foot. Along Route I-495 in the suburbs, 25 miles from the central business district, prices are less than $1.00 per square foot. Some of Boston's manufacturing losses have been to the Boston area suburbs. Others have been out of state. Textile firms once were clustered in Massachusetts. Labor costs are now cheaper in the south, and manufacturers do not have to confront unions in the south so frequently. Numerous firms that once called Boston home no longer do so. The story is similar elsewhere. In the fall of 1976, Dallas Chamber of Commerce representatives came to Chicago to discuss the economic virtues of Southwest "Metroplex," the Dallas–Fort Worth region, with Chicago-area industrialists. The Dallas officials called the discussions "productive." Chicago civic leaders found them otherwise.

THE CONSEQUENCES OF ECONOMIC MIGRATION: METROPOLITAN DISPARITIES

Metropolitan Fragmentation

The dual migration of people and production to the suburban areas has produced significant socioeconomic disparities between central cities and suburbs, reinforced by the fragmentation of metropolitan

Table 4.3   Number of Governments in the United States

	1972	1967	1962
Total	79,269	81,299	91,237
U.S. government	1	1	1
State government	50	50	50
Local governments	78,218	81,248	91,186
Counties	3,044	3,049	3,043
Municipalities	18,517	18,048	18,000
Townships	18,991	17,105	17,142
School districts	15,781	21,782	34,648
Special districts	23,885	21,264	18,323

SMSAs with largest number of Governments, 1972

Chicago	1172
Philadelphia	852
Pittsburgh	698
New York	538
St. Louis	483
Houston	304
San Francisco–Oakland	302
Portland	298
Indianapolis	296
Denver	272

Source: U.S. Bureau of the Census, Census of Governments, 1972 (Washington, D.C.: Government Printing Office, 1975).

governments. By "fragmented," we mean that there are scores or hundreds of governments within a single metropolitan area. Municipalities, counties, school districts, and special districts abound, each overlapping the other. Table 4.3 reports some sobering data on the number of urban governments in the United States generally and in several particular SMSAs. One of the authors of this book who lives in the multiplicity of Chicago-area governments receives an annual tax bill, fortunately neatly consolidated and tabulated, for nine separate local government jurisdictions.

The policy consequences of this multiplicity of urban governments are to reinforce economic and social disparities among governments within the metropolis. Typically these disparities are most extreme when comparing central city and suburban communities. As we shall see, there are poor suburbs as well as poor central cities, and rich central cities in comparison with their suburbs are not uncommon. But the tendencies are clear. These disparities are illustrated by the personal-income data in Table 4.4. Incomes reflect both demand and supply aspects of the urban political economy. Viewed as reflecting demand, they indicate certain needs associated with poor housing, inadequate health care, and other aspects of poverty, plus the various demands that are made by middle- and upper-income taxpayers; viewed as reflecting supply, they indicate the resources potentially available to policy makers. To be sure, income levels are only imperfect measures of supply and demand, as urban governments rely not on income taxes but mainly on property taxes. The income figures in Table 4.4 must therefore stand as a rough approximation of the disparities in needs and resources within the metropolis. As we can see from those figures, central cities have a larger share — though by no means a monopoly — of poor people, whereas the suburbs contain a

Table 4.4   Metropolitan Area Families with Incomes Over $15,000 and Under $5,000, 1971

| | Percent of families | | Ratio of well-to-do to poor |
	Over $15,000	Under $5,000	
White			
Central City	26.7	15.7	1.701
Outside Central City	33.2	11.3	2.938
Black			
Central City	11.3	35.6	.317
Outside Central City	16.9	28.0	.604

Source: Statistical Abstract of the United States, 1974 (Washington, D.C.: Government Printing Office, 1973), p. 331.

larger proportion of the well-to-do. The ratio of well-to-do (those with incomes in excess of $15,000) to poor (those with incomes below $5,000) people is smaller in central cities than in outside-central-city areas. That is, in central cities the poor outnumber the well-to-do, whereas suburbs have more than half again as many well-to-do as poor persons. To the extent that the poor have more need for government services and the affluent have more ability to pay, it is clear that central cities have a disproportionate share of problems and that suburbs have a considerable advantage in resources. In the words of the Advisory Commission on Intergovernmental Relations, "one set of jurisdictions (usually the central city) has the problems and the other set of jurisdictions (usually the suburbs) has the resources."[5]

The central city, for example, contains:

1. more crime, necessitating heavier expenditures on law enforcement
2. older buildings and housing, necessitating more costly fire protection
3. more poverty and more unemployment, necessitating higher welfare expenditures
4. more aged persons, necessitating greater public assistance to the aged
5. more substandard housing units, necessitating more public housing
6. higher traffic counts, necessitating more highway expenditures and traffic control
7. more students from culturally disadvantaged backgrounds, necessitating more compensatory-education programs in schools

One disparity that tends to increase certain public expenditures in the suburbs is the larger incidence of school-age children there and the larger proportion who actually attend public schools. The economic resources represented by well-educated adults also translate themselves into demands for expensive children's schooling. An additional characteristic strains suburban economies: high growth rates. When cities are called on to provide programs to compensate for a decline in their private sectors, suburban governments must serve the demands resulting from their growth.

Socioeconomic disparities between cities and suburbs are reflected in the public expenditures and taxation patterns of urban governments (for further discussion of spending and taxation, see Chapter 9). Suburban residents are able to escape not only many problems but also much of the tax burden of city residents. The average suburbanite pays local taxes amounting to about 5.4 percent of his income, whereas the average city resident contributes about 7 percent of his income to municipal coffers. Cities in the largest SMSAs spend much more per capita on such noneducational functions as police, fire protection, urban renewal, public housing, streets and roads, public health, and welfare than do the suburbs. Suburban areas spend a great deal more money on education than cities do. Thus, it is not surprising that the most common reasons given for the flight to suburbs include "lower taxes" and "better schools."

This analysis suggests that the judgment that the central city has the problems and the suburbs the resources, though oversimplified, is not unreasonable. The central cities have a concentration of "high-cost citizens" and enterprises, whereas outside central cities have the advantage of resources. Central cities, like the Red Queen in *Through the Looking Glass,* must run very fast just to stay in the same place. Still, extreme images of either central cities or suburbs should be avoided. Any depiction of central cities as composed exclusively of huddled and starving masses is misleading. Any image of suburbs as composed of lawyers, doctors, and bankers is equally misleading. We describe *tendencies,* not iron laws. If fact, there are substantial differences among metropolitan areas in central city–suburban disparities.

Central City–Suburban Disparities: A Comparative Analysis

Most central cities score worse on quality-of-life indicators than their suburbs. A few, such as San Diego, Seattle, and Houston, actually show up better than their suburbs. One effort to construct a "hardship index" for central cities is by Richard Nathan and Charles Abrams of the Brookings Institution.[6] They developed a composite index, using 1970 census data on unemployment, age structure, education, income level, crowded housing, and poverty. Their hardship scores for 55 of the 65 largest SMSAs are contained in Table 4.5. The indexes are weighted so that scores over 100 indicate an advantage to the suburbs, whereas a score less than 100 shows a central-city advantage. As Nathan and Abrams emphasize, "The most important point that emerges is that the relatively greater disadvantaged central cities are concentrated among older cities in the northeastern and north central regions."[7] Newark (which Louis ranked as the "worst American city" in an article we summarized in Chapter 1, pp. 5–6), is worst off, and places such as Cleveland, Chicago, St. Louis, and Baltimore are in the greatest hardship group. Every single city where suburbs are worse off is outside the northeastern region.

Special Problems of Poor Suburbs

Not all metropolitan disparities are between central cities and suburbs. We pointed out in the last chapter that suburbs come in various types and forms. Some are rich, but others are very poor, often poorer than their central cities. The assumption of suburban affluence finds a sharp challenge in the periphery of the largest metropolitan areas. Contrasts between upper-class white and working-class black or racially mixed suburbs appear for the communities near Chicago, Detroit and Los Angeles included in Table 4.6. For the people at the

Table 4.5   Index of Central City Hardship Relative to Balance of SMSA for 55 SMSAs

Primary centray city of SMSA	Central city hardship index	Primary central city of SMSA	Central city hardship index
Newark	422	Pittsburgh	146
Cleveland	331	Denver	143
Hartford	317	Sacramento	135
Baltimore	256	Minneapolis	131
Chicago	245	Birmingham	131
St. Louis	231	Jersey City	129
Atlanta	226	Oklahoma City	128
Rochester	215	Indianapolis	124
Gary	213	Providence	121
Dayton	211	Grand Rapids	119
New York	211	Toledo	116
Detroit	210	Tampa	107
Richmond	209	Los Angeles	105
Philadelphia	205	San Francisco	105
Boston	198	Syracuse	103
Milwaukee	195	Allentown	100
Buffalo	189	Portland, Oreg.	100
San Jose	181	Omaha	98
Youngstown	180	Dallas	97
Columbus, Ohio	173	Houston	93
Miami	172	Phoenix	85
New Orleans	168	Norfolk	82
Louisville	165	Salt Lake City	80
Akron	152	San Diego	77
Kansas City, Mo.	152	Seattle	67
Springfield, Mass.	152	Ft. Lauderdale	43
Ft. Worth	149	Greensboro, N.C.	43
Cincinnati	148		

Source: Richard Nathan and Charles Adams, "Understanding Central City Hardship," *Political Science Quarterly,* 91 (Spring, 1976), Table 1.

lower end of these comparisons, there may be problems even more severe than in the central city ghettos. Poor people in poor suburbs suffer from their own lack of political visibility. Also, residents of an independent poor suburb lacks access to property taxes collected from affluent neighborhoods. Thus they must endure abysmal levels of public service, without the easy access to special schools, city colleges, and cultural activities that are open to those residents of the central-city ghetto who are motivated to seek them.

Table 4.6 Suburban Contrasts in Chicago, Detroit, and Los Angeles

	Percent white	Median years education of adults	Median family income	Percent below low-income level	Median value owner-occupied homes	Percent unemployment	Serious crimes per 1,000 population	Property taxes per capita	Current government expenditures per capita
Chicago									
Highland Park	97.6	14.1	$20,844	2.1	$46,509	2.1	21.8	$ 48	$106
Northbrook	99.4	14.3	19,994	1.7	48,337	1.4	9.5	NA	NA
Wilmette	98.9	15.2	21,784	2.3	46,461	2.7	14.4	51	89
Harvey	68.8	11.7	11,329	7.0	17,117	3.8	72.5	26	69
Maywood	57.9	12.1	12,150	6.0	19,380	4.3	34.2	16	54
Detroit									
Birmingham	99.6	14.1	17,297	2.1	31,736	2.6	20.9	95	152
Southfield	99.3	12.7	18,140	2.4	36,235	3.3	39.4	62	97
Highland Park	43.4	11.2	8,715	14.5	13,466	8.0	99.6	108	449
Inkster	55.2	11.7	11,280	8.4	17,242	6.2	78.6	44	93
Los Angeles									
Beverly Hills	98.5	13.0	20,303	4.5	71,336	4.5	4.7	86	286
Compton	26.1	11.8	8,722	17.1	17,682	9.8	12.9	19	72

Source: County and City Data Book, 1972 (Washington, D.C.: Government Printing Office, 1973).

In each of the comparisons that appear in Table 4.6, the affluent white suburbs have family incomes averaging about twice those in the lower-income black or racially mixed suburbs, and the white communities have higher levels of education, lower unemployment, and much lower crime rates—in some cases as much as one-eighth the crime in the poorer suburbs. The proportion of families in the wealthy suburbs below the low-income level is one-third to one-ninth that in the poor suburbs, and the value of homes is two to four times greater in the wealthy suburbs. These social and economic traits of the private sector often translate into parallel differences in local taxes and expenditures, thereby permitting the wealthy to have more generous public services as well as all their private advantages. One exception to this pattern occurs in Highland Park—outside of Detroit—where industrial properties provide a tax base to push local spending per capita above that in the white communities of Birmingham and Southfield.

THE UNDERSIDE OF THE URBAN
POLITICAL ECONOMY

Completing the irony of the urban economy are the migrants from rural areas who have come to the city for a better life. Today this migration comes largely from the black-belt counties of the South, from the all-white counties of the southern Appalachians and the Ozarks, from Puerto Rico and other Caribbean islands, from Mexico, and to some extent from Indian reservations.

The urban economy once had plenty of jobs for new migrants. Factories and construction were more dependent on hand labor than they are today, and the municipal government employed large numbers of menial laborers. There are still many such opportunities, but their proportion of the urban economy has diminished markedly. Literacy is increasingly required for even the lowest-paid and least permanent jobs. The spread of the labor movement and union control of apprenticeship programs mean that today's ethnic newcomers suffer from institutionalized discrimination by fellow workers as well as by prospective employers.

Economists often describe themselves as practitioners of the "dismal science" because they focus on problems resulting from scarce resources. When Professor Frank G. Davis writes about the economics of urban black communities, he is even more dismal than is customary for his discipline. He identifies five traits in the economies of urban ghettos:[8]

1. Nonwhite workers' salaries are approximately 58 percent of whites'. Even after adjusting for white–nonwhite differences in education, age, region, and size of city, the income of nonwhite urban males is only 81 to 87 percent of their

white counterparts'. This differential of 13 to 19 percent represents the elements that discriminate against non-whites in the urban setting.
2. There is a net *outflow* of capital resources from the ghetto. This reflects: purchases made by black businesses (mainly small retail and food shops) from outside the ghetto; imports of goods and exports of profits by white-owned businesses; and the export of black labor to employers outside the ghetto.
3. The high concentration of low-income residences attracts small-scale, low-profit retail activities, but excludes manufacturing opportunities due to land scarcity and high land values.
4. Black-owned businesses tend to be smaller and financially more precarious than the "white-enclave" businesses, thus minimizing any hopes for a burgeoning of black capitalism.
5. Industries locate in the low land-value suburban areas, imposing transportation costs on black laborers that make the wages for unskilled labor uneconomic for ghetto blacks. "The result is the simultaneous existence of job vacancies and unemployed black labor."[9]

Several additional traits mark the larger economy in which the ghetto exists, and have striking consequences for ghetto residents:

1. Investments in industry emphasize technological changes that reduce the need for unskilled labor.
2. Economic growth for industry in the larger society makes black laborers redundant in high-productivity, high-paying manufacturing jobs, and forces them to compete for jobs in low-productivity, low-paying service industries where blacks are already concentrated. The result of this growth sequence is an inflation in the prices that blacks must pay for consumer goods, along with a lag in the incomes of unskilled workers.

Davis examines the promise of black capitalism for the ghetto but remains pessimistic. The structure of black enterprise does not seem likely to generate a large volume of business or high rates of employment. There remains the problem of residential land values that prohibit large-scale industrialization in the ghetto. Davis finds that manpower training programs have not reached the mass of unemployed blacks: over a 6-year period on-the-job trainees included only 1.4 percent the estimated number of black unemployed.

Some programs increase the number or the wealth of black entrepreneurs, but leave untouched the major forces producing black poverty. "Mere substitution of black capitalists for white capitalists under present conditions of resource use is far from an optimum economic condition of ghetto development and growth and could have only minimal effects."[10] Davis's own prescription emphasizes the community ownership of ghetto resources. He would have the sectors of manufacturing and distribution controlled by the community, with the retention of profits as well as labor wages in the community. This is not the place to provide a detailed criticism of Davis's proposals. However, we would be remiss as political scientists if we did not point to the likely opposition from aspiring black capitalists, as well as from the white politicians who would be asked to authorize grants of capital and the regulatory actions needed to establish such ventures.[11]

From an employment perspective, the problem is a complex one, but it can be simply stated: There are fewer and fewer jobs to accommodate more and more people. Two graduate students in geography devised an ingenious method to measure the decline of jobs in black Chicago neighborhoods.[12] They took the Illinois manufacturing directory and mailed return-receipt-requested letters to several thousand firms in black areas of Chicago. What they discovered was that in a two-year period firms with over 7000 jobs and several million dollars in capital had moved out of the neighborhoods, some entirely out of the state. There are simply fewer jobs in such areas than there used to be. This is one important reason why unemployment rates in ghetto areas are typically twice the national average.

WHY URBAN WEALTH DOES NOT TRANSLATE INTO FISCAL RESOURCES

Metropolitan areas are wealthy; their governments, ironically, are often poor. The inaccessibility of urban wealth to urban policy makers is a function of several problems: (1) an unequal distribution of needs and resources throughout urban areas; (2) legal limits on the kinds and amounts of revenue that local authorities may collect; (3) the "monopoly" of income taxes and sales taxes by federal and state governments; and (4) the failure of local officials to tax or borrow up to the legal limits.

The Unequal Distribution of Needs and Resources

The fragmented metropolis produces wealth in one place even as it may leave unmet needs somewhere else. The unequal distribution of needs and resources results from what Anthony Downs calls the "Law of Cultural Dominance," and the fragmentation of governments throughout metropolitan areas. Downs believes that most middle-class families want their own values to dominate the home environment, so that "everyday life should be primarily a *value-reinforcing* experience for both adults and children, rather than a *value-altering* one."[13]

Local governments vary greatly in the resources that their residents provide, as well as in the residents' demands for public services. The suburb that is thick with industrial and commercial properties has high tax revenues for its local government but minimal demands for schools and other social services. The purely residential suburb, however, faces high demands for school expenditures but has no source of revenue except private home owners. If the incomes of home owners are high, they can devote ample resources to their children's schooling. Yet residential suburbs that are predominantly working class in composition are often characterized by many children and low incomes and property values. When such communities are new and rapidly growing, they must bear the burden of adding new school buildings and facilities, as well as the operating costs of established programs. Some working-class communities adjoin municipalities with a high incidence of industrial or commercial properties. The industrial complex is likely to draw its labor force from the working-class town; yet the industries' property taxes support only the schools that lie within their own municipality.

In jurisdictions that have more resources than their services demand, some remain untapped. In fact, because metropolitan areas are not governed by integrated institutions, abundant resources lie unused within short distances of unmet service needs.[14]

Legal Limits on Kinds and Amounts of Taxation and Indebtedness

State constitutions and statutes restrict local authorities to certain kinds of revenues and to certain levels of taxation and indebtedness. Local governments in most states are restricted to taxes on property; charges for city-operated services like water, trash removal, sewage, gas, and electricity; and limited borrowing for capital improvements (for example, construction of buildings and highways or the purchase of major equipment). In several states, local governments also tax their residents' incomes, the retail sales of local merchants, or both. But these taxes are typically low: 1 percent is a common upper limit on local income and sales taxes. Some cities also collect revenues from local "wheel taxes" (on automobiles) or levies on motel and hotel rooms. These taxes, too, typically make only small total contributions to local government resources. The property tax is the single major source of support.

Property taxes may apply to *real* property (land and buildings); *personal* property (clothes, furniture, and other such possessions); and *intangible* property (stocks, bonds, bank accounts). The reluctance of both citizens and officials to reveal their resources in full detail precludes thorough assessment of personal and intangible property, however, and these taxes are widely evaded. It is common for the amount of a local government's debt and the level of its property taxes to be limited to a certain proportion of the assessed value of the real property in the jurisdiction. "Assessed value" is flexible, however, and can be increased to permit more revenues either from taxation or borrowing when the need arises. Nevertheless, legal limits are important in the minds of many officials and citizens, who may keep city budgets low when the limits are approached, even if there are still some options to increase total valuation.

The set of taxes that is legally available to a local government may not be adequate for its revenue potential. Some resort communities could raise significant funds through local amusement or restaurant taxes, and some jurisdictions with large upper-income populations might benefit significantly from local progressive income taxes. The state legislatures, however, decide which taxes can be raised by local authorities, and the individual communities are often left with revenue possibilities not suited to their resources.

The Monopoly of Income and Sales Taxes by Federal and State Governments

One reason for the restrictions on local governments' use of income and sales taxes is the heavy use of these same taxes by federal and state governments. It is said that the latter governments use up almost all the revenues that are potentially available from these sources. Although this allegation is neither clear nor even established as fact, a number of authorities do believe that two levels of government cannot make simultaneous heavy use of the same form of taxation.

Through a series of tacit understandings — as well as through the legal restrictions that state governments have imposed on their municipalities — the federal government has become the chief user of the personal and corporate income taxes, state governments rely heavily on sales taxes, and local governments are left with the tax on real property. In 1970–1971, personal and corporate income taxes accounted for 56 percent of federal revenue; sales taxes accounted for 40 percent of revenues collected by state governments; and property taxes accounted for 55 percent of revenues collected by municipalities.

It has not always been so. Tax *specialization* came after the Depression of the 1930s and may reflect the overall increase in taxes that characterized this period. Before the Depression both state and local governments were major users of the property tax, but the states left that revenue source to municipalities during the 1930s, and they themselves became increasingly dependent upon retail sales taxes. State governments earned almost 45 percent of their revenues from property taxes in 1902. By 1940, however, this had dropped to only 5 percent, and by 1974 it was only 1.5 percent.

As most local governments are left without a major source of tax revenue other than real-property taxes, they find themselves unable to tap large segments of the local economy for support. Much of the wealth in the local community takes the form of profits from retail sales and personal and corporate incomes, but in most places this wealth is not subject to local taxation. Moreover, many earners and retail spenders live outside the community in which they earn or spend their incomes, and they pay property taxes to their communities of residence. The burden lies especially heavily on central cities. As noted, the central city faces heavy demands for social services, transportation, fire and police protection, and housing; yet the incomes of its wealthiest business and professional people are not (in most cases) subject to local taxation, and purchases made in the central business district are (in most cases) taxed only by the state government. The tax options of most central cities do not match their economic resources, and so there may be starvation of public services in the presence of enormous private resources. Some state governments have loosened the controls on localities' use of nonproperty taxes. Yet the general picture is still one of constraint, with most local governments relying on the unpopular and regressive levy on real property as their major taxing device.

The Failure of Local Governments to Tax or Borrow to the Legal Limits

Governments in some communities do not tax or borrow to their legal limits, even while they fail to satisfy prominent demands for service. Also some officials compete with other jurisdictions for the location of industrial or commercial establishments by offering the incentive of low taxes. The reason given is that high taxes will discourage a firm from locating in a jurisdiction or even prompt an established firm to move elsewhere. Actually the availability of manpower, transportation facilities, electric power, and clean water—plus recreational and educational opportunities for the staff—often have more to do with management's decision about location than does the simple factor of the tax rate. Yet local authorities are tempted to compete for industries by means of their tax rates. When different communities in the same urban area do compete over tax rates, an occasional firm may be induced to choose a low-rate community or even to leave a community whose taxes rise significantly above those in a neighboring jurisdiction. In this case the firm can still recruit its labor force from the surrounding towns, and its officers can live in those surrounding communities with the most attractive amenities. Also, if a large firm is persuaded to settle—or stay—in a community because of a low tax rate, the taxes from that firm alone may nevertheless be sufficient in their total magnitude to permit a low tax rate for the community's home owners.

The failure of local governments to tax or borrow up to their legal limits does not result solely from the preferences of municipal officials. Sometimes community leaders may urge tax increases or bond issues to pay for needed services, only to run up against intense popular opposition. Forty-two of the 50 states require that local governments obtain the consent of their citizens in referenda before issuing bonds for improvements in streets, sewers, schools, and other public fcilities. Twelve states require consent by extraordinarily high majorities, ranging from 55 percent to two-thirds of the electorate, before capital investments may be undertaken. The proportion of referenda in which local electorates reject such investments has increased in recent years. The voters of Youngstown, Ohio, may hold the record for negative referenda. They defeated proposals for schools taxes on 6 consecutive occasions before the fall of 1968, when the schools ran out of money and shut down for most of the term.

The Auxiliary Devices of Intergovernmental Aid and Special Districts

Although officials face severe problems arising from the inaccessibility of urban wealth, two major devices, the *special district* and *intergovernmental grants and loans,* offer partial solutions to their problems.

THE SPECIAL DISTRICT   The special district broadens the tax base that can be used to support public services in an urban area by joining together an extensive area for the provision of a particular service. Special districts are—as the name implies—created for special purposes. They do not provide the full range of local services. Rather, each provides one basic service or a group of closely related services. The most common special districts are school districts; others include districts for water, sewage, or both; trash collection; police, fire protection, or both; parks; libraries; hospitals; and transportation, bridges, and port facilities.

Most metropolitan areas have several of these districts. The largest and best known is the Port of New York Authority. Each district may have its own borders, not necessarily coterminous with the borders of others. A school district, for example, may include one set of municipalities (or some whole municipalities and parts of others) and may partly, but not entirely, overlap a water-and-sewer district that covers a different part of the metropolitan region. Where special districts have proliferated in this manner, they can provide individual services on the basis of the resources that lie within their extensive boundaries. They appeal to those who prefer that financial support for services be tied directly to the receipt of those services.[15]

Because of the confusion that arises from a variety of separate jurisdictions, however, citizens cannot easily determine which districts provide which services to their homes, much less how they may influence the policies made by the authorities of each district. The governing bodies of many special districts are boards appointed jointly by the councils or mayors of several municipalities, by the state governor, or both. The indirect lines of responsibility, as well as the confused geographical boundaries, help to isolate special districts from voter control.

INTERGOVERNMENTAL AID   Intergovernmental aid permits urban governments to receive some of the revenues raised within their jurisdictions by the income and sales taxes of the federal and state governments.[16] One advantage of intergovernmental aid is that federal and state authorities can extract revenues from urban areas without imposing differential tax rates that might drive away industry from these jurisdictions. Because they are not troubled by the unequal distribution of needs and resources throughout a metropolitan area, state and national governments can use a wider variety of taxing and borrowing mechanisms than local authorities. Admittedly only a portion of the revenues raised from an urban area is returned to that area by state and federal governments, because much of this wealth must be used to support a variety of federal and state programs, including national defense and financial aid to small-town and rural citizens.

Until 1972 all federal aid came as funds for particular programs. Now, with the passage of the Revenue Sharing Act, the federal government has committed approximately $6.1 billion per year to state and local governments for purposes selected by the recipients within the broad terms of the legislation. Local governments are assured of two-thirds the annual allotments, with the funds for individual localities coming on the basis of population, the per-capita income of local residents, and the level of local taxes. Communities with *large* populations, *low* income, and *high* local tax effort benefit from the formula. Along with revenue sharing, there remain over 1000 separate federal aid programs that help to fund specific activities. Some of these (e.g., public housing, urban renewal, crime control) channel money directly from Washington to municipal authorities. Most other programs provide aid to state governments, which in turn offer some of the funds to municipalities, urban school districts, and other urban units. The nature of these aids varies considerably from one program to another.[17] Some programs are designed to redistribute resources from "have" to "have not" areas; others substitute the resources raised by superordinate governments for those raised locally; others are provided with only portions of the funds needed and are designed to stimulate local authorities to put more effort into raising money through their own taxes or service charges; and others are meant to add resources to those that the municipalities have raised for certain programs from their own resources.

There are systematic variations in the state-to-state intergovernmental aids among states. Some state governments assume a large part of the responsibility for financing public services and use aids to municipalities in order to accomplish their objectives.[18] Others provide only minimal state aids, and leave to the local communities the task of supporting whatever services their citizens desire. Not all local officials, however, feel that the disbursement of state money is equitable, even in the former case.

For a long time, state and federal aid exacerbated the disparities between central cities and suburban governments. Aid policies were based on formulas that favored suburbs, despite their greater wealth. As of 1965, per-capita aid to cities and suburbs was nearly identical ($78 per capita).[19] But since the mid-1960s both federal and state aids have shifted in the direction of cities over 500,000. The period 1964–1973 saw per-capita federal aid increasing 25 percent more and per-capita state aid increasing 28 percent more in these larger cities than in smaller cities.

Coping

Local officials must make ends meet. Payroll costs typically run to three-fourths of the municipal budget, and city employees must be paid. It is politically difficult to cut back on local services. Appeals to higher governments for assistance are frequent. But city officials must constantly cope with needs for meeting current budgets. Arnold Meltsner describes the situation in Oakland as one in which property taxes have reached their political limits. They operate on the principle that "small taxes are hidden taxes."[20] Many of the tax increases appear on cigarettes, sewer service charges, business licenses and permits, hotel rooms, and other minor charges. Yet, "because the revenue problem is always there and is never considered to be solved, search is recurring and open ended. . . . Oakland officials feel they do not have many options, [and] they have chosen the low-yield, low-political-cost revenue sources."[21] These are coping strategies, used in city after city.

In some municipalities officials actively solicit business investments in industrial or commercial developments, because they add to the value of real property and tax revenues. Such campaigns are, of course, likely to be more effective in some communities than in others, because geographical location in relation to the sources of supply and labor and to markets is important to industrialists, as is the availability of water, electric power, and transportation facilities. In many cases these tangible needs of a prospective investor outweigh any arguments — or even temporary tax concessions — that local authorities can provide.

Local authorities are not prohibited from trying to alter provisions of the state constitution or statutes that keep their fiscal position weak.

Debt and tax limitations, for example, as well as the formulas for distributing state aid, are subject to change. Recent increases in the representation of urban areas in state legislatures may also aid the city's efforts to reduce its fiscal impediments. Yet in some states reapportionment has only heightened city–suburb conflicts in the legislatures; it may even have ousted certain rural legislators who were allies of the cities. The process of reapportionment is complex and cannot be said to have uniform influence on city–state relations across the country.[22]

SUMMARY

The metropolis is the area in which the wealth of the United States is produced and concentrated. Yet we have described in this chapter "the irony of urban wealth" — the paradox of private wealth amid public poverty. The irony of urban wealth parallels the story of the political sociology of the American city discussed in Chapter 3. As people have decentralized within the metropolis, so has production. One result is significant social and economic disparities between central cities and their suburban areas. The central-city hardship index, constructed by Nathan and Adams, showed that a few central cities were better off than their suburbs, but that most were disadvantaged *vis-à-vis* their suburbs. Suburbs are, of course, not alike. Poor suburbs are often more severely disadvantaged even than central cities. In both poor suburbs and many central cities, the underside of the urban economy includes problems of joblessness, the demise of small businesses, and difficulties in capital formation.

Consequently the political economy of American cities is often characterized by a set of coping behaviors. Local officials are faced with a fragmentation of needs from resources, legal and political limits on tax levels, and the monopoly of tax sources by state and federal governments. What they try to do, therefore, is make ends meet by creating special districts, by the constant appeal for intergovernmental aid, and by persistent campaigns for industrial recruitment and promotion. When major tax sources are exhausted, city officials try minor ones. All in all, the political economy of metropolitan areas produces significant constraints on the ability of local governments to respond to urban problems.

Notes

1. Jane Jacobs, *The Economy of Cities* (New York: Vintage, 1970).
2. Edgar M. Hoover and Raymond Vernon, *Anatomy of a Metropolis* (Garden City, N.Y.: Doubleday, 1962), chap. 2.
3. Wilbur Thompson, "A Preface to Suburban Economics," in Louis H. Masotti and Jeffrey K. Hadden, eds., *The Urbanization of the Suburbs* (Beverly Hills, Calif.: Sage, 1973), p. 411.

4. This discussion of Boston is derived from Andrew Hamer, *Industrial Exodus from the Central City* (Lexington, Mass.: Heath, 1973).
5. Advisory Commission on Intergovernmental Relations, *Fiscal Balance in the American Federal System,* Vol. 2. (Washington, D.C.: Government Printing Office, 1967), p. 6.
6. "Understanding Central City Hardship," *Political Science Quarterly, 91* (Spring 1976) 47–62.
7. Ibid., p. 50.
8. Frank G. Davis, *The Economics of Black Community Development: Analysis and Program for Autonomous Community Development* (Chicago: Markham, 1972).
9. Ibid., p. 104.
10. Ibid., p. 114.
11. On the economics of the urban poor, see also Carolyn Shaw Bell, *The Economics of the Ghetto* (New York: Norton, 1972).
12. Charles M. Christian and Sari J. Bennett, "Industrial Relocations from the Black Community of Chicago," in Michael R. Greenberg, ed., *Readings in Urban Economics and Spatial Patterns* (New Brunswick, N.J.: Center for Urban Policy Research of Rutgers University, 1974), chap. 9.
13. Anthony Downs, *Urban Problems and Prospects* (Chicago: Markham, 1970), p. 34.
14. See the arguments in Robert C. Wood, *1400 Governments* (Garden City, N.Y.: Doubleday, 1964).
15. On special districts and their rationale, see John C. Bollens, *Special District Governments in the United States* (Berkeley: University of California Press, 1957).
16. For an overview of intergovernmental aid, see Deil S. Wright, *Federal Grants-in-Aid: Perspectives and Alternatives* (Washington, D.C.: American Enterprise Institute for Public Policy Research, 1968).
17. See, for example, Richard Musgrave, *Essays in Fiscal Federalism* (Washington, D.C.: The Brookings Institution, 1965).
18. Ira Sharkansky, *The Politics of Taxing and Spending* (Indianapolis, Ind.: Bobbs-Merrill, 1969), chap. 4.
19. Advisory Commission on Intergovernmental Relations, op. cit., p. 84.
20. Arnold Meltsner, *The Politics of City Revenue* (Berkeley: University of California Press, 1971), p. 105.
21. Ibid., pp. 8–9.
22. On reapportionment, see Ira Sharkansky, "Reapportionment and Roll-Call Voting: The Case at the Georgia Legislature," *Social Science Quarterly, 51* (June 1970), and the references cited there.

PART THREE

Politics
and Policy Making
in the City

5

THE CITY POLITIC: POLITICAL ACTION AND LINKAGE INSTITUTIONS

An old cliche says that "you can't fight city hall." In fact, we discover that urban political participation is quite low. Whether through contacting or conventional modes of participation, political action at the urban level is less than at state or national levels. In this chapter we will examine the city politic, particularly mass behavior in policy process. We emphasize that urban political behavior can be best understood in terms of "exit" or "voice" options. Each is a response to dissatisfaction with the neighborhood or the city government. Mass political behavior, however, is not very effective unless it is organized behavior. Consequently it is important to examine "linkage institutions" in urban politics. These include

- the interest group
- the political party
- the election
- political protest
- mobility or "exit"

How well these linkage institutions "work," how closely they bind elites to mass preferences, and what policy consequences they have are the principal issues that we raise in this chapter.

Q. I am 74 years old and reside on the city's Northwest Side. Recently I painted three sides of my building and took down the storm windows. When I started to paint the fourth side, my neighbor came over and ordered me off his property. My problem is I can't finish the job without putting my ladder on his property. The City Hall information office referred me to the clerk's office in the Civic Center and they sent me to the Chicago Bar Association, which charged me $10 and told me it would take a lot of money to fight it out in court. Can you help?
    — J.S., Northwest Side

A. Your neighbor told this column that the dispute could have been resolved had you talked to him first. Instead, he contends, "he wanted to stick it to me" by filing numerous complaints with the building department, the Albany Park police station, and "he even took me to court." Your "sneaky" actions have cost him over $1,200, he said, adding, "I definitely do not want him on my property. He is

painting these swastikas all over the place and putting up red and black crosses in his yard," he added. Perhaps, seeing this in print might convince both parties that continued escalation won't end this feud. But, then, our mediation didn't help either.
— "Action Line," Chicago *Tribune,*
    26 June 1975

Such is the stuff of urban political conflict. Every political system provides channels — all more or less imperfect — for resolving political conflict or at least permitting citizens to raise issues in hopes of resolution. Collectively these modes of participation and agenda setting comprise the *input process* in the urban political system, and constitute the subject of this chapter. The input process encompasses all activities in which individuals and groups use time, information, money, skills, votes, and other resources to secure favorable political outcomes.

Here we focus on mass politics, as distinguished from elite politics. The ways in which elites handle inputs will be the subject of subsequent chapters (Chapter 7 in particular). Linkage institutions, however, provide ways in which mass opinions and participation are aggregated to reach the attention of decision makers. Simply because the city is a large institution, a group shouting simultaneously is not very effective. We suggest that there are five linkages between masses and decision makers in urban politics: (1) political parties, (2) interest groups, (3) elections, (4) protest, and (5) mobility. Singly or in combination they represent the processes by which preferences and demands will be registered. If they do not work, elites will feel free to go their own way. How effective these linkages are, how well they communicate mass sentiments and control elite behavior, is a matter of much dispute. Our analysis, therefore, is both descriptive and cautiously evaluative.

PARTICIPATION IN
CITY POLITICS

"You can't fight city hall" is a hallowed cliché in American politics. But judging by the available evidence, relatively few urbanites take advantage of their opportunities to change things at city hall. Unfortunately it is difficult to collect firm data on the actual rates of participation in local elections, simply because local records are not aggregated into any national repository. But available evidence is suggestive nonetheless. It suggests that turnout in local elections is perhaps no more than one-half that of national elections. In the 1976 presidential election over 60 percent of the adult population voted for its presidential favorite; in the typical state election, something like one-half the eligible population troops to the polls. Though 47 percent of the American population claims "always" to vote in local elections,[1] the evidence suggests that some have faulty memories. Probably no more than one-third of the eligible population turns out in municipal elections that are not held concurrently with state or national contests.[2]

Voting, however, is not the only form of participation in politics. In a major study of political participation in the United States, Verba and Nie categorized 12 separate types of participation.[3] They emphasized that participation was *specialized*, rather than generalized. Among the five types of participants identified in Table 5.1 there was little overlap; except for the "complete activists," most people fell neatly into one of the participatory types and not another. But it is also important to emphasize that fully one-fifth of the population (22 percent, to be exact) were simply inactive in all forms of political participation. Chances are that if we examined only participation in local politics, the proportions of inactives would rise significantly, and the levels of participation would decline.

Participation in community politics may be seen as a function of both *macro* (community) and *micro* (individual or subcommunity) factors. The probability of participation will vary both from individual to individual and from community to community. Unless participation is viewed from both perspectives, a one-sided picture results. Even if two people resemble each other in social characteristics, they may participate differently, depending on whether factors in the political environment operate to facilitate or to hinder political activism.

Table 5.1   Types of Participants in American Politics

Type	Percent of population
Inactives	22
Voting specialists	21
Parochial participants	4
Communalists	20
Campaigners	15
Complete activists	11
	93
Unclassifiable	7
	100

Source: Derived from data in Sidney Verba and Norman Nie, *Participation in America* (New York: Harper & Row, 1972), chap. 4.

Table 5.2   Correlates of Participation in Community Politics[a]

Macro factors		Micro factors	
1. Form of government		1. Social class	
Mayor-council or commission	+	Higher	+
Manager	−	Lower	−
2. Form of election		2. Stakes in policies	
Partisan	+	High	+
Nonpartisan	−	Low	−
3. Type of constituency		3. Ethnicity	
Ward	+	Ethnic	+
At large	−	Nonethnic	−
4. Party system		4. Mobility	
Strong	+	High	−
Weak	−	Low	+
5. Community stability			
Stable	+		
Unstable	−		
6. Intensity of conflict			
High	+		
Low	−		

[a] A plus sign indicates that the characteristic identified is usually associated with higher participation rates; a minus sign indicates that the characteristic is ordinarily associated with lower participation in community politics.

The aggregate level of participation in any given community is a product both of the kinds of individuals found in the community and of the characteristics of the community and its socioeconomic and governmental systems. A listing of some of the more significant correlates of participation in community politics, divided into macro and micro categories, appears in Table 5.2. It is important to note that this list conceals the interaction and interrelations among the various factors. It is difficult to isolate the effect of any one of these elements from the others, and it is the sum of various factors that produces a higher or lower level of participation, rather than any one factor taken independently.

Micro Explanations of Participation

Participation varies with *individual* attributes and attitudes. These are the micro-level explanations of political participation. Some people have social and economic attributes, and attitudes associated with their attributes, which incline them to more vigorous levels of participation. Many of these are well known to our readers, and we need not rehash them at length. Perhaps the most significant single correlate of participation in American life is one's social-class status. As Daniel Patrick Moynihan once neatly summarized it, the relation between status and political activism is "high–high; low–low." Verba and Nie's national study of the correlates of participation found overrepresentations among the complete activists among precisely those groups one would expect: the better educated, the wealthier, and the members of higher-status occupational groups.[4]

At the urban level these findings generally, though not universally, repeat themselves. One study of local political involvement, using data from four Wisconsin cities, revealed that two measures of social class (educational attainment and occupation) were among the three most important factors associated with political activity, and Robert A. Dahl's study of New Haven found a 34 percent difference in the proportions of high- and low-income people who were "highly active" in local politics.[5] A study of voting on bond referenda in Atlanta revealed a positive, but not very strong, relationship between indicators of socioeconomic status and turnout, and investigators of the St. Louis metropolitan area did not find class significant in differentiating between high and low participators. In Toledo a powerful correlation between class and participation was noted.[6] At the urban level there is thus some variability in the relationship between class and voting

President Carter and Mayor Daley in Chicago. Is the Daley political machine still intact after his death?

turnout. Variations may reflect peculiarities of election campaigns, the community itself, or the measurements of both class and participation used.

The stakes perceived in local public policies are another factor that seems to affect participation. By *stakes*, we mean the material or ideological gains and losses that the voter perceives as likely to result from the activities of local government. The fact is that for most Americans city hall is more distant, politically speaking, than is Washington, D.C., despite American rhetoric about "government close to the people." But for some urbanites local public policy can be calculated in a profit-and-loss column. Businessmen, realtors, contractors, developers, and municipal employees are far more likely than is the average person to see local politics as relevant to their pocketbooks. Developers, realtors, and landowners are affected by decisions about urban renewal, zoning, and economic development. Contractors and suppliers are affected by nearly every capital-outlay decision, and municipal employees have obvious economic interests in municipal decisions. Because most local taxes are tied to property values, home owners may see greater stakes in local politics than others do (though they probably see lower stakes than street contractors do). Alford and Scoble have noted that "home ownership is apparently a form of politically relevant group membership, vesting the individual with tangible interests perceived as impinged upon by local politics quite apart from more conventional interests of high social status."[7]

Mobility, race, and ethnic affiliation also relate to local participation. Mobile people are less active participants for two principal reasons. First, legal residence qualifications for voting in most American elections disenfranchise people who have recently moved. Second, highly mobile people also have fewer roots in the community, fewer social ties, and less information about local political affairs.

The ethnic affiliation, or identification, of an individual seems also to be indicative of his political activism. *Ethnics* (an ethnic, for our purposes, means either an immigrant or, more commonly nowadays, the son or daughter of immigrants) are more likely to participate than are native Americans. A study of St. Louis found that 77 percent of the German community in the city and 80 percent of residents of southern and eastern European ancestry had voted at least once in municipal elections, whereas only 61 percent of "old stock" Americans and 62 percent of blacks reported having ever voted in such an election.[8] Robert E. Lane, in discussing the "way of the ethnic in politics," has noted:

In a real sense, the seat of ethnic politics is the local community, not the national capital. This is evidenced by the fact that although ethnic groups often vote no more frequently than native white Protestants in national elections (with the Jews excepted) and sometimes less frequently, they usually vote more frequently in local elections.[9]

In the heydey of the political machine, ethnic groups were crucial elements in the party leaders' victory package. "Ticket balancing" still occurs in cities with large ethnic populations, and politicians often woo ethnic voters with promises of symbolic group-related rewards.

Macro Explanations of Participation

Understanding participation levels solely by focusing on individual attributes is, however, misleading. The overall rate of electoral turnout is a function not only of the mix of individuals within the city, but also of the structural attributes of the community and its political institutions. Robert R. Alford and Eugene C. Lee assembled the most complete data available on electoral turnouts from a macro perspective.[10] Drawing on the resources of the International City Management Association, they conducted a survey of city clerks in all American cities with more than 25,000 people and collected data on electoral participation in the most recent municipal election. Their findings can be summarized by this set of propositions:

1. "Reformed" political institutions (i.e., council-manager governments, nonpartisan and at large elections) are associated with *lower* turnout rates. (We shall later in this chapter (see pp. 124–126) investigate the political consequences of electoral reform on political life in the city.)
2. Higher proportions of ethnicity in the city are associated with *higher* rates of political participation.
3. Higher levels of educational attainment in the city are associated with *lower* rates of participation.
4. Communities with stability and continuity, indicated by their age and their mobility rates, have *higher* rates of participation.
5. Cities in the Northeast have especially high, and cities in the south especially low, rates of participation.

Contrasting the macro- and micro-explanations of participation suggests that certain factors work differently, depending on the level of analysis. That is the case with educational attainments, for example. At the individual level, Moynihan's "high–high; low–low" dictum holds. The opposite inference can be drawn, however, about the relationship between the level of education in the community as a whole and its overall turnout rate. Curiously, the more educated its people are, the lower a community's participation. What appears to be happening is that education is related to the class composition, and thus to

the level of social conflict, within the community. A socially homogeneous community, whether composed mostly of white-collar executives or of blue-collar union workers, generates fewer political conflicts and thus fewer incentives to participate in politics. In those communities with very high educational attainments—the prototypical
dormitory suburb—excessive local politicking is viewed as distasteful, and civic participation remains low-keyed. For this reason we indicate in Table 5.2 the "intensity of conflict" as a major determinant of
community participation rates.

Other macro-level characteristics also play a role. One is the nature
of the local party system. A few cities possess vigorous local party
organizations, but others are nonpartisan in fact as well as in name. A
strong party need not "vote headstones" in order to increase turnout.
They can frame issues, engage in personal contact, and link candidates with voters through the medium of party identification. Katz
and Eldersfeld found that an active local party can produce as much as
a 10 percent change in the division of the vote—certainly enough to
capture a close election.[11] In the remaining machine-dominated cities,
such as Chicago, a precinct leader's personal and political fortunes are
quite literally tied to the size of the vote that he or she delivers on
polling day.

If individuals vary in their participatory propensities, then so do
communities. On the basis of our evidence, one might conclude that
cities such as Boston, Albany, New York, Altoona, Cleveland, Buffalo,
and Chicago might have higher rates of participation in their local affairs than cities such as Miami, Wilmette, San Jose, Austin, and Beverly Hills.

Another Form of Participation:
Contacting and Getting Results

For most Americans, local governments are service institutions, not
places for settling great issues of the day. One may choose between
Nixon and McGovern or Carter and Ford on the basis of war and peace,
probusiness or prolabor sentiments, or farm versus city orientations.
Local governments, however, are supposed to "get things done," picking up the garbage, providing fire and police protection, fixing potholes in streets, telling neighbors to fix houses in disrepair, and generally making services available to citizens. Participation in national
politics may be expressive, but participation in local politics is more
typically instrumental. One reason that overall participation in municipal elections is so low may be simply that citizens perceive the city as
a service provider rather than as a political institution. They may not
be altogether wrong in those perceptions.

Thus, contacting officials is an important alternative form of urban participation. Citizens who find that contacts and requests for service get immediate results are likely to return incumbents to office; citizens met with sullen, "bureaucratic," and delayed responses are a power to be reckoned with in the next election. We suggest that the most effective contacting occurs in two very different kinds of cities. One is the classic machine city, where the precinct captain is in business 24 hours a day, eager to spur the service bureaucracies to individual attention, even providing free garbage cans to citizens who complain about the rough treatment their cans receive from clumsy sanitation workers. The other type of city where the complaint-contact process is perhaps most efficacious is the polar opposite of the machine city. In the professionalized, bureaucratic city, local government is expressly a service institution. Well-paid, thoroughly trained, and highly educated police officers answer calls promptly and with courtesy; the city manager has an open line to inquisitive — even angry — citizens; garbage is collected with tender, loving care; and potholes are repaired within 48 hours of complaint. Such places are most likely to be upper-middle-class suburbs, where citizens can (and do) pay for the same individualized and quality services from the public sector that they can get from their specialty shops rather than from discount houses.

Yet if participation in local elections is rather low, the practice of contacting as participation is surprising low as well. Eisenger studied the pattern of citizen contacts with national, state, and local officials in Milwaukee. Only a minority of his sample of citizens (33 percent of whites and 11 percent of blacks) had made any recent contact with public officials.[12] The most common source of contacts was the scope and quality of public services, from snow removal to garbage pickups. The most common recipient of the call or contact was an elected official, who was supposed to nudge the service bureaucracy into responsiveness. In Milwaukee and elsewhere, participating through the contact route is almost a "whites only" business and is skewed sharply toward individuals of higher-social-class status.

One reason for this racial and class bias in the contacting system is that middle-class citizens are both more experienced and more effective in dealing with bureaucracies, of which the government is a conspicuous example. As Sjoberg and his associated observed in exploring the relationship between bureaucracy and the lower class, "First and foremost, the lower-class person simply lacks knowledge of the rules of the game. Middle-class persons generally learn how to manipulate bureaucratic rules to their advantage . . . ."[13] Because information is class-biased in the political system, middle-class persons are more likely to know either the name of the agency responsible for the problem or of some elected official whose reelection depends on citizen responsiveness.

EXIT, VOICE, AND POLITICAL LINKAGE: TOWARD A THEORY OF MASS POLITICS IN THE CITY

The Concept of Linkage Institutions

In the old, and mostly imaginary, New England town meeting, people could thrash out their differences in a face-to-face forum. The differences were probably not very great in any case, simply because community homogeneity was high. We do not operate town meetings in American cities today. With participation as low as it is, few would show up anyway. Urban political life has become more institutionalized, more bureaucratized, and more organized. It depends on secondary instead of primary institutions to identify interests and forge issues. A few efforts to create "spontaneous" citizen participation, either through indigenous neighborhood action groups in poor areas or through citywide "Goals for Podunk" schemes, have mostly ended in cooptation, low turnout, or never-ending meetings. Those who romanticize an imagined past of grassroots organization or fantasize an unlikely future of civic rejuvenation are often disappointed.

Let us face clearly the fact that cities are large, complex social organizations. How, then, can citizens satisfy their policy preferences? Transmitting mass opinions to elites is not an easy matter. Citizens cannot easily assemble *en masse* to shout their preferences. Communication of mass sentiments is carried on through institutional mechanisms or processes that we call *linkage institutions*. With politics what it is, linkage processes can operate only if support is given to political leaders or withdrawn systematically in reponse to leaders' policy behavior. The rational assignment or withdrawal of political support is not very effective by a lone citizen. Acting in concert, a lonely voice is multiplied. That brings us to the importance of linkage institutions, which are the formal and informal structures through which citizens (the "masses") channel their policy preferences to policy makers (the "elites").

Mass opinion can be communicated to elites through five major means. We will discuss each one in the remainder of this chapter. They are:

- the *interest group,* in which aggregates of citizens with common interests combine to influence policy making
- the *political party,* in which alternative choices of leaders and policies are offered to voters
- the *election,* in which individual citizens can have a say about who shall occupy policy making positions;

- *political protest,* in which citizens not otherwise satisfied can make themselves heard, either peacefully or violently
- *mobility,* in which citizens can literally move in search of policy makers and policies more to their liking

These are not mutually alternative modes of political action. Elections, for example, often attract interest groups and political parties. Interest groups can use various forms of political protest, some very low-key such as speech making and assembling crowds, some more colorful such as leaving dead rats on the mayor's doorstep to protest housing conditions, and some quite dramatic such as street violence. Mobility is a form of political linkage available at the local but not the national level. Unavailing other alternatives, citizens can simply move, hoping to improve their satisfaction with urban policy. But mobility itself is a way of flagging policy makers that something may be wrong.

Exit, Voice and Political Action

In economist Albert O. Hirschman's short book *Exit, Voice, and Loyalty: Responses to Decline in Firms, Organizations, and States,* he poses this simple question:[14] What happens when a firm, an organization, a political party, or even a government starts to deteriorate? A firm's customers begin to decide that the product they have always bought is declining in quality; a political party watches its adherents become independents or shift to the other party; an organization sees its members moving elsewhere to satisfy their needs or talents. Hirshman wants to know whether such declines are inevitable downward spirals — into bankruptcy for a firm or historical footnote for a forgotten political party — or whether they may be only "repairable lapses." What, then, do people do when a firm, party, or organization is no longer satisfying their preferences? How do organizations respond to dissatisfaction with their policy outputs?

According to Hirschman, responses to decline can take two forms: *exit* or *voice.* Consumers (or party adherents or organizational members) can exit altogether. They can seek alternative suppliers (or another party or another organization). Or they can exercise their voice option by complaining, making their dissatisfaction known, individually or collectively, to responsible officials. Either way, the voice option gives the firm, party, or organization "one more chance" to change its ways or watch the disaffected consumers ultimately resort to the exit option. How organizations, firms, and parties respond to exit and voice by consumers and members will determine their future.

It should already be clear that there is a strong parallel to urban political action in this argument. As with Hirschman, we need not worry about citizens who are perfectly content with the substance of urban policy. The urban political system satisfying everyone will probably contain very little citizen action. Those who are dissatisfied with one policy or many policies are the ones who take the voice or the exit options. Two examples will suffice. Citizens in Boston were confronted with court-ordered desegregation of the city's high schools, including a large-scale school busing program. Opponents of the desegregation utilized their voice options often in most vocal ways. Protest is the ultimate form of voice, and demonstrations, even violent ones, marked the opening of the Boston schools on a desegregated basis. But protest was not the only form of voice used. Groups were formed and old ones, such as those supporting long-time busing opponent City Councilwoman Louise Day Hicks, were energized. Group activity spilled over into electoral activity on behalf of antibusing candidates. But Hirschman's perspective reminds us that there is another form of response to policy dissatisfaction, namely exit. Some Bostonians simply abandoned ship, selling their homes and moving to greener (or "whiter") suburbs. Mobility is not a neutral political action. The phrase "white flight" suggests that one common response to dissatisfaction over desegregation was white movement away from desegregating school systems.[15] Still others exited in another way by sending their children to private schools.

Reactions to crime in an urban neighborhood are another example of the use of exit and voice. When crimes rates soar, citizens confront two options: organize or leave. Some neighborhoods have protested to city officials and demanded more police protection. In Minneapolis, for example, one black neighborhood has organized a "Soul Patrol" to give citizens protection from rougher elements and also to guard against excessive use of police force. Elsewhere the fear of crime has promoted exit. People who can afford to exit often flee to avoid crime and disorder.

Families are not the only ones who make decisions about "switching" instead of "fighting" when they are dissatisfied. Industries and firms have and same options. Corporations that supply thousands of jobs and pay substantial taxes have potent weapons to use against city governments. When taxes become too high, or regulations too stringent, firms can threaten to move elsewhere. United States Steel's Gary, Indiana, plant has resisted air pollution regulations for decades by threatening to move out or close down, thereby depriving thousands of workers of jobs.[16] Worries about the exist of a large employer or a big taxpayer can make city officials very mindful of the corporate exercise of voice.

Figure 5.1 portrays graphically the linkage institutions of exit and

Figure 5.1   Exit, Voice, and Political Linkage

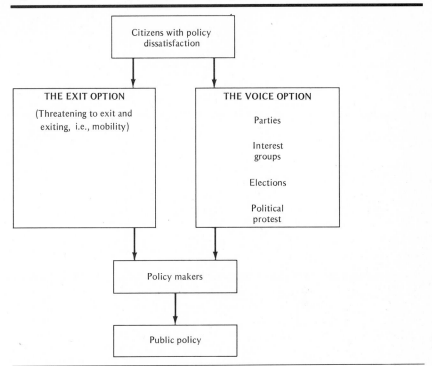

voice. There we list four institutions that can express voice: parties, elections, groups, and protest. How they operate and how effectively they operate are questions that we examine in the remainder of the chapter. We also emphasize, however, both the threat of and the actual use of the exit option. Citizens, groups, and firms dissatisfied with urban governmental policy have a last resort open to them in mobility. Mobility is not merely a sociological phenomenon; it is also a political one.

INTEREST GROUPS AS LINKAGES

Using Organizations to Maximize Voice: The Interest Group

Arthur Bentley was the first proponent of the *group theory of politics* in modern political science. So convinced was he that all political life could be explained by the interaction of groups that he claimed: ". . . when the groups are adequately stated, everything is stated. And when I say everything, I mean everything."[17]

According to Bentley an individual is merely the sum of his group interests, and government constitutes merely the equilibrium of group interests at a given time. Numerous political scientists have expanded, qualified, or elaborated on Bentley's formulation, but the original outline of the analysis of groups and political life was his. Bentley himself despised "definition-mongers," sneering that "he who likes may snip verbal definitions in his old age, when his world has gone crackly and dry."

Part of the difficulty with definitions that may have troubled Bentley is that the words *interest* and *group* seem either redundant or, from another perspective, contradictory. If we conceive of a political group as an organized body of people designed to influence public policy, *interest* becomes a meaningless adjective, for it is hard to imagine such a group without shared interests. On the other hand, if we emphasize the adjective *interest,* then it is equally clear that all interests are organized into groups or, at least, that some clearly are better organized than others. A consumer, a poor man, and a commuter each has an interest in common with fellow consumers, poor people, and commuters, but no group—or at least not a very effective one—represents this interest. The term *interest group,* therefore, subsumes two somewhat distinct ideas. The degree to which a particular interest is in fact organized as a group to influence public policy is an empirical question.

More specifically, we conceive of a political group as an organization attempting to influence public policies through application of political resources. From either an individual or group perspective, an interest emcompasses a set of preferences about the direction of public policy. The essential difference between groups and interests is that interests are psychological, whereas groups are sociological, phenomena. Interests may be more or less organized into groups; groups may share more than one interest.

Given what we said earlier in this chapter about the low level of political participation, it is not surprising to discover that only a fraction of urbanites belongs to any political-interest group. Table 5.3

Table 5.3   Self-reported Membership in "an Organization Working on City Problems," by Social Class

	Upper	Upper middle	Lower middle	Upper lower	Lower lower	Total
Yes	26.0%	24.8%	15.7%	10.9%	5.7%	14.3%
No	74.0%	75.2%	84.3%	89.1%	94.3%	85.7%

Source: Pooled data from Urban Observatories 10-city study of citizens attitudes toward local government.

draws on a question asked citizens in ten Urban Observatory cities. People were asked if they were a member of "an organization working on city problems." Less than 15 percent of the respondents are self-proclaimed organization men and women. Clearly there is a class bias in political organization membership. One-fourth of upper-class citizens were members, but only 1 in 20 lower-lower-class citizens were. Perhaps the important implication, however, is that overwhelming majorities of all social classes were nonmembers of organizations. Presumably many people choose to follow the old adage about "letting George do it" or believe the other old adage that "you can't fight city hall."

But some people whose stakes in local politics are particularly strong are well organized. We argued in Chapter 4 that urban politics is often a politics of economics. One should be safe in guessing, therefore, that economic-interest groups were the strongest in the city. Table 5.4 confirms those suspicions by reporting a study of city council members in the San Francisco Bay Area. Anyone who suspected that the Chamber of Commerce was an important local political group will find those suspicions confirmed by the evidence there. Moreover, it is clear that the categories of "economic groups" and "special interests" are somewhat overlapping, with economic groups like developers, unions, and merchant associations exhibiting strong economic interests. Let us focus on some of the most commonplace and crucial urban-interest groups, including businessmen, ethnics, minority groups, labor, reformers, municipal employees, neighborhood groups, and environmentalists. Our discussion of each is not exhaustive, but

Table 5.4   Most Influential Pressure Groups Named by City Councilmen

Type of organization	Frequency of mention
Economic groups (e.g., Chamber of Commerce, taxpayer groups, neighborhood groups)	43%
Civic groups (e.g., PTA, League of Women Voters, church groups, press, service clubs)	31
Special interests (e.g., conservation associations, builders, developers, senior citizens, unions, merchant associations)	23
Semi-official and official bodies (e.g., planning commission, advisory committees, etc.)	2
Total	100%

Source: Adapted from Local Interest Politics: A One-Way Street, by Betty H. Zisk, copyright © 1973, by The Bobbs-Merrill Company, Inc. Used by permission of the publisher. The data represent answers by San Francisco Bay Area city councilmen. Total rounded to 100%.

we show the principal interests of each and make some assessment of their effectiveness as urban interest groups.

Businessmen, or, Power to the Dollar

If a community has some behind-the-scenes "power structure" that makes the "big decisions," chances are that its membership is coterminous with the economic elite. Still, generalizing about the role of businessmen in the 80,000 units of local government in the United States is hazardous, for the term *businessman* subsumes the owner of a local nightspot as well as the half-million-dollar-a-year Detroit automobile executive.

Economic interests unite most businessmen some of the time (as in the desire to reduce the tax burden on local business), some businessmen all of the time, but rarely all businessmen for very long. Downtown merchants are interested in policies on mass transportation, urban renewal, and economic development that would infuse new life into the central city. Businessmen in the outlying areas tend to oppose such costly undertakings. Small businessmen, especially those who are downwardly mobile in the status system, are often hostile to downtown interests like department-store owners. Realtors are more concerned with zoning and subdivision regulation than with revitalizing sagging downtown areas. Businessmen who provide services over a wide area within the community — major wholesalers and producers, for example — are more interested in community growth, regardless of the direction that it takes.

The two interests most likely to be shared by most businessmen are the quest for lower taxes and the desire to secure economic growth for the community. The first interest is hardly monopolized by the businessmen and may be overstated in any case. Charles Gilbert, in a study of government in the Philadelphia area, noted that "in interviews, industrialists commonly aver that local and county taxes are a small part of the cost of doing business." Moreover, he reminds us that local taxes, because they are deductible from federal taxes, cost industry only 52 cents on the dollar.[18] We do not mean to suggest that businessmen are enthusiastic about high taxes, but they may be no more antagonistic to higher taxes than are, say, homeowners. Moreover, businessmen, especially those in larger firms, see a need to make local communities as attractive as possible, in public services, as a means of increasing livability both for them and for their prospective employees.

Businessmen are perhaps most unified and vocal in their support for public policies promoting economic growth. More economic growth not only means more sales; it is also a visible and measurable sign of progress, especially to those accustomed to measuring progress in economic terms.

The political resources of businessmen and corporations are formidable. Using voice options, businessmen have access to important resources like funds, organizations (sometimes through the Chamber of Commerce), and social status. Businessmen are mostly from the upper and middle classes who participate in politics beyond mere voting. Most local office holders, particularly in small and medium-sized communities, are recruited from the business and professioal sectors.[19] Corporations also have extra clout in exercising the exit option. Communities need jobs and taxes, and corporations provide both. Dependence on the resources that firms provide increases the seriousness of threats to exit. City officials will take that extra step to "improve the business climate" or "create jobs," policies which accrue to the advantage of the business sector.

Labor Unions, or, The Surprising Ineffectiveness of Labor Power

Given the visibility and alleged importance of labor unions in national politics, it is surprising to discover the variability in their political influence at the urban level. Detroit is a one-industry city dominated by automotive manufacturers and the United Auto Workers. The UAW has played a fairly active role in local politics through its Committee on Political Education (COPE). But it appears to be much less effective in local affairs than in influencing Michigan state politics.

Kenneth E. Gray and David Greenstone, in their penetrating study of labor influence in Detroit, St. Louis, and Houston, concluded that "despite its power, COPE has had relatively little success in [Detroit] politics."[20] This study indicated that voters and politicians alike tend to view COPE as a self-interested group that does not represent the city as a whole. Also, and perhaps more significantly, Detroit's nonpartisan electoral system weakens the hold of union leaders on their followers. Even when the rank and file do know the union's candidates, many are reluctant to support leader-endorsed liberals for fear of increased property taxation and the possibility that such candidates will enact housing-integration ordinances.

The interests and stakes of trade unions, as well as their political resources, help to account for their minimal (or variable) influence on local policy. As organizations, unions have relatively low stakes in local public policy. The key decisions, which are of concern to *all* union members, are those related to wages and hours, safety requirements, right-to-work laws, and purchasing power. These decisions are made not in city halls but by states and the federal government. Said a leader of one union in Toledo: "City government is not as important for us. We've got to think about state and national issues. The state is in many ways the most important, I think, since it handles workmen's compensation, unemployment, and such things."[21]

During an earlier era when local police broke up strikes and jailed picketers, unions were more concerned about local politics. Today the overriding concerns of unions as a whole are focused on higher levels of the American federal system. Many significant local political issues tend to divide rank-and-file unionists in ways that would permit no clear leadership position to prevail. Race relations, integration of schools and neighborhoods, and taxation are especially divisive issues. As these issues involve no direct threat to the interests of the union as an organization, leaders typically avoid taking sides. Much more than businessmen, unions have conflicting interests among their memberships. There is simply less incentive to get involved when the issues will not only divide your own membership, but are not critical to organizational goals anyway.

Yet there is one kind of labor union whose influence is potent indeed in local politics. That is the union of municipal employees, whether teachers, police officers, firefighters, or sanitation workers. Strikes and threatened strikes, wage hikes and demands for wage increases, have become routine business in many cities.

Municipal Employees, or,
Strikes Are a Potent Weapon

Once when New York City was negotiating with its uniformed employees, Michael J. Maye, president of the Uniformed Firefighters Association, was quoted as almost shouting to reporters: "They say there's no money for us. Well, fire protection has gone from 4 percent to 3 percent of the budget. There's a drain all right, and who's getting it? We know. Welfare has gone from 10 percent to 22 percent—there's plenty of money for that."[22] This anecdote illustrates something already obvious to most urban dwellers, that city employees can be potent interest group and often have resources to get their way. They are in competition with other groups for scarce budget dollars. The 4.5 million employees of local government in the United States have high stakes in urban politics. Typically, more than three-fourths of the urban budget goes for salaries and wages. Payrolls in the local government sector have risen much faster than other wages, doing better than inflation in almost every city, at least until the fiscal crunch came in the mid-1970s. Some even blamed "excessive" demands of unionized employees for the fiscal crisis in New York City and elsewhere.

The growth of public employee unions has been the only source of recent growth in the American labor movement. In the 1950s, a union of police officers or sanitation workers was almost unheard of. By the mid-1970s, nearly one-half of all city employees were members of a union or other employee organization. In the biggest cities, nearly all employees are unionized. Some are members of the American Federation of State, County and Municipal Employees, an affiliate of the AFL-CIO. Teachers are often members of the American Federation of Teachers or a bargaining unit of the National Education Association. Some local employees are Teamsters union members, but still others are members of independent local groups. One historic technique of unions has been the strike, and work stoppages have grown with municipal unionization. Police officers in Oklahoma City dramatically tossed their badges on the city hall steps before walking off the job. Garbage piled up on Baltimore streets for days when sanitation employees struck for higher wages. Countless school districts are lucky to start the year on time. In 1965, fewer than 50 cities saw work stoppages. This year, close to 500 public-employee strikes can be expected. These strikes are often technically illegal, but cities sometimes discover sudden "epidemics" among employees involved in wage negotiations. (Among police officers, this phenomenon is often called the "blue flu.")

Like working people everywhere, municipal employees are concerned about wages, working conditions, and job security. These worries have been heightened by the wave of near-bankruptcies of city governments. Detroit, for example, faced with a deficit of $44.3 million, fired 1200 city employees, including several hundred fire and police officers. This financial threat to job security makes unions even more sensitive about their political power. Sometimes unions will trade additional job security for less than they would like in wages. Municipal unions, strong for years in northeastern cities, now are raising these sorts of issues in cities all across the country.

Ethnic Groups, or, Whatever You Do, Don't Lose the Polish Vote

American cities, particularly those in the Northeast, have long been potpourris of ethnic groups. To sympathetic observers, the city has been the great "melting pot." To nativist critics, it has been the "garbage can." Stepping off the boats at Ellis Island and other processing centers, millions of immigrant families were tagged with new names and sent packing to relatives already settled in cities. They became formidable voting blocs in an era of universal manhood suffrage, and leaders of the nascent urban machines were delighted to see them. Democratic (and some Republican) political organizations still draw heavily on the urban ethnic vote. Both parties take notice of Columbus Day, Polish-American Week, or Oktoberfest. When Gerald

Ford boldly announced in the 1976 presidential debates that Eastern Europe was not under Soviet domination, Republicans feared the loss of Polish, Czech, Lithuanian and other ethnic groups concerned about the freedom of the old countries. Ethnic politics is far from dead. Mark Twain is said to have grumbled, upon reading his own obituary, that "the reports of my death are greatly exaggerated." The same may be said about the widely touted theory of the *assimilation* of urban ethnic groups.

According to the assimilation theory, second- and third-generation European immigrants have become so thoroughly socialized into American middle-class culture that their political behavior and attitudes are scarcely distinguishable from those of direct descendents of the Mayflower pilgrim. Robert Dahl studied ethnic politics in New Haven and found that it passed through three stages.[23] In the first stage, group members vote very much alike. In the second, socioeconomic status begins to play a more important role, and group members even find their ethnic status a source of embarrassment. Finally, considerable heterogeneity develops, and ethnic groups disappear as potent political forces, as ethnic solidarity becomes a subject for historians. These observations square with other facts about urban ethnic groups. There were an estimated 1400 foreign-language newspapers in the United States in 1914; today there are fewer than 400. No longer are European ethnic groups' crowded neighborhoods called "little Italy" or "little Dublin." As have other Americans, second- and third-generation ethnics have moved to the suburbs and up the socioeconomic ladder.

Yet ethnic politics has a tenacity that defies demographic evidence about assimilation, absorption, and homogenization. Raymond Wolfinger reexamined ethnic voting patterns in New Haven and found a remarkable persistence of ethnic voting. His "mobilization theory" of ethnic politics argues that the "strength of ethnic voting depends on both the intensity of ethnic identification and the level of ethnic relevance in the election." The most important expression of ethnic relevance is the presence of an ethnic name on the ticket. But, because "middle-class status is a virtual prerequisite for candidacy for major office" and because "an ethnic group's development of sufficient political skills and influence to secure such a nomination also requires the development of a middle class,"[24] ethnic voting solidarity will not appear until some members of the group become candidates for middle-class status. The peak of ethnic solidarity in elections thus will come not during the first generation — when the group is uniformly of the lower class and subject to manipulation and cross pressures from competing factions — but during the second and third generations. This theory seems better able to explain why, in New Haven at least, there was an increasing solidarity of ethnic groups behind their parties over time. It also embodies recognition of political-leadership skills as a crucial ingredient in ethnic politics.

Ethnic politics, unlike the interests of businessmen, unions, or municipal employees, is largely *status* politics. Placement of a group leader on the ballot provides vicarious status mobility to all members of the group. Hiring members of the group for civil service jobs (e.g., in Chicago, different municipal departments are still dominated by different ethnic groups) provides group status. Conflict over status becomes more vigorous if there are several dominant ethnic groups in the city. Indeed, the rise of black consciousness has heightened the solidarity of older ethnic groups. That many police departments include large numbers of Italians, Irish, Polish, and other ethnics heightens the friction between police and blacks. It is often the older ethnic neighborhood, which is in the path of an expanding black neighborhood, that exacerbates tensions between the European ethnic group seeking to protect its "turf" and the black community seeking to expand its living space.

Reformers: The Never-ending Battle for "Good Government"

Edward C. Banfield and James Q. Wilson formulated an influential theory of city politics in their book *City Politics*, based on the presumed conflict between "ethnic" and "Yankee" values.[25] Ethnic groups exhibit, they claimed, *private-regarding* values, which emphasize personalistic politics, oriented toward the family, group, or subculture, and involving a political style similar to that provided by the machine. Bargaining, trading off, jobs, club politics, with perhaps a bit of private advantage on the side, figure prominently in the private-regarding style. The *public-regarding* style, however, is said to reflect principles of abstract morality, honesty, efficiency, professional management, and an aversion of "politics." Upper-class, Yankee reformers deplored the machine and its ethnic base. They favored at large elections, nonpartisan elections, council-manager government, and the civil service. Whether or not Banfield and Wilson's controversial theory accurately depicts urban politics, the conflict between reformers and ethnic politicians has been long standing.[26]

Nearly every major city has its reform group. New York has the Citizen's Union; San Antonio had a group literally called the Good Government League; and Chicago has a group of business and professional people assembled into Chicago United . Nearly always, such groups are dominated by upper-class people seeking to institutionalize the values of "good government." (Because of these perennial cries for "good government," critics of the early reformers sometimes called them the "goo-goos.") Often they are liberal in political philosophy, although their critics might snidely call them "limousine liberals." Most seem to share certain predispositions about local government:

1. an aversion to "politics" as a means of arriving at public-policy decisions and specifically to political parties and organized interest groups
2. a holistic conception of the community as a whole to which special interests should be clearly subordinated
3. a strong preference for professional management of community affairs, implying preference for public policy making by technical experts like the city manager
4. a strong faith in the efficacy of structural reform

The reformers became prominent in the latter years of the nineteenth century. They have remained so ever since, although there are some differences between the early and latter-day reformers. Businessmen, traditional groups, local chambers of commerce, and upper-class people were in the forefront of the early battles for reform. Harold Stone, in his survey of early adoptions of the council-manager plan, found in Jackson, Michigan, that "most of the campaign work [for the plan] was done through the Chamber of Commerce, which enlisted the support of all the Protestant reform agencies in the city." In Rochester, New York, the campaign for manager government was "supported by the leading industrialist of the city, George Eastman, by the Bureau of Municipal Research which he financed, and by most of the civic, reform, and business associations of the city."[27] (One leader of the Rochester Communist Party also supported the manager plan, believing that it was one stage through which politics would have to pass before the dictatorship of the proletariat could be achieved.) Almost as surely as the manager plan was supported by traditional and business interests in the city, it was opposed by trade unions and ethnic groups.

Considerable overlap exists between businessmen and reformers, but the two groups are not quite identical. Businessmen seek economic advantage through urban policy. Reformers peddle ideas about the proper way to run a government. They are instinctively opposed to politics, which they see as "seamy," and favor political reforms to make government more "honest" and "efficient." Robert Agger and his associates, in their study of four American communities, summarize the political mentality of the reform group when they describe the rise of "community conservationists," who see the "values of community life maximized when political leadership is exercised by men representing the public at large rather than 'special interests'."[28] But reformers always have trouble persuading people that their conception of the "public at large" is not just another "special interest."

Neighborhood Groups: Exit and
Voice at the Grassroots Level

If the "voice" option is to be a reality, it must be nurtured at the "grassroots" level. Some neighborhood groups persist for years, are effectively led, provide articulate linkages of citizen preferences to policy makers. Indeed, the worst enemy of neighborhood organization is the fear of exit by those whose voices could be effective. What happens when a neighborhood starts to decline often goes like this: Almost imperceptibly, signs of decay are noticed. Streets become a little dirtier; stores begin to close early and then close altogether; houses are carved up into apartments or rooms for rent; young people move away; mortgage money is hard to get; perhaps the "wrong kind" of people begin to move in; crime becomes more prominent; the quality of homes deteriorates. Citizens faced with neighborhood decline normally confront the exit or voice options. Some citizens, often the young and upwardly mobile, will move, perhaps to the suburbs. Their departure may almost guarantee the continued deterioration of the area. Whether citizens choose the exit or voice response to neighborhood decay largely determines the future of the area.

Sometimes citizens choose the voice option, although it is often an uphill struggle. It is easiest to organize groups around specific *threats* to neighborhood integrity. Thus neighborhood groups are often ad hoc, organized in response to some perceived challenge. Among the most common threats are a proposed change in zoning ordinances, an "invasion" by other racial or ethnic groups, a threatened closing of a neighborhood school, a new highway proposed through the area, or sudden increase in street crime. Articulate, politically sophisticated neighborhood groups can often fight someone else's view of "progress." More typically, however, they lack staying power, as many potential leaders are siphoned off through the exit process.

There is an incredible variability from city to city in the number and potency of neighborhood associations. San Francisco has an estimated 212 groups, ranging from a league of Arab grocers to gay groups.[29] Most southern and midwestern cities have less group activity. Several factors combine to encourage organization or the grassroots. It seems clear that:

1. Cities that use ward or district elections will have stronger neighborhood associations.
2. Neighborhood organization is strongest in *middle*-class areas, because upper-class people will quickly exit and lower-class people are not very organizable.
3. Where threats to neighborhood viability are specific and dramatic, rather than slow and imperceptible, organization is encouraged.

Minority Groups: From Conciliation
to Confrontation to Fragmentation

As we showed in Chapter 3, the urbanization of the black American population is perhaps the most profound change since the abolition of slavery. In 1910, 9 out of 10 blacks lived in the South, primarily in the poor countryside. Today more than 7 in 10 blacks live in the SMSA, almost all in the central city.

Because of the lower income and educational levels of most blacks, we expect to find them participating in politics at lower levels than white. This hypothesis is only partially supported. In fact, if we compare black and white citizens of similar socioeconomic status, *blacks participate in politics at higher levels than whites.*[30] Blacks and whites are almost identical in self-reported membership in "an organization working to solve city problems," despite the lower social status of blacks.

To what degree does voting strength affect urban policies benefiting blacks as a group? The right to vote has been touted as "the most powerful instrument ever devised by man for breaking down injustice and destroying the terrible walls that imprison men because they are different from other men."[31] Such claims make good politics but poor social science. Participation through voting is but one of many means of enunciating political preferences, and public policy is determined by more than occasional elections. The importance of the vote in a scheme of ordered liberty notwithstanding, any claims for the efficacy of the franchise in achieving group goals should be subjected to careful empirical examination.

William R. Keech assessed the strengths and limitations of black voting as a political resource in a study of Durham, North Carolina. Durham blacks have voted for many years and have skilled leadership and vigorous political organization. Still, Keech noted, "the really striking gains of Durham's Negro minority have come through resources other than votes." Some policy decisions are influenced by votes, but "the vote is a far more potent instrument for achieving legal justice than social justice. The gains [that are] most susceptible to Negro voting have consistently been those which most clearly involved fair and just administration of exiting laws. Social justice, however, demands more than this."[32] People have different perceptions of *social justice*, but, if the concept includes such things as comparable incomes for comparable jobs, courteous and equal treatment by fellow citizens, and opportunities for economic advancement, the vote in urban elections does not win social justice. The vote is much more influential in reducing disparities in treatment in the public sector than it is in changing behavior in the private sector through governmental action. Other strategies like litigation, boycotts, and demonstrations seem to be more effective than the vote in securing basic social changes.

These strategies in the 1950s and early 1960s reflected a politics of conciliation. Led by Martin Luther King, civil-rights groups pressed for integrationist goals and worked vigorously through traditional linkage institutions like elections, parties, and groups. The mid-1960s, however, witnessed the rise of challenges to the integrationist stance. "Black power" leaders such as Stokeley Carmichael, H. Rap Brown, Eldridge Cleaver, and Malcolm X opposed integration efforts as injurious to black solidarity.

Black power leadership groups in American cities vigorously opposed coalition politics. Statements and definitions of black power are as numerous as are its proponents (multiplied, perhaps, by its critics). One of the most articulate and widely read statements was that of Stokeley Carmichael and Charles V. Hamilton. Their fundamental premise is a distinction between "individual" and "institutional" racism. This distinction parallels the difference between micro and macro levels of analysis in city politics. They contend that:

When a black family moves into a home in a white neighborhood and is stoned, burned or routed out, they are victims of an overt act of individual racism which many people will condemn — at least in words. But it is institutional racism that keeps black people locked in dilapidated slum tenements, subject to the daily prey of exploitative slumlords, merchants, loan sharks, and discriminatory real estate agents.[33]

Individual racism is direct, specific, and visible; individuals can be singled out and held culpable. *Institutional racism* is covert, indirect, collective, and nonspecific; it is difficult to pin responsibility upon a single group or individual. Carmichael and Hamilton have argued that even achievement of the traditional black goal of integration can deal only with individual racism. They note that it is possible to *assimilate* individuals but that only groups can be *integrated*. Individual assimilation merely siphons off the fortunate few who might otherwise have provided a source of leadership for the black community. Instead of integration, the black power philosophy rests upon the "fundamental premise" that "before a group can enter the open society, it must first close ranks."[34] In these authors' view coalitions have failed in the past because Blacks have permitted white coalition partners to define the interests of both parties. Black power rests upon the Machiavellian notion that "a prince ought never to make common cause with one more powerful than himself." Black power proponents said, "enter coalitions only *after* you are able to stand on your own."[35]

The "confrontationist" strategy of black power, however, no longer galvanizes a large segment of the black community. The assassinations of Martin Luther King and Malcolm X, the relative obscurity of Stokeley Carmichael and the bizarre conversion of the one-time ex-patriate Eldrige Cleaver into a pin-striped spokesman for Ameri-can virtues have set black politics on its ear. By the mid-1970s, both the civil rights movement and the black power movement had lost much of their momentum. "Community control" – an important sym-bol of black politics then – is a dormant issue today. Black political in-terests today seem fragmented and not significantly different from white interests. Issues like service delivery (which we examine in Chapter 10), schooling, housing opportunities, and transportation are on black as well as white political agendas. Blacks continue to be in-terested in the symbolic representation afforded by black mayors. But once in office, black mayors face pretty much the same problems as white mayors.[36]

Environmentalists, or, Don't Put Your Nuclear Power Plant Near Me

Environmentalists are a new, and potentially very powerful, entrant on the interest-group scene. As ubiquitous as the problems they attack and the "progress" they oppose, environmentalists can be found in freeway controversies, opposing new airports, maintaining open spaces against encroachment, and fighting skyscrapers. Colorado en-vironmentalists successfully protested the Winter Olympics; San An-tonio environmentalists fought a freeway that would have run within 90 feet of the zoo's bear pits (see our case study on pp. 344–346); San Francisco environmentalists advocated limitation of skyscrapers; and environmentalists everywhere have battled against the automobile and the nuclear power plant. These causes have not endeared envi-ronmentalists to civic leaders accustomed to measuring municipal progress by the number of new sewer connections. While business and reform ideologies assume growth is the key to urban survival, en-vironmentalists see growth as further exploiting or despoiling scarce resources.

Most Americans are, at least in the abstract, environmentalists. In opinion polls a majority of Americans have described themselves as "deeply concerned" and another third as "somewhat concerned" about air and water pollution. Abstract interest, however, is not always translated into concrete action. Environmentalism is a public-interest issue like consumerism, and there is often a tendency to "let George do it" (or Ralph Nader or the Sierra Club) when the interest is an ab-stract and long-term problem. Local interest groups concerned with environmental despoilation are, therefore, often small, but vocal, mi-norities. We shall have more to say about environmental politics and policy in Chapter 14.

Interest Groups as Linkages

Political scientists are hardly in agreement about the power of groups to influence public policy. But there is good reason, we think, to reject literal acceptance of Bentley's observation that, "when the groups are adequately explained, everything is explained." This argument is true only if the trivial and tautological sense that, if attitudes, values, parties, electoral mechanisms, bureaucratic premises, and the like are defined as *groups* or *group-determined,* then everything indeed can be explained by explaining groups. If *everything* is a *group,* then the concept of *group* can explain everything.

If we restrict ourselves to a more narrow and commonsensical meaning of the term *interest group* to denote formal organization, however, we do not find that interest groups are all-powerful. One of the most penetrating studies of policy making at the national level examined the influence on tariff policy of such associations as the Chamber of Commerce, the National Association of Manufacturers, the League of Women Voters, and the AFL-CIO; it found them surprisingly ineffectual.[37] More pertinent to city politics, John P. Crecine studied budgetary policies in three cities and found that decision makers rarely received any pressure from specific groups. When groups did argue for particular financial commitments, decision makers tended to believe that most requests were reasonable but that "you can't do everything everybody wants."[38] In a study of San Francisco Bay Area city councils, groups were found to play an important role on occasion, but their influence depended heavily on the attitudes of councilmen toward the legitimacy of the group's activity.[39] These findings do not invalidate the assumption that groups are important elements in community decision making, but they cast doubt on any theory of urban politics that assumes the primacy of interest groups in determining the use of community resources.

As a representational mechanism, therefore, the interest group is (like the party and electoral system) limited. One of the interest group's most significant limitations derives from the paucity of group membership in a city. Mythology to the contrary, the United States is hardly a nation of joiners. The vast majority of American citizens belong to no political organization. This does not mean that they will go unrepresented, but the nonparticipant remains at the mercy of someone else's good will. There is, moreover, a strong correlation between group membership and socioeconomic status. Some, in other words, are better organized than others. Chambers of Commerce is more tightly organized than the local consumers' associations; schoolteachers are better organized than the poor; transportation industries are typically more organized than commuters. Even if a group is well organized, many city councilpersons reject pressure and prefer to follow their own consciences. Thus a number of interests in the city are not well organized into groups, and, even when they are, an organization does not assure effectiveness in shaping policy.

THE POLITICAL PARTY
AS LINKAGE

At the national level the political party is an important — some political scientists think the most important — linkage institution. The party aggregates many expressions of voice. The Democrats and Republicans may not be so sharply distinguishable as some would like, but party identification remains the best predictor of both individual and congressional voting behavior and also of presidential programs. Whether the urban political party contributes much to holding decision makers accountable to public opinion is debatable. To understand why, we must examine old party organization in cities and what little current party organization exists.

The Machine: An Example, A Definition, and Some Nostalgia

In the 1890s, Chicago's Nineteenth Ward, where Jane Addams and her associates established the famed Hull House, contained 50,000 people of 20 different nationalities, crammed together in a few square miles of dingy tenements.[40] Most were immigrants, and, because of universal manhood suffrage, most of the men were voters.

The political boss of the Nineteenth Ward was Johnny Powers, a short, stocky Irishman and one of the most powerful figures in Chicago city politics. As chairman of the finance committee of the Chicago City Council, he used his position to manipulate public-utility franchises and the jobs of thousands of city employees. Powers ran for office on a year-round basis: bailing a son or husband out of jail, fixing matters with a judge, buying funerals through his standing account at the undertaker, buying turkeys at Christmas, and keeping 2600 residents of the ward on the city payroll. Public policy under the Powers machine was "personalized." There was no commitment to alter the conditions that had produced the need for his patronage and favors and little concern for the niceties of honest and efficient municipal government.

This whole system was disturbing to the women of Hull House. They tried to defeat Powers in the elections of 1895, 1896, and 1898. But Powers and his associates survived every challenge from Hull House and its reformist allies. Following the second unsuccessful attempt in 1896, Powers gave a municipal position to nearly every man who had campaigned actively against him. He appointed a printer who was also an opposition leader to a clerkship at city hall, a driver from the opposition camp to the city police barns at a lucrative salary, and the opposing candidate himself to a comfortable position in the city construction department. It was difficult to defeat a man with such political resources. Reform of the Nineteenth Ward had to wait for forces stronger than Miss Addams and her colleagues.

Johnny Powers's operation in the Nineteenth Ward was one example of the urban party machines that dominated many American cities during the years of rapid urbanization and immigration. The party machine is both the best-known and the least-understood aspect of urban political life. Banfield and Wilson have defined it as a "party organization that depends crucially upon inducements that are both specific and material."[41] Specific inducements are those (such as jobs in city government) that can be given to some and withheld from others; material inducements are those that are monetary or readily convertible into money. This definition, however, understates the importance of nonmaterial inducements in generating support for the machine. Banfield and Wilson themselves have noted that one very important resource of the ward captain was "friendship."

Fred I. Greenstein has offered the following more general definition of the machine from a structural and functional point of view.[42]

1. There is a disciplined party hierarchy led by a single executive or a board of directors.
2. The party exercises effective control over nomination to public office, and through this it controls the public officials of the municipality.
3. The party leadership—which quite often is of lower-class social origins— usually does not hold public office and sometimes does not even hold formal party office. At any rate, official position is not the primary source of the leadership's strength.
4. Rather, a cadre of loyal party officials and workers, as well as a core of voters, is maintained by a mixture of material rewards and nonideological psychic rewards—such as personal and ethnic recognition, camaraderie, and the like.

It is almost fashionable these days to romanticize the political machine. Unlike Shakespeare's Julius Caesar, where the good that men did was oft interred with their bones, writers often exhibit nostalgia about the machine. Reformers saw the machine as an object of moral disdain, chiefly because of its presumably shady operations with public tax dollars. Revisionist views of the machine have emphasized that a little corruption universally occurs in developing governments, whether an American city or developing nations.[43] The machine was said to provide a welfare function for the dispossessed and did so with a personalism and intimacy that welfare bureaucracies have never equalled. Fires, unemployment, illness, crime, and other human miseries were opportunities for politicians to help the disadvantaged and collect their votes in return. They also, their defenders say, provided an avenue of upward mobility for ethnic groups, helped them to become socialized in American culture, found them jobs, and gave them a measure of social status. Political clubs were effective ways for Irishmen, Poles, and other ethnics to get ahead. Bosses offered jobs, favors, and status in exchange for votes. Machines thus performed certain "latent functions," as Robert Merton calls their activities, which were performed by no other social institution before the days of legal aid, unemployment compensation, and social security.[44] If only, some go on to claim, we had organizations such as the machines today, instead of faceless bureaucracies, the cities would be better off.

Perhaps that argument is correct. No ward heeler worth his salt would let a family be evicted from their house if he could help it; the modern urban bureaucracy would perhaps bring the rulebook to the eviction. Frankly we think the political machine to be a more complex institution than its defenders — even its critics — portray. The myth of the machine has almost begun to outrun the reality.

The Myth of the Machine

The popular image of the machine is a mixture of myth and reality, with perhaps a larger dose of myth than reality. The machine of popular lore rests on an immigrant, ethnic political base; it was found mostly in older northeastern cities such as New York, Boston, or Chicago; it was supposedly corrupt and engaged in hanky-panky with public monies; it was roundly despised by right-thinking businessmen and loved by the "down-and-out"; and it was unique to the American city. On almost all counts these elements of the machine myth are either wrong or greatly overstated, as we indicate in Table 5.5.

One of the most prevalent myths about the machine is that it was, as Theodore Lowi once claimed, "peculiar to the American city."[45] Yet rural counties throughout the South (and even in the North) have machines as well oiled as any ever present in a city. Machines and remnants of machines, such as the Byrd organization in Virginia, the Long organization in Louisiana, and the Kennedy organization in Massachusetts, exhibit the same characteristics as city machines. Even political organizations in developing countries often resemble American urban machines. Nor do machines necessarily thrive on ethnic politics. Cities such as Milwaukee with heavy ethnic concentrations have never had much of a machine, and places with few ethnic voters like Kansas City and Memphis had famous machines. What strikes us on close examination is the *variability* of machine politics rather than its constancy.

There is but one common denominator of the organization that we

Table 5.5   **The Machine: Myth and Reality**

Myth	Reality
1. The machine was almost always based on the ethnic vote.	1. Dead wrong. Machines thrived in places like Kansas City (the famous "Pendergast machine") where ethnics were few, whereas other places with ethnic concentrations never developed effective machines.
2. The machine was almost always Democratic.	2. More often than not, yes, but Republican machines have been potent in cities in New York, Pennsylvania and elsewhere.
3. The machine was almost always corrupt.	3. It depends on "how corrupt is corrupt?" Some, such as Tammany Hall, were unbelievably corrupt in certain periods; others were no more corrupt than city and state governments not dominated by a machine.
4. The machine was "peculiar to the American city," especially big, older, northeastern cities.	4. Certainly not. Probably more machines exist in rural counties and state governments than in cities; nor are two fabled machines—in Kansas City and Memphis —in old, northeastern cities.
5. Machines were despised by businessmen and loved only by the ethnics.	5. Wrong on both counts. Businessmen often developed close ties to the machine (as is still true in Chicago) and the electoral base included ethnics, blacks, and old-stock Americans.
6. The machine is dead.	6. Increasingly true, but not entirely; remember Chicago.

call the political machine: It is a nonideological electoral organization, depending heavily on lower-class votes. Machines are almost never ideological. They are rather broad umbreallas that are large enough to cover every shade of opinion and interest. They are principally electoral organizations, interested in winning to enjoy the fruits of office. Perhaps most important—and illustrating that political discourse is often a matter of language—the word *machine* is normally reserved for organizations dependent on lower-class voters. We almost never describe an upper-class electoral organization as a "machine."

When an organization of essentially upper-middle-class people, such as the Good Government League in San Antonio, manages to elect 79 of 81 candidates it nominates over a 20-year period, we still do not call it a machine. Being a machine is almost a matter of the language that we use to describe a political organization.

The Machine as Linkage and the Supposed
Demise of the Machine

The machine as a means of linking policy preferences of the masses with policy decisions of the elites was at best second-rate. A hod of coal at Christmas is nice, but the machine had little interest in ending poverty. In fact, *the machine depended on maintenance of a lower-class clientele to stay in business.* Raymond Wolfinger, assessing machine politics in New Haven, emphasizes that "the individual voter's support for the machine is not likely to be rewarded by its leaders' formulation of policy programs. Machines do not pay off their rank-and-file supporters with social polities, nor are they pressed to do so."[46] Rather, machine politicians may form close alliances with those who prefer weak enforcement of housing codes and shoddy public services. The poor hardly gain from such alliances, for, as Wolfinger observes, "where money talks, the poor are silent." An overall assessment of the machine and the disadvantages might emphasize that the poor may benefit individually from machine activities, but rarely collectively.

If urban history books typically recount the "rise of the machine," books on urban politics document "the demise of the machine." The urban party machine survives today principally as an anachronism. There are several reasons why the machine has declined almost everywhere. Affluence has meant a general decrease in the relative values of the rewards available through the machines. In affluent society, menial jobs such as census taker and city sanitation worker will not buy the votes they once did. The rise of the welfare state also emasculated the machine. Unemployment compensation, social security, and other benefits are more certain and more generous than were the occasional turkeys, hods of coal, and small favors handed out by a friendly neighborhood precinct captain. The Depression was a double blow to the machine, straining its scarce resources as well as leading to a federally organized, financed, and supervised welfare program that the party organization could not match. At the same time the machines were losing their welfare role, local governments had to perform a new range of services. Municipal governments hired skilled technicians and professionals. Party hacks cannot handle complex decisions, intricate financial procedures, computerized police protection, and other technical matters. As public management becomes more complex, mismanagement becomes increasingly embarrassing.

The impact of the reformers, and the institutions they advocated, also dealt heavy blows to the machine. Nonpartisanship made it more difficult for voters to know who was behind the names on the ballot and for the machines to keep unwanted candidates off the ballot. Elections at large organized politics around whole constituencies, rather than neighborhoods whose precinct captains could know voters by name. They also raised the costs of machine campaigning.

Furthermore, the advent of manager governments and the professionalization of city bureaucracies through the civil-service system removed the office of mayor from the arena of public choice, lessened the importance of political premises in decision making, and substituted the trained skills and judgments of professional managers. Civil-service reforms, as they took hold at the local level, increasingly removed middle- and low-level jobs from patronage.

The Chicago Machine

Wolfinger, though, has cautioned against proclaiming the death of the machine prematurely.[47] No one who lives in Chicago would be willing to write an obituary for the machine. There the "greatest mayor Chicago ever had," Richard J. Daley, maintained a strong machine by using all the traditional devices but also by adapting to countless reform programs.[48] Daley succeeded where others failed partly by conspicuously supporting business interests and thereby defusing reformist sentiment. City finances are strong compared with other big cities, and civic boosterism is encouraged. The machine has always suffered periodic defeats. An aggressive U.S. attorney (now Illinois governor), James Thompson, prosecuted and jailed countless Daley friends and aides. But the mayor hung in there, recalling the advice of an earlier Chicago boss, Ed Kelley: "If you don't run them, they'll run you." Only age appeared to be the mayor's natural enemy; he died suddenly in 1976.

The Chicago machine has relied on all of the traditional blandishments to turn out the vote. Each precinct—there are more than 3000 in all—has its own captain, who in turn has several assistants. Precincts are organized into wards, fifty altogether, and ward committeemen are typically more powerful than the ward's alderman. The competent committeeman can predict his ward's vote and turnout on election day with an accuracy which would rival the Harris or Gallup organizations. Committeemen can get sewers repaired, turn on fire hydrants for kids on hot summer days, find jobs for deserving and loyal constituents, play ombudsman roles with the city bureaucracies, make small loans to suddenly needy citizens, and get new garbage cans for citizens whose cans have been abused by careless sanitation men. These sorts of favors make the machine a public service organization even more than it is an electoral organization.

The machine, of course, has nurtured stories about its supposed electoral invincibility. Yet one should hardly be surprised to find Chicago a heavily Democratic city, even if it did not have a strong Democratic organization. Its demographic profile—heavily black, working class, Catholic, labor union, and ethnic—fit neatly most of the characteristics of the Democratic voter. Chicago, after all, is not the only big city to turn out comfortable Democratic majorities. When unchallenged, the machine rolls up lopsided majorities for its candidates. But when it has been challenged—and it has increasingly been challenged in recent years—it scrambled for every vote. Michael Bilandic, who as Acting Mayor, succeeded Richard J. Daley faced substantial opposition in his 1977 primary election. Alderman Roman Pucinski drained away some Polish votes from the city's largest ethnic minority and State Senator Harold Washington pulled some black votes. But for an obscure and definitely noncharismatic local politician who had been active in politics for less than six years, Bilandic managed to accumulate an impressive 50 percent of the primary vote.

How the machine managed to pull off two significant victories in close contests is illustrated by the data in Table 5.6. In the mayoral primary of 1975, Mayor Daley survived a challenge from black State Senator Richard Newhouse and independent, antimachine alderman William Singer. In 1977s primary, Bilandic beat back a challenge from a Polish and a black opponent. Even in almost all-black wards, Daley

Table 5.6   Voting in Chicago: The 1975 and 1977 Mayoral Primaries, Selected Wards

	Daley, 1975 (percent)	Bilandic, 1977 (percent)
Black wards[a]		
3	48	57
6	43	41
17	55	43
Strongholds		
1	70	70
11	87	87
Heavily ethnic[b]		
36	67	46
40	51	44
50	50	46
Independent		
43	37	45
44	47	50

[a] 95 percent or more black.
[b] 50 percent or more foreign stock.

and Bilandic managed to hold their black opponents to bare majorities. Even with a Polish candidate Bilandic was able to garner nearly half the votes from the most heavily ethnic (typically Polish) wards. And even against a visible, well-financed, and articulate independent running in 1975, Daley collected a third to half the votes in the most independent-minded wards. But the machine has historically relied on several stronghold wards. Most notable among them is the 11th ward, locally known as Bridgeport. Every mayor since 1933, including Daley and Bilandic, has hailed from Bridgeport, a white enclave in an encroaching black area, near the old Chicago stockyards. With less than a 9th-grade median education, Bridgeport voters turn out in extraordinarily large numbers. They also, along with several other stronghold wards, deliver their almost unanimous support for the organization's candidates. Chicago politics has always been like a giant jigsaw puzzle, where each piece must fit into a larger whole. So long as the organization can rely upon its stronghold and hold opponents to minimums even in the opponents' strongholds, the organization can deliver. With the passing of Mayor Daley the machine went right back to work.

ELECTIONS AS LINKAGES

Electoral participation is the most widely touted form of "voice." Democratic theory emphasizes the critical role that elections supposedly play in assuring political linkage. If voters participate, and vote wisely, policy makers will always fear electoral retribution if they do not respond to mass preferences. This perception of elections as "mandates" to elected officials depends on several assumptions. It requires, at a minimum, that:

1. Citizens must have opinions on issues and knowledge about which leaders will pursue policies they favor.
2. Citizens must vote, and electoral participation — whether high or low — must be *representative* of the population.
3. Elections must offer clear choices between viable and *competitive* candidates.
4. The persons elected must be those who actually have the power to execute policies.
5. Those elected must feel some compulsion (such as fear of defeat at the next election) actually to adopt policies satisfactory to their constituents.

It is difficult to say how well these criteria are met in the urban electoral marketplace. Some would say they are not met very well. We have already seen, for example (see pp. 90–95), that participation in urban politics is rather low and unrepresentative. We will show in Chapter 7 that communities with behind-the-scenes "power structures" do not meet the fourth condition. Electing a slate, in other words, which itself is at the mercy of a nonelected elite, does not make elections mandates. In this section we examine several important features of the urban electoral process to see how they affect elections as linkages.

Nonpartisanship and Elections at Large

The political machine was anathema to municipal reformers. Not only did it affront their ethical values, but it also violated their conceptions of policy making by professional management ("There is no Democratic or Republican way to pave a street"). The machine was an institution that capitalized on social cleavages within the electorate and was therefore also at variance with the reformers' belief in the interest of the community as a whole.

The institutional choices that reformers advocated to eliminate the pernicious effects of the machine were the *nonpartisan election* and the *constituency at large*. In a nonpartisan election candidates are not identified on the ballot by party affiliation. A constituency at large includes the whole city, and candidates run in the entire city rather than as representatives of geographically bounded wards or districts. Today 64 percent of U.S. cities use the nonpartisan ballot, while only 36 percent use party labels on the ballot.[49] Most nonpartisan cities also use at-large elections.

Nonpartisan at-large systems are likelier to be found in some kinds of cities than in others. Council-manager cities are more likely to use nonpartisan and at-large elections, whereas mayor-council cities are more likely to retain the ward and partisan systems. About 85 percent of manager cities use the nonpartisan ballot, whereas only about 50 percent of mayor-council cities are nonpartisan. Region seems to be another differentiating factor. Cities in the Northeast are much more likely to use partisan and ward systems; those in the South and West lean toward nonpartisan, at-large ballots; and those in the Midwest are more evenly split.

The introduction of nonpartisanship, especially when coupled with elections at large, has a number of consequences for urban politics. To a significant degree the nonpartisan ballot fulfills the expectations of its designers. It weakens the traditional party structure and isolates local politics from national political tides. There are only a few exceptions (e.g., Chicago) to the rule that strong local party organization does not coexist with the nonpartisan ballot. In Newark, for example, the political party plays an active role in partisan contests for the state legislature but is dormant in nonpartisan municipal elections.[50] Nonpartisanship also tends to split the systems of campaign finance and condidate recruitment, with one set of funds and candidates for local nonpartisan office and another for partisan political posts. This split has reduced the grassroots organizational capacities of the political party and has made it difficult for the parties to permit aspiring politicians to get their feet wet in local office, thus retarding the development of a national party system. On the other hand, it was not until the local party strongholds were finally broken, in part through the influence of nonpartisanship, that a nationally organized party system could have much meaning, a fact less frequently recognized by critics of nonpartisanship. The dominance of parochial machines was a major impediment to the national organization of the party. Until recent decades the national conventions were largely congresses of fiefdoms, without much genuine power, and even today machines play a major role at conventions. Somewhat ironically, therefore, nonpartisanship has had a mixed effect on the national party system. It has helped to create the conditions (the demise of the local machine) under which national party government could in fact develop, but it has made it difficult for a national party to organize itself at the grassroots level.

At the voter level the nonpartisan ballot at large has increased the information cost to the voter, increased the financial cost of elections, and altered the structure of participation in local elections. The political party in the American system is a great economizer for most voters, because party labels tell something (though certainly not everything) about the candidates and their policy goals. When those party labels are unavailable, voters' information declines and their frustration increases. The party is not only a cue giver; it is an organizer. Parties get out the vote. In New Haven, with vigorous parties, 60 percent of the population is contacted by one or both parties during a campaign, compared with only 10 percent of the population nationally.[51] Without a party to provide cues and organizational support, other cues must be used. Two of the major factors are name familiarity and ethnic identification. Italians will vote for a Mosconi, Irish for an O'Meara, and Latins for a Rodriguez.

Electoral turnout is significantly lower in nonpartisan cities than in partisan cities. Reduction in the size of the electorate in the nonpartisan city is not across the board or random but is concentrated particularly in lower-income groups and among those voters who would normally vote Democratic.[52] This group of voters relies most heavily on partisan affiliation as a cue to voting, and has fewest alternative sources of political information (such as press reports, personal knowledge of the candidates, civic-club ties, and so on). Nonpartisan elections therefore attract larger proportions of middle- and upper-class citizens and a relatively smaller proportion of working-class citizens than do partisan elections. Another consequence is that the combination of nonpartisanship with elections at large lessens the ability of minority groups to engage in bloc voting.

These factors suggest that nonpartisanship probably increases the representation of middle-class interests in urban politics. The "voice" of certain groups—e.g., business people, Republicans, upper-income voters, people who read newspapers regularly—is a bit louder in nonpartisan than partisan cities.

At-Large Elections and Minority Representation

Having a representative from one's own group, whether it be women, corporate executives, Poles, or blacks, certainly helps a group's voice. Institutions that reduce such representation will not be popular with groups whose numerical strength is greater than the offices held by group members. At-large elections may have those effects, especially on minority representation. Let us see why.

Imagine the typical American city with a high level of residential segregation and seven council members to elect. It can elect all by wards or all at-large, meaning that every voter votes for seven council candidates. Candidates are not confined to particular wards or districts. The logic of the hypothesis suggests that if black citizens constitute, say, 20 percent of the population, they should surely be able to elect at least one councilman in the ward system. But under the at-large system, every black voter could vote for a black candidate and be outvoted by the white majority. Moreover, because it is often more expensive to run a citywide race, fewer minority candidates will be able to enter.

There is considerable evidence to support the hypothesis, although it is not universally valid. Karnig investigated "black council penetration"—the ratio between black share of the population and black share of council seats—in 139 cities.[53] The average score for all the cities was .528, suggesting that blacks have only about half their "share" of seats. More than one-third had no black representation at all. Two main factors operate to lower black council penetration— southern location and at-large elections. In northern ward cities black representation is almost exactly commensurate with black population (.983). But in southern at-large cities it is only one-third of the proportion of blacks in the population.

Black leaders and civil-rights groups have challenged several at-large systems in court. In *Chavez* v. *Whitcomb* the Supreme Court refused to hold against at-large elections unless specific discrimination could be proved. Other courts, though, have found discriminatory effects. On 17 January 1975, for example, a federal district judge ordered the city of Dallas to abandon at-large elections because of their discriminatory effects. The days of the at-large election—one of the basic institutional changes advocated by reformers—may be numbered.

Participation, Parties, Elections, and Linkage

If the purpose of elections and parties is to identify and represent mass interests in urban decision making, they fall rather short of their goal. The party, historically the great institution of democratization, has been a poor performer at the local level. Whereas the machine had its virtues (as well as its vices), it paid little attention to representation of public interests. Moreover, the machine did little to uplift the socioeconomic conditions of its constituents. To have done so would have been suicidal, for the machine depended on its ability to parlay the plights of people into political power. In the post-machine era, the party has been weak or ineffectual, especially in most nonpartisan cities. In most urban areas the parties do not offer even their traditional minimum choice between Tweedledum and Tweedledee. If national parties are pilloried as disorganized, ideologically fuzzy, and inattentive to issues, then the role of the local party is even worse as a representative mechanism.

Still, *participation does matter*, particularly for lower-status citizens. Susan B. Hansen analyzed the *concurrence* of citizen with elite opinions in 64 randomly selected American communities. Both elite and mass samples were asked to identify the principal problems facing their community. In some cities there was a high level of concurrence, with leaders and citizens picking the same set of problems. Elsewhere, leaders' views and citizen views differed sharply. Certain factors were associated with higher levels of concurrence:

1. Concurrence was higher in communities *with partisan than nonpartisan electoral systems.*
2. Concurrence was higher in communities *where elections were competitive and closely fought.*
3. Concurrence was higher in communities *where participation was higher.*

Particularly significant is that participation seems to bring leaders' views more into line with lower-class citizens. Upper-status people normally find leaders more in agreement with them. But participation by cross sections of the electorate reduces this bias of the representational system. Hansen's summary is worth quoting:[54]

[These conclusions] may offer grounds for optimism: democratic practices such as participation and competition for office operate as they should do to improve linkage between leaders and citizens. But the long-term outlook is less optimistic. Trends toward nonpartisan elections, atrophied political parties, and lack of electoral competition at the local level suggest that conditions for effective citizen participation in American communities may no longer obtain.

We concur in that assessment of the effect of participation.

EXIT AS A POLITICAL LINKAGE

A tobacco company once used a series of ads proclaiming, "I'd rather fight than switch." Hidden in that message are the final two modes of political linkage at the urban level: exit and protest. Exit is an option not generally available at the national level. Citizens dissatisfied with their nation's policy may grumble, but they rarely emigrate. Americans, at least, do not. But citizens dissatisfied with *local* politics and policies may simply choose to move. Exit involves bailing out or the search for greener pastures. Several economists have described a fragmented metropolis as a system of competitive service suppliers. If taxes are too high or services too poor in one place, the citizen-consumer can move to another community.[55] Millions of American families have done just that, seeking better schools, lower taxes, or finer public amenities. One important explanation for suburbanization has been exit in search of better services or lower taxes. Within the city, people may abandon a particular neighborhood because of its crime rate, its lack of services, or its deteriorating conditions. These people would rather switch than fight.

But how can exit function as a political linkage? In the private marketplace a decline in customers should signal trouble to a firm. The wise organization will respond to customer exit by improving its products or services. The foolish organization will ignore the loss of its customers, and the capitalist system will ensure its demise. City governments, of course, are not capitalistic firms. Indeed, they may be only dimly aware that processes of decay are reversible. But municipal officials justify numerous policy initiatives as "reversing the tide of neighborhood decay," "retaining the middle classes in the city," or "attracting more investment." All of these are in partial response to exits from the city. Schemes for "urban homesteading," special neighborhood crime-control programs, and tax incentives for new business are examples of efforts to stem the exodus.

Three principal deficiencies of exit as a linkage mechanism exist. First, *widespread exit skims off a potential leadership cadre.* If those who could use their voice most effectively are the first to leave, then those left behind will be the least able to be heard. This is too often the case. A neighborhood shows initial signs of deterioration, and citizens with substantial investment in the neighborhood leave before their property values decline. Businesses with the capital to relocate do so, leaving least successful businesses behind. Exiting, then, may set in motion a spiral of further exiting.

A second problem with exiting is that *policy responses to massive exiting may be slow and ineffectual.* Crime and school problems are common reasons for abandoning a neighborhood. Yet (as we will see in Chapters 11 and 12) these problems cannot readily be solved merely by pouring money into a neighborhood. And (as we will see in Chapter 9 on the urban fiscal crisis) city governments may lack the resources to respond vigorously to population exodus.

The third difficulty in the exit option is its *class bias*. Exiting is not free — or even cheap. Pulling up stakes and relocating cannot be done without resources. With the price of new housing soaring, relatively few can take advantage of it. Racial discrimination reduces exit options for still others. An elderly family may be the most constrained of all. Tied by sentiment to an older neighborhood and often short of financial resources, older people are least likely to utilize the exit option. The ability to exit depends on one's resources. Those who stay need even louder voices.

PROTEST AS A POLITICAL LINKAGE

Those who do not switch *may* stay to fight. Almost by definition, protest is a weapon of groups that are weak in conventional political resources. Protest — violent and nonviolent — has a long history in American cities. Not all protest, of course, is violent, nor is all violence protest. Unfortunately neither the causes nor the consequences of protest are more than dimly understood. Speculation abounds about the effects of protest on policy, but there is little hard evidence at present. A few things about the nature of protest activity, however, are clear.

In the first place, it seems that protest is a more complex activity than is commonly believed. Michael Lipsky argues that our understanding of protest movements cannot be satisfactory unless we pay attention to a multiplicity of actors.[56] The participants in any protest activity are not limited to the activists themselves and to the elite whom they wish to influence, but depend on crucial third parties. All protest activities will wither on the vine without a means of communicating sentiments. The mass media thus plays a crucial role in focusing attention on grievances. The activists typically intend to energize sympathetic third parties, who in turn can be expected to bring pressure on decision makers. Martin Luther King, Jr., we presume, had little hope of winning over diehard segregationist southern governors, mayors, and elites. His success depended on his ability to lay bare and expose injustices to crucial third parties, particularly the national elite and the federal government. This is also true of protest movements at the local level, which depend on their capacity to focus attention on the evils they experience, and to develop within the community a network of third parties who will enter the conflict on their side.

Nonviolent protest is at least as old as Henry David Thoreau, yet as contemporary as rent strikes, welfare sit-ins, political demonstrations,

and antiwar marches. The late Saul Alinsky developed protest strategies to the level of an art form, complete with rehearsed scenarios,
the use of the dramatic (e.g., carrying live rats to councilmen's doorsteps in one campaign), and the insistence on a sustained thrust. But
although it may be increasing in usage, protest strategy has remained
highly unpopular with most Americans. Despite the horrors of what
Chicago lawyer (and former Illinois governor) Daniel Walker called a
"police riot," most Americans felt that Mayor Daley's police used *too
little* or the *right amount* of force on demonstrators at the 1968 Democratic convention. A majority of Americans contend flatly that they
would *disapprove* of even a lawful protest march, *sanctioned by local
authorities.*[57] If nonviolent protest is to be effective, it will surely be in
spite of, rather than because of, the attitudes held by a majority of
American citizens.

Sometimes people confuse protest with violence. Not all protest is
violent—in fact, very little of it is—and not all violence is protest.
Peter Eisenger suggests that protest "is a device by which groups of
people manipulate fear of disorder and violence while at the same
time they protect themselves from paying the potentially extreme
costs of acknowledging such a strategy."[58] He collected data on protest
incidents in 43 cities and discovered that all but 6 percent of 120 incidents were carried out entirely peacefully. Protest, he concludes, is
likely to occur most frequently in political systems that are neither
"open" nor "closed," but in-between. Cities in which institutions
(such as partisan elections) encourage normal channels of conflict resolution are less likely to see protests. And cities in which institutions
severely restrict normal participation, which are the most repressive,
are also unlikely to witness much protest.

Protest, then, is one weapon among many in articulating demands.
It is "voice" at its most vocal. Sometimes protest, though, takes the
form of violent behavior.

Violence and Urban Politics

Violence has long been associated with urban life. The prophet
Ezekiel observed that "the land is full of bloody crimes and the city is
full of violence," and his words still ring true. The American city has
been the site of slave revolts, antiblack violence, labor–management
conflict, anti-Catholicism, and draft protest. The Civil War draft riots
in the 1860s would easily match the anti-Vietnam riots of the 1960s.
One student of civil violence, Ted Robert Gurr, has ranked the United
States seventh among a list of 113 countries in the level of its domestic
violence.[59] The enduring issue evoking urban violence, then as now,
seems to be racial conflict.

Race riots did not begin in the 1960s with Watts, Detroit, Cleveland, and Newark. Racial conflagrations in East St. Louis in 1917 and in Detroit in 1943 matched in deaths and destruction most of the severe riots of the 1960s. Stanley Lieberson and Arnold R. Silverman counted 76 major racial disorders between 1913 and 1963.[60] The earlier riots differed from those of more recent vintage, however, in being mostly initiated by whites and involving direct violence against individual blacks or black groups. Most were responses to perceived transgressions of the legal or social taboos of racial segregation. The riots of 1963–1968 (which by one count numbered 283 among cities of over 25,000 population) were more commonly outbursts generated within the ghettos themselves and directed against aspects of white society (particularly the police and ghetto merchants), rather than against whites as individuals or groups.

Whites and blacks, surveyed separately by the National Advisory Commission on Civil Disorders (the Kerner Commission), were sharply divided on the "causes" of the riots. Two-thirds of the whites thought that some particular group of "undesirables" — radicals, looters, or Communists — had provoked the riots. This micro-level explanation attributes riots to the perniciousness of men. Blacks, on the other hand, almost universally offered macro-level explanations of the riots, as results of social-structural factors, especially discrimination and unemployment. It thus appears that the premise of *institutional racism* is prominent in black explanations for the riots. It follows from the varying perceptions of causes that whites and blacks also favor different policy responses to the riots. When asked what could be done to prevent further rioting, Whites most frequently responded that "more police control" is essential, whereas blacks preferred changes in the social and economic structures.[61]

A number of white Americans (and their public officials) pictured the "typical" rioter as part of the "criminal element" or as "radical." This view, sometimes dubbed the *riffraff theory* of riot participation, includes three premises about riots: (1) Only a tiny fraction (1–2 percent) of the ghetto community participated in the riots; (2) most rioters were riffraff — unattached youths, people with criminal records, the unemployed, disoriented migrants from the rural South who are unable to adjust to an urban environment; (3) the black community as a whole deplores the violence, seeing it as pointless and counterproductive.[62] This theory is comfortable for white middle-class Americans and their public officials, but it is not supported by studies of riot participants. Evidence suggests that between one-third and one-fifth of the ghetto community participated in major riots. And, instead of being drawn largely from the criminal elements in the ghetto, the typical rioter was not much different from his fellow ghetto residents. Robert M. Fogelson and Robert B. Hill's study for the Kerner Commission found that the "typical" rioter:

1. was slightly better educated than were other ghetto residents
2. was likely to have been born in the community in which the riot occurred
3. was usually employed, although at a job requiring little education
4. had an income about equal to that of other ghetto residents
5. was no more likely than other ghetto residents to possess a "record"

After an examination of rioters in Newark and Detroit, Nathan S. Kaplan and Jeffrey M. Paige concluded that

the rioters are not the poorest of the poor. They are not the hard-core unemployed. They are not the least educated. They are not unassimilated migrants or newcomers to the city. There is no evidence that they have serious personality disturbances or are deviant in their social behavior. They do not have a different set of values.[63]

The rioter was not an atypical member of the ghetto community.

The third tent of the riffraff theory is that the riots are condemned by most blacks. Yet, despite the fact that a number of ghetto residents suffered personal or material losses during the riots, a significant minority approved of them, and a majority saw them as protests that would ultimately have positive results. In the aftermath of the Los Angeles riots, "a large minority (about one-third) approved of the rioting, and most black residents of the riot area felt it had been a meaningful protest, and most were optimistic about its effects on their life situation."[64] Blacks, whether or not they supported the riots, thought that the riots had helped to dramatize their plight.

The Policy Consequences of Violence and Protest

Does violence or protest make any difference in attaining the goals sought by an aggrieved group? One can easily construct two diametrically opposed hypotheses. One would suggest that *violence always boomerangs.* By antagonizing and alienating the very people whose support is needed, protestors "turn off" their potential constituencies. Alternatively one could hypothesize that *under certain conditions protest, and even violence, can secure policy objectives* just as voting or pressure group activity can secure objectives. Surely the activities of a generation of civil-rights activists contributed to the Civil Rights Act of 1964 and the Voting Rights Act of 1965.

Fortunately several political scientists have made serious efforts to assess the impact of protest and violence. In Eisenger's study of incidents in 43 cities, he assessed the outcome of the protest.[65] In the majority of cases (54 percent) *no concessions were made* to protestor demands. Yet in the rest of the cases protestors could claim some gain, either by delaying intended action or by securing concessions. One example of the unsuccessful protestors is described by Michael

Parenti.[66] In Newark one neighborhood used countless hours of activity, physical and written protests, to protest the lack of a stop light at a dangerous intersection. A similar problem was solved in a matter of days in another neighborhood. Protestors in Boston were generally unsuccessful in stopping school busing. On the other hand, groups in many cities have been successful in preventing the closing of neighborhood schools or the passage of a highway through a neighborhood.

It is much more difficult to assess the impact of violence on public policy. The effect of violence is highly problematic. Nonetheless, Susan Welch examined the expenditure levels of cities that had major racial riots during the 1960s and contrasted them with cities that did not experience major riots. What she found was remarkable: Riot cities tended significantly to increase *police expenditures* but not other expenditures. As she put it, "Cities experiencing riots, more than other cities, increased expenditures in areas assumed to be concern to those demanding control and punishment of rioters, and to a much lesser extent in areas assumed to be of concern to those rioting."[67] Clearly the riots provoked more police expenditures (including an array of riot-control equipment) but not much more health, education, and welfare expenditures by cities.

Protest and violence, as we have suggested, are extreme forms of "voice" in expressing mass preferences to policy makers. They are very common in the American city. Typically groups weak in conventional resources are most likely to resort to them. Protest is used when other means of expressing policy preferences seem unavailable or exhausted. But protest can be a calculated strategy, oriented toward specific policy goals and sometimes producing success. When protest slips into violence — although normally it does not — chances of achieving intended policy changes seem to diminish. Evidence on the policy consequences of violence is meagre, but it suggests that violence may evoke policy responses designed to repress further violence. There is a fine line, sometimes, between protest and violence, but differences in policy consequences may be very significant.

CONCLUSIONS

We have reviewed in this chapter the *input process*, the mechanisms by which opinions and interests are channeled into the political system. Perhaps the most significant point to emerge from this discussion is how limited is the informational input from large numbers of groups and individuals. Political participation, whether through elections or in more active forms, is much lower in local political life than in state or national politics, for reasons that we have tried to indicate. Not only is individual participation somewhat low, but institutional and organizational devices for presenting interests are also not so well developed at the local level as they are at higher levels of government. Labor unions, for example, though quite active in national politics, play only minor roles in most cities. Because of the influence of non-partisanship and other factors, political parties may be active in national and state elections but may be quite dormant in municipal contests (except in a few cities). Generally the relatively low participation levels, coupled with the fragmentary channels of interest articulation, make the costs of political information—information about groups and individuals and their policy preferences—quite high. Because of the incompleteness and distortion of information processed through input mechanisms, municipal decision makers can rarely obtain more than a fragmentary sense of community preference about public policy.

The preferences of mass publics for policy change can be communicated to elites through *linkage institutions,* which afford the opportunity for either *voice* or *exit.* Voice includes institutions such as parties, groups, and elections, as well as the more vocal forms such as protest and violence. Each institution can link mass preferences to elite decisions to change policy. Sometimes elections work to change policy by changing the elite in power. Yet each of these institutions has significant limitations as a means for registering mass sentiment. Groups disheartened about more normal modes of representation, (e.g., parties and elections) may resort to protest and violence. These highly visible forms of linkage can sometimes make policy changes more likely, although they can also reduce the chances of goals being realized.

One mode of expressing preferences—exit—is unique to the local level. Dissatisfied citizens may simply move elsewhere in search of better policies. The reasons for urban mobility are numerous. But they often are responses to citizen dissatisfaction with schools, crime, or other service conditions. People may seek more opportunity by moving elsewhere, but they may also be registering complaints as surely as if they voted against the incumbent officials. The city has an open boundary and mobility is easy for many Americans—but not, of course, for all. Some who cannot afford to switch may stay behind to fight.

Notes

1. For this estimate, and for a thorough treatment of participation generally, see Sidney Verba and Norman Nie, *Participation in America* (New York: Harper & Row, 1972), Table 2.1.
2. Robert R. Alford and Eugene C. Lee, "Voting Turnout in American Cities," *American Political Science Review,* 62 (September 1968), 796–813.
3. Verba and Nie, op. cit., chap. 4.

4. Ibid., chap. 6.
5. Robert R. Alford and Harry Scoble, "Sources of Local Political Involvement," *American Political Science Review, 62* (December 1968), 1192–1206; Robert A. Dahl, *Who Governs?* (New Haven: Yale University Press, 1961), p. 283.
6. Alvin Boskoff and Harmon Zeigler, *Voting Patterns in a Local Election* (Philadelphia: Lippincott, 1964), pp. 130–131; John C. Bollens et al., *Exploring the Metropolitan Community* (Berkeley: University of California Press, 1961), chap. 11; and Howard Hamilton, "The Municipal Voter: Voting and Nonvoting in City Elections," *American Political Science Review, 65* (December 1971), 1135–1140.
7. Alford and Scoble, p. 1203.
8. Bollens et al., chap. 11.
9. Robert E. Lane, *Political Life* (New York: Free Press 1959), p. 239.
10. Alford and Lee, op. cit.
11. Danial Katz and Samuel J. Eldersfeld, "The Impact of Local Party Activity on the Electorate," *Public Opinion Quarterly, 25* (Spring 1961), 1–24.
12. Peter K. Eisenger, "The Pattern of Citizen Contacts with Urban Officials," in Harlan Hahn, ed., *Urban Affairs Annual Reviews: People and Politics in Urban Society,* vol. 6 (Beverly Hills, Calif.: Sage, 1972), pp. 43–69.
13. Gideon Sjoberg et al., "Bureaucracy and the Lower Class," *Sociology and Social Research, 50* (April 1966), 330.
14. (Cambridge: Harvard University Press, 1970). A provocative application of Hirschman's theory to urban politics is found in John M. Orbell and Toro Uno, "A Theory of Neighborhood Problem-Solving: Political Action vs. Residential Mobility," *American Political Science Reivew, 66* (June 1972), 471–489.
15. On the "white-flight" hypothesis, see our discussion in Chapter 12.
16. Matthew Crenson, *The Unpolitics of Air Pollution* (Baltimore: The Johns Hopkins Press, 1971).
17. Arthur Bentley, *The Process of Government* (Cambridge, Mass.: Harvard University Press, 1967; orig. published 1908), p. 208.
18. Charles Gilbert, *Governing the Suburbs* (New York: McGraw Hill, 1967), p. 145.
19. Bryan T. Downes, "Municipal Social Rank and the Characteristics of Local Political Leaders," *Midwest Journal of Political Science, 12* (November 1968), 514–537; Heinz Eulau and Kenneth Prewitt, *Labyrinths of Democracy* (Indianapolis: Bobbs-Merrill, 1973), p. 265.
20. Kenneth S. Gray and J. David Greenstone, "Organized Labor in City Politics," in Edward C. Banfield, ed., *Urban Government* (New York: Free Press, 1961), p. 372.
21. Schley R. Lyons, "Labor in City Politics: The Case of the Toledo United Auto Workers," *Social Science Quarterly, 49* (March 1969), 827.
22. Quoted in *The Brookings Bulletin,* Fall 1971, p. 1. On municipal unions see also Raymond D. Horton, *Municipal Labor Relations in New York City: Lessons of the Lindsay-Wagner Years* (New York: Praeger, 1973); Sam Zagoria, ed., *Public Workers and Public Unions* (Englewood Cliffs, N.J.: Prentice-Hall, 1972); and the several books reviewed by Felix Nigro, "Urban Government and the Unions," *Urban Affairs Quarterly* (June 1974).

23. Dahl op. cit., pp. 34–36.
24. Raymond Wolfinger, *The Politics of Progress* (Englewood Cliffs, N.J.: Prentice-Hall, 1974), p. 49.
25. *City Politics* (Cambridge, Mass.: Harvard University Press, 1961).
26. For one penetrating critique of Banfield and Wilson's theory, see Raymond Wolfinger and John O. Field, "Political Ethos and the Structure of City Government," *American Political Science Review* 60 (June 1966), 306–326.
27. *City Manager Government in the United States* (Chicago: Public Administration Service, 1940), pp. 25, 35.
28. Robert Agger, Daniel Goldrich, and Bert E. Swanson, *The Rulers and the Ruled* (New York, Wiley, 1964), p. 21.
29. On group politics in San Francisco, see the study by Frederick M. Wirt, *Power in the City* (Berkeley, Calif.: University of California Press, 1974).
30. Verba and Nie, op. cit., p. 156.
31. Lyndon B. Johnson, while signing the Voting Rights Act of 1965, quoted in *Newsweek*, 16 August 1965, p. 15.
32. William R. Keech, *The Impact of Negro Voting* (Skokie, Ill.: Rand McNally, 1968), pp. 105, 107.
33. *Black Power* (New York: Vintage, 1967), p. 4.
34. Ibid; p. 44.
35. Ibid., p. 81.
36. See Michael D. Preston's "The Limits of Black Urban Power: The Case of Black Mayors," in Louis Masotti and Robert L. Lineberry, eds., *The New Urban Politics* (Cambridge, Mass.: Ballinger, 1976), chap. 5.
37. Raymond A. Bauer et al., *American Business and Public Policy* (New York: Atherton, 1964).
38. John P. Crecine, *Governmental Problem-Solving: A Computer Simulation of Municipal Budgeting* (Skokie, Ill.: Rand McNally, 1969).
39. Betty H. Zisk, *Local Interest Politics: A One-Way Street* (Indianapolis, Ind.: Robbs-Merrill, 1973).
40. Our discussion of the Nineteenth Ward is based on the account in Allen F. Davis, *Spearheads for Reform* (New York: Oxford University Press, 1967), chap. 8.
41. Banfield and Wilson, op. cit., p. 115.
42. Fred I. Greenstein, "The Changing Pattern of Urban Party Politics," *The Annals of the American Academy of Political and Social Science, 353* (May 1964), p. 3.
43. For an important perspective from comparative politics, see James C. Scott, "Corruption, Machine Politics, and Political Change," *American Political Science Review, 63* (December 1969), 1146–1148. These and other views of the machine's "corruption" are assessed by Martin Shefter, "The Emergence of the Political Machine: An Alternative View," in Willis D. Hawley et al., *Theoretical Perspectives on Urban Politics* (Englewood Cliffs, N.J.: Prentice-Hall, 1976), chap. 2.
44. Robert K. Merton, *Social Theory and Social Structure* (New York: Free Press, 1967), pp. 60–82; Edward M. Sait, "Machine, Political," *International Encyclopedia of the Social Sciences* (New York: Macmillan, 1933), vol. 9, p. 659.

45. Theodore Lowi, "Machine Politics—Old and New," *The Public Interest* (Fall 1967), 83.
46. Wolfinger, op. cit., p. 120.
47. Ibid., pp. 106–118.
48. The best books on the Chicago machine and especially its leader are by television commentator Len O'Conner, *Clout: Mayor Daley and His City* (New York: Avon, 1975), and by political scientist Milton Rakove, *Don't Make No Waves, Don't Back No Losers* (Bloomington: Indiana University Press, 1976). For a characteristically acerbic view, see Mike Royko *Boss* (New York: Signet, 1971).
49. Willis D. Hawley, *Nonpartisan Elections and the Case for Party Politics* (Berkeley: University of California Press, 1972), p. 17.
50. Gerald Pomper, "Ethnic and Group Voting in Nonpartisan Elections," *Public Opinion Quarterly, 30* (Spring 1966), 79–97.
51. Wolfinger, op. cit., p. 76.
52. Robert Salisbury and Gordon Black, "Class and the Party in Nonpartisan Elections: The Case of Des Moines," *American Political Science Review, 54* (1963), 584–592; Banfield and Wilson, op. cit., p. 159.
53. Albert K. Karnig, "Black Representation on City Councils: The Impact of Reform and Socio-Economic Factors," *Urban Affairs Quarterly, 12* (December 1976), 223–242. See also Ernest Patterson, *Black City Politics* (New York: Dodd Mead, 1974), chaps. 5, 6.
54. Susan B. Hansen, "Participation, Political Structure, and Concurrence," *American Political Science Review, 69* (December 1975), 1198.
55. This is a major theme in the "public choice" approach to metropolitan governance, such as Robert L. Bish and Vincent Ostrom, *Understanding Urban Government: Metropolitan Reform Reconsidered* (Washington, D.C.: American Enterprise Institute for Public Policy Research, 1973).
56. Michael Lipsky, *Protest in City Politics* (Skokie, Ill.: Rand McNally, 1970), esp. chap. 1.
57. Phillip E. Converse et al., "Continuity and Change in American Politics," *American Political Science Review, 63* (December 1969), 1105.
58. Peter K. Eisenger, "The Conditions of Protest Behavior in American Cities," *American Political Science Review, 67* (March 1973), 14.
59. Ted Robert Gurr, "A Comparative Study of Civil Strife," in Hugh Davis and Ted Gurr, eds., *Violence in America*, vol. 2 (Washington, D.C.: Government Printing Office, 1969), p. 448. See also Gurr's *Rogues, Rebels, and Reformers: A Political History of Urban Crime and Conflict* (Beverly Hills, Calif.: Sage, 1976).
60. Stanley Lieberson and Arnold R. Silverman, "The Precipitants and Underlying Conditions of the Race Riots," *American Sociological Review, 30* (December 1965), 887–898.
61. See the discussion of white and black perceptions of the riots in Angus Campbell and Howard Schuman, "Racial Attitudes in Fifteen Cities," in National Advisory Commission on Civil Disorders, *Supplementary Studies* (Washington, D.C.: Government Printing Office, 1968), chap. 5.
62. Our discussion of the riffraff theory is based on data in Robert M. Fogelson and Robert B. Hill, "Who Riots?" in National Advisory Commission on Civil

Disorders, *Supplementary Studies* (Washington, D.C.: Government Printing Office, 1968), chap. 3.

63. Nathan S. Kaplan and Jeffrey M. Paige, "A Study of Ghetto Rioters," *Scientific American, 219* (August 1968), 19.
64. David O. Sears and T. M. Tomlinson, "Riot Ideology in Los Angeles: A Study of Negro Attitudes," *Social Science Quarterly, 49* (December 1968), 502; Campbell and Schuman, op. cit., p. 49.
65. Eisenger, op. cit., p. 17.
66. Michael Parenti, "Power and Pluralism: The View from the Bottom," *Journal of Politics, 32* (August 1970), 501–530. For several cases of protest in New York City, see Jewell Bellush and Stephen M. David, eds., *Race and Politics in New York City* (New York: Praeger, 1971).
67. Susan Welch, "The Impact of Urban Riots on Urban Expenditures," *American Journal of Political Science, 19* (November 1975), 757.

6

STRUCTURES OF URBAN GOVERNANCE — FEDERAL, STATE, AND LOCAL

Governing urban America does not take place in municipal governments alone. Rather, urban governance is part of a complex network of intergovernmental relations. The city has become the weakest link in the federal system, and its autonomy has been eroded by policies at the state and federal level. In this chapter, we

- discuss the city in the federal system and show how choices made "upstairs" constrain the policy decisions of urban citizens and elites
- emphasize the issue of centralization–decentralization as a major source of controversy in urban government
- examine the internal structure of municipal governments, showing that the choice of government structures has significant consequences for policy decisions.

The design of government is a subject of considerable controversy. One dramatic example occurred in Mobile, Alabama, where a federal judge ordered the city to change its form of government. Mobile was one of the few cities to use a commission form of government (see pp. 166–167), where three city commissioners rotated as mayor during their four-year term. Judge Virgil Pittman noted that blacks constituted one-third of the population. But only a handful of city employees and representatives on city committees and boards were black. He ordered the city to abandon the commission form with at large elections and institute a mayor-council form with nine council members elected from single-member districts. The city appealed the ruling, claiming that, as the mayor put it, the judge "has become a dictator."[1]

The Mobile story illustrates the twin themes of this chapter: (1) The form and structure of city government are not neutral matters but are of major importance and conflict; and (2) the federal government, including congress, the executive, and the courts, now provides significant inputs into the local government system.

CITIES IN THE FEDERAL SYSTEM: THE STATE ROLE

Cities and States

The structure of government established by the Constitution recognizes the nation, the states, and the people; the Constitution provides certain guarantees to each. There are no provisions for local governments. Municipalities were considered to fall under the umbrellas of their states and to be subject to whatever powers and restrictions the state constitutions and laws provided. The charter of a municipality is the state statute that affects it most directly, but other state actions also apply. They include general laws pertaining to all local governments and numerous local bills pertaining to specific municipalities. The standard interpretation of local government powers is Dillon's rule:

It is a general and undisputed proposition of law that a municipal corporation possesses and can exercise the following powers, and no others: First, those granted (by the state) in express words; second, those necessarily or fairly implied in or incident to the powers expressly granted; third, those essential to the accomplishment of the declared objects and purposes of the corporation — not simply convenient, but indispensable. Any fair, reasonable, substantial doubt concerning the existence of power is resolved by the courts against the corporation, and the power is denied.[2]

This severe standard resolves even reasonable doubts against the local government.

Where the state constitution is restrictive in its general grant of power to municipalities, the state legislature is a busy enactor of local laws; it may approve specific sites for local schools and other public facilities, condemn private property, and define local employees' salaries and working conditions. Under this kind of arrangement, the legislators who represent an urban area become an important — if informal — adjunct to the local government; they can modify those items that municipal officials ask them to introduce in the legislature and can select proposals to steer personally through the legislative process.

Even the most permissive state constitution restricts the nature and extent of local government taxation or indebtedness. All typically limit municipalities to property taxes and perhaps to small levies on retail sales and personal incomes. In an era when the most dramatic social demands are made in urban communities, the governments most closely affected by these demands do not have the authority to raise sufficient revenues from local resources. Local officials lack access to the wealth from high personal incomes and lucrative commercial transactions if they cannot tax income or sales. In New Mexico, before the state adopted home-rule provisions for city governments, it took state laws to:

1. permit cities to destroy weapons and narcotics confiscated by police
2. authorize cities with populations over 100,000 to acquire and operate their own bus systems
3. allow municipalities to discontinue water service to customers who had not paid their bills
4. permit cities to zone for flood control

About half of the states have written provisions into their constitutions that are designed to increase the discretion of local officials. The term *home rule* suggests a large grant of authority to local governments, but this image is more generous than the actual grant of authority. The home-rule movement began in Iowa in 1851, and such provisions were first adopted into a constitution in Missouri in 1875. By 1960 it had become part of the constitutions of 23 states, and cities in 21 of these states had taken advantage of its provisions. When a city operates under home-rule provisions, it can change its own powers and operations without first going to the state legislature for consent. The mechanism for changing local powers is typically a citizens' referendum. Some home-rule cities can change the form of their local governments, including the nature of local elections; can annex fringe areas; and can regulate public health, safety, and morality.

The practical significance of home rule is not so great as many of the reformers originally anticipated. State reins on local authorities remain short and can be tightened at the convenience of the state legislature. Some local authorities view their narrowly defined home-rule provisions as disadvantageous in that they preclude some imaginative efforts that would be permitted by more broadly defined provisions. Yet home-rule provisions may raise a psychological deterrent to state legislators. The broad connotations of the term may benefit cities, especially during an era when urban problems and reapportionment at the state level may heighten legislative support for local authorities. At the least, home-rule provisions relieve local officials of the nuisance of having to go to the state legislature for many detailed enactments.

Cities are not without some clout in their competition with state governments. Some of this power is intangible and reflects only the revered position of local control and home rule in American traditions. Cities also benefit from whatever attachments there are to political accountability as a mode of governmental organization. Insofar as local residents are thought to be most aware of their needs, they are considered to be the most suitable governors of local activities. Much of the time, however, such strengths are not sufficient to free the cities from the hard bonds of law and precedent that subordinate them to the states.

Recently cities have gained some ground in their competition with the states. Their victories — which promise even greater gains in the future — include a series of federal court decisions, since *Baker* v. *Carr* in 1962, that have vastly improved the representation of urban areas in state legislatures and an increasing willingness in Congress to establish grant-in-aid programs that are national–local in character and involve only minimal participation for state governments. Although the impact of legislative reapportionment on state governments' treatment of the cities is yet to be demonstrated, it has at least increased urban representation in the legislatures. Optimists predict increased state sensitivity to urban needs and more permissive legislation pertaining to city revenues. The federal government started to provide direct aid to the cities through housing legislation in the 1930s, and more recently there have been substantial increases in federal aid to cities for primary and secondary education, preschool classes, job training, highways, mass transit, and community action, as well as the assurance that cities will receive a share of federal revenue sharing. But the evidence also shows an increasing generosity of state governments in aiding their largest cities.

State Aids to Local Government

Aside from the local property tax, the state is the biggest supplier of urban government revenues. The array of state aids to municipalities includes many patterned after federal aids to state and local governments. But state aids emphasize shared taxes and *bloc grants* (for broadly defined types of programs), rather than grants-in-aid for specified projects. A fixed portion of taxes revert to the local government in whose jurisdiction they were collected. As bloc grants and shared taxes are used by most states, they provide more freedom to local governments than do federal grants-in-aid. They are awarded not for specified projects or in response to detailed applications but go automatically to local governments according to certain criteria and may be used for any programs within generally defined areas (e.g., education, roads and streets) or even for any local government activities. State aids are generally free, and no matching by locally raised revenues is required. For the most part, local governments receive state aid as a matter of right; there are few application procedures and few limitations on expenditures. The financial relations between state and local governments are not, however, free from diputes over local and state control.

State governments use various criteria to allocate financial aids to each local government. Some redistribute economic resources from have to have-not communities; some merely return to communities certain proportions of state taxes collected there; some reward communities that make some effort to use their own resources in support

Table 6.1   State-Government Portions of State-Local Total Tax Revenues, Fiscal 1972–1973

United States	56.2%		
Alabama	74.8	Montana	49.2
Alaska	66.9	Nebraska	48.3
Arizona	59.5	Nevada	56.5
Arkansas	75.1	New Hampshire	43.4
California	48.1	New Jersey	41.4
Colorado	50.4	New Mexico	79.8
Connecticut	51.1	New York	50.1
Delaware	78.6	North Carolina	73.9
Florida	66.0	North Dakota	59.9
Georgia	65.7	Ohio	52.5
Hawaii	76.1	Oklahoma	66.0
Idaho	65.3	Oregon	50.3
Illinois	53.4	Pennsylvania	63.1
Indiana	50.3	Rhode Island	59.3
Iowa	55.5	South Carolina	77.4
Kansas	51.7	South Dakota	44.6
Kentucky	75.6	Tennessee	62.0
Louisiana	70.4	Texas	57.1
Maine	57.4	Utah	66.2
Maryland	56.9	Vermont	61.1
Massachusetts	49.5	Virginia	60.7
Michigan	61.4	Washington	65.3
Minnesota	64.7	West Virginia	76.2
Mississippi	76.0	Wisconsin	61.5
Missouri	54.3	Wyoming	55.8

Source: U.S. Bureau of the Census, *State Government Finances in 1974* (Washington, D.C.: Government Printing Office, 1975).

of certain programs; some award funds equally according to arbitrary criteria (such as population); and some rely on special considerations of emergency or agreements between state and local agencies.

States vary widely in the responsibilities that they take themselves and those that they require local governments to undertake. Some states support the entire costs of junior college systems and shoulder major shares of public school budgets. Others let local government undertake these tasks. Table 6.1 shows the division of fiscal labor between states and local governments in 1972–1973. In New Mexico the state government was very dominant, raising 79.8 percent of all state and local revenues. New Jersey was at the other extreme, where only 41.4 percent of state-local revenues were collected at the state level. Generally, in well-to-do states such as New York, Ohio, Illinois, and

Pennsylvania, local governments carry more of the load. The South tends toward centralization.

State aids to cities are on the increase, especially to big cities. Table 6.2 shows that large cities are doing better than they were in 1960, both in per-capita terms and in percentage of local revenues coming from states. Since 1960, large cities have increased their state aid by more than 7 times. Now it is smaller cities that can complain about being second-class citizens.

Also during the 1960s and 1970s an increasing number of states changed their constitutions to permit local governments greater freedom in raising their own revenues. Cities still rely most heavily on the property tax. As of 1974, however, the local governments in 26 states collected a sales tax, and local governments in ten states collected an income tax. In most cases, the state revenue department actually collects the revenues for the locality, according to options chosen by the local units. Further state efforts have improved the administration of local property taxes. Forty states make periodic comparisons between market values (as determined by actual sales) and local property assessments. These sales-assessment studies can help local governments and their citizens in several ways: They can indicate areas of inequality in tax assessments between communities; they can equalize the distribution of those state aids that go to communities on the basis of local property values; and they can reduce tax competition between adjacent communities in metropolitan areas.[3]

Table 6.2   State Aids to City Governments, 1960 and 1973–1974

City Size	1960		1973–1974	
	Per-capita state aid	State aid as percentage of city revenue	Per-capita state aid	State aid as percentage of city revenue
1,000,000 plus	$35.95	17.8	$266.65	35.3
500,000–999,999	23.48	16.4	86.18	18.3
300,000–499,999	14.11	13.2	72.84	19.7
200,000–299,999	12.28	11.4	68.26	19.1
100,000–199,999	14.77	14.2	59.68	18.9
50,000–99,999	13.91	15.0	46.93	17.5
25,000–49,999	11.27	14.3	} 32.82	17.7
less than 25,000	8.62	17.0		

Sources: U.S. Bureau of the Census, Compendium of City Government Finances in 1960 (and 1973–74). (Washington, D.C.: Government Printing Office, 1961 and 1975).

The Increase in State Centralization

States have changed in recent years. They have recently taken on more and more of the fiscal responsibilities that once belonged to cities. G. Ross Stephens has analyzed what he calls "the erosion of local authority." He examined state and local shares of public expenditures and found that states assume a larger burden than they did in the past. In almost all states the state share increased, while the local share decreased between 1960 and 1970. He puts the argument forcefully:[4]

Our political creed regarding the importance of local self-government had some validity at the turn of the century when local government was a really active level in comparison to the states and the nation. If revenues from own sources are a measure of independence, local government has become a mere shadow of its former self—the "action" is at the higher levels of government.

We are not prepared to go as far as Stephens would in this line of argument. Although it is true that state fiscal centralization has increased, his own data show an increase from 56 to 61 percent of fiscal responsiblity from 1957–1969. This does not exactly signal the death throes of local government. Cities still retain major responsibilites in schooling, law enforcement, recreation, and other public services. Some have expressed the hope that revenue sharing to local govern-

U.S. mayors at New York City's Gracie Mansion discuss the role of cities in the federal system.

ments will make them more vital partners in the federal system. We do agree that what cities do is heavily determined by what states do.

THE NEW FEDERALISM AND CITIES

The Cities Go to Washington

At one time cities, states, and the federal government operated pretty much independently. States passed a little money along to the cities, but cities had virtually no ties to the federal government. That is certainly no longer the case, because the federal government has become deeply involved in the governance of urbanites.[5] A few years ago the *New York Times* published a 1243-page volume entitled *Guide to Federal Aids to Cities and Towns.*[6] The number of federal programs, together with guidelines and regulations, has become so elaborate that most cities have hired full-time grant coordinators. Their job is to stay abreast of what is available and help the city government get its share. Among the numerous programs the *Times* guide listed as available were

- machine tool loans to vocational schools
- flood insurance
- mental health training
- assistance for export promotion
- disaster relief
- urban renewal
- support for crime labs
- airport development
- historical preservation grants
- school breakfast programs, and
- support for chamber music concerts

Local governments have now become organized to pressure the federal government for more funds. The National League of Cities, the National Association of Counties, the United States Conference of Mayors, and the International City Management Association are the "Big Four" local lobbies. Together with their counterparts at the state level, they are the "PIGs" — an acronym for "public-interest groups."[7] They function like all other interest groups. They have professional staffs who see members of Congress and press for urban-oriented legislation; they conduct research; and they represent a conduit of information about new programs and regulations to their members. In addition, almost all professional heads of local departments (police chiefs, urban renewal officials, personnel officers, housing officials, airport directors, and so on) have Washington-based associations. Increasingly, the larger cities are hiring full-time Washington "liaison officers," whose job is as much to lobby as provide liaison. Urban lobbyists descended in droves on Jimmy Carter as soon as he was elected, pressing for more urban aid.

One of the crowning achievements of these urban lobbyists was the revenue-sharing legislation in 1972 (see discussion on pp. 149–151). When prospects for revenue sharing—no-strings-attached federal aid to cities, counties, and states—appeared bleak in 1970, the PIGs conducted a vigorous campaign with members of the incoming Ninety-Second Congress.[8] The urban lobbies, combined with the National Governor's Conference and the Council of State Governments (collectively called the "Big Six"), sent letters to all congressional candidates, urging their support of revenue sharing. Shortly, 400 incumbents and challengers responded, and 93 percent registered their support. That kind of lobbying, combined with vigorous efforts of the Nixon administration, paid off in passage of the State and Local Fiscal Assistance Act of 1972. Revenue sharing was a godsend to local officials confronted by deteriorating urban tax bases and increased taxpayer resistance. Today states still give more aid to cities than the federal government. But revenue sharing and other monies from Washington are increasing the federal contribution more rapidly. Increasingly, city officials view Washington like the nephew views the rich old aunt —the interference is resented, but the money is welcomed nonetheless.

Direct Federal Aid to Cities:
From Categorical Grants to Revenue Sharing

Grant-in-aid programs to states and localities actually have a long history.[9] But the 1960s saw them mushroom. In 1975 they amounted to $52 billion. Cities actually benefitted more than states. Because states passed along some of their federal aids to cities, the local governments fared even better than direct federal grants to cities indicate. Table 6.3 shows how $35.9 billion in federal grants and other aids to urban areas were distributed through numerous programs during 1975.

By far the largest chunk of federal monies comes as *categorical* aid. Each categorical program has a specific purpose; they do not offer general budget support for local expenditures. Most are characterized by *shared costs* and *shared administration*. Recipient localities usually must provide some of their own resources to support the program and must administer it according to prescribed standards. Categorical money is not "free" for the asking. Some leading examples include highway assistance, aid to airports, school aid, alcohol and drug abuse programs, and urban renewal. Not all cities apply for all grants. To do so requires commitment of urban government's scare resources. But most cities find it in their interest to get what monies are available.

Table 6.3   Federal-Aid Outlays in SMSAs (in Millions of Dollars)

Function and program	1961 Actual	1964 Actual	1969 Actual	1975 Estimate
National defense	10	28	30	38
Agriculture and rural development:				
Donation of surplus commodities	128	231	313	299
Other	27	40	104	141
Natural resources and environment:				
Environmental protection	24	8	79	2,603
Other	30	10	101	249
Commerce and transportation:				
Economic development	—	158	104	331
Highways	1,398	1,948	2,225	2,678
Airports	36	36	83	232
Urban mass transportation	—	—	122	586
Other	1	5	5	117
Community development and housing:				
Funds appropriated to the President	—	—	432	183
Urban renewal	106	559	786	863
Public housing	105	136	257	1,023
Water and sewer facilities	—	36	52	104
Model cities	—	—	8	209
Other	2	17	75	783
Education and manpower:				
Consolidated education grants	—	—	—	1,337
Elementary and secondary	222	264	1,262	556
Higher education	5	14	210	30
Vocational education	28	29	179	280
Employment security	303	344	449	315
Comprehensive manpower assistance	—	—	—	1,220
Manpower activities	—	64	530	369
Other	3	7	333	990
Health:				
Health resources	48	66	216	545
Health services	47	82	219	458
Alcohol, drug abuse and mental health	4	8	77	530
Preventive health services	—	—	—	38
Medical assistance	—	140	1,731	3,989
Other	—	4	54	—

Table 6.3   Federal-Aid Outlays in SMSAs (in Millions of Dollars) continued

Function and program	1961 Actual	1964 Actual	1969 Actual	1975 Esti- mate
Income security:				
Rehabilitation services	37	61	247	669
Public assistance	1,170	1,450	3,022	4,820
Child nutrition, special milk, and food stamps	131	168	482	3,484
Other	3	16	148	429
General government:				
Law enforcement (including law-assistance)	—	—	17	656
National Capital region	25	38	85	361
Other	—	9	27	65
Other functions	—	2	—	29
General Revenue Sharing	—	—	—	4,322
Total aids to urban areas	3,893	5,588	14,045	35,931

Source: *Special Analysis, Budget of the United States Government, Fiscal Year 1975* (Washington: Government Printing Office, 1974, p. 212). Note that "1975 estimates" represent the requests being made by the President in this submission to Congress.

Urban officials are not always happy with categorical grants. Federal rules and regulations mandate expenditures for only certain purposes and the paperwork in applying and monitoring compliance can be staggering.

The year 1972 saw a major new departure from categorical federal aid. Revenue sharing was designed to be no-strings-attached money for states, counties, and cities.[10] An automatic allocation formula is set down by statute, and the Treasury Department simply sends a check by first-class mail.

Revenue sharing differs most dramatically from traditional federal aids in its lack of "strings." The money goes to communities as a matter of right, without detailed applications. Recipients can spend the money at their discretion, subject only to the following restrictions:

1. Local governments must spend their allotments within certain "priority" areas: public safety, environmental protection (including sanitation), public transportation, health, recreation, libraries, social services for the poor and aged, financial administration, and "ordinary and necessary" capital expenditures.
2. Discrimination on the basis of race, color, national origin, or sex is not permitted in any program financed with revenue-sharing funds.

3. Funds may not be used to match federal funds provided under other grant programs.
4. Construction workers paid with revenue-sharing funds must be paid at least the wage prevailing on similar construction activity in the locality.
5. Recipient governments must publish plans and publicly account for the use of revenue-sharing funds.

The State and Local Fiscal Assistance Act of 1972 provided for the distribution of $30.2 billion to 39,000 state and local governments over a five-year period. Congress, after some controversy, extended the legislation in 1976. In some respects revenue sharing is the classic political compromise with a little bit for everybody. That three thousand counties, 18,500 municipalities, and 17,000 townships receive aid has the effect of spreading revenue sharing monies rather thinly. Almost 9 in 10 eligible local governments have populations of fewer than 10,000.[11] Though the formulas favor poorer jurisdictions over richer ones, they do not favor big cities over small ones. Thus, revenue sharing probably contributes to the maintenance of a governmentally fragmented metropolis. However widely touted and popular revenue sharing has been with local officials (not surprisingly), it is important to remember that it is a small drop in a large bucket. Allen D. Manvel notes that "the $6.2 billion distributed as shared revenue in fiscal 1975 amounts to only two percent of the federal budget and less than two and one-half percent of all spending by state and local governments during this period."[12]

Revenue-sharing proponents talked extensively about the possibility for genuine local initiative and innovative programs if only monies were made available without cumbersome rules and requirements. What, then, did urban governments do with their newfound treasures? Generally they spend shared revenues pretty much like they spend their own revenues. Law enforcement got the lion's share, with transportation in second place — much as with the regular urban budget.[13] A University of Michigan study notes that "local officials do not look upon revenue sharing as an opportunity to start new, innovative programs, but rather as an additional source of revenue that does not have to be extracted from local sources."[14] The one unexpected catch in revenue-sharing monies, though, was the nondiscrimination provision. Shared funds could not be used to support local activities that discriminated because of race or sex. The Treasury Department's enforcement of that stipulation ranged from lax to negligible, but local groups sometimes took city governments to court. On a suit filed by the Afro-American Patrolman's League, federal judge Prentice Marshall found discrimination in police-hiring practices in Chicago and escrowed $95 million in revenue-sharing funds for the city. Federal judges found several southern cities guilty of service discrimination against black citizens and held up payments. Interestingly, the 1976 extensions of the legislation *strengthened* the civil-rights provisions of the act.

Indirect Federal Aids

Not all federal aids to cities come in the form of checks to city governments. Many of them are indirect. These indirect aids have nonetheless profoundly shaped the landscape of the American city. Housing policy is a prominent example. The Federal Housing Administration has for years guaranteed loans primarily to new, single-family homes. Aid is technically given to banks in the form of loan guarantees, but it rebounds to the benefit of middle-income families purchasing new housing in the suburbs.[15] In fact, the F.H.A. long had explicit policies against guaranteeing loans in "socially incompatible" neighborhoods, which had the effect of virtually excluding minority families from assistance. F.H.A. policies are an indirect federal aid to urbanites—at least to some urbanites—even though aid does not go to the local government itself.

Many taxpayers do not recognize the subtle federal aids that are written into the income-tax code. In computing income subject to federal taxation, a citizen can deduct any amounts paid as state or local income or sales, excise, or property taxes. Furthermore, any income received from interest on state or local government bonds is not subject to federal taxation. These provisions lessen the impact of state and local taxes and permit state and local agencies to pay lower than commercial interest rates for the money that they borrow.

Several other federal programs provide indirect, or subtle, forms of aid to state or local agencies. The direct provision of federal benefits to institutions or private citizens relieves states and municipalities of demands for services that otherwise would come to them. In this category are federal grants, loans, or loan guarantees to institutions of higher education for the construction of instructional facilities and dormitories; loans and scholarships to the students of these institutions; and federal insurance payments for the aged and disabled.

One New Element: Cities and the Courts

We have already met in this chapter several cases of urban involvement with another branch of the federal government—the courts. For many years it sufficed to discuss federalism in terms of the relations of cities to Congress and the federal bureaucracy, but no longer. Federal courts have appeared as a major new actor on the urban scene. The federal judge in Alabama who ordered a new structure of government, the federal judge in Chicago who escrowed revenue-sharing funds, the federal judges all over who ordered school busing have all played major input roles in urban decision making. City officials used to worry about the federal bureaucrats peering over their shoulders. Now they also worry about the federal judge. Some examples would include:

- A state judge in Newark who actually jailed five members of the city council for refusing to assess property at realistic levels. The judge stated that "the Newark Municipal Council is charged with the obligation of obeying the laws of the state and complying with the orders of the court," whereas the council members stated that "homeowners will not remain in this city and be unjustly taxed."
- the federal judge who ordered a new form of government in Mobile because the present one discriminated against minorities in the electoral process
- the decision of Judge Skelly Wright in Washington, D.C., ordering the equalization of public school expenditures in white and black neighborhoods
- the decisions in Detroit, Boston, and elsewhere requiring school busing
- the decision of the New Jersey Supreme Court in June 1976, ordering the closing of the state's public schools that did meet court-ordered requirements for equal financing
- the decision of federal Judge Sarah Hughes (who swore in Lyndon Johnson after the assassination of John F. Kennedy) that the city of Dallas must modernize its jails to avoid "cruel and unusual punishment"

Many, though not all, of these decisions involve civil-rights issues. But they all involve an expanded role of the courts in limiting local officials discretion. The courts are the newest entrant—though in the long run, a most significant one—in threatening the demise of urban autonomy.

CENTRALIZATION AND DECENTRALIZATION AT THE METROPOLITAN LEVEL: HORIZONTAL INTERGOVERNMENTAL RELATIONS

The Centralization–Decentralization Controversy

The structure of urban government at the metropolitan level is a fragmented one. We showed in Chapter 4 that most metropolitan areas are composed of a central-city government, plus dozens, scores, or even hundreds of local governments. The pattern typically is one large government, many small governments. Many metropolitan reformers believe that:

- the best solution to problems of metropolitan areas is the consolidation of many units of government into a few large units of government

This centralist strategy has long been advocated by those who see suburban governments as exploiting central cities. They believe that fiscal equity and political responsiveness would both be enhanced by metropolitan reorganization. Their preferred strategy is that each metropolitan area would have a single overarching government.[16] This regionwide government would be responsible for regionwide problems and would be able to draw on tax resources in one area to meet service needs in another area.

Others prefer a different strategy for urban government structure. Instead of a few large governments advocated by metropolitan reformers, they prefer many small governments. They advocate "neighborhood government" or "community control."[17] Their logic runs as follows: Indigenous neighborhood groups can best determine their own needs. Citizen preferences for police protection or school curriculum may vary from black to Latino to Anglo neighborhoods of a city. Thus, imposing a uniform governmental structure on all citizens will violate some citizen's preferences. So it is desirable to let spatially homogeneous areas have the major input on their own governance and policies. These community-control advocates contend that:

- urban problems are best solved at a neighborhood level, so that the creation of a large number of small jurisdictions should be encouraged.

Figure 6.1 indicates the range of centralization–decentralization alternatives. At one extreme, of course, is complete centralization with a unitary form of government (as in Britain or France) at the national level. Although the United States has certainly moved toward greater nationalization, few advocate this extreme in centralization. Many authorities do favor greater metropolitan consolidation to solve problems of equity and service coordination. Still others, particularly people in the "public choice" school, favor a fragmented system similar to the status quo. But others want far more decentralization than that. Advocates of "community control" and "neighborhood government" favor a very large number of relatively autonomous local governments, coterminous with the urban neighborhood. We shall see as we examine these alternative policy perspectives that each position requires crucial tradeoffs among alternative values.

Figure 6.1   Centralization–Decentralization Alternatives

EXTREME CENTRALIZATION			EXTREME DECENTRALIZATION
Federal control of metropolitan areas/problems	Metropolitan consolidation: a few very large governments	Metropolitan fragmentation: a large number of smaller governments	Neighborhood control: a very large number of small governments

The "Metropolitan Problem"

Metropolitan areas are the most frequent settings for horizontal relations among local officials, reflecting the high population density and the demands for policy that are thus generated, as well as the proximity of many separate governments with policy problems that depend partly on one another's actions. In Chapter 4 we discussed the social and economic differences between central cities and their suburbs and mentioned some features that hinder the smooth coordination of local activities in metropolitan areas. Here we return to the subject of metropolitan areas, this time to focus on problems and opportunities in governmental integration.

The number and density of governmental units in metropolitan areas (see Table 4.3 in Chapter 4) are the primary conditions that beg for coordination. The Chicago SMSA has the dubious distinction of containing the most units. Its 1172 jurisdictions were divided among school districts, counties, municipalities, townships, and special districts.

The "metropolitan problem" has been studied and decried by a generation of urban scholars. The fundamental problem they identify is the *noncongruence of policy-making units and problem units.* Municipal borders follow railroad tracks, creeks and rivers, streets and alleys, and other artificial lines of demarcation; but problems of crime, pollution, poverty, transportation, and so forth do not respect these boundaries. Lineberry[18] has identified four basic aspects of governmental fragmentation in the metropolitan area: externalities, fiscal and service inequities, absence of political responsibility, and lack of coordination.

EXTERNALITIES   Because the metropolis is an interdependent system, policies undertaken by independent municipal corporations or special districts may produce changes, sometimes unintended, in other parts of the total region. Economists call such consequences *externalities,* or, more descriptively, *spillover effects.* Land-use and zoning policies are examples. Sophisticated manipulation of zoning requirements is regularly used to produce the most desirable mix of residents and commerce, while shifting burdens to other areas in the metropolis, particularly to the central city. The "zoning game" may thus be used to maximize the benefits to one's own community while shifting the costs to other "players," particularly the less fortunate ones (see our discussion of the zoning game in Chapter 14, p. 361). Although zoning decisions especially illustrate the spillover effects of municipal policies, decisions in numerous other functional areas, including crime prevention, transportation policy, pollution control, schooling, and industrial attraction, may also entail externalities for other communities.

FISCAL AND SERVICE INEQUITIES   We noted in Chapter 4 the problems resulting from the segregation of economic needs and resources in the metropolitan area. To reiterate by example, in Detroit 25 suburban school districts spent up to $500 more per child per year to educate their children than did the city of Detroit. In the central city of Detroit, on the other hand, nearly one-third of the public-school buildings were built during the administration of President Ulysses S. Grant.[19] One New Jersey community had an assessed valuation of $5.5 million per pupil, and a neighboring community had a valuation of $33,000 per pupil.[20]

ABSENCE OF POLITICAL RESPONSIBILITY   When there is a plethora of governmental units, citizen control of decision makers is diffused. A citizen of Fridley, Minnesota, a Minneapolis suburb, is expected to exercise informed control over 11 local governments, in addition to the state and national governments. In the absence of an overarching metropolitan government there is no policy-making body to hold accountable for broad metropolitan problems or for failures arising from governmental action or inaction. Such fragmentation of the citizens' attention can hardly contribute to responsible democratic government.

LACK OF COORDINATION   The construction of public policy requires at least minimum coordination both among functions and among decision-making units. The absence of both types of coordination in the metropolis suggests that it will be unable to realize all the benefits of coherent policy and the consequent economies of scale that larger units should be able to secure. If communities fail to coordinate air-pollution control, for example, a municipality downwind may have the most advanced regulation yet still suffer the effluence of its upwind neighbor.

Policy Alternatives
to Metropolitan Fragmentation

1. *"Consolidate, and if you can't consolidate, at least coordinate."* *E pluribus unum*—"out of many, one"—has been a long-standing response to the problems attendant on metropolitan fragmentation. Consolidation of metropolitan-area governments into one or a very few overarching governments is the hallowed solution of a generation of metropolitan reformers. An areawide governing authority would have power over the metropolitan region as a whole. This would enable it, so the argument goes, to (1) even out fiscal and service inequities by drawing on the resources of the whole metropolitan area; (2) coordinate policy for the entire region so that one community would not create externalities for nearby communities through its self-serv-

ing policies; and (3) plan intelligently for regionwide development, optimizing land-use decisions, coordinating policies to reduce the brunt of decay, and managing growth at the periphery. A few (a very few, actually) metropolitan areas have followed the advice of the metropolitan reformers to create variants of a metropolitan regional government. Notable among them are Nashville, Jacksonville, Miami, Minneapolis–St. Paul, and, to the north, Toronto and Winnipeg.[21] Yet on the whole, a generation of urging and exhortation to reorganize has not brought many major reforms. Of the few reforms that have taken place, most of them have been in the South.

Adhering firmly to the philosophy that half a loaf is better than none, or that even a slice or two will do, metropolitan reformers have taken a fallback position: If you can't consolidate, then coordinate better. The major contemporary vehicle is the so-called "COG," an acronym for Councils of Governments. COGs were mandated by federal policy that requires that local governments applying for federal assistance, loans and grants, shall have to funnel their requests through an areawide agency. It must be composed of representatives of municipalities and other local governments throughout the metropolitan region. Such congresses of ambassadors are commonly called COGs and have acronyms sometimes more interesting than their function — for example, ABAG, the Association of Bay Area Governments, or ACOG, the Association of Central Oklahoma Governments. Though the COGs have the authority to *disapprove* federal grant applications by local governments within the region, there is rarely much incentive to do so. They have neither autonomous taxing power nor power to compel the elimination of fiscal disparities, externalities, nor to supersede local policies.[22]

It would not overstate the case by much to claim that the efforts to reorganize metropolitan government, based on arguments for efficiency, equity, and economy, have reached a blind alley. The idea of creating a single government for metropolitan Cleveland, metropolitan Buffalo, or metropolitan Denver has exhibited so little political feasibility that it is scarcely advocated any more.[23] Whites in suburbs have opposed being thrown in with a central city whose problems they succeeded in escaping. Municipal employees and their unions fear loss of job security with the uncertain consequences of governmental tinkering. And the most recent addition to groups opposing reform are central city blacks, who would sacrifice their voting majorities or pluralities if they were consolidated into a superordinate government of the entire metropolitan area. In one of the most notable city–county consolidations of recent years, Jacksonville, Duval County, Florida, such fears were dramatically fulfilled. In Jacksonville before consolidation, blacks were an impressive 41 percent of the city's population, on the verge of electing a black mayor. After the consolidation with Duval County, the black population of the new consolidated government was scarcely half that. It is not really surprising, therefore, that—what with opposition from suburban whites, central-city blacks, and municipal employees and unions—metropolitan reform as a policy alternative founders on the rock of political feasibility.

2. *"For heaven's sakes, don't create larger governments, but more smaller ones."* If the historic policy alternatives espoused by metropolitan reformers have favored fewer governments (preferably as few as possible), some economists have generally tended to prefer the opposite solution—as many governments as possible in order to maximize consumer choice within the metropolitan area. Political scientists, concerned with goals such as organizational efficiency, equity, and administrative symmetry, have favored the areawide government approach. Economists, who prefer to maximize goals such as consumer sovereignty and economy of scale, have advocated a kind of "metropolitan marketplace" model where competition is preferred to monopoly. Political economists Robert Bish and Vincent Ostrom state the problem as follows:[24]

Instead of assuming that fragmentation of authority and overlapping jurisdictions are the source of the contemporary urban crisis, we urge the opposite proposition be entertained as a serious hypothesis—that the absence of fragmented authority and multiple jurisdictions in large central cities is the principal source of institutional failure in urban government. The absense of neighborhood governments makes it difficult for residents of urban neighborhoods to organize so that common problems can be handled in routine ways.

According to the public choice or political economy perspective, the *last thing we should want* is more gargantuan metropolitan governments, so large in size that they would be as bureaucratically run and as politically responsive as big city governments are now. To create a metropolitanwide government for the Allentown-Bethlehem-Easton, Pennsylvania, area would entail a government of .5 million people. To create a metropolitan area for the New York metropolitan region would require a government of almost 20 million. Far better would it be to decentralize so that there were fewer massive city governments, not more.

The Demand for Decentralization: Community Control and Its Critics

Centralists believe that the present structure of urban governance is much too fragmented and cite equity and efficiency reasons for more centralization. At the other extreme are those who favor more decentralization of urban governance. These people advocate community control or, as it is sometimes called, neighborhood government. Fainstein and Fainstein in "The Future of Community Control" argue that the decentralist movement has two important rationales. The first advocates smaller governments on grounds of traditional democratic theory. "According to this model," they suggest, "individuals become alienated from government and society unless they can effectively participate in the determination of public policy as it affects them most directly."[25] This advocacy cuts across racial lines. Included are those who believe that bureaucracies have become powerful and insensitive instruments of social regulation, unresponsive to needs of particular neighborhoods. Boston's use of "little city halls" allegedly to bring government "closer to the people" is one way of realizing these objectives. But more important would be creating neighborhood boards with real budgetary and personnel authority 'to operate schools, police protection, and other urban services.

The second motivation has been based on a race-conflict model. It "stresses the utilization of the homogeneous black neighborhood as a vehicle for the mobilization of political power."[26] Writers such as Stokeley Carmichael and Charles Hamilton have been vigorous advocates of community control as an outgrowth of a black power ideology.[27]

Many black leaders, pessimistic about the prospects for integration, see community control as the most immediately practical alternative. The late Whitney Young, executive director of the National Urban League, argued that "community control is the most crucial issue right now. Institutions have failed because control isn't in the hands of the people who live in the communities."[28] Bayard Rustin, on the other hand, has argued that "black community control is as futile a program as black capitalism. . . . The truth of the matter is that community control as an idea is provincial and as a program is extremely conservative."[29] To white segregationists the demand for black power over neighborhood institutions poses equally difficult issues. Some favor the idea as a diversion from further housing and educational integration, but others fear a new militance arising from black control.

Although the concept of community control has implications for law enforcement, urban renewal, housing, model cities, public welfare, and other policies, education has so far been the main target. New York City, Detroit, and other cities have experimented with decentralization of public-school systems. Within carefully drawn limits of city and state standards, neighborhood school boards have been granted certain powers to establish programs and to hire and fire teaching personnel. A distinction should be made, however, between purely administrative decentralization and community control. Decentralization may include no more than the geographical reshuffling of administrative personnel and tasks from a central office to field offices. Store-front city halls may possess real power or may be no more than outposts of the central bureaucracy. Decentralization of administrative organization may or may not imply that power has been redistributed to community groups. Bringing bureaucrats into physical proximity does not bring them under neighborhood control. Many urban police departments are decentralized at the precinct level, but advocates of community control do not have this sort of geographical decentralization in mind. Community-control supporters advocate a measure of actual policy control of city-government operations and decisions that affect themselves, their children, and services that they require. Suburbanites, they argue, have genuine power to shape the policy and direction of their schools, police forces, tax systems and other concerns; central-city neighborhoods should enjoy the same kind of citizen influence over public policy.

Douglas Yates emphasizes that community control and neighborhood centralization come in many guises.[30] Self-help organizations, neighborhood field offices and "little city halls," community advisory councils, ombudsman structures, and other structural arrangements may all give some power to neighborhoods. The real question, he contends, is, *What is being decentralized to whom with what policy impacts?* The whole idea of community control — that different neighborhoods really have different needs and policy preferences — mitigates against easy generalizations about impact. One insightful study of the community action agencies in the war on poverty found very different levels of success in the five largest cities. New York's community action agency seemed to enjoy the most impact, with Chicago's having the least impact and Detroit, Los Angeles, and Philadelphia in between.[31] The success of the participatory model depends upon factors like creative neighborhood leadership, adequate resources, and issues to galvanize participation.

Community control has been a bitterly debated issue in many cities. Alan Altshuler has identified several major sources of opposition to the community-control movement, and it is a formidable list indeed.[32] Many public officials oppose community control because it threatens to undercut their own control over city budgets and policies. The established municipal bureaucracies — teachers, policemen, welfare workers, and others — see neighborhood control of service personnel as threatening to their jobs. Municipal employees' unions such as the American Federation of Teachers have been active opponents of modest schemes for neighborhood control of schools in New York City. Contractors who do a major portion of their business with city governments fear disruption of their established relations with city hall. Large numbers of whites oppose any program that might contribute to disruption of the status quo in race relations.

From the point of view of blacks, community control contains a built-in dilemma: the tensions between resources and control. Blacks already control the political system of Newark, where they constitute a majority of the electorate and elect the mayor. But there they have been unable to secure resources needed for change, as Newark is teetering on the brink of public poverty. The dilemma between control and resources is illustrated by Figure 6.2. Ideally, advocates of community control prefer a situation depicted by cell A, that is, a high degree of control over generous resources. Unfortunately the availability of human and economic resources in the ghetto is limited. Some integrationists argue that a program relying exclusively on neighborhood resources would doom minorities to a permanent poverty of public services. Fiscal resources sufficient to maintain only symbolic programs are no substitute for ghetto needs for heavy investment in education, extraordinary levels of law-enforcement activity, and a high level of additional public services. On the other hand, advocates of community control maintain that the present system is simply minimal control over minimal resources (Figure 6.2, cell D), and this is the worst possible arrangement. Almost any change, therefore, represents an improvement.

Our own view is that the future of community control will depend strongly on the combination of indigenous political leadership *and* access to resources. Yates puts it simply in saying that "neighborhood structures will be effective only if their resources are commensurate with their tasks and costs."[33] The political-economy approach in this book is consistent with the argument that political control without adequate economic resources is ephemeral indeed.

Centralization–Decentralization in Perspective: An Issue for Urban Governance

Political thinkers from Aristotle, through Madison, to contemporary political scientist Robert Dahl have written about the optimal size of the political community. Those such as Aristotle and Dahl who favored smaller governments have made familiar arguments about the political democracy and responsiveness of smaller governments.[34] Those such as Madison who have advocated larger governments stress the tyranny of the majority in small constituencies. These arguments translate into the debate about the structure of urban governments. Metropolitan reformers stress the ability of large, metropolitanwide governments to draw on metropolitan tax bases and redistribute to meet needs in all areas. They see confusion and chaos in different jurisdictions, which may create tax havens and wall off rich from poor. Public choice advocates favor more competition among governments, viewing the multiplicity of metropolitan governments almost like a marketplace where citizens can pick and choose the government best meeting their needs. "Exit" in that model serves a positive function.

Figure 6.2   The Dilemma of Control vs. Resources in the Issue of Community Control

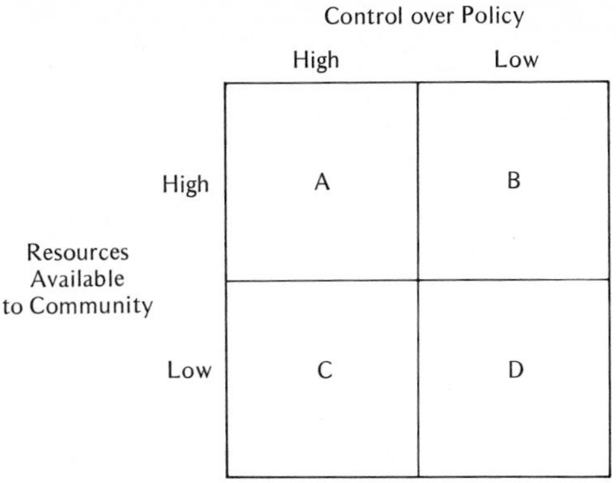

Control over Policy

		High	Low
Resources Available to Community	High	A	B
	Low	C	D

Still a third group, advocates of more community control, want strong decentralized government responsive to neighborhood needs. Some neighborhoods, they contend, have been slighted for years by unresponsive municipal bureaucracies, and seizing control of their own institutions is the best alternative to that dominance. We do not in this book peddle any one of these views. But we do return here to our political-economy stance, emphasizing that control over nonexistent resources is not much control at all. *Who controls* the structure of urban governance is important, but so is *what they can control.*

STRUCTURES OF MUNICIPAL GOVERNANCE

City governments in the United States represent a mix of centralist and decentralist elements. They are certainly not so decentralized as community-control advocates would like. But neither are they as centralized, covering large areal jurisdictions, as metropolitan reformers would prefer. The structure of American municipal institutions has long been shaped by conflicts between "reformers" and their opponents. The numerically dominant municipal institutions — manager government, nonpartisan elections, and at-large constituencies — are a product of the reform movement and its desire for "professional management" and "political accountability."

The Impact of Reformism

The way in which a government is structured is not an ideologically neutral matter. Formal structures advantage some interests and disadvantage others. The municipal reform movement was in its heyday during the Progressive era at the turn of the century. Its leaders were often upper-class businessmen, intent upon ridding the city of all vestiges of the political machine. Some cities were easy marks for the advocates of reform; others have retained traditional institutions to this day. The reformers pressed for a battery of institutional changes including manager government, at-large constituencies, nonpartisan elections, civil-service systems, budgeting, referenda, primary elections, and competitive bidding on city purchases. Reformers, according to one historical analysis, "had a much better chance of success if their city was small, young, ethnically homogeneous, and of relatively high socioeconomic status."[35]

Today we can think of cities as being more or less reformed according to their institutional forms and structures. A city containing most of the structural changes advocated by Progressive-era reformers we would call a "reformed" city; one that still maintained partisan elections, wards, a mayor-council system, and other older elements we would call "unreformed." Lineberry and Fowler classified cities in terms of the degree of reformism present in their governing institutions.[36] They focused on three principal reform features: manager government, nonpartisan elections, and at-large constituencies. These were distinguished from their unreformed counterparts: mayor-council government, partisan elections, and ward constituencies. They divided cities into four types:

1. cities with no reformed institutions (i.e., the structure of government is mayor-council; the type of election is partisan; and constituencies are ward)
2. cities with one reformed institution
3. cities with two reformed institutions
4. cities with three reformed institutions (i.e., the structure of government is council-manager; the type of election is nonpartisan; and constituencies are at-large)

Table 6.4 indicates some of the variation among American cities in the degree of governmental reformism. There has been some research into the kinds of cities that have adopted each form of government. Table 6.5 shows the distributions of various features by size of city over 5000 population. Unreformed mayor-council forms dominate in both the smallest and largest cities, whereas the council-manager and commission forms together dominate the middle-sized ones. Council-manager forms are by far the most common among reformed institutions. Commission forms are a small minority and are concentrated in medium-sized cities.

The choice of governmental, electoral, and constituency structures is not trivial. Lineberry and Fowler argue that unreformed structures maximize a political system's *responsiveness* to groups and interests in the population. Manager governments, nonpartisan elections, and at-large constituencies tend to insulate decision makers from potential

Table 6.4   Reform Scores for Selected American Cities

	Form of government	Election type	Constituency type
0 = no reformed institutions (i.e., government is mayor-council, elections are partisan, and constituencies are ward)			
Binghamton, NY	Mayor-council	Partisan	Ward
Burlington, VT	Mayor-council	Partisan	Ward
1 = one reformed institution, 2 unreformed institutions			
Chicago, IL	Mayor-council	Nonpartisan	Ward
Louisville, KY	Mayor-council	Partisan	At-large
2 = two reformed institutions, 1 unreformed institution			
Camden, NJ	Mayor-council	Nonpartisan	At-large
Boston, MA	Mayor-council	Nonpartisan	At-large
Boise, ID	Mayor-council	Nonpartisan	At-large
St. Petersburg, FL	Manager	Nonpartisan	Ward
Skokie, IL	Manager	Partisan	At-large
Springfield, MA	Mayor-Council	Nonpartisan	At-large
3 = reformed (i.e., government is manager, election type is nonpartisan, and constituency type is at-large)			
Anaheim, CA	Manager	Nonpartisan	At-large
Austin, TX	Manager	Nonpartisan	At-large
Portland, ME	Manager	Nonpartisan	At-large
Raleigh, NC	Manager	Nonpartisan	At-large
Santa Ana, CA	Manager	Nonpartisan	At-large
Tacoma, WA	Manager	Nonpartisan	At-large

Source: International City Management Association, *Municipal Yearbook* (Washington, D.C.: ICMA, 1976), Table 1/1.

Table 6.5   The Incidence of Government Forms in 200 Cities of over 50,000 Population

Institutional form	Reformed		Unreformed	
Form of government	Manager	45%	Mayor-council	43%
	Commission	12		
Type of election	Nonpartisan	67	Partisan	33
Type of constituency	At large	63	Ward or mixed[a]	37

[a] Includes a small proportion of cities that use a combination of ward and at-large elections.

Source: Robert L. Lineberry and Edmund P. Fowler, "Reformism and Public Policies in American Cities," *American Political Science Review,* 61 (September 1967), 705–706.

conflicts of urban life and give professional managers and bureaucracies more power. Karnig, for example, discovered that civil-rights groups were more successful in obtaining favorable policy outputs in unreformed than reformed urban governments.[37] Specifically, political reformism seems to have these impacts on patterns of urban participation and decision making:

- Mass participation is typically lower in reformed communities than in unreformed communities.
- Representation of minority groups is usually less in reformed communities than in unreformed communities.
- Municipal bureaucracies have more power and autonomy in reformed systems, and elected decision makers have corresponding smaller bases of power.
- Decision making in reformed systems is more likely to be made on the basis of "professional management" criteria than on narrowly "political" grounds (or, in other words, "bureaucratic politics" comes to replace "electoral politics" as the key arena of decision-making).

The Three Types of Governmental Structures

MAYOR-COUNCIL FORMS   The classic model of local government combines an elected mayor with an elected council. Figure 6.3 portrays the relations of a typical mayor and council with the voters and with the departments of the city government. Depending on the predominant influences at work in the initial design or later modification, these structures may reflect emphasis on political accountability or professional management. Offices may be filled through partisan or nonpartisan ballots; the personnel of administrative departments may

Figure 6.3   Simplified Government Structure in a Strong Mayor–Council City

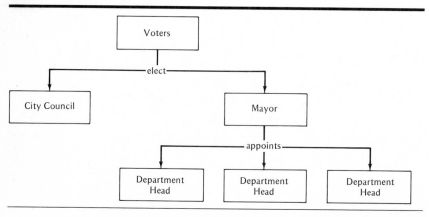

be selected by the chief executive according to political criteria or according to professional personnel standards and protected by a merit system; the legislators may be elected at large or from individual wards.

Mayor-council cities may also differ in the formal powers given to the mayor and council. In *weak-mayor governments,* the selection of department heads and the responsibility for administrative policies are usually given to boards or commissions, whose members are chosen by direct election or by the mayor and the council. Mayors can also be weakened by being denied a veto over the actions of the council or by being required to share responsibility for preparing the budget with the entire council or a council committee. An individual executive can also be made stronger or weaker by virtue of the staff he is allowed to hire. Where he is permitted an extensive, well-paid, and professional cadre of assistants, he can use the high-quality information they provide to assert himself in dealings with the council or administrative departments.

A local government reflecting the primary influence of political accountability would tie the mayor and council to the voters and minimize the authority of any local official to make policy on his own initiative. It would have partisan elections for the mayor and council, councilmen elected from wards, selection of administrators according to political criteria, control of departments by the elected chief executive, but budgeting and other policy-making functions shared by the mayor and the council.

THE MANAGER FORM   The extreme expression of the professional-management doctrine is the council-manager form of government. This form is depicted in Figure 6.4. It typically combines a small council, elected at large by nonpartisan ballot, along with a professional administrator who is selected by (and responsible to) the council. There is often also a mayor, who performs ceremonial functions as head of the local government. He may preside at meetings of the council, represent the city on public occasions, and sign legal documents for the city. He may be elected by the voters or selected by the council from among their own members. The typical manager has the power to appoint (and remove) the heads of administrative departments; to prepare the budget for the council's consideration and to allocate funds after the budget's approval; and to make investigations, reports, and policy recommendations to the council on his own initiative or at its request. The professional-management ideal is even more nearly realized when administrative personnel are selected on the basis of professional competence and protected from political dismissal and when the manager has the budget and authority to hire competent staff.

Figure 6.4   Simplified Government Structure in a Council–Manager City

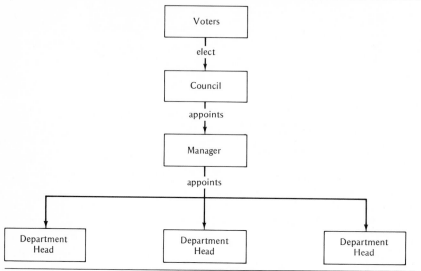

As the council-manager plan was originally designed, the manager was expected to administer but to remain assiduously aloof from politics or policy making. In recent years, however, it has become evident that the manager is inevitably involved in controversial issues. Even the most careful manager encounters politics when he conducts policy-oriented research for the council, formulates a budget for the council's deliberation, interprets the council's preferences in allocating funds to departments, or seeks to change a department's procedures in rendering service. The manager's role in policy making is heightened when the council depends on his professional judgment. Council members are typically part-time officials not professionally trained to make policy decisions nor to supervise their implementation. Although most—if not all—managers do involve themselves in politically charged issues, they differ markedly in style. Some shape the basic policies of their governments and enlist the aid of interest groups, private citizens, and councilmen in their efforts. Others work more narrowly through official channels. Managers have no tenure in their positions; they can be dismissed by majorities of their councils or forced to resign by intensely hostile minorities. Some managers define success by their ability to remain in office, whereas others define it by the innovations they have guided through local politics.[38]

THE COMMISSION FORM   The third form of local government, the city commission, departs radically from the distinctive American pattern

Figure 6.5   Simplified Government Structure in a Commission City

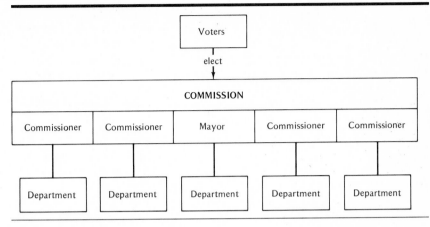

of separate legislative and executive branches. This structure is por-
trayed in Figure 6.5. It consists of a small group of elected commissioners, each heading an administrative department, as well as sitting
as a member of the local legislature. There is no strong executive, although one member of the commission is designated the nominal
head of government. In some cities, the chairman's position rotates
periodically among the commissioners. At one time this form of government was the darling of good-government reformers. It was first
developed in Galveston in 1900 and was in use in 108 cities by 1910.
It is said that commission cities suffer from a lack of administrative integration. Separately elected department heads and the absence of a
real central authority provide no focus of coordination. Vote trading
and "you stay out of my department, and I'll stay out of yours" characterize the style of government. The plan has lost its appeal to reformers, most of whom have switched their allegiance to the council-
manager form. The commission is now used by only 37 cities with
populations over 50,000 plus a smattering of smaller cities, mostly in
the South.

Formal Fragmentation and
the Myth of Hierarchy

American cities are governed by a highly fragmented authority structure. This fragmentation comes from two factors, both of which we
have explored in this chapter: the fragmentation of metropolitanwide
government into scores or hundreds of independent governments and
the formal fragmentation and dispersion of powers within the city government itself. It is erroneous to think of the urban mayor as being
analogous to the President of the United States in a smaller context. A

president has scope of power and political resources to control subordinates that are simply unavailable to municipal decision makers.

President Lyndon B. Johnson is said to have commented in one of his most harried moments that "things could be worse. I could be a mayor."[39] A mayor of Milwaukee once observed that "the central city mayor survives only when he has the psychological capacity to handle at one time three man-eating gorillas of crises and two of the paper tigers that, it seems at times, are thrown upon his back just to test him."[40]

Much of the difficulty in appraising our mayors is that we are influenced by the *myth of hierarchy*, which does not describe American city government. Although the President and most governors have at least nominal hierarchical controls working for them, American cities are surrounded and beset by formal pluralism.[41] In the first place, city governments are only one of multiple types of governments in urban areas. Milwaukee County has 46 taxing units of local government: the City of Milwaukee; 18 suburban municipalities, "each proudly waving its own flag of suburban independence emblazoned, 'Don't invade me' "; 22 suburban school boards; 2 sewage commissions; 2 city school boards; as well as the county government.[42] Even if a mayor reigned supreme in his own bailiwick, he would thus be at best a feudal lord in a castle, beset by numerous other claimants to the throne.

Within what we call city government, there is also fractionalization of power, with the mayor being both limited in his powers and compelled to share responsibilities with other decision-making agencies, particularly the council and perhaps also a manager. Also there may be other decision-making officers elected by the public and thus not beholden to the mayor.

CONCLUSIONS

The structure of urban governance, we have argued, is not a matter resolved outside the political process. How governments are set up has consequences for whose interests are represented and what policies are made. Perhaps the most enduring source of conflict has been over centralization or decentralization of local authority. Centralists tend to favor areally inclusive governments, preferring a few large governments to many small ones. Decentralists want to maximize local control, even at the neighborhood level. Centralists generally deplore fragmentation; decentralists often welcome it.

A great deal of centralization has already occurred in urban governance. Both the state and federal governments have assumed larger and larger roles in urban policy making. Cities are constitutionally the "creatures of the states," and state governments regulate their behavior as well as provide them aid. But in recent years the expanding federal role has been more crucial. Hundreds of categorical grant programs—plus the recent investments in revenue sharing—have made cities far more dependent on the federal government. Federal aid comes directly to city governments and indirectly to urban residents. And when the fiscal crunch comes, city officials look increasingly at the munificent federal tax base as a source of remedies to their problems.

At the metropolitan level the centralist–decentralist tension has been played out in the dispute over metropolitan reform. For two generations centralists have advocated consolidation of metropolitan governments but rarely with much success. The reform tradition has, however, been challenged both by public-choice theorists and by community-control advocates, each of whom favors a large number of small governments. Although both groups land on the same side, they arrive there from very different motivations. Public-choice theorists want to maximize exit options and intergovernmental mobility; community-control advocates want to maximize voice options, especially for minority groups concentrated in central cities.

The fragmentation of metropolitan governments is paralleled by the decentralized structures of municipal governments themselves. The municipal reform movement etched major changes in the structure of city government, advocating manager governments, nonpartisan elections, at-large constituencies, and other reforms. Emphasizing professional management premises, the reformers were successful in a majority of American cities in introducing new forms of governing. These changes—like all structures—have not been neutral, but have served to make the city more bureaucratically governed and, according to some, less "responsive" to interest groups and citizens.

Notes

1. *New York Times,* 13 November 1976, p. 1.
2. Quoted in Duane Lockard, *The Politics of State and Local Government* (New York, Macmillan, 1963), p. 132.
3. See Ira Sharkansky, *The Maligned States* (New York: McGraw Hill, 1972), pp. 146–147.
4. G. Ross Stephens, "State Centralization and the Erosion of Local Autonomy," *Journal of Politics,* 36 (1974), 74.
5. See Douglas M. Fox, ed., *The New Urban Politics: Cities and the Federal Government* (Pacific Palisades, Calif.: Goodyear, 1972); James L. Sundquist, *Making Federalism Work* (Washington, D.C.: Brookings, 1969); and Frederic N. Cleaveland, et al., *Congress and Urban Problems* (Washington, D.C.: Brookings, 1969).
6. (New York: Quadrangle Books, 1971).

7. William P. Browne and Robert H. Salisbury, "Organized Spokesmen for Cities: Urban Interest Groups," in Harlan Hahn, ed., *People and Politics in Urban Society* (Beverly Hills, Calif.: Sage, 1972), chap. 10; Donald Haider, *When Governments Come to Washington* (New York: Free Press, 1974).

8. The role of the PIGs in revenue sharing is told in Richard P. Nathan and Susannah E. Calkins, "The Story of Revenue Sharing," in Robert L. Peabody, ed., *Cases in American Politics* (New York: Praeger, 1976), chap. 2.

9. See Wallace E. Oates, *Fiscal Federalism* (New York: Harcourt, Brace, Jovanovich, 1972); and George F. Break, *Intergovernmental Fiscal Relations in the United States* (Washington, D.C.: Brookings, 1967).

10. On revenue sharing, see Paul R. Dommel, *The Politics of Revenue-Sharing* (Bloomington, Ind.: Indiana University Press, 1974); Otto G. Stolz, *Revenue-Sharing: Legal and Policy Analysis* (New York: Praeger, 1974); and David Caputo and Richard L. Cole, *Urban Politics and Decentralization: The Politics of General Revenue-Sharing* (Lexington, Mass.: Heath, 1974).

11. National Science Foundation, *General Revenue Sharing: Research Utilization Project* (Washington, D.C.: Government Printing Office, 1975), p. 17.

12. Cited in ibid., p. 30.

13. Ibid., pp. 38–40.

14. Ibid., p. 51.

15. On the role of.the FHA, see Gary Orfield, "Federal Policy, Local Power, and Metropolitan Segregation," *Political Science Quarterly, 89* (March 1975), 777–802.

16. For differing views on metropolitan reform, see the collection of papers in Alan K. Campbell and Roy W. Bahl, eds., *State and Local Government: The Political Economy of Reform* (New York: Free Press, 1976).

17. On community control, see Alan Altshuler, *Community Control* (New York: Pegasus, 1970); and Milton Kotler, *Neighborhood Government* (Indianapolis: Bobbs-Merrill, 1969).

18. Robert L. Lineberry, "Reforming Metropolitan Governance: Requiem or Reality?" *Georgetown Law Journal, 58* (March–May 1970), 675–718.

19. National Advisory Commission on Civil Disorders, *Report* (Washington, D.C.: Government Printing Office, 1968), p. 241.

20. Robert C. Wood, *1400 Governments* (Garden City, N.Y.: Doubleday, 1961), p.55.

21. For a discussion of these metropolitan reforms, see Lineberry, op. cit.

22. For a review of COGs, see Nelson Wikstrom, "Councils of Government: A Review of Twenty Years," paper delivered at the National Conference on Public Administration, Chicago, Ill., 1–4 April 1975.

23. On the political dimensions, see Vincent L. Marando, "The Politics of Metropolitan Reform," in Campbell and Bahl, eds., op. cit., chap. 2.

24. Robert Bish and Vincent Ostrom, *Understanding Urban Government* (Washington, D.C.: American Enterprise Institute for Public Policy Research, 1973), p. 95.

25. Norman I. Fainstein and Susan F. Fainstein, "The Future of Community Control," *American Political Science Review, 70* (September 1976), 905. See also Peter K. Eisenger, "Support for Urban Control Sharing at the Mass Level," *American Journal of Political Science, 17* (November 1973), 669–694.

26. Fainstein and Fainstein, op. cit., p. 906.

27. Stokeley Carmichael and Charles V. Hamilton, *Black Power* (New York: Vintage, 1967).
28. Quoted in Altshuler, op. cit., p. 61.
29. Bayard Rustin, "The Failure of Black Separatism," *Harper's,* January 1970, p. 28.
30. Douglas Yates, "Political Innovation and Institution Building: The Experience of Decentralization Experiments," in Willis D. Hawley et al., *Theoretical Perspectives on Urban Politics* (Englewood Cliffs, N.J.: Prentice-Hall, 1976), chap. 6.
31. J. David Greenstone and Paul E. Peterson, *Race and Authority in Urban Politics* (New York: Russell Sage Foundation, 1973), chap. 1.
32. Altshuler, op. cit., chap. 3.
33. Yates, op. cit., p. 158.
34. For Robert A. Dahl's reflections on this issue, see his presidential address to the American Political Science Association, "The City in the Future of Democracy," *American Political Science Review, 61* (December 1967), 953–970.
35. Richard M. Bernard and Bradley R. Rice, "Political Environment and the Adoption of Progressive Municipal Reform," *Journal of Urban History, 1* (February 1975), p. 170.
36. Robert L. Lineberry and Edmund P. Fowler, III, "Reformism and Public Policies in American Cities," *American Political Science Review, 61* (September 1967), 701–716.
37. Albert K. Karnig, "Private Regarding Policy, Civil Rights Groups, and the Mediating Impact of Municipal Reforms," *American Journal of Political Science, 19* (February 1975), 91–106.
38. On city managers in politics, see Ronald O. Loveridge, *City Managers in Legislative Politics* (Indianapolis: Bobbs-Merrill, 1971).
39. *Newsweek,* 13 March 1967, p. 38.
40. Henry Maier, *Challenge to the Cities* (New York: Random House, 1966), p. 190.
41. For some qualifications on the hierarchical controls available to the president and governors, see Ira Sharkansky, *Public Administration* (Chicago: Markham, 1972), chap. 4. The point is that mayors have even fewer such controls, not that they are the only American chief executives who lack them.
42. Maier, op. cit., p. 23.

7
POWER
AND LEADERSHIP
IN THE CITY

"Who governs?" is an enduring but unsettled question in the study of urban politics. The men and women who have power sometimes occupy positions of formal authority, but often they do not. In a few cities an informal power structure may operate behind the scenes and be relatively invisible to the public. Still other cities seem dominated by their organized bureaucracies, with weak mayors and rubber-stamp councils seemingly incapable of exercising much clout. In this chapter we describe the varied patterns of power in the American city. Specifically we:

- introduce a theory of power in the city that includes three principal elements: private-sector elites, elected decision makers, and municipal bureaucracies
- describe the principal roles and resources of each of these three elements of urban power
- provide an overview of the urban decision-making process

Often the most unlikely people end up as power holders, the mighty figures who literally remake the urban landscape. The late Richard J. Daley of Chicago was born to an Irish steelworker behind the stockyards of that city. One of his first jobs was herding cattle in those yards, a cowboy in the city; from there he went to night school, earned a law degree while working full time, and played ward politics. More than anything else, it was a series of lucky accidents that pushed him to the mayoralty of the nation's second city. Few would have expected on his accession in 1955 that he would wield power greater than perhaps any other urban official in the twentieth century. Perhaps his only rival was New York City's Robert Moses, a man who held a long list of public offices and an even longer list of public edifaces to his credit. At the beginning of Robert Caro's massive (1246-page) and magisterial biography of Moses, a map of New York City is presented, showing Moses' responsibility for Lincoln Center, the New York Coliseum, the United Nations headquarters, Shea Stadium, Jones Beach State Park, countless public housing projects, hundreds of miles of parkways and freeways, parks, bridges, tunnels, and other public projects. Rising well above his early days as a prosperous (but never really employed) municipal reformer, Moses became the most prominent reshaper of urban landscapes in modern times.[1]

In this chapter we focus on power and leadership in the city. Michael Korda wrote a popular — and possibly not altogether serious — book entitled *Power: How To Get It, How To Use It,* in which he contends that "all life is a game of power. The object of the game is simple enough: to know what you want and get it."[2] One hopes that more is involved in the pursuit of power than this. The uses to which power is put determine the nature of urban policy and the quality of life in the city. Moses, for example, vastly expanded the number of parks and beaches in the New York metropolitan region and made automobile transportation infinitely easier. But in doing so he also wedded the city to the car and displaced perhaps as many as a half a million New Yorkers from their homes.[3]

In our opinion no subject in the study of urban politics is as unsettled as questions related to power and leadership. Vigorous disputes have raged between those contending that American cities are "elitist" and others arguing that they are "pluralist." Those disputes have typically overlooked an important element of urban power, the organized and hierarchical urban bureaucracies. We describe here a theory of power in the city. Our theory includes three basic elements: private-sector elites, elected urban decision makers, and the municipal bureaucracies. We suggest that power is likely to be variable from place to place and from time to time. It is important to examine each of these elements individually, showing the roles and resources of each. We also outline, toward the end of this chapter, the urban decision-making process. There we show how different elements of power interact to produce policies.

TOWARD A THEORY OF POWER IN THE CITY

The Concept of Power

Power is a commonplace analytical focus for political scientists, political activists, and ordinary citizens. It is as ancient as Aristotle and as current as black power. It is as ambiguous as it is ubiquitous, as elusive as it is useful. There is much controversy over the definition of power, but most contemporary efforts are based on that of the German sociologist Max Weber: " 'Power' is the probability that one actor within a social relationship will be in a position to carry out his own will despite resistance, regardless of the basis on which this probability rests."[4] One of the most penetrating students of power in American communities, Dahl, has relied on Weber's formulation: "My intuitive idea of power, then, is something like this: *A* has power over *B* to the extent that he can get B to do *something that* B *would not otherwise do.*"[5]

Power can be a micro (individual) property or a macro (community) property. It is both a capacity of the individual to alter his environment and a capacity of the community itself to manipulate the economic, social, and cultural spheres in which the individual operates.

Formal decision makers (those who hold significant public offices) may or may not be the "real" decision makers in a political system. Sociologist C. Wright Mills won considerable notoriety with his argument that "the power to make decisions on national and international consequence is now so clearly seated in political, military, and economic institutions that other areas of society seem off to the side and, on occasion, readily subordinated to these."[6] Mills argued that elected office holders are essentially subject to historic decisions made by the big three institutions of government bureaucracies, military commanders, and economic elites. Whether Mills was right or wrong need not concern us here, but his implication that power may not always reside with the occupants of formal positions is clearly relevant to the study of urban politics. The degree to which formal office holders actually exercise power is a most significant empirical matter.

Three Theories of Power in Urban Politics

One school of thought holds that American cities are typically dominated by "power structures." It is very similar to the argument of Mills about power at the national level. The earliest and still the most significant argument along these lines was Floyd Hunter's study of Atlanta, Georgia.[7] Hunter's method, which inspired countless others, involved using a panel of informants to identify the most influential men in the community that he studied. The informants might be either a random sample of the population or a specific panel believed to be particularly informed about local decision making (as newspaper editors or chamber-of-commerce officials would be). By culling newspaper accounts of community decision making and organizational rosters and minutes, Hunter arrived at a list of 175 possible leaders and then submitted this list to a panel of informants. These informants were told to pare down the list, and 40 people were finally identified as the community "influentials" of Atlanta. Once the list of 40 had been compiled, Hunter interviewed as many of its members as possible in an effort to identify the "top leaders." The principal question he asked each person on his list was, "If a project were before the community that required *decision* by a group of leaders — leaders that nearly everyone would accept — which 10 on this list of 40 would you choose?" Twelve men were identified consistently enough by the 40 "reputational leaders" to convince Hunter that they constituted the top leaders in the community power structure.

The key leaders in the power structure of Atlanta were men from the private, rather than the public, sector. Only 4 of the 40 on the original list had roles in the public sector. Most held positions in commerce, banking, manufacturing, and the professions. Not only were the political officeholders a small proportion of the total leadership, but also, Hunter argued, they were mainly second-level leaders, whose major responsibility was execution of decisions made by economic "dominants." The political and governmental realm was thus secondary to the economic one. In Atlanta, according to Hunter:

the dominant factor in political life is the personnel of economic interests. It is true that there is no formal tie between the economic interests and the government, but the structure of policy-determining committees and their tie-in with the other powerful institutions and organizations of the community make government subservient to the interests of these combined groups. The government departments and their personnel are acutely aware of the power of key individuals and combinations of citizens' groups in the policy-making realm, and they are loath to act before consulting and "clearing" with these interests.[8]

The picture of community power painted by Hunter and other reputationalists is one in which realities of power are at variance with the democratic theory of political accountability. Instead of decision making by elected office holders, power is wielded by economic dominants who are relatively invisible to the public and are not subject to electoral control. Rather than a wide distribution of political power among the citizens, power is held by a relatively small upper class.

Advocates of an elitist theory of community power find ample evidence to support their case. Longtime Dallas mayor Erik Jonsson was the epitome of the business elite in politics. Jonsson was founder and chairman of the board of Texas Instruments, an important electronics and computer firm headquartered in Dallas. Like many businessmen in positions of power, he favored economic growth for the metropolitan region. The vast Dallas–Fort Worth Regional Airport—so large that it covers more land than Manhatten Island—was a pet project of his. Even after his term as mayor had ended, he remained chairman of the airport board. Even in New York City, which had rarely been associated with elite dominance, the city's financial collapse was followed by creation of powerful boards, largely composed of financial and business leaders, to oversee the city's finances. Elitists typically see these kinds of decisions as demonstrating the capacity of private-sector elites to dominate urban policy making.

A second school of thought is sometimes called "pluralism." It rests upon a very different set of assumptions—and produces very different conclusions—than Hunter's reputational study of Atlanta. Pluralist scholars emphasize the need for careful analysis of actual decisions in order to identify patterns of power. The decisional approach was stimulated by the work of Robert Dahl and his associates at Yale University.[9] It is also called the *event analysis,* or *decision-making* approach (after its method), the *political-science* approach (after its academic proponents), and the *pluralist alternative* (after its usual findings).

The decisional approach begins with the selection of certain key issues in the community and then identifies the people who seem significant in affecting their outcomes. Current decisions may be selected by the researcher from meetings, newspaper accounts, and interviews of participants. Past decisions may be reconstructed through similar procedures and from the minutes of past meetings.

Dahl identified three basic issues in New Haven during the period of his study: school decisions, an urban-renewal decision, and political nominations. His principal conclusions about power in New Haven are: first, that a leader in one issue area was not likely to be influential in another and that, if he was, he was probably a public official and most likely the mayor; and, second, that leaders in different issue areas did not seem to be drawn from a single homogeneous stratum of the community.[10] No identifiable, cohesive elite dominated by economic and social notables appeared in Dahl's study of New Haven. The power structure included multiple centers. Different sets

Los Angeles Mayor Tom Bradley's "open office" — an effort to make government accessible to the people.

of decision makers operated in each arena, and the arenas were bridges only by the mayor. In New Haven, Dahl concluded, economic and social notables had "relatively little direct influence on government decisions."[11] As public officials tended to be the major power brokers, it followed that there was a high degree of mass control over decision makers. Such political accountability is unlikely when decision making is controlled by an elite in the private sector.

In Dahl's New Haven, power was centered in elected public officials. This is a very different picture of power from that painted by elitists. Where elected officials dominate, the mayor's office plays an important political brokerage function. The successful mayor will offer some policy gains to various groups but will never yield fully to their demands. Group politics flourishes in pluralism. Mayor Daley was a pluralist *par excellence*. The Chicago school board, which the mayor appoints, was always carefully balanced with representatives of business and labor, Irish, Poles, blacks, and other ethnics, Catholics, Jews, and Protestants. The pluralist welcomes this multiplicity of power centers. To the pluralist an open system is one in which many groups can get some of their policy demands answered, but no single group (especially not an economic elite) can succeed in shutting out the others.

Pluralism without strong leadership, however, may be called "hyperpluralism." We emphasized in the last chapter that few cities have powerful mayors. Many cities, instead, are characterized by having many contending groups but very little power centralized within anyone's hands. San Francisco is prototypical. Frederick Wirt's study of San Francisco politics describes its political pattern as hyperpluralistic.[12] Group politics in San Francisco is perhaps more complex and fascinating than in any American city. Groups of Arab grocers, gay-rights advocates, ecologists, and more conventional interest groups make up a complex mosaic of interests. Yet power in the city is fragmented. City and county governments are coterminous, and conflicts between city and county law enforcement authorities are not uncommon. Numerous boards and commissions operate relatively independently of the mayor. An appointed city administrator serves a longer term than the mayor and cannot be easily removed. City bureaucracies, increasingly unionized, exert power over work rules and service decisions. Members of the Board of Supervisors (the city council) spend much of their own time planning mayoral campaigns. Hyperpluralism exists where numerous centers of power vie for policies without centralization anywhere to referee such conflicts.

Still, something is missing from these two theories of urban power. Urban public bureaucracy is often the hidden element in local decision making. Neither in Hunter's Atlanta nor in Dahl's New Haven is much attention paid to municipal bureaucracies. Francis Rourke even remarks that one might never know, from reading Dahl's *Who Governs?*, that New Haven had a bureaucracy.[13] Yet virtually every policy decision of urban government depends for execution on the capacities and willingness of the bureaucracy. Few important decisions are self-executing. But bureaucrats do more than simply implement policy. They are a highly attentive and interested public with unusually high stakes in policy outcomes; they form an interest group that favors certain policy directions.[14] We have previously met the municipal bureaucracy in our discussion of its roles as urban interest group and decision maker. It is often dominated by two motivations: first, the desire to maintain its autonomy, security, and freedom from political interference, and second, an interest in program expansion. These motivations give bureaucrats both conservative and expansionist interests in the policy process. Sayre and Kaufman found that in New York City "bureaucratic groups, especially as they mature in their organization and in their self-awareness as cohesive groups, share with all other groups the aspiration to be self-sufficient and autonomous. In fact, bureaucracies appear to present one of the strongest expressions of this general tendency."[15]

As it is so often, New York City may be *sui generis*. There city bureaucracies are protected by one of the nation's strongest civil-service systems, with entrance examinations scored to three decimal places and virtual tenure accrual after six months on the job.[16] Strong municipal unions protect employees from the mayor and city council. In the city's public school system the decisions taken at 110 Livingston Street, the offices of the school administration, trickle down to neighborhood schools. Bureaucracies resist changes in work rules taken to improve productivity. They dominate by their monopoly of routine decisions. We will show in Chapter 10 how bureaucratic decision rules have more to do with the delivery of municipal services than any other factor. This seems especially true in New York City, where every recent mayor has reported a losing battle against bureaucratic power.

But New York City lacks one crucial bureaucrat found in cities that use the council-manager plan of government. The city manager is almost always more than a mere administrator. One survey of city managers reported that more than 90 percent claimed "always or nearly always" to set the city council's agenda, three-fourths claimed "always or nearly always" to play a leading role in municipal policy making, and more than 60 percent claimed "always or nearly always" to initiate new municipal policies.[17] Clearly people often overestimate their own importance, and possibly city managers are no exception. But because the code of professional ethics of city managers clearly forbids their policy-making role, these estimates can be taken seriously. Most American cities are council-manager cities. Hence the authority of city managers cannot be lightly dismissed. In many places, the city manager is a "de facto mayor," making policy decisions and shaping urban goals. There is no analogue to their role at the national or state level. But on the urban level the city manager is frequently the major actor in making urban policy.

We have then three theories of urban power. One holds that power is likely concentrated in private-sector elites governing in their own interest. This "elitist" perspective finds support in discovering how much power corporate executives (such as the leaders of United States Steel in Gary, Indiana) or bankers wield in city politics. The second theory is often called "pluralism" and emphasizes group politics. Pluralism may coexist with strong or weak elected leadership (Chicago under Mayor Daley and San Francisco under almost any mayor are polar examples). But most critical local decisions are made through electoral and official channels. The third perspective emphasizes that power is often relatively invisible, because it is concentrated in the masters of routine, the urban bureaucracies. City managers in council-manager cities and service bureaucracies everywhere have vast powers that ultimately determine the shape of urban policy. Our own view is that the accuracy of these theories is variable from place to place and from time to time. We suggest, therefore, a triangular notion of power in the city.

A Triangular Model of Power in the City

Combining three perspectives on urban power, we suggest that American cities vary not along a single dimension from "pluralistic" to "elitist," but rather along three dimensions. Figure 7.1 depicts our argument visually. There we show three poles of power: bureaucrats,

Figure 7.1   A Triangular Model of Community Power

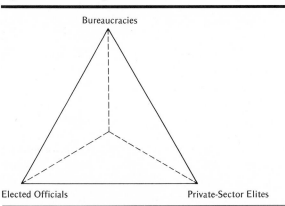

Bureaucracies

Elected Officials   Private-Sector Elites

private-sector elites, and elected decision makers. Probably no American city contains one element that completely overawes the others. Rather, cities vary in the degree to which one or the other element dominates. Floyd Hunter's Atlanta may represent an extreme case of dominance by private-sector elites. Yet Dahl's New Haven and Mayor Daley's Chicago concentrated power in the hands of elected officials. This is not to say that private-sector elites or public bureaucracies were impotent in New Haven or Chicago. But it does suggest that elected officials were more powerful *vis-à-vis* other elements than may have been true in Atlanta. Finally, New York City is often cited as a case of bureaucratic dominance. Countless medium-sized cities exhibit a mixed pattern of power in the bureaucratic sector and the private-elite sector. In those communities, public office holding may be no more than grudging "public service," mayors and council members serve part time, have no staffs, and tend to defer to city administrators and the Chamber of Commerce. To be sure, it is unlikely that we will ever be able to measure power so precisely that we can locate any city mathematically on the vectors of Figure 7.1. Our argument is suggestive but not empirically verifiable. It does, however, stress that power patterns vary from place to place.

They also vary from time to time in a single city. Many students of community power have stressed that patterns of power change over time. Dahl, for example, showed how power in New Haven had passed from the old elites — he called them the "patricians" — to newer ethnic groups.[18] A "bifurcation" of power had occurred, in which the economic and political elites were no longer fused.[19] Agger, Goldrich, and Swanson studied power structures in four communities over several years and concluded that the nature of power could change quite frequently over time.[20] And, of course, few observers would conclude that Atlanta politics today is the same as Hunter described it in the early 1950s. The demographic changes we described in Chapter 3 took their toll in Atlanta's power structure. The city, like many other large central cities, became heavily black, resulting in the election of Maynard Jackson as Atlanta's first black mayor. The private-sector elite of Atlanta is certainly alive and well (though Jimmy Carter took some of its members to Washington with him), but Maynard Jackson would not figure prominently in a theory that bankers, industrialists, and financiers dominate local politics. Demographic changes may be slow, but they are very sure ways of altering the character of urban power.

Perhaps in most cities the most significant alteration in the pattern of power has been the rise of the bureaucracies to a position of near-hegemony. Theodore Lowi describes the rise of "the new machines," which are the urban bureaucracies fortified by civil service protection and unionization.[21] The new machines thrive on the decentralized power in city halls. The party machine once provided a semblance of centralization of authority. But we have shown earlier how machine politics was typically defeated by reform politics. We have also noted the formal fragmentation of the municipal governments that survive the machines. This fragmentation is characterized by relative decentralization, weakening of the formal and political powers of the mayor's office, and proliferation of independent boards and commissions. The disappearance of the machines left in its wake considerable disorganization of the policy-making process. City government is characterized not by absence of political resources but by their dispersion in countless hands; centralized leadership from political officials is difficult to obtain. One effect of this dispersion is that the greatest single combination of organized resources now resides in public bureaucracies. They are, according to Lowi, the new machines in urban politics: "The legacy of Reform is the bureaucratic city-state," in which cities "become well-run but ungoverned."[22] The new machines are different from the old machines in their low tolerance for inefficiency and corruption. They also have a resource base of formal authority rather than votes. But, according to Lowi,

[t]he New Machines are machines because they are relatively irresponsible structures of power. That is, each agency shapes important public policies, yet the leadership of each is relatively self-perpetuating and not readily subject to the controls of any higher authority.

The New Machines are machines in that the power of each, while resting ultimately upon services rendered to the community, depends upon its cohesiveness as a small minority in the midst of the vast dispersion of the multitude.[23]

Many of the old machines were run by the mayors. Now, however, any mayor with an innovative turn of mind must confront the new machine, in which he is permanently denied membership.

PRIVATE-SECTOR ELITES:
THE URBAN "POWER STRUCTURE"

Private-sector elites may be very powerful in some cities under some circumstances. In other cities and under other circumstances, they may be only one actor among many. Not surprisingly some policy issues touch the interests of private-sector elites and energize them to action. Greer, for example, shows how United States Steel resisted efforts by the city of Gary and the State of Indiana to control pollution at its Gary works.[24] Maintaining economic viability of downtown areas is another issue that evokes elite participation. Almost every city has a chamber of commerce, and major cities have organizations of leading economic notables to exert influence on economic decisions. Henry

Ford, Jr., chairs the Detroit organization of leadership in the private sector. Often these groups favor visible, brick-and-mortar projects such as office buildings, civic centers, theater complexes, and highways. In Detroit, they pushed the construction of the Renaissance Center. Yet leaders of these groups often live in suburbs rather than in cities, which may reduce their influence on a central city's mayor and council. Some issues matter very little to private-economic elites. The character of urban neighborhoods or urban schools matters little to economic elites who have taken or can easily take the exit option. One study of the distribution of municipal services to neighborhoods in San Antonio, Texas, hypothesized that areas with large numbers of power-structure members would receive better services. But the relation between the neighborhood's share of power holders and the services it received was nonexistent.[25]

The power of power structures is itself variable rather than constant from city to city. There has been a massive outpouring of research on the question of urban power structures. One book-length bibliographical review has even appeared to summarize this massive research effort. The yield of this research has enabled us to make some definitive statements about the variation in American urban power structures. Let us, therefore, examine the antecedents and consequences of structures of urban power.

Antecedents and Consequences of Variations in Power Structure

ANTECEDENTS   Are certain kinds of communities more likely than others to have monolithic power structures? Does the structure of community power make any difference in the kinds of public policies pursued by local government? These questions have received considerably less attention than have questions of the shape or structure of power and the mere identification of power holders. Nor is either of them easily answered. In some obvious respects, however, there are remarkable similarities between Atlanta and New Haven. Both have recently been governed by mayors nationally regarded as progressive. Both are central cities where parks are built, police patrol neighborhoods, fires are fought, and hospitals and public utilities are maintained. Although neither city is usually singled out as an extreme case of discrimination, racial disorders have occurred in both. What are the antecedents and consequences of variations in community power structures, and can they be identified?

This question can be answered more directly if we classify power structures on a continuum ranging from monolithic to pluralistic, as indicated in Figure 7.2. Although several classification schemes have been suggested,[26] the one adapted from Charles M. Bonjean's and

Figure 7.2   Four Dimensions of Power Structure

"Pluralist" Structure	DIMENSION	"Monolithic" Structure
Leaders hold public or associational office	LEGITIMACY ←——→	Leaders do not hold public or associational office
Leaders are recognized by general public	VISIBILITY ←——→	Leaders are unknown to general public
Leaders do not form a cohesive, interacting group	COHESIVENESS ←——→	Leaders form a cohesive, interacting group
Leaders are specialized and exercise power in one or a few policy areas	SCOPE OF ←——→ INFLUENCE	Leaders are general and exercise power in most or all policy areas

Source: Adapted from Charles M. Bonjean and David M. Olson, "Community Leadership: Directions of Research," *Administrative Science Quarterly, 8* (December 1964), 291–300.

David M. Olson's analysis of power structures captures the major disagreements among the researchers; it uses the dimensions of *legitimacy, visibility, scope of influence,* and *cohesion.*[27] The two models of pluralistic and monolithic power structures represent extreme points on a continuum. It is doubtful that any existing power structure is completely monolithic or pluralistic. Given the classification scheme, the question then becomes, what variables are associated with power structures that tend toward one or the other extreme? Several antecedents of power structures may be suggested in the form of propositions.[28] These propositions are only tentative generalizations rather than absolute laws of social structure. Each community possesses certain features that make it unique and imperfectly comparable with other communities. What is really important may be not the presence of particular factors but their combination and interaction in a particular setting. Moreover, these generalizations are derived from a wide assortment of studies that differ among themselves on the most appropriate methodology for studying community power. The propositions, therefore, are better viewed as tools for analysis than as iron laws of power distribution in the city.

1. The larger the number of inhabitants in a community, the more pluralistic is the power structure.

The evidence from case studies is mixed. However, Terry N. Clark's analysis of decision-making structures in 51 cities has revealed a moderate relationship ($r = .384$) between community size and a measure of pluralistic decision-making structures.[29] The smaller the community, the greater is the probability of dominance by a monolithic structure. One study of a tiny upstate New York village has identified a small clique of influentials who controlled the village government.[30] On the other hand, the relationship between size and type of power structure is not perfect. Reputational studies of Atlanta and Dallas have concluded that monolithic power structures dominate those communities.[31] Size per se may be less important than certain structural characteristics associated with size. Large cities are ordinarily more socially and economically heterogeneous. It may be this heterogeneity, rather than size alone, that is associated with pluralistic power structures. We can frame this argument in terms of a porposition.

2. The more diversified the economic system within a community, the more pluralistic is the power structure.

The evidence for proposition 2 ranges from a slight tendency to strong support.[32] The logic of the proposition suggests that multiple economic centers in the private sector produce alternative resource bases for competition in community decision making. One particular feature of the economic structure that seems relevant to the structure of power is the degree of industrialization.

3. The more industrialized the community, the more pluralistic is the power structure.

Almost by definition, industrialization will broaden the economic base of a community beyond commercial and service-oriented enterprises and will introduce another potential center of power in the economic system. Moreover, industrialization is usually (at least outside the South) associated with labor unions, which offer an additional source of power in community decision making.[33] The implication can also be framed as a proposition.

4. The stronger labor unions are in a community, the more pluralistic is the power structure.

One other proposition relates community power distribution to the economic system.

5. The larger the proportion of absentee-owned enterprises in a community, the more pluralistic is the power structure.

Perhaps the most monolithic power structure ever identified was that in "Middletown," where a single local family owned the major source of livelihood for the town's entire population and dominated nearly all facets of community life.[34] In cities dominated by absentee ownership, the executives of such nonlocal firms tend to have lower stakes in community activities and to play less active roles.

Social heterogeneity parallels economic differentiation in its association with more pluralistic forms of power.

6. The more socially heterogeneous the community, the more pluralistic is the power structure.

However, a community where elites do not value political equality and mass participation is unlikely to fit proposition 6. A community dominated by racists is not a likely candidate for social pluralism. So:

7. Pluralism is promoted by community and, particularly, elite attitudes emphasizing widespread participation and political equality.

A well-developed network of secondary associations — civic groups, social clubs, ethnic and religious organizations, political-action groups, and so on — provides multiple channels for expression of opinion, as well as an organizational basis for alternative leadership structures.[35] Another proposition therefore follows:

8. The larger the number of secondary associations in the community, the greater is the probability of pluralism.

There has been too little research on the relation between governmental structure and power structure to permit confidence in any generalization. Nonetheless, several writers suggest that governmental reformism, particularly nonpartisanship, is associated with monolithic power structures.

9a. Nonpartisanship is more commonly associated with monolithic structures of power.

9b. Competitive party politics is more commonly associated with pluralistic structures of power.

John Walton found a strong relationship between competition among local parties and pluralism in community power.[36] Clark's study of 51 communities went even further in relating reformism to monolithic structures.[37]

10. The higher the level of reformism of political institutions (form of government, type of elections, and type of constituencies), the more monolithic is the decision-making structure.

The degree of governmental reform was the strongest predictor of power structure in Clark's 51 cities. Certain features of the reformist syndrome seem to produce less pluralism in community decision making. Among them may be the elimination of competition among parties through the nonpartisan ballot, the depoliticization of the mayor's office, and the reduction in working-class voting turnout associated with reformed institutions.

A significant consequence of community power structure is its impact on citizen participation, as several studies have indicated.

11. Competition among different elements of the power structure is a necessary condition for widespread citizen participation.

Agger, Goldrich, and Swanson concluded that "a competitive political leadership is necessary . . . for the existence of a power structure of the mass type."[38] If the cohesion dimension of leadership changes from competitive to consensual, the distribution of political power in the community will thus change from relatively broad to relatively narrow. This finding is consistent with much writing by democratic theorists who stress competition among elites as the sine qua non of democratic government.[39]

CONSEQUENCES FOR POLICY   Whatever the nature or source of a community's power structure, its relation to the level or distribution of urban public policies is not well established. In discussing the consequences of power structure, Bonjean and Olson deplored the fact that "even fewer studies have been concerned with consequences of leadership structure characteristics than with antecedents."[40] This neglect is particularly unfortunate if, as we believe, the central task of urban political analysis is the understanding of policy outcomes.[41]

Perhaps power structures do not make much difference in the outputs of community political systems. Many decisions by local governments are automatic responses to the requirements of state and federal statutes and prior financial commitments. Regardless of the concentration or dispersion of power, local governments are constrained by Dillon's rule, by tax rates and municipal indebtedness, and by the laws and administrative rulings of states and the federal government. Yet several hypotheses suggest variations in the effects of power structure on policies. Cities with monolithic power structures may furnish fewer public services to poor neighborhoods (unless, of course, the power structure is public regarding), may emphasize economic-development over social-welfare policies, and may tax and spend at lower than average levels. But until we have more data, we cannot demonstrate that policy choices in monolithic cities are notably different from those in pluralistic cities.

Why Power Structures Have Fallen on Hard Times

Perhaps there was once a time when some crowd at the civic club could dictate policy behind the scenes. Our view is that the clout wielded by economic elites in urban politics is frequently exaggerated. But even if we concede the capacities often attributed to an urban power structure, we still suggest that they wield less power than they once did. Let us examine three cases — Atlanta, Dallas, and San Antonio — whose power structures were reputedly among the most cohesive and dominant, and see what hard times have befallen them.

Atlanta was the subject of the book that actually coined the phrase *community power structure.* Hunter's book included a chapter on black leadership structure in Atlanta. When the research was conducted—before the Supreme Court had even outlawed school segregation—the black community was pitifully weak. He described the infrequent contacts between black and white leaders as "stealthy," where whites feared recognition of their contacts with blacks and blacks going hat in hand to whites for favors.[42] But things have changed in Atlanta. The election of black mayor, Maynard Jackson, and the appointment of a black Atlanta congressman, Andrew Young, as Ambassador to the United Nations, have altered significantly the role of black Atlantans. Economic elites are not without influence in contemporary Atlanta. But national forces such as the civil-rights movement have altered the once-dominant role of economic elites. The changing patterns of urban demography have also changed the face of power in Atlanta. The suburbanization of whites and the increasing black share of the electorate have operated to change the community power structure of Atlanta.

Dallas and San Antonio long had power structures as formidable as the one that Hunter described in Atlanta. For almost 40 years Dallas was strongly influenced by the Citizens Charter Association, a group dominated by social and economic elites. Typical of the calibre of people leading the CCA was long-time Dallas mayor Erik Jonsson. As chairman of the board of Texas Instruments, he was a forceful spokesman for business interests in the city. Yet over the steady opposition of the CCA, Mayor Wes Wise held his office, beating a CCA-sponsored candidate by a 43,488 to 28,699 margin in 1975.[43] The CCA still held an edge in council seats. But just before the 1975 local election a federal judge ordered the city to abandon at-large elections because they unconstitutionally discriminated against minority voters. In the future, black voters—never as enthusiastic about the CCA as white voters—will probably elect a larger share of local officeholders.

A similar story can be told about San Antonio. Long dominated by the Good Government League, the city's political system seemed to change significantly by the mid-1970s. The electoral success of the GGL had once rivaled that of the old-style political machine. Since its inception in 1954 until the municipal elections of 1973, the GGL-backed candidate was successful in 77 of 81 local council races.[44] The GGL was not a secret cabal or a casual organization. It was a formal, permanent organization, with stable leadership, solid financing, and an elected board of directors. It maintained its offices in a savings and loan association building partly owned by the GGL's long-time mayor. Powerholders in the city were typically well known. One city newspaper even runs an annual listing of the 10 most powerful people and organizations in the city and invites its readers to send in their own nominations. Yet again, as in Dallas and Atlanta, the GGL fell on hard times. New organizations of chicano and black voters were formed to challenge the GGL's hegemony. One institutional device permitting continued GGL dominance was the at-large election, but under pressure from the Justice Department, the city moved toward a single-member district system in 1975. Eventually, in early 1977 the GGL folded. New groups came to share power with the remnants of the GGL leadership.

We think that several factors have combined to weaken the traditional hold of power structures. One — and it appears in all three of our cases — is the growing power of minority groups in big-city politics. Changing demography has abetted the political clout of blacks and Latinos in urban elections. Federal policy has also played a role. Court decisions striking down voting discrimination and even at-large elections have weakened the ability of citywide power structures to control elections. Moreover, many potential members of the economic elite have taken the exit option, vacating the city and moving to the suburbs. While people can be influential in places where they cannot legally vote, their power is nonetheless blunted. It is probably too soon to sound a death knell for the cohesive urban power structure first described by Floyd Hunter in Atlanta. But times change, and changing times take a toll even of the powerful.

ELECTED DECISION MAKERS: THE COUNCIL

The Councilmember

It is difficult to describe a *typical* councilmember. They come from varying income, educational, occupational, and ethnic backgrounds; have different views about municipal government; and, depending on the particular states and municipalities in which they hold office, exercise different powers and responsibilities. Yet we can gain perspective on the city councilmember by positing some typical characteristics and then suggesting factors responsible for deviations from those characteristics. Typically, a councilmember is male, middle-aged, a businessman or professional, relatively well educated and well-to-do, white, active in civic associations, and Republican. A study of councilmembers in St. Louis County revealed that 70 percent were at least high-school graduates and that 53 percent had completed college. About one-half were from managerial, professional, or proprietary occupations, and another 22 percent were from white-collar occupations.[45]

The use of ward or at-large elections also affects the composition of the council. Ward systems tend to increase the representation of lower socioeconomic groups and minorities. Sloan found that cities using ward systems elected larger proportions of councilmembers from minority groups than did cities using at-large elections.[46] The at-large system increases the costs of elections and forces all contenders to run before a constituency of the whole. Minority-group candidates in many cities thus face a white Protestant majority. Even when minority-group candidates are successful, under the at-large system they are usually the more moderate ones.

Factors other than these class and election procedures influence the types of people chosen for the council. Some of these factors are specific to a particular city or even to a particular campaign. But among the more general ones are: (1) the degree to which labor unions and ethnic and racial groups are organized and involved in local politics, (2) whether the city pays councilmembers enough to sustain working-class representation on the council, (3) whether the party system facilitates representation of various social groups, and (4) whether a covert power structure recruits or prevents recruitment of certain kinds of candidates.

Roles and Resources

RESPONSIBILITIES   *The New York Times Magazine* once entitled a story about a New York councilman "Man in a Wind Tunnel."[47] Its focus was the multiple pressures constantly buffeting an officeholder in the nation's largest city. In smaller and less heterogeneous communities these pressures are less intense. A better analogy is perhaps life in a partial vacuum. Whatever the appropriate metaphor, the council and its members are legally responsible for making all ordinances pursuant to state law and the municipal charter. Yet this statement leaves much unsaid, just as a description of the U.S. Congress solely in terms of its constitutional responsibilities would be incomplete or even misleading.

In the broadest sense, the city council makes policy for the city; that is, it chooses among alternative courses for taxing people, spending money, and the like. In a narrower sense the formal powers of the council vary a good deal from one form of government to another. The council operating in the council-manager city is supposed to make policy but to leave questions dealing with administration to the city manager and his administrative agencies.

The council-manager plan enshrines the alleged dichotomy between policy and administration. In the strong mayor-council form of government, the initiative for policy is still more likely to come from the mayor than from the council, although the latter is not confined so narrowly as in the council-manager city. The scope of the council's power is probably greatest in the weak-mayor system. Here the mayor shares power with other elected officials, and the council itself sometimes appoints officials, prepares the budget, or performs tasks that are considered administrative in other forms of government. A commission government fuses legislative and administrative authority in the council; each councilmember is also the administrator of some particular branch or department of the city government. Commissioners are prone to mind their own bailiwicks and to let others do the same, which promotes mutual noninterference at the council level.

As do all legislative bodies, the municipal council performs an important representative function. Yet different councilmembers will have different views about the proper role of the representative, and the formal structures of municipal government foster particular styles of representation. In the ward system, representation is likely to mean a narrow bricks-and-mortar orientation: Ward councilmembers tend to look after their constituencies' desires for paved streets, parks, school facilities, and other tangible outputs of municipal government. In one Michigan city using the ward system, one councilman shouted to another at a meeting, "You bastard, you had three more blocks of black-topping in your ward last year than I had; you'll not get another vote from me until I get three extra blocks."[48] One New York City councilman, explaining his approach to the city budget, said:

. . . the first thing I look for is the budget items involving my district. Are we getting what we're entitled to? Are we being shortchanged on a library or not getting a school we were promised? . . . It's only after I've done all I can for my own area that I look into the rest of the budget.[49]

In the constituency at large, a councilmember's political future depends less on material gains for a small area. A councilmember at large can afford to affiliate with broad social, economic, or political interests, rather than binding himself or herself to geographical interests.

ROLES   The ways in which a municipal councilmember attempts to represent the constituency depend on his or her representational role. Political theorists debate the extent to which a representative should be either a trustee or a delegate. The trustee role emphasizes the representative's obligation to vote according to conscience and best judgment, regardless of whether his or her vote happens to follow constituents' preferences. The delegate role obligates the representative to vote according to the perception of constituents' sentiments, regardless of personal views.

Studies of city councilmembers suggest overwhelming support for the trustee orientation toward representation.[50] Almost three-fourths of St. Louis area councilmembers said that they made decisions on the basis of their own judgment or principles. Councilmembers seem to prefer their own to their constituents' thinking on matters of public policy, and Downes has hypothesized that this attitude may reflect councilmembers own beliefs that "they act as councilmen in their spare time and receive little or no monetary compensation." Therefore they can "ignore the blandishments of neighborhood, ward, or other specialized interests."[51] It may also reflect the very imperfect information on public preferences that councilmembers receive. When input institutions such as elections, parties, and interest groups provide vague or conflicting intimations of public opinion, the councilmember may find it easier to use personal judgment as a guide to policy.

Partly because most councilmembers have trustee orientations, they are relatively free to ignore the sentiments of their constituents. But Kenneth Prewitt finds that they also share an ethic of *volunteerism,* which further immunizes them from the necessity of responding to constituent attitudes.[52] It is easy for a councilmember whose political ambitions are negligible to vote personal policy preferences and to ignore constituents' wishes. Prewitt's councilmembers hold elected offices but are not always veterans of tough contests. About one-fourth of the councilmembers in his sample had been initially appointed to their offices on a predecessor's resignation, and if they ran for reelection it was with the advantages of an incumbent. Further, only a minority expressed a wish for a political career extending to higher offices.[53]

When asked if it was easy or difficult to go against majority preferences in policy making, one councilman said: "Easy, I am an independent type of individual. I don't feel the weight of voter responsibility. I am not all fired up for a political career." Such councilmembers do not fear the ballot, which makes electoral accountability and reprisals difficult. Although volunteerism may be more widespread in suburban, middle-class areas than in big-city politics, its prevalence does not make it easier for the electorate to control local government.

RESOURCES   The city councilmember's major political resource is his legal authority to make policy. Whatever influence other elements of the city's political system may have, it is still the legal responsibility of the council to pass ordinances (consistent, of course, with the city's own charter and the laws of the state), to enact the city budget, to hire and fire the manager in a council-manager city, and so forth. Councilmembers may also possess as individuals great political skill, some prestige, and experience in the procedures of decision making. But most are limited in their resources of time and information, particularly technical information. Serving as a city councilmember is a full-time job only in the largest cities. Elsewhere he must divide his time between his private occupation and his public service. Staff assistance is minimal or nonexistent on almost all city councils. Individual council members find it tempting, and necessary, to rely on the recommendations of their professional city manager or department administrators, or the full-time mayor who can rely, in turn, on the advice of staff assistants. Moreover, councilmembers face increasingly complex and technical policy issues with only their own wits and political wisdom to guide them. Many of these issues are too broad in scope for the council—or any other city officials—to tackle by themselves. Issues such as air and water pollution and mass transportation involve areawide coordination and a scale of financial resources that make state and federal governments the prime actors, and may reduce city councils to the role of observers.

ELECTED DECISION MAKERS: THE MAYORS

The Variability of the Mayoral Role

It is easy—but very misleading—to draw analogies between an American mayor and other chief executives such as governors and presidents. Both the formal powers and the informal clout in the mayor's office vary from city to city and from occupant to occupant. Understanding the mayor, therefore, is partly a matter of understanding why some mayors are strong in spite of weak formal authority, while others remain weak even where they command significant formal resources. Mayor Sam Yorty of Los Angeles used to respond to critics of his lackluster leadership by stressing how little formal authority the mayor had.[54] The late Mayor Daley, on the other hand, was mayor in a technically weak-mayor system but hardly lacked informal resources. A strong Democratic organization, of which Daley was the chairman, gave him plenty of "clout."

It is therefore important to distinguish between the *formal authority* and the *political resources* available to the mayor. The formal authority derives from several factors. Other things being equal, the mayor has more formal authority when he or she:

- is directly elected
- has a veto power over council legislation
- plays some role in the budget-making process
- has the power to make appointments of key department heads and other city officials
- serves a longer term of office

Not all mayors can claim these formal powers. A majority of American mayors, for example, do not possess the power to veto council legislation. Although most mayors in mayor-council cities are elected, almost half the mayors in council-manager cities are elected by the council rather than directly by the voters. Staff resources are typically weak except in the largest cities. The mayor's "staff" in a city of a half million people may consist of a couple of secretaries, and aide or two, and a press secretary.

The differences between the mayors in a strong-mayor city and in a weak-mayor city are, of course, matters of degree. A weak mayor can rarely be called a chief executive. He shares administrative power with separately elected officials, with independent boards and commissions, and with the council itself. Often he has no central role in budget making but shares power equally with other officials. In Milwaukee, for example,

> ... the mayor does not prepare an executive budget as is done in cities of the "strong mayor" type. Instead, a number of cooks are involved in the making of the budget pie. The Budget Department goes over requests with individual department heads, usually paring their requests sharply. The formal budget is prepared at hearings conducted by the Budget Examining Committee of the Board of Estimates, on which the mayor serves as chairman, together with the council's Finance Committee, the Comptroller, and the Budget Supervisor as secretary.[55]

In a strong-mayor city, the mayor plays a more crucial role in both policy initiation and administration. He typically dominates the budget-formulation process and key administrative appointments. To be sure, these formal differences do not always predict accurately the power relations at city hall. Sometimes, as in Chicago and New Haven, politically strong mayors operate within weak-mayor systems. Still, however, the formal powers of the mayor make it easier or more difficult for him to influence policy making.

Probably the most important structural feature explaining variation in formal powers of the mayor is whether the city is council-manager or mayor-council. The weakest mayors in mayor-council cities are likely to be stronger even than the strongest mayors in council-manager cities. The mayor who coexists with a city manager is typically shorn of formal authority. Only half of them are directly elected; 7 in 10 have no veto power; almost all are part time and are paid so little that they cannot devote full energies to the mayor's office.

The *political resources* available to the mayor are not the same thing as his or her formal authority. No political resource is more important than an electoral organization. Mayors who have potent electoral organizations can rely on external support even when formal authority may be weak. Typically these organizations depend on one of three kinds of political bases. Some mayors depend on a party machine. Obviously the mayor of Chicago and other cities with strong party organizations fit this pattern. Other mayors have depended on a private-sector elite. Mayors of Atlanta, Dallas, San Antonio, and other cities with a dominant power structure relied on the slate-making and financial powers of an economic elite. Increasingly, though, mayors are depending on a racial or ethnic organization. Black mayors such as Maynard Jackson in Atlanta or Tom Bradley in Los Angeles have nurtured political organization in black communities. With a political organization behind the mayor, he or she can depend on support from a stable constituency. Mayors who win election solely on the basis of personal followings must spend a large part of their time worrying about reelection. Personal followings have an ephemeral quality about them.

A Typology of Mayoral Leadership

We have been focusing on two elements that contribute to a mayor's leadership capabilities, the formal authority of the office and the political resources available to the mayor. If we combine these — as in Figure 7.3 — we have a fourfold typology of mayoral leadership. The typology is meant only to be suggestive, not definitive. For one thing, there is no neat line separating strong from weak authority, nor strong from weak political resources. Nonetheless, there are clearly two polar opposite types of mayoral leadership. One we call the "ribbon cutter," simply because mayors weak in both formal authority and political resources are likely to be more ceremonial than actual political leaders (much like, say, the Queen of England). The ribbon cutter is a common role in council-manager cities. But some larger cities have mayors who are really little more than ribbon-cutters. Jeff Pressman describes the office and its occupant in Oakland, California. "In the

Figure 7.3   A Typology of Mayoral Leadership Roles

	Formal Authority	
	Strong	Weak
Political Resources — Strong	"Power brokers"	"Frustrated activists," "Conservatives"
Political Resources — Weak	"Frustrated activists," "Conservatives"	"Ribbon cutters"

nongroup, nonpartisan, and non-electoral political system of Oakland," he says, "it is entirely possible for a 'nonpolitical' civic reformer like John Reading to attain the position of mayor without really trying for it."[56] Once in office, Reading discovered that exercising effective leadership without many formal powers and few political resources was difficult indeed.

The polar opposite of the ribbon cutter is the *power broker,* rich in formal authority and in political resources as well. In the light of what we have already said about the relative weakness of mayors' powers in comparison with those of governors and presidents, it is not surprising that this cell of our typology is not filled with many mayors. In fact, we find it difficult to think of more than a half dozen examples. Mayor Richard Lee of New Haven seems to qualify, if we are to believe the laudatory reports written about his political leadership skills.[57] The power-broker cell is now emptier after the death of Richard J. Daley of Chicago. Mayor Daley would have found it hard to comprehend the political system of Oakland. Though technically Chicago is a weak-mayor structure, Daley actually capitalized on the multiplicity of boards, commissions, and other elected officials. His appointment powers were vast. Every major municipal appointment was cleared with "the man on five" (the mayor's office was on the fifth floor of City Hall), and hundreds of minor ones passed across his desk. Even those whom he did not appoint, he nonetheless helped select through his control of the Cook County Democratic Organization. The mayor presided over the city council, a body of 50 aldermen almost all of whom owed their office to Daley's machine. The handful of independent and Republican aldermen were drowned in a sea of points of order, which the mayor usually found meritorious. University of Illinois, Chicago Circle political scientist Richard Simpson, an independent alderman, even found that critical council meetings were scheduled during his clases. Despite his malapropisms ("we must rise to higher and higher platitudes," "the police are not here to create disorder, the police are here to preserve disorder") and his uncharismatic style, "the man on five" was an urban power broker *par excellence.* Private-sector elites came to him for positions on the school board; blacks depended on his support for their political futures; ethnic neighborhoods and labor unions needed his support for their demands. To be a power broker, one must first have power. Mayor Daley had it, used it, and — one supposes — took it to his grave with him on 20 December 1976.

Most American mayors fall between these two extreme types. Mayors generously endowed in formal authority may be weak in political resources, or vice versa. Or they are only modestly endowed on both. The result is a mayoral role we call the "frustrated activist" or the "conservative." Such a mayor will discover that his or her grandest schemes and political promises are soon drowned in incremental budgeting, a plethora of independent boards and officeholders, lack of authority over the council, or other limitations. The combination of weakness on one dimension and strength on the other can also yield a conservative leadership style. Mayor Yorty never wanted to make dramatic changes in urban policy and always rationalized his conservatism by emphasizing his incapacity. Perhaps the oversupply of frustrated activists and conservatives explains why the urban mayor's office is so often a political dead end. Kotter and Lawrence studied 20 urban mayors and found that 17 had ambitions for higher office. Not one, however, made it.[58] Very few nationally prominent politicians got their start as a mayor (Hubert Humphrey, the former mayor of Minneapolis, is one exception). John Lindsay, Sam Yorty, Kevin White, Richard Hatcher, Carl Stokes, and Moon Landrieu are all competent politicians. But no higher call ever came.

The New Black Mayors

A changing urban demography has put a new group of black mayors in office. Carl Stokes of Cleveland, Kenneth Gibson of Newark, and Richard Hatcher of Gary were among the first to break the color barrier and steer the rocky urban ship of state. Listed in Table 7.1 are black mayors in cities over 25,000 population in 1974. It does not seem essential for black populations to be substantial to elect a black mayor. In a few cities (such as Berkeley, California and Boulder, Colorado) black mayors were selected by overwhelmingly white electorates. But these places are often bastions of liberalism or university communities. Among the larger cities with black mayors, Los Angeles elected Tom Bradley when blacks were less than one-fifth of the electorate. But generally the correlation between percent black and the election of a black mayor is a strong one.

Michael Preston analyzed these new black mayors and discovered that their problems and powers were not much different than their white counterparts elsewhere. In fact, he speculates that high expectations may lead to unrealistic beliefs about what black mayors can accomplish. "Black mayors," he concludes, "face severe limitations that will restrict what they can accomplish. . . . Where high expectations exist and performance is low, the growth of electoral politics as the new cutting edge will surely diminish."[59] Maynard Jackson of Atlanta, for example, immediately confronted resistance to his goals by service bureaucracies. His efforts to fire the city's police chief were vigorously resisted. Kenneth Gibson in Newark has discovered that the urban political economy of deterioration is as real for black as for white mayors. All black mayors have found it necessary to appease white as well as black constituents.

Table 7.1   Percent Black Population in Cities
of over 25,000 with Black Mayors, 1974

City	Percent Black
Prichard, Alabama	46
Berkeley, California	20
Compton, California	65
Los Angeles, California	16
Boulder, Colorado	*
Atlanta, Georgia	46
East St. Louis, Illinois	63
Gary, Indiana	48
College Park, Maryland	3
Detroit, Michigan	37
Grand Rapids, Michigan	9
Highland Park, Michigan	46
Inkster, Michigan	44
Pontiac, Michigan	23
Ypsilanti, Michigan	16
East Orange, New Jersey	46
New Brunswick, New Jersey	17
Newark, New Jersey	48
Chapel Hill, North Carolina	8
Raleigh, North Carolina	20
Cincinnati, Ohio	24
Dayton, Ohio	27
Washington, D.C.	64

* Less than one percent.

THE BUREAUCRACIES

Maynard Jackson's frustrating efforts to dislodge the Atlanta police chief show how much power bureaucracies can exhibit. In a council-manager city, bureaucracies are even more powerful than in the mayor-council city. Bureaucracies dominate the urban decision-making process because they control critical resources. They are typically protected by a strong civil-service system, often called a "merit system," which ensures job security and protects them from "political interference." One indication of the potent policy-making role of bureaucrats is its frequent appearance in subsequent chapters dealing with urban policy outputs. Chapter 10, for example, will show the dominant role of urban bureaucracies in the allocations of municipal services. Our discussion of the police emphasizes the role that police discretion plays in law-enforcement policy. Bureaucratic rules and routines give the budget-making process (discussed in Chapter 8) an incremental character. Let us now, therefore, take a look at the "new machines," in Lowi's words, which have come to exert considerable clout in urban policy making.

The City Manager

The city manager is a professional city administrator who is also chief executive in the council-manager city. The professional organization of city managers is the International City Management Association (formerly the International City Managers' Association). For many years, the ICMA has provided a model city charter, which outlines the ideal relations between the manager and the council and is the basis of numerous actual city charters and many state enabling statutes.

The city manager is hired by the council, serves at its discretion, and is subject to removal at any time by a majority vote of the council. In the early days of the council-manager plan, most managers were civil engineers by training. Today most city managers have been trained in graduate programs of public administration. They are familiar with financial administration, personnel management, municipal law, and planning. Like many professionals in American society, city managers tend to be highly mobile. Only a minority are hometown boys. The career of a typical manager might include work as a staff assistant to an established manager, then a post as assistant city manager, then appointment as manager in a small town, and, finally, similar posts in larger or more prestigious communities.

The official responsibilities of a manager are specified in the city charter. They include: (1) overseeing the execution of policy made by the council, (2) preparing and submitting the budget to the council, (3) appointing and removing the principal department heads (the police and fire chiefs, the personnel and budget officers, and so on), and (4) making recommendations on policy to the council. It is the last point that receives the most varied interpretations. The underlying philosophy of the manager plan specifies the responsibility of the council to make policy and of the manager to administer it. The manager is expected to shun interference in the policy choices of the council. The most egregious violation of the managers' code of ethics is participation in partisan politics. But if the manager is expected to make recommendations to the policy-making council, where is the line drawn between the roles of manager and council?

In practice, of course, there is no clear line between policy and administration. The manager's persuasiveness in his policy recommendations can make him the most powerful figure in a city's policy-making process. Matters ordinarily regarded as administrative are laden with policy implications. The cumulative effect of bureaucratic, or administrative, decisions — many of which are made by the manager's subordinates in the operating units of the city government — may be as significant as any general policy selected by the mayor or council. For example, police treatment of minority groups may have more effect on minority-group attitudes toward law enforcement than does any policy of equal treatment enunciated by the city council.

The Manager's Roles and Resources

In order to define more precisely the roles and behavior of the city manager, Deil S. Wright conducted a survey of 45 managers in cities with populations larger than 100,000. "The behavior of city managers," he wrote, can be "fully and exhaustively characterized by three role categories: managerial, policy, and political."[60] The first managerial role involves his relation with the municipal bureaucracy, including supervision and control of policy administration and personnel. The policy facet of the manager's role includes his relation with the city council, particularly as he is the source of policy recommendations. His political role includes efforts as a community leader and as a representative of community needs and interests before the local council, the community at large, and other units of government. Wright's survey of managers uncovered variations in the ways that they view and perform these three roles.

In his performance of the managerial role, "the capacity of the manager to control the bureaucracy is linked to his abilities to secure information, allocate resources, and impose sanctions (or grant rewards)."[61] The major formal resources available to him in his administrative capacity are his professional staff, his control over the budget, and his power to appoint and remove department heads. Each of these resources may be used to impose constraints and to offer incentives to the municipal bureaucracy. In most council-manager cities, the manager has nearly complete autonomy in his performance of the administrative role. This autonomy is, more than any other factor, at the core of the council-manager system. Many managers guard their administrative autonomy jealously.

The underlying philosophy of the council-manager plan is more ambiguous about the role of manager in policy initiation and recommendations. Still the manager does play a significant role in initiating policy. Wright has concluded that the manager is the dominant policy initiator in most council-manager cities. More than two-thirds of the managers that he surveyed said they set the agendas of the city councils. This task helps them to control the kinds of questions that are raised and the policy options that are considered. The same proportion of managers reported that most items considered by the council were on the agendas at the behest of managers. The city manager is probably the major source of information for any city council. He bears most of the responsibility for creating the "menu" of policy alternatives to be considered. The council will not accept everything on the menu, but the menu does set forth the policies likely to be considered seriously.

Wright has divided the manager's political-leadership role into two components: vertical (extracommunity representation) and horizontal (intracommunity leadership). In dealing with other units of government (particularly the states and the national government), the manager interacts with state or federal bureaucrats. The mayor usually serves as spokesman to elected state or national officials. On the horizontal dimension the manager plays a major role in representing and explaining community policies to the public at large. He ordinarily has no special expertise or information on the political interests of the community, however. His information is technical, not partisan.

Wright found that the manager is most at home in his administrative role, and he devotes most of his time to administrative tasks. Managers report that they obtain more personal and job satisfaction from their administrative than from their other roles.[62] This attitude reflects their basic professional orientation toward efficient management and delivery of public services and towards detailed financial accounting and personnel administration. Their skills are administrative, and their major resource is technical expertise. Their commitments are greatest in matters of capital improvements (bricks and mortar) and established programs. They shoulder responsibility for the formulation of social policy and the burdens of community leadership with less enthusiasm and, perhaps, with less competence. Karl Bosworth wrote some years ago that "the manager is a politician."[63] This view is a useful corrective to myths about apolitical managers. In Wright's study, however, managers appear primarily as administrators; they are more interested in administrative than in political responsibilities.

Ronald O. Loveridge adds to our understanding of city managers with his information from the San Francisco Bay area. He finds that managers espousing a political role for themselves are more likely than self-perceived administrators to have majored in the social sciences in college and to have pursued graduate training in public administration. They are also more likely to be newcomers to local government. Managers oriented to administrative roles, in contrast, are more likely to have begun work without a college degree, and to have moved up in municipal administration through such jobs as public works director, building inspector, city engineer, or personnel director.

Loveridge finds that managers and council members differ sharply in their views of proper managerial behavior. Whereas most of the managers (even those feeling most comfortable as administrators) claim some prerogatives as policy leaders, council members express the older view of management as being strictly administrative and subordinate to the council. The result of these disharmonious views is compromise; neither party acts within the strict boundaries of his role conception. Managers sense the limits of activity that council members will permit; they feel out the situation; work behind the scenes; advise council members in private; educate the council in regard to issues and alternative policies; and generally seek to maintain the council's support. Specific strategies of the manager include the introduction of his policies in the budget that he recommends to the council; writing formal reports to introduce new issues onto the council's agenda; and selecting an outside consulting firm to make recommendations. With each of these actions and astute manager may appear to be removed from the debate about major policy changes, even while he induces the council to consider a problem, defines the terms of its consideration, and structures the presentation of alternatives to highlight his own preferred course of action.[64]

Bureaucratic
Roles and Resources

Expertise — knowledge of how to lay out a highway network, how to fight fires, how to organize an educational system — is the major resource of the technical specialist. Bureaucrats resist encroachments on expertise as a premise of decision making. They also follow strategies that help to maintain autonomy. By insisting on stringent rules for entrance, promotion, and seniority in the bureaucracy, they reduce the opportunities of elected officials to appoint political and nonprofessional department heads. The appointment of someone other than a career public servant is regarded as political manipulation. Another strategy is the demand for participation in policy formulation. Police administrators seek to impress their own judgments about law enforcement upon the council; school administrators do the same with educational policy, and so forth. As a source of technical information, bureaucracies almost always play some role in policy formulation. It is seldom that policy makers consciously pursue policies that are opposed by the concerned administrative heads. It seems to be more often that the formal policy makers seek — and accede to — the advice of administrators on matters of program formulation.

At the same time that bureaucrats resist disruption of their established ways of doing things and seek to "minimize innovation and change,"[65] they often seek to expand their budgets and activities. There is no better spokesman for the interests of policemen than the local Policemen's Benevolent Association or its equivalent. Bureaucrats are their own best lobbyists, although they also commonly align themselves with organized clients and other interest groups. Educational administrators and teachers seek the support of parent-teacher associations, and planners often seek the support of the local Chamber of Commerce. A major source of pressure for expansion comes from the agency itself and its administrative heads.

By far the most important bureaucratic resource in directing actual policy is its control over the day-to-day execution of programs. Some people think of bureaucrats as neutral automatons who merely carry out policies laid down at higher levels, exercising no choice or discretion. In reality, according to Sayre and Kaufman,

it is in execution that the bureaucrats have their most nearly complete monopoly and their greatest autonomy in affecting policy. They give shape and meaning to the official decisions, and they do so under conditions favorable to them. Here the initiative and discretion lie in their hands; others must influence them.[66]

Many bureaucrats—from department heads to the lowest clerks—possess considerable discretion. In fact, studies of traffic-law enforcement and ticketing policies by John A. Gardiner and of local welfare administration by Martha Derthick suggest that top administrators enjoy striking degrees of discretion.[67] Gardiner noted extreme variations in the number of traffic tickets dispensed in cities with nearly identical populations. Boston and Dallas both have populations of about 700,000, but in one year Dallas policemen wrote twenty-four times as many tickets as did those in Boston! No doubt some of this variation may be attributed to variations in state laws and local traffic ordinances or to different habits of Boston and Dallas drivers, but it is unlikely that such factors account for such a large differential. In fact, between two adjacent Massachusetts cities with similar populations (Cambridge and Somerville) there was a 700 percent differential in ticketing rates. The most important factor accounting for wide differences in law-enforcement policies has proved to be the attitude of the police chief toward traffic ticketing. "In general, the rate of enforcement of traffic laws reflects the organizational norms of a police department—the extent to which superior officers expect and encourage particular policies regarding ticket-writing."[68] Gardiner has reported the change in one New England city from a police chief who viewed detective work as the only really important police function to another who was a zealous advocate of traffic enforcement. During the last year of the first chief's tenure the whole force wrote 480 tickets. After the new chief took over, the figure shot up to 4569, which shows the influence of administrative discretion on the performance of lower-level bureaucrats.

Opportunities for discretion are not monopolized by senior bureaucrats and agency heads. Street-level bureaucrats such as teachers, police officers, and social workers often exercise discretion in crucial matters for their clients or citizen contacts.[69] Social workers can facilitate or discourage an application for public assistance; school teachers can be supportive or severe in dealing with students having little motivation. James Q. Wilson has analyzed the discretion of beat patrolmen.[70] He discovered that officers have relatively little discretion when they confront clear transgressions of unambiguous laws: armed robberies, murders, dope peddling, and so on. But, in maintaining order and dealing with transgressions against vague standards of public peace and serenity, their discretion increases. In the case of a clear violation, an officer approaches the situation by enforcing the law; in other matters, he is free to handle the situation.

In the final analysis, however, the bureaucrat is not totally free to do whatever he wants. Lower-level bureaucrats—as the traffic-ticketing study indicates—are clearly constrained by the expectations of their superiors, and even their superiors have only finite amounts of discretion. Bureaucrats are not neutral automatons, but neither are they wholly independent in their actions. Certain kinds of policies or circumstances permit greater discretion than do others. When administration can easily be routinized, there is less room for discretion. The maximum welfare payment, the speed that breaks the legal limit, and attendance in school are subject to exact specification. On the other hand, bureaucratic decisions involving determination of what constitutes undesirable behavior as grounds for eviction from a housing project or how to handle a scuffle outside a bar do not lend themselves to uniform responses. In much of the administrative process there are continuing attempts at routinization in order to minimize the discretion of subordinates.

URBAN POLICY MAKING:
AN OVERVIEW

Describing urban policy making is much more difficult than describing policy making at the national level. After all, there is only one national government; there are thousands of local communities. What is true of one may not be true of any other. We did offer, however, a suggestive model for understanding the shape of power in the city. It assumed that three principal elements—private sector elites, elected decision makers, and bureaucracies—were likely to be the key actors in urban-policy choices. Cities may vary in terms of their dominance by one or another group. Cities may also vary over time, with a private-sector dominance gradually being replaced either by elected officials or by massive service bureaucracies. Our view is that the most important change in the structure of urban power has been the rise of the latter institution, fortified by their monopoly of routine decisions and relatively insulated from political control (more on this argument appears in Chapter 10). Let us, however, examine briefly some of the most obvious attributes of urban policy making *generally*. There has been a constant tension in American cities between those who would make decisions more "rational" and those who settle for more "political" decisions. We suggest that there are good reasons why urban decision making is not likely to be very comforting to the former group.

Why Urban Decision Making Is Rarely "Rational"

Rationalism receives wide respect in our social system. The demands of a completely rational decision are severe, however. It is costly to be perfectly rational, and few decision makers have sufficient resources to inform themselves about all possible opportunities and all possible consequences of each opportunity. Five major reasons why decisions in public (or private) bodies rarely measure up to the exacting standards of pure rationality include:

1. the sheer pressures of time
2. the costs of obtaining adequate information about the various acceptable goals and policies
3. The mixture of sometimes incompatible or incommensurable goals that are pursued simultaneously within an urban system
4. structural features of the political system that frustrate coherent and coordinated policies
5. the constraints of political feasibility

These five items are not entirely separable in practice, but each does impose its own limitations on pure rationality, and each is worth separate consideration for analytical purposes.

TIME PRESSURES   Most features of the urban environment that we consider to be problems — high population density, inadequate transportation, pollution, decay — did not appear overnight and will not be eliminated overnight. But policy makers are pressed for action, for policies, and for solutions. Planners and other bureaucrats may be able to look to the future and to deal with models covering spans of several decades; politicians, however, must look to the next election. Academicans have time for reflection, but decision makers are expected to act with dispatch. The press of time is an obvious enough problem, and it is probably the first and paramount reason why public policies cannot be formulated according to the rational model. There simply is not enough time to accumulate the information, survey all the possible alternatives, and select from among them.

COSTS OF INFORMATION   A second factor that makes rational decision making impossible is the high cost of obtaining information. There are basically two types of information: political (on the needs and preferences of the community and interests within it) and technical (on the most efficient ways of reaching goals). Anthony Downs has listed three conditions that generally prevent bureaucracies and other decision-making bodies from acquiring the types of information required by the rational model:

1. Information is costly because it takes time, effort, and sometimes money to obtain data and comprehend their meaning.
2. Decision makers have only limited amounts of time to spend making decisions, can consider only a certain number of issues simultaneously, and can absorb only certain amounts of data on any one problem.
3. Although some uncertainty can be eliminated by acquiring information, an important degree of unpredictability is usually involved in making decisions.[71]

Not only is information costly to gather and process, but also different types of information may imply contradictory policy decisions. A common problem is that political information implies different decisions from those implied by technical information. Technical information on access, noise, and similar criteria may suggest the location of a new airport in a particular district, but political information may suggest that it would be wiser to choose another site.

As capacities for obtaining information are limited by the availability of resources, the important questions are, When does a decision maker stop gathering information? And when does he stop assessing what he has gathered? The answer to both these questions may be never. But at some point in the formulation of a new policy, the information-search process will have to be replaced by the decision and action process. Often decision makers will cut off their search when they discover a mode of operation that involves the least profound change in their established programs. They do not search all possible alternatives until they find the one best mode of operation. Instead they search until they find something that will work, that will provide some relief from the perceived difficulties without threatening undesirable unrest within the bureaucracy and among other decision makers and interest groups. In the words of one student of decision making, the search proceeds until the participants can "satisfice."[72] It is simply too expensive (and the demands for action are too great) to search until the one optimum combination of goals and policies has been identified.

INCOMPATIBLE AND INCOMMENSURABLE GOALS   Urban (and other) governments pursue numbers of policies simultaneously, some of which are almost certain to be incompatible with others. This fact is certainly not surprising and is perhaps fortunate when we realize that

governments serve multiple interests and respond to numerous demands for service and conflict resolution. At least in the abstract, there
is some inconsistency in community policies that encourage the
dispersion of population to the urban periphery, whereas other policies are aimed at salvaging a decaying downtown area. Sometimes,
however, such inconsistent goals must be served by a single policy or
agency. An example is urban renewal. Among the goals that some people think it should accomplish are such disparate efforts as improving
the city's tax base, attracting new industry, reversing suburban migration by providing middle-income housing, and improving the housing
plight of low-income families. It is clear that a single urban-renewal
program cannot serve each of these goals equally; even if it could, it
would fall short of any strict standard of rational policy making.

Not only are goals of a community or a particular agency sometimes
in conflict, but they are even more consistently incommensurable. By
incommensurable, we mean they are difficult or impossible to compare. There is both insufficient consensus on the goals themselves and
a highly inefficient system for their measurement. Each of these factors impedes comparability. Decision makers have little notion of
whether another dollar invested in urban renewal would reap more
payoffs than would another dollar invested in education. Even if the
goal is supported by a relative consensus, as is the reduction of
poverty, there is still incommensurability among policies. There is no
very clear evidence that any one strategy for reducing poverty will be
more effective than would any other strategy. Because most goals and
policies do not lend themselves to ready measurement, it will be
nearly impossible to meet standards of rationality that require comparison between alternative goals and policies.

If rational decisions require the capacity to organize public processes of selection toward certain goals rather than others, the structure of urban government is not geared to maximize rationality. Instead there are countless local governments in a metropolitan area, as
well as the state and federal governments, each of which may be pur-
suing different policies to achieve the same or different goals. Within
the city government itself, fragmentation of legal authority means that
various decision makers can each pursue different strategies and
policies, without too much concern for checkmate by superior authority.

Political Feasibility

In the last analysis, the determination of what to do about a particular
problem is made not by what is rational but by what will "sell" to the
electorate and to political influentials. Public attitudes toward taxation
are likely to be a major constraint upon any purely rational approach to

problem solving. Feasibility depends to a considerable degree upon familiarity. According to Ralph Huitt, "what is most feasible is what is purely incremental, or can be made to appear so. : . . Paradoxically, it is politically attractive to tout a proposal as 'new' so long as it is generally recognized that it is not new at all, but a variation on a familiar theme."[73] Elected officials are rarely willing to sacrifice their chances for reelection upon the altar of rationality, especially when justifications abound in democratic theory for adhering to the voice of the people. Perhaps the most rational way to grapple with the problem of poverty in the American system is through a form of guaranteed high-level income for all. Politically, however, such a proposal is likely to generate enough hostility to be considered unfeasible by most politicians, even if they might support the notion on other grounds.

Although politicans are said to seek power, the complexity of their environments may make it difficult to reach a decision. Deciding what is *feasible* may be as difficult as deciding what is *right*. It is often advantageous for decision makers to avoid conflict and delay decision. William L. C. Wheaton suggests that conflict avoidance is a common strategy in urban decision making:

Public officials delay decisions interminably, attempting to appraise the balance of power pro and con. They may defer decision indefinitely if the balance is approximately equal, and will reach decisions only when there is clearly preponderant support for one position. . . . Frequently decisions may be referred to experts or to other levels of government so that local public officials can evade responsibility or place it elsewhere.[74]

SUMMARY

The structure of urban power determines the shape of urban policy. In this chapter we presented a conception of urban power that depended on the interaction of three elements. The first of these was the private-sector elite. Many of those who studied community power structure, following Hunter in Atlanta, argued that private-sector elites called the shots in most cities. These elitists pointed to the influence of business and financial interests in critical urban decisions. The second element was elected decision makers, including mayors and council members. Another group of urban scholars emphasized the "pluralism" of local communities. In pluralistic cities, interest groups dominated and mayors often tended to play a brokerage role. Elsewhere a sort of "hyperpluralism" prevailed where interest groups were active but city officials were weak. We examined the roles and resources of urban mayors and city councils, emphasizing that mayors' powers are determined both by their formal authority and by their political resources. The third element in the urban decision-making process is the urban bureaucracy. Some cities

— New York is a common example — are said to be dominated by their civil-service institutions. But in all cities, these "new machines" play a significant role, protected as they are from political interference and secured by civil-service regulations. The interaction of these three elements means that urban policy making is rarely very "rational" and that the touchstone of success is typically "political feasibility."

Notes

1. Robert A. Caro, *The Power Broker: Robert Moses and the Fall of New York* (New York: Alfred A. Knopf, 1974).
2. Michael Korda, *Power: How to Get It, How to Use It* (New York: Ballantine, 1975), p. 4.
3. Caro, op. cit., pp. 19–20.
4. Max Weber, *The Theory of Social and Economic Organization,* T. Parsons, ed., (New York: Free Press, 1957), p. 152.
5. Robert A. Dahl, "The Concept of Power," *Behavioral Science, 2* (July, 1957), 202.
6. C. Wright Mills, *The Power Elite* (New York: Oxford University Press, 1956).
7. Floyd Hunter, *Community Power Structure* (Chapel Hill: University of North Carolina Press, 1953).
8. Ibid., pp. 100–101.
9. Robert A. Dahl, *Who Governs?* (New Haven: Yale University Press, 1961). For other analyses of New Haven in the Dahl tradition, see Nelson Polsby, *Community Power and Political Theory* (New Haven: Yale University Press, 1963); and Raymond Wolfinger, *The Politics of Progress* (Englewood Cliffs, N. J.: Prentice-Hall, 1974).
10. Dahl, *Who Governs?, op. cit.,* p. 183.
11. Ibid., p. 233.
12. Frederick Wirt, *Power in the City* (Berkeley: University of California Press, 1975).
13. Francis Rourke, *Bureaucracy, Politics and Public Policy* (Boston: Little, Brown, 1969), p. 60.
14. Edward C. Banfield and James Q. Wilson, *City Politics* (Cambridge, Mass.: Harvard University Press, 1963), pp. 207ff.
15. Wallace Sayre and Herbert Kaufman, *Governing New York City* (New York: Russell Sage, 1960), p. 405.
16. E. S. Savas and Sigmund G. Ginsburg, "The Civil Service: A Meritless System?" *The Public Interest, 32* (Summer 1973), 70–85.
17. Robert J. Huntley and Robert J. Macdonald, "Urban Managers: Organizational Preferences, Managerial Styles, and Social Policy Roles," *Municipal Yearbook* (Washington, D.C.: International City Management Association, 1975), 149–159.
18. Dahl, *Who Governs?* op. cit.
19. See also Robert O. Schulze, "The Bifurcation of Power in a Satellite City," in Morris Janowitz, ed., *Community Political Systems* (Glencoe, Ill.: The Free Press, 1961), 19–80.
20. Robert Agger, Daniel Goldrich and Bert E. Swanson, *The Rulers and the Ruled* (New York: John Wiley, 1964).

21. Theodore Lowi, "Machine Politics—Old and New," *The Public Interest, 9* (Fall 1969), 83–92.

22. Ibid., p. 86.

23. Ibid., p. 87.

24. Edward Greer, "Air Pollution and Corporate Power: Municipal Reform Limits in a Black City," *Politics and Society, 4* (1974), 483–510.

25. Robert L. Lineberry, *Equality and Urban Policy: The Distribution of Municipal Services* (Beverly Hills, Calif.: Sage, 1977).

26. The most extensive and potentially useful ones are found in Agger, Goldrich, and Swanson, pp. 73–93.

27. Charles M. Bonjean and David M. Olson, "Community Leadership: Directions of Research," *Administrative Science Quarterly, 8* (December 1964), 291–300.

28. For a more extensive listing of propositions derived from the literature on community power structure, see Terry N. Clark, "Power and Community Structure: Who Governs, Where, and When?" *The Sociological Quarterly, 8* (Summer 1967), 291–316.

29. Clark, "Community Structure, Decision-Making, Budget Expenditures, and Urban Renewal," *American Sociological Review, 33* (August 1968), 576–594.

30. Arthur Vidich and Joseph Bensman, *Small Town in Mass Society* (Princeton, N.J.: Princeton University Press, 1958).

31. For Atlanta, see Hunter, op. cit.; for Dallas, see Carol E. Thometz, *The Decision-Makers* (Dallas: Southern Methodist University Press, 1963).

32. John Walton, "Substance and Artifact: The Current Status of Research on Community Power Structure," *American Journal of Sociology, 71* (January 1966), 684–699; Clark, "Community Structure, Decision-Making, Budget Expenditures, and Urban Renewal," p. 586.

33. Note, however, that, as we argued in Chapter 5, labor unions are typically much less active in local politics than in state and national politics.

34. Robert S. Lynd and Helen M. Lynd, *Middletown in Transition* (New York: Harcourt Brace Jovanovich, 1937). Middletown is a pseudonym for Muncie, Indiana.

35. The importance of secondary associations is emphasized by Agger, Goldrich, and Swanson; see especially pp. 272ff.

36. John Walton, "Vertical Axis of Community Organization and the Structure of Power," *Social Science Quarterly, 48* (December 1967), 355–357.

37. Clark, "Community Structure, Decision-Making, Budget Expenditures, and Urban Renewal," p. 586.

38. Agger, Goldrich, and Swanson, pp. 662ff.

39. Joseph A. Schumpeter, *Capitalism, Socialism, and Democracy* (New York: Harper & Row, 1947), pp. 232ff; and Seymour M. Lipset, *Political Man* (Garden City, N.Y.: Doubleday, 1960), chap. 2.

40. Bonjean and Olson, p. 299.

41. For examples of research that attempts to link the structure of community power with public policies, see Clark, "Community Structure, Decision-Making, Budget Expenditures, and Urban Renewal;" Agger, Goldrich, and Swanson, op. cit.; and Amos Hawley, "Community Power and Urban Renewal Success," *American Journal of Sociology, 68* (January 1963), 422–432.

42. Hunter, op. cit., p. 127.

43. On Dallas, see Thometz, op. cit., and *New York Times,* April 13, 1975. p. 21.
44. Lineberry, op. cit., p. 56.
45. Bryan T. Downes, "Municipal Social Rank and the Characteristics of Local Political Leaders," *Midwest Journal of Political Science, 12* (November 1968), 514–537.
46. Lee Sloan, "Good Government and the Politics of Race," *Social Problems, 17* (Fall 1969), 161–175.
47. M. Arnold, "John Santucci Is a Man in a Wind Tunnel," *The New York Times Magazine,* April 16, 1967, pp. 56–70.
48. Oliver Williams and Charles Adrian, *Four Cities* (Philadelphia: University of Pennsylvania Press, 1963), p. 264.
49. Arnold, p. 62.
50. Downes, p. 528.
51. Ibid.
52. Kenneth Prewitt, "Political Ambitions, Volunteerism, and Electoral Accountability," *American Political Science Review, 64* (March 1970), 5–17.
53. Kenneth Prewitt, *The Recruitment of Political Leaders: A Study of Citizen-Politicians* (Indianapolis: Bobbs-Merrill, 1970), chap. 8.
54. John C. Bollens and Grant B. Geyer, *Yorty: Politics of a Constant Candidate* (Los Angeles: Palisades Publishers, 1973). See also, on recent mayors, Carl B. Stokes, *Promises of Power: A Political Autobiography* (New York: Simon and Schuster, 1973); Ann L. Greer, *The Mayor's Mandate* (Cambridge, Mass.: Schenkman, 1974); and Wolfinger, op. cit.
55. Henry W. Maier, *Challenge to the Cities* (New York: Random House, 1966), p. 114.
56. Jeffrey Pressman, "Preconditions of Mayoral Leadership," *American Political Science Review,* 66(June 1972), p. 522.
57. On Mayor Lee, see Alan R. Talbot, *The Mayor's Game* (New York: Harper & Row, 1967), and Wolfinger, op. cit. On Mayor Daley, the writings are vast. Outside Chicago, the most widely-read Daley biography is Mike Royko's rather nasty *Boss* (New York: Signet, 1971), which Mrs. Daley once succeeded in having removed from her neighborhood supermarket's book rack. A much more careful book is Len O'Conner's, *Clout* (New York: Avon Books, 1975). A more sympathetic treatment is found in Milton Rakove, *Don't Make No Waves, Don't Back No Losers* (Bloomington, Indiana: Indiana University Press, 1975).
58. John P. Kotter and Paul R. Lawrence, *Mayors in Action* (New York: John Wiley, 1974).
59. Michael Preston, "Limitations of Black Urban Power: The Case of Black Mayors," in Louis H. Masotti and Robert L. Lineberry, eds., *The New Urban Politics* (Cambridge, Mass.: Ballinger, 1976), p. 129. See also Charles H. Levine, *Racial Conflict and the American Mayor* (Lexington, Mass.: D. C. Heath, 1974).
60. Deil S. Wright, "The City Manager as a Development Administrator," in Robert T. Daland, ed., *Comparative Urban Research* (Beverly Hills, Calif.: Sage, 1969), p. 218.
61. Ibid., p. 219.
62. Ibid., p. 236.

63. Karl Bosworth, "The Manager Is a Politician," *Public Administration Review,* *18* (Summer 1958), 216–222.

64. Ronald O. Loveridge, *City Managers in Legislative Politics* (Indianapolis: Bobbs-Merrill, 1971), especially chaps. 4 and 8.

65. Sayre and Kaufman, op. cit., p. 407.

66. Ibid., p. 421.

67. John A. Gardiner, "Police Enforcement of Traffic Laws: A Comparative Analysis," in James Q. Wilson, ed., *City Politics and Public Policy* (New York: Wiley, 1968), pp. 151–172; and Martha Derthick, "Intercity Differences in Administration of the Public Assistance Program: The Case of Massachusetts," in Wilson, ed., pp. 243–266.

68. Gardiner, p. 161.

69. Michael Lipsky, "Toward a Theory of Street-Level Bureaucracy," in Willis D. Hawley, et al., *Theoretical Perspectives on Urban Politics* (Englewood Cliffs, N.J.: Prentice-Hall, 1976), chap. 8.

70. James Q. Wilson, *Varieties of Police Behavior* (Cambridge, Mass.: Harvard University Press, 1968).

71. Anthony Downs, *Inside Bureaucracy* (Boston: Little, Brown, 1967), p. 3.

72. Herbert Simon, *Administrative Behavior* (New York: Macmillan, 1961).

73. Ralph Huitt, "Political Feasibility," in Austin Ranney, ed., *Political Science and Public Policy* (Chicago: Markham, 1968), p. 274.

74. William L. C. Wheaton, "Integration at the Urban Level," in Philip Jacob and James V. Toscano, eds., *The Integration of Political Communities* (Philadelphia: Lippincott, 1964), p. 132.

PART FOUR
Public Policies and Their Impacts

8

URBAN PUBLIC POLICY: ASKING THE RIGHT QUESTIONS

Public policies are directed at public problems. But policy choices are shaped by political factors that we have examined throughout this book. The great migrations associated with the political sociology of urban areas (discussed in Chapters 3 and 4), the political process (discussed in Chapter 5), and the urban elites (discussed in Chapter 7), combine to make policy. We now will examine policy outputs of urban governments. In this brief chapter, we provide an overview of urban policy and perspectives on policy outputs. We suggest that five key questions should constantly be asked about urban policy, specifically:

- What choices are made and why?
- Who benefits and who loses?
- What difference does money make?
- What is the impact of public policy?
- How shall urban policies be evaluated?

In the preceding chapters we dealt with basic features of the urban environment, the political input process, and decision making. We now turn our attention to the outputs and impacts of the urban political system: the efforts of urban governments to affect their environments. This chapter introduces the concept of public policy as a response to urban problems. All public policies involve hard choices, and all represent opportunity costs: A dollar invested in improving the schools is a dollar that cannot be invested in improving transportation or controlling pollution. Frequently in the city, policies are advocated and adopted with little insight into their impacts. Policy makers often fail to evaluate the impacts and effectiveness of policy choices and ignore the spillover effects of particular policies. Our purpose in this chapter is to elucidate the nature of public policy and to point up issues involved in the analysis and evaluation of policy.

THE NATURE OF PUBLIC POLICY

A concern with policy is the common denominator in the writing of the classic political philosophers on the one hand, and the activities of

215

urban mayors and administrators, on the other. As political scientists we recognize that there are disagreements about the kinds of policies that governments *should* enact; we also recognize that political scientists use the term *public policy* in different ways. A simple definition of policy states that it is "the important missions of government." This, or course, leaves unspecified the meanings of *important* and *missions*. It also leaves out any indication of the varying ways that people may view policies. In merely dealing with the problem of describing government expenditures, for example, an economist may focus on the sums allocated to programs described according to how they will affect the economy; economic stabilization activities (e.g., unemployment insurance, industrial promotion); income redistribution activities (e.g., health, welfare); resource allocation activities (e.g., highways, police).[1] An administrator may focus on the allocation of funds to various governmental agencies: highway department, police department, schools, sanitation department, fire department. A political scientist may emphasize the perspectives of the decision makers. Political scientist Austin Ranney has described the components of policies as:[2]

1. *a particular object or set of objects* — some designated part of the environment (an aspect of the society or physical world) that is to be affected
2. *a desired course of events* — a particular sequence of behavior desired in the particular object or set of objects
3. *a selected line of action* — a particular set of actions chosen to bring about the desired course of events; in other words, not merely whatever the society happens to be doing toward the set of objects at the moment, but a deliberate selection of one line of action from among several possible lines
4. *a declaration of intent* — some statement by the policy makers, whether broadcast publicly to all who will listen, or communicated secretly to a special few, on what they intend to do, how, and why
5. *an implementation of intent* — the actions actually undertaken vis-à-vis the particular set of objects in pursuance of the choices and declaration

Some policy analysts broaden the term *policy* to include the *effects* that government actions have on the populations that they are designed to serve. Some of these effects are encompassed by the terms *outputs, outcomes, spillover effects, impacts* or *feedbacks* of policy. David Easton, a progenitor of systems analysis in political science, draws a distinction between *outputs* (roughly, what governments do) and the *outcomes* of these outputs (roughly, what consequences follow from the outputs).[3] Still others use the term *policy* to refer to broadly interrelated government decisions. When we label officials liberal, moderate, or conservative, we use shorthand forms to denote the ways in which specific decisions coalesce into broad policy directions.

Policy-making institutions and personnel convert inputs from the environment into policies that then produce outputs, impacts, and feedback. The major policy-making actors and processes are found in the formal structures of local government and their occupants (mayors, managers, school boards, the bureaucracy); informal community power structures; the procedures used by officials to make their policy decisions; and the commitments, predispositions, and beliefs that shape these officials' decisions. As we saw in Chapters 5 through 7, these features are not fixed. They include many varieties of behaviors, which differ with the kind of issue that is introduced and the ways in which inputs flow from the environment. Among the features that may be found in the conversion process are conflicts between formal rules of procedures and the practices followed by officials; clashes among various officials from different agencies or branches of local government; clashes between decision makers and representatives of interest groups who make innovative demands; and decision makers' use of routine procedures to simplify complex and numerous demands.

In the description of the policy process we present in this and in the following chapters we treat policy sometimes as a dependent variable and sometimes as an independent variable. In the former instance, we are interested in the *dependence* of policy on features in its environment; we look for evidence on how variations in educational policies, for example, are influenced by variations in its environment. Likely correlates of educational policy are the social characteristics of the community, the economic resources available to the decision makers, and the policy predispositions of the community elite. When we consider policy as an independent variable, we seek its influence on the environment. We ignore, for the moment, the influence of environment on policy by abstracting policy elements from their surroundings and considering them independently from other sources. We then assess the impacts of policy on its environment by treating certain environmental characteristics as dependent variables.

FIVE ISSUES IN POLICY ANALYSIS

Public policy is the focal point of urban politics. Both masses and elites invest their political resources to achieve changes in policy or to preserve the status quo. Typically the questions raised about policy choices are deceptively simple: Is policy X good or bad? How much will it cost? Who's going to pay for it? Actually such questions are not very meaningful by themselves and without further specification. Policy analysts have attempted recently to develop some basic conceptual tools for the analysis of policy and to bring them to bear on urban policy. In our opinion, policy specialists have raised five basic questions about urban public policy.

What Choices Are Made and Why?

The making of public policy involves choices among alternatives. Except in a theoretical and ideal world, one free from political factors and with unlimited resources, all choices involve costs. Costs are not only monetary but social, psychological, and political as well. Economists rightly emphasize the importance of a choice perspective:

Economics can be said to be no more than the study of the costs and benefits of the choices among alternatives; it remains "the dismal science" because it says again and again that societies and individuals face hard choices among alternatives, and that there are few opportunities that have no costs.[4]

Few choices are *free* choices. Choosing among alternatives is what urban politics is all about. Each choice among policy alternatives is constrained by both macro and micro features of the policy environment. The availability of human and economic resources represents a constraint on any policy; one cannot spend money one does not have. The limits of information are a serious constraint on many policy alternatives.

Urban officials are under constant pressures to cope with changes in their social and political environments. We show in the next chapter how the urban revenue-raising process has reacted to important trends in the urban economy. These choices are *constrained* choices. Officials are not free to enter the fiscal restaurant and order any meal they like. The racial disorders of the 1960s, the energy crisis of the 1970s, the bitter winter of 1976–77, and other traumas command attention and limit options. In the future, as we argue in Chapter 14, there will be further constraints from shortages of energy in cities. The strategies of urban governance are often strategies designed to *cope*, to get by from one budget year to the next, and to put off major decisions in hopes that they will go away.

Who Benefits and Who Loses?

The burdens and benefits of urban policy fall differentially on the urban landscape. Public policies can make the rich richer and the poor poorer; or they can redress social and economic inequalities by giving advantages to the disadvantaged. For each policy alternative, we can ask: Who benefits and who loses?

A few urban policies are *pure public goods* that cannot, by definition, be differentially distributed. Public goods can be enjoyed by one person without diminishing the consumption of the same good by another person. In principle a public good reaches everyone in a jurisdiction, at least indirectly. Some theorists reason that the public nature of a good (or a *bad* in the case of things such as pollution) provides the major justification for governmental activity rather than leaving its distribution to free-market operation. Yet the definition of a public good is not precise, and economists use the concept even when they insist that local governments produce no public goods in their pure form.[5] A few governmental policies come close to being pure public goods. Pollution control and fluoridation are examples. If citizen *A* receives cleaner air from pollution control, citizen *B* will automatically receive it as well.

Many public policies can be delivered differentially to citizens but still have aspects of the pure public good. Some neighborhoods may have good, and others poor, schools even while education in general rebounds to the benefit of the community as a whole.

How urban public services are distributed is the subject of Chapter 10. Some claim that the poor are usually shortchanged in public service allocations. We examine some evidence about the distribution of urban services to groups and neighborhoods. Other questions related to who benefits are addressed in the discussion of urban policy and inequality in Chapter 11.

What Difference Does Money Make?

Few public policies, other than purely symbolic expressions of intent, do not involve expenditure of public money. The questions of the total size of the public budget and of desirable tax burdens are among the most critical issues in most urban political systems. Each substan-

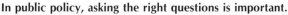

In public policy, asking the right questions is important.

tive policy involves the question of finance. Officials pay a great deal of attention to budget making, and expenditures are widely viewed as a common denominator with respect to items that actually produce service. Although spending does not by itself meet popular demands for service, it does buy many of the things that produce service. We shall examine spending and taxing issues in Chapter 9.

Yet both citizens and policy makers often assume that more money produces better services. The problem of urban crime evokes calls for more police expenditures and officers; problems of teenage joblessness are met with calls for better schooling and more school spending; problems of transportation are met by demands for more mass transit expenditures. We investigate the connection between resources and services at several places in these policy chapters. We discuss, for example, the relationship between school spending and learning, between the levels of police patrol and crime rates, and between expenditures and the quality of services rendered. We repeatedly point out the fact that resources expended may not be strongly tied to policy impact.

What Is the Impact of Public Policy?

The output of a public policy does not necessarily accomplish its goals. Although the elements of a service may be provided by a local agency, they may not have their intended impact on the problem. Impacts represent the effects that a service has on the target population and on other features of the environment. Impacts may be intended or not. Some impacts are planned and anticipated by policy makers. Others—we call them *spillover effects*—represent the unanticipated products of policy. Unintended impacts arise because the urban system consists of interrelated parts that influence one another and because information about all the potential effects of a policy is unavailable. An elusive hope of policy makers is to design public policies whose major consequences are intended and whose unintended impacts are either minimal or benign.

Spillover effects or externalities affect parties not directly conceived as objects of public policy. An example of a *negative externality* is the traffic congestion spawned by a new housing project or a sports arena. Yet a *positive externality* may come as a result of the public spirit generated by a winning team that has been attracted to town by the construction of a new stadium. Often it is a negative externality generated by private enterprise (sometimes called a *public bad*)—such as industrial pollution—that prompts a local government to formulate new policies. All of the public policies that we discuss in Chapters 9 through 13 have spillovers, sometimes benign and sometimes undesirable. Urban renewal (discussed in Chapter 13) is one such example. All citizens may benefit from an improved local tax base spurred by a revitalized downtown, but other externalities of urban renewal, particularly the problem of relocating the families living in an area to be renewed, will burden certain elements of the population. A principal concern of policy analysis is to specify as precisely as possible the spillover effects of policies on urban populations.

There may be no question for the policy maker that is more important than policy impact. Policies may not accomplish the intended impacts. In Chapter 11, for example, we discuss an important experiment that casts doubt on the policy impact of police patrol. Some impacts are extremely difficult to assess. One example is the impact of the so-called war on poverty, which we discuss in Chapter 12. But for each policy we want to know what difference it made.

How Shall Policies be Evaluated?

Policies can be evaluated in terms of two principal issues: Are the goals pursued by the policy desirable social ends? Do the policies actually accomplish the stated goals? If one dissents from the goal ostensibly furthered by a policy, the issue is simple. Matters are usually more complex, however, because most policies are advocated in terms of seemingly consensual and even noble goals. Policies are said to eliminate poverty, improve consumer choice, provide jobs, improve opportunities, and so on. The tough question is usually, therefore, whether the policy actually accomplishes its goal — and whether it accomplishes the goal more effectively and at less cost than would alternative policies.

Increasingly, policy evaluation depends on measurement. The rising status of precise measurement and quantitative analysis is evident, not only in academic studies of the causes and implications of certain policies — what might be called *basic research* — but also in applied studies that attempt to measure various cost-benefit ratios of public policies.

Cost-benefit analysis and planning-programming-budgeting (PPB) are techniques currently being touted by some government management specialists. Cost-benefit analysis attempts to estimate the costs of each policy option, including as many spillover costs as can be identified, and to sum up the benefits of each policy. Decision makers then use the results in the choice of alternatives.[6]

Ultimately, though, policies will be evaluated in terms of citizen goals. We cannot prejudge those assessments; we can, however, offer relative assessments of cities in terms of some goals. Some cities have more fiscal strain than others (see pp. 256–257); some cities have higher cost housing than others (see pp. 368–369); some cities have more significant poverty problems than others (see pp. 322–323).

These relative rankings should assist in understanding that the quality of life in the American city is closely tied its policy constraints and choices.

Notes

1. Dick Netzer, *Economics and Urban Problems: Diagnoses and Prescriptions* (New York: Basic Books, 1970), p. 170.
2. Austin Ranney, "The Study of Policy Content: A Framework for Choice," in Austin Ranney, ed., *Political Science and Public Policy* (Chicago: Markham, 1968), p. 7.
3. David Easton, *A Systems Analysis of Political Life* (New York: Wiley, 1965), pp. 351–352.
4. Netzer, op. cit., p. 5.
5. See Werner Z. Hirsch, *The Economics of State and Local Government* (New York: McGraw-Hill, 1970), p. 1.
6. An excellent summary of cost-benefit and PPB techniques can be found in Aaron Wildavsky, "The Political Economy of Efficiency," in Ranney, op. cit., pp. 55–82. The best single-volume compilation of materials is that of Fremont J. Lyden and Ernest G. Miller, eds., *Planning Programming Budgeting: A Systems Approach to Management,* 2d ed. (Chicago: Markham, 1972).

9

SPENDING, TAXING, AND THE FISCAL CRISIS

Urban governments, it is often claimed, face a fiscal crisis of unprecedented proportions. Even though New York City is most newsworthy, city after city finds it difficult to make ends meet. Many of the traditional revenue sources, particularly the property tax, have reached their political limits. Inflation cuts into city income as surely as it reduces family incomes. City finances are strained everywhere. In Chapter 4 we discussed the "irony of urban wealth." In this chapter we show the connections between the irony and the fiscal crisis of the American city. Specifically we:

- emphasize that the fiscal crisis of the American city is a function of its relationship with the political sociology and political economy of the metropolitan area
- show how city finances are increasingly dependent on decisions made in state capitals and in Washington, D.C.
- explain the complex politics of revenue raising
- show how both macro and micro elements affect urban budget decisions

The United States Conference of Mayors meets annually to discuss common problems and to present a united front on issues of urban interest. The 1976 meeting was held in Milwaukee and attracted 300 American mayors from large and small cities. Keynoting the gathering, Mayor Moon Landrieu of New Orleans reported a survey of 136 big-city mayors. Four out of five reported that their cities were "grappling with financial problems." Landrieu called it a "new economic crisis in America." There was a special urgency attached to the impending bankruptcy of New York City, but the problems were not confined to Gotham. Detroit was cutting city employees by 20 percent, while Philadelphia was hiking taxes by 30 percent. The Chicago public schools had just closed 11 days early to save money. Mayor Pete Flaherty of Pittsburgh reported that his fiscal austerity program had helped maintain a solid financial rating but that taxes would have to be increased anyway. Even the mayor of Beverly Hills, Donna Ellman, reported that her prosperous city had spent $2 million more than its income and would be making personnel and service cutbacks.

These were grim times for urban budget makers, mayors, and taxpayers. Costs were climbing, demands of municipal unions for pay increases were unceasing, inflation was eating away at the tax dollar, and citizens vetoed so many referenda that most cities simply stopped holding bond elections. Why the cities were in such a state is a major concern of this chapter.

A lot of money is at stake in urban politics. In 1974–1975, total revenues of local governments in the United States were $60 billion. Of this sum, two-thirds was raised from local sources, and another third was received from federal, state, and other local governments. In the past 10 years, total resources climbed by an average 11 percent per year. These sums are of great interest to the municipal officials who distribute public largesse to those seeking governmental contracts and to those of us who must pay the bills. Builders of roads and schools, city employees, and suppliers of equipment and services pay close attention to the decisions of local financial officers. These decisions are never far removed from concern with taxes, for local governments are very close – sometimes perilously close – to their taxpayers. The property tax is the prime source of local revenues, and of all the taxes used by American governments it seems to provoke the sharpest and longest-lasting controversies.

URBAN FINANCES IN A FEDERAL SYSTEM

An Overview: Federal, State, and Local Finances

The national government is the greatest tax collector, collecting almost three times as much revenue as local governments. Yet Washington spends much of its money on national defense and international affairs. Much of the national budget for domestic programs goes to states and localities in the form of grants, loans, and revenue sharing. State governments are now in second position as raisers of tax revenue. Like the national government, however, much of its money goes to intergovernmental transfers. Local governments receive transfers from both Washington and their state capitals. Most of the spending on domestic programs – and thus most of the program implementation – occurs at the local level. It is true that state governments increased their share of program implementation during the 1962–1970 period. Yet ours is still a system of program administration that rests heavily on the shoulders of local officials.

Table 9.1 provides an overview of the domestic sector and the place of local governments within it. Local governments increased their expenditures from $14.5 billion in 1954 to nearly $83 billion in 1976. As a percentage of the gross national product, they increased from 4 to

Table 9.1   Changing Patterns of Federal, State, and Local Domestic Expenditures, 1954–1976

Year	Federal		State		Local	
	Amount	Percent of GNP	Amount	Percent of GNP	Amount	Percent of GNP
1954	$22.7	6.2	$12.7	3.5	$14.5	4.0
1964	$54.2	8.5	$27.3	4.3	$30.8	4.8
1974	$194.5	13.8	$85.6	6.1	$71.8	5.1
1976 (est.)	$265.7	15.8	$102.3	6.1	$82.7	4.9

Note: Only federal domestic expenditures included; all dollar amounts in billions.
Source: Advisory Commission on Intergovernmental Relations, *Significant Features of Fiscal Federalism, 1976 Edition* (Washington, D.C.: Government Printing Office, 1976), Table III, p. 11.

nearly 5 percent. But local governments have lost out *relatively* to state and national governments. National government expenditures increased as a percentage of the GNP about two and a half times, while state shares of the GNP nearly doubled. The local government, however, is playing a greater role in policy implementation rather than in direct revenue raising. Grants-in-aid to local government typically require local administration of shared funds. The administrative side of local authority has diminished less than the revenue-raising function.

URBAN REVENUES AND TAXES

Where Do Local Governments Get Their Money?

Urban governments draw on four major sources of revenue: locally collected taxes, intergovernmental aid, consumer charges for public services, and borrowing. Within these major categories the following specific choices must be made: Which kinds of taxes should be collected and how much of each? What services should the municipality provide on a charge basis? How high should service charges be? What federal or state aids can the municipality obtain? And how much and what forms of indebtedness should it incur? Revenue policies provide clear examples of policy outputs that have direct feedback to decision makers. Subsequent revenues reflect decisions on tax rates, service charges, and borrowing and the burden that taxpayers are willing to bear.

Figure 9.1   Trends in City General Revenue from Selected Major Sources: 1966–1975 (Billions of Dollars)

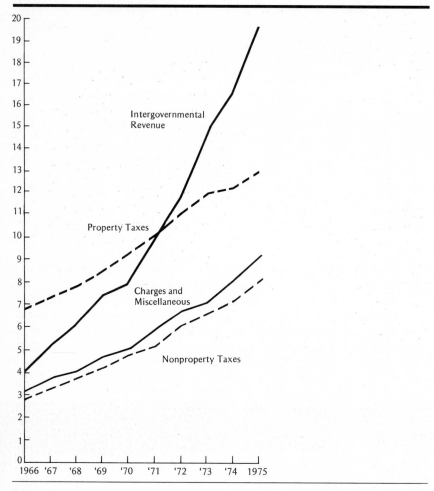

Source: U.S. Bureau of the Census, *City Government Finances in 1974–75* (Washington, D.C.: Government Printing Office, 1976), Figure 1, p. 2.

Figure 9.1 shows the major trends in local revenues. All the major sources listed there — intergovernmental aid, property taxes, charges and miscellaneous sources, and nonproperty taxes — have increased since 1966. One revenue source, though, has been skyrocketing. Intergovernmental assistance increased from 24 percent to almost a third of local revenues. Federal aid is still a smaller share than state aid, but it is growing more rapidly. The number of categorical federal aid programs numbers in the hundreds, and revenue-sharing monies come without strings attached. Both are important sources of revenues sorely needed by hard-pressed local officials.

The property tax remains the most important *local* source of local revenues. In 1975, municipal governments collected $13 billion in property taxes, more than twice as much as from all other local taxes combined. In fact, local government's dependence on the property tax has not changed much throughout the twentieth century. Property taxes comprise about the same percentage of local government tax receipts as they did in 1902.

State aid is almost exactly equal to the property tax as a source of local revenue. Municipalities got about $13.1 billion in aid from their state governments in 1974–1975. It takes the form of grants for specific functions (schools, roads, or other services), grants to support general local government (the use of which is determined by local officials), and state tax money that is returned to the jurisdictions where it is collected. Federal aid is a smaller, but rapidly growing source of local assistance. Federal aid is composed of a large number of categorical programs (aid given for specific purposes such as airport construction or public housing) and a smaller share of general revenue sharing.

The third and fourth most prominent forms of city-government revenue are service charges and borrowing. In 1974–1975, city governments raised $17.3 billion in charges and utility revenues and another $5.8 billion from long-term debt. The most important sources of

"Big MAC" Chairman Felix Rohatyn, Governor Hugh Carey, and Mayor Abraham Beame discuss New York City's fiscal crisis.

charges and fees were utilities, especially water and electric systems. Other sums come from hospital charges, rents from public housing, tolls, license fees, and charges for school lunches.

These figures reflect only general patterns; they do not take account of the complexity that pervades local-revenue policies. The main source of complexity arises from the position of local governments as creatures of the states.

The States and Local Revenues

The powers of cities to tax are heavily circumscribed by the legal constraints of Dillon's rule (see Chapter 6, pp. 140–141). Cities may tax only for such purposes and in such manners as are specifically allowed by state law.[1] Although state legislatures may require cities to perform a multiplicity of functions, there is no necessary guarantee that tax resources will match legal responsibilities. Cities cannot determine on their own to adopt a sales tax or an income tax if state law has not explicitly authorized the levy of such taxes. Even if they are authorized, their upper limits may be specified. Sometimes the uses of each tax are also specified in detail by the legislature. These restrictions make local governments the legal children of American federalism.

Few municipalities collect sales or income taxes because most states forbid such levies. The property tax, the only major tax allowed by all state governments, is the mainstay of local governments. Furthermore, state governments limit the total amounts even of these taxes that may be raised. They regulate the levels of property taxes, the kinds of properties that are subject to property taxes, and the amounts that local authorities can borrow.

Tax and debt limits are typically based on the amount of *assessed valuation* in a community: the total value of property as local officials have established it for purposes of taxation. The constitution of Alabama, for example, forbids local governments to raise more than 1.25 percent of the total assessed valuation within their jurisdictions in taxes; that of Washington limits taxation to 4 percent; the debt limit of Indiana municipalities is 2 percent of assessed value; and that of Pennsylvania (except for Philadelphia) is 7 percent.[2] Local authorities can exercise some discretion in the face of these limits simply by increasing the assessments on property within their jurisdictions when they reach the current limits of taxes or indebtedness imposed on them.[3] However, such manipulations usually do not escape the notice of tax-wary citizens' groups, and there are high political costs in manipulating assessments in order to increase taxes. State governments also require tax exemptions and deductions for certain kinds of property. Several states give concessions to veterans, the aged, certain kinds of industrial plants, and "homesteads" (single-family homes occupied by their owners). States also exclude from the local tax base or require special tax rates for farm properties, automobiles, and other forms of personal property.[4] Certain properties of churches and non-profit organizations, as well as state and federal properties, are exempt from local taxation. The City of New Haven, the home of Yale University, has only a little more than half the actual property within the city limits on its tax rolls. Tax-exempt properties nevertheless add to the total service burden of the city, for they require transportation arteries, police and fire protection, and other "free" public services. Taxable properties in cities having government, medical, and educational centers thus must bear added burdens.

Urban Taxes and the Problem of Equity

Taxes are never very popular. Benjamin Franklin carped that "nothing in life is certain but death and taxes." Today we might all agree, but some would add that death is more equitable. Tax *equity* is an issue that often figures in local politics. Equity can be defined as fairness, equality, or distribution of appropriate burdens. The issue of equity is complicated by long-standing philosophical disputes about equality, as well as by immediate questions of whose pocketbook is to be tapped. In principle an equitable tax is one that distributes the costs of public service in a fair manner among economic groups. But equity is not simply resolved by an *equal* assignment of taxes among citizens or business firms. There is debate over the wisdom of *progressive* versus *regressive* taxation. Those who advocate progressive taxes argue that burdens should be equal only among those with equal economic resources and that people with large incomes should pay, not only more taxes than people with small incomes, but also higher percentages of their incomes. Some observers favor progressive taxes on incomes, combined with regressive taxes in other areas, because they think that this combination will spread the burden throughout the community most fairly. Regressive taxes, which take larger percentages of the incomes of the poor than of the rich, are defended on the grounds that they leave more resources in the hands of the wealthy, who are likely to promote economic growth with their investments. Regressivity is also supported by those who claim that the poor reap the greatest benefit from domestic spending and should pay for what they get.

In debates about taxation, the subject of equity cannot be considered apart from the *incidence* and *burdens* of taxation and their subsequent impacts on individuals and the local economy. The incidence of a tax—the ultimate payer—is not apparent in the statute that defines the rates and the items to be taxed. When a property tax is first levied, it falls on the property owner. If he is a landlord, however, he can shift the tax to his tenants by increasing his rents accordingly. The original justification and still-current defense of property taxes is that higher taxes are placed on properties of higher value. But, because poor people spend larger-than-average percentages of their incomes for housing, property taxes take larger shares of the incomes of the poor than of those of the relatively well-to-do. Property taxes generally have a regressive impact, although their regressivity can be modified somewhat if certain low-income groups (e.g., the aged) are given special exemptions.

Urban taxation tends to be regressive. Even those local taxes other than property taxes that are commonly used — income and sales taxes — are not progressive in their application at the local level. Sales taxes are generally regressive because they take larger shares of the incomes of poor men, who must spend most of their incomes buying basic necessities that are subject to the tax. At the federal level, of course, income taxes are moderately progressive. Income taxes at the local level, however, tend to take fixed proportions of incomes, typically 1 percent. Considering the whole system of taxation, in which state and local regressivity works against the progressivity of the federal income tax, the American taxation system is not so progressive as is sometimes supposed.

Joseph Pechman and Benjamin Okner of the Brookings Institution studied the overall effects of the American tax structure on income.[5] They estimated the tax incidence of various kinds of taxes. Federal taxes, of course, were progressive, taking larger shares of the rich family's income than the poor family's income. There is some slippage through "tax loopholes" for the very rich, but the system as a whole is clearly progressive. State and local taxes, however, are so regressive that they counterbalance the progressive effect of the federal income tax. Overall, therefore, most American families — whether their income is $3,000, $30,000, or $300,000 — pay about 34 percent of their income in taxes. The regressivity of the local property tax is perceived by taxpayers as well as by economists. The Advisory Commission on Intergovernmental Relations commissioned a survey about the fairness of different taxes. They asked "which do you think is the worst tax, that is, the least fair?" Here are the results, with the percent of the public most disliking each tax:[6]

1. local property tax   45%
2. federal income tax   19%
3. state income tax   13%
4. state sales tax   13%
5. don't know   10%

Issues of tax equity, incidence, and burdens at the local level are complicated further by the wide disparities in assessing the tax base of real property. This is an inexact science at best, and among the 66,000 local governments that levy property taxes there is a great variety of talent and predisposition that produce variations from statutorily defined levels of incidence and burden. Individual property owners can benefit—or suffer—because of an assessor's incompetence, because the taxpayer has—or has not—made a contribution to the party of an elected assessor, or because the taxpayer fits a social or economic classification that the assessor feels should be given an especially high or low assessment.

Still the question of tax burdens cannot be dismissed after examination of only the revenue side of government. Although the classic defense of progressive taxation defines the regressive tax as inequitable, certain regressive taxes seem somewhat more equitable because of the expenditures that they support. Local taxes on property and retail sales are regressive in the burdens they impose, but they also help to support such services as public education, health, recreation, and welfare, which provide important benefits to lower-income citizens. Before final answers about tax equity can be determined, we need an analysis of benefits. One such effort has been made by Walter Heller, former chairman of the President's Council of Economic Advisers. Heller estimated that "the state-local expenditure pattern is strongly [progressive], declining steadily [in the benefits offered] from an estimated 43 percent of income for the poorest families to 6 percent for families with incomes about $10,000." He emphasized that "study after study has confirmed the unmistakable pattern of substantially progressive federal taxes and expenditures, strongly regressive state local taxes, and strongly progressive state–local expenditures."[7] The progressive character of the expenditure patterns of state and local governments operates to counterbalance, at least in part, the regressivity of their tax systems.

The Limits of the Property Tax and the Search for Alternatives

In many local communities the property tax has been exhausted as a source of revenue increases. Citizens will rise up in a "taxpayer's revolt" at the mention of a tax increase. Philadelphia Mayor Frank Rizzo promised an administration with no new tax increases. When some hints were dropped that he was changing his position, local voters launched a massive recall petition. (A recall election is a device by which local voters can vote to dismiss an officeholder, a power reserved at the national level to Congress through the impeachment process.) Such fears strike close to the electoral futures of local officeholders everywhere.

Local officials know, too, that raising property taxes often produces no net increase in tax yield. If taxes increase, people may be more inclined to use their exit options. Newark is a case in point. A state judge in 1976 ordered city officials to undertake certain policies to bring them into compliance with federal law. But to undertake those policies, the city would have to raise its already staggering property taxes (a homeowner with a house valued at $20,000 was paying $2000 in property taxes). The city council refused, and the judge sentenced its members to jail for contempt of court. Officials in Newark and elsewhere fear that escalating tax rates only drive more people to suburban tax havens. If people do exit in large numbers, there may be no net increase in taxes collected. In Newark and elsewhere, the widespread abandonment of apartment buildings and houses has resulted partially from tax hikes too great to bear. St. Louis contains areas in which 16 percent of all living units are abandoned; in the East New York section of Brooklyn, abandonment rates range from 6 to 10 percent.[8] Such units do not pay property taxes at all. Instead they are a drain on the city because they attract vandals, gangs, and arsonists.

Making ends meet is a constant challenge. Oakland's revenue politics indicates how city officials try to cope with limited revenue sources. There "officials believe the property tax is exhausted." So they resort to dozens of nickel-and-dime taxes, "chopped up by commodity to make them palatable, [seeking] the path of minimal taxpayer resistence."[9] In each case the question is whether the revenue yield would be worth the opposition from some small constituency whose taxes were being increased. The city raised hotel occupancy taxes to the chagrin of the tourist trade; it increased cigarette taxes over the objections of tobacco wholesalers. Once in a while it hit everyone for a small increase, as when it adopted a sewer service charge. Coupled with an increase of "hidden" taxes, city officials constantly pressured municipal bureaucracies to hold down costs, refused to permit new hiring, and tried to get services to "pay their own way." Taxpayer revolt was a constant spectre that had to be balanced against the desires of municipal employees to receive salary and wage increases. The result was a coping strategy, where the wolf was never far from the door.

Urban Revenues and the Political Economy of American Cities

Local governments face both a revenue bind and a crush of demands for public expenditures. As we emphasized in Chapter 4, urban areas are the centers of most concentrations of American wealth, yet much of that wealth is inaccessible to local governments. Such factors as legal limitations upon the objects and levels of taxation, the hostility of taxpayers, debt limitations, and the reluctance of local officials to take advantage of their fiscal options contribute to the *revenue incapacity* of local governments.

Any hints that local governments propose to increase revenues are usually followed by veiled threats from local industries to move elsewhere and by sharp warnings from business groups that high-tax communities cannot be expected to attract industry and residents. The fact is that a number of studies indicate that the level of state or local taxes is but one of many factors, and often not the most important one, in determining industrial location.[10] One economist has noted the paradox that

the influence of tax considerations on the location decisions of business is grossly overstated . . . [but] its impact on state and local taxation is not. . . . Fear of losing business to another jurisdiction haunts the mind and stills the pen of the state and local lawmaker, and special pleaders have developed the skill of exploiting this fear to a high art.[11]

It would not, however, be fair to lay at the doorstep of local businessmen the sole responsibility for pressures for low taxes. Also culpable are local electorates, municipal officials reluctant to take political risks, and state legislators unwilling to increase local-revenue options. At least in terms of taxing, local governments are close to the people, and the property tax hits — quite literally — very close to home.

URBAN EXPENDITURE PATTERNS

The other side of the fiscal coin is expenditures. They are of interest to political scientists and citizens for several reasons. First, budgets indicate relative priorities among public choices. Charles A. Beard once wrote:

In the purposes for which appropriations are made the policies of the city government are given concrete form — the culture of the city is reflected. Indeed, the history of urban civilization could be written in terms of appropriations, for they show what the citizens think is worth doing and worth paying for.[12]

More recently Louis H. Masotti and Don R. Bowen have noted that "the community budget can be viewed as public policy spelled out in dollars and cents, and that budget decisions represent the allocations of certain kinds of values."[13]

Second, expenditures are of interest because they purchase certain levels of public services through which the municipality can make an impact on its environment. Educational expenditures buy teachers, schoolbooks, and classrooms in an effort to raise the educational achievement and community aspirations. Police expenditures purchase policemen, cars, paddy wagons, radios, radar equipment, and laboratory devices, all of which are designed to help apprehend transgressors of the law. Expenditures are therefore important as means of procuring certain kinds of output intended to have impact on the environment.

Third, local expenditures are of interest because they have considerable influence on the economic system as a whole. That local governments spend about 5 percent of the GNP makes them a potent influence on levels of inflation or deflation and on economic growth.

Where All That Money Goes

In 1974–1975, city governments spent a total of $48.7 billion on a wide range of services. Table 9.2 details the distribution of city expenditures by major categories of public function. Municipal governments have a very wide range of expenditure categories. Few separate items require more than 10 percent of the typical city budget. Only educa-

Table 9.2   Local Government Expenditures, 1974–75

Function	Amount (millions of dollars)	Percent	Per capita amount (dollars)
Total general expenditure	48,678	100.0	358.65
Education	7,164	14.7	52.78
Police protection	5,281	10.8	38.91
Public welfare	3,846	7.9	28.34
Highways	3,861	7.9	28.45
Fire protection	2,901	5.9	21.37
Sewerage	3,415	7.0	25.16
Hospitals	2,735	5.6	20.15
Parks and recreation	2,274	4.7	16.75
Interest on general debt	2,294	4.7	16.90
Housing and urban renewal	1,752	3.6	12.91
Sanitation other than sewerage	1,763	3.6	12.99
General control	1,440	2.9	10.61
Financial administration	819	1.7	6.03
General public buildings	845	1.7	6.23
All other functions	8,288	17.0	61.07

Source: U.S. Bureau of the Census, *City Government Finances in 1974–75* (Washington, D.C.: Government Printing Office, 1976), p. 2.

tion and policing account for as much as 10 percent each of total city expenditures. These major items accounted for $52.78 and $38.91 per capita, respectively.

Table 9.2, however, shows only the aggregate patterns of municipal expenditures. The data suffer from several limitations. First, there is wide variation among states in the division of labor. Some state governments perform functions that in others are operated by city governments. In some states, for example, welfare payments are made entirely from state contributions while elsewhere cities contribute to the welfare function. There is also wide variation in responsibilities among different kinds of local government. Education is the major variable. In some states, particularly in the East, city governments are responsible for the operation of public schools and sometimes for colleges and universities. New York City's $2.6 billion-dollar school budget (which alone accounts for about 40 percent of all municipal governments' spending on education) constitutes a very large proportion of its total expenditures. But in cities in the Midwest, South, and West school expenditures are typically made by special school districts. What in one state may be performed by municipal governments is thus performed in other states by counties, special districts, or the state governments themselves. The endless variations in distribution of responsibility among and within states make it risky to generalize about typical local expenditure patterns. The expenditure categories listed in Table 9.2 provide only a rough overview of the ways that city governments allocate their budgets.

Urban Expenditures and the Federal System

It is increasingly impossible to separate programs into neat categories of federal, state, or local sponsorship. There are very few programs relevant to urban America that do not involve the federal system as a whole. Education is predominantly a local matter, but assistance to public and higher education is the largest single item in state budgeting, and federal aid to local schools has increased significantly in recent years. Quiet residential streets are built mostly with local money, but state and federal assistance is significant in building major traffic arteries, particularly those connected to the interstate-highway program. The federal government helps to build local hospitals and airports and to train policemen. Housing and urban-renewal programs receive federal and local funds, as well as state aid in some states. Because most of these programs are funded by more than one level of government, any neat effort to sort them by layers of the federal system will be misleading. The federal system is deeply embedded in the expenditure options of local governments.

Grants-in-aid and restrictions on expenditures mean that local governments are not entirely free to make any set of decisions that suit their fancies. State governments require local authorities to perform certain functions in specified ways. Except for general revenue sharing, federal aid comes with strings attached. Grants are provided for specific purposes, and local governments that do not conform to requirements find their grants terminated. The rules and legislation of state and federal governments thus establish numerous constraints on local policy.

COMMUNITIES AND BUDGETS: A MACRO PERSPECTIVE

Some cities spend more money than do others. In one sense this difference results merely from financial decision makers' consciously choosing to spend and tax at certain levels. But in a broader sense the level of spending is shaped by the socioeconomic, political, governmental, and legal structures of the community and its environment. In this section, we describe some of the community characteristics most commonly associated with variations in expenditures.

A great deal of research by economists and political scientists has investigated the relationships between community characteristics and levels of expenditures.[14] Some of the principal findings are summarized in Table 9.3. Each suggests a hypothesis about the relationship between a socioeconomic attribute and higher or lower spending. Among the most important correlates are these:

INCOME   As with families, so too with communities: The higher the income, the greater the level of expenditures, other things being equal. Cities vary widely in their income levels. Biloxi, Mississippi, contains less than 2 percent of its population with incomes over $25,000 annually; in Edina, Minnesota, more than 30 percent of the families earned $25,000 annually. Places such as Edina can afford higher levels of expenditures than places like Biloxi.

ECONOMIC BASE   A manufacturing economy is associated with higher expenditures for two reasons. First, industrial properties provide a lucrative tax base and thus more money for the municipality to spend. Second, industrialization brings heavy service demands for police and fire protection, roads, and public utilities.

DENSITY   The effects of population density seem to vary with the service examined. Density is associated with higher expenditures per capita on traffic control, law enforcement, fire protection, and sanitation. But it is associated with lower expenditures for transportation.

Table 9.3 Summary of Relations Between Socioeconomic Variables and Municipal Spending Levels[a]

Variable	Relation to municipal spending
Income	
High	+
Low	−
Economic base	
Manufacturing	+
Other	−
Density	
High	?
Low	?
Growth rate	
High	?
Low	?
Owner occupancy	
High	−
Low	+
Metropolitan type	
Central city	+
Outside central city	−

[a] A plus sign indicates a relationship generally identified as a positive. A minus sign indicates a relationship generally identified as negative. A question mark indicates a variable about which findings are incomplete or mixed.

GROWTH RATES   Growth cuts two ways. Sometimes expenditures are increased to meet demands of growth. Capital expenditures for schools, streets, and parks are likely to be high in a new community. But a high level of expenditures may also be a response to deterioration. Neighborhood reconstruction, crime-prevention expenditures, and the costs of servicing dependent populations may be expensive items in the budget of a declining city. It is the *kinds* of expenditures most directly affected by growth or decay.

OWNER OCCUPANCY   The greater the degree of home ownership in a community, the lower municipal expenditures usually are. Lineberry and Fowler have offered two principal explanations for this:

1. Owner occupancy is correlated (almost by definition) with lower urban population density. High density, bringing all manner of men together in the classic

urban mosaic, may itself be correlated with factors which produce demands for higher expenditures — slums, increased need for fire and police protection, and so on.

2. No doubt self-interest (perhaps "private-regardingness") on the part of the home owner, whose property is intimately related to the tax structure of most local government, may account for part of this relationship.[15]

Whatever the underlying explanation, the incidence of home ownership in a community is one of the major negative correlates of municipal expenditures.

CENTRAL CITY/SUBURBAN LOCATION   We emphasized in Chapter 4 that the political economy of American cities adds to the burdens of central cities. They are faced with a greater proportion of the burdens — traffic, poverty, poor housing, crime, decay — necessitating public expenditures. Suburban governments, on the other hand, are mercifully free of many of these problems and can keep public budgets lower. But outside central city areas do contain larger proportions of school-age children and thus have higher educational expenditures than do central cities.

OTHER SOCIOECONOMIC FACTORS   There are countless other socioeconomic factors — incidence of poverty in a community, type of industrial activity, general age of buildings, whether the climate necessitates snow removal, and so forth — that may affect expenditures of city governments. Any attempt to catalogue all the possible elements that impinge on the level of spending would stretch the boundaries of an introductory text too far. We have discussed a few of the socioeconomic factors on which the most research has been done. Our listing does not imply lesser significance of an array of unmentioned factors that might influence spending levels.

Governmental and Political Factors and Spending

As public officials write budgets, authorize city appropriations, and collect taxes, it might be possible to claim that only governmental and political factors affect local budgeting. This view is, however, a narrow one that denies the significant relations between community characteristics and municipal spending levels. Numerous community characteristics, from the resource base to the amount of snowfall, may affect public expenditures. But it is inappropriate to attribute all inter-municipal variations in spending levels to socioeconomic forces. There are important factors in the political process and the structure of government that bear upon the level of local spending. Some of these relations are summarized in Table 9.4.

STATE–LOCAL EXPENDITURES   Different states use different divisions

Table 9.4   Summary of Relations Between
Government Variables and Municipal
Spending Levels[a]

Variable	Relation to municipal spending
State–local centralization	
State responsibilities greater	−
Local responsibilities greater	+
Intergovernmental aid	
High	+
Low	−
State debt and expenditure limits	
Restrictive	−
Unrestrictive	+
Previous expenditures	
High	+
Low	−
Degree of government reformism	
High	?
Low	?
Participation in local politics	
High	?
Low	?
Party competition	
High	?
Low	?

[a] A plus sign indicate a relationship generally
identified as positive. A minus sign indicates a
relationship generally identified as negative. A
question mark indicates a variable about which
findings are either incomplete or mixed.

of labor among governments. Some states spend very large proportions of total state and local revenues and have broad responsibilities
for provision of public services. In other states, local governments are
assigned many of these responsibilities. West Virginia, Delaware, and
Kentucky are highly centralized states, making 61, 55, and 59 percent
of total state and local expenditures, respectively. At the other extreme, New York and Minnesota are highly decentralized states; local
governments account for 77 and 71 percent of state and local expenditures, respectively. The greater the responsibilities assigned to the
local governments, the more cities will spend. Alan Campbell and
Seymour Sacks found such arrangements between state and local governments to be the most significant predictor of the level of local expenditures.[16]

INTERGOVERNMENTAL AID   Because resources determine the amounts of money available to local governments, the amounts of intergovernmental aid received are positively correlated with expenditures. The most significant question about state and federal assistance is its *substitution effect* on local efforts. Opponents of intergovernmental assistance frequently claim that aid simply reduces local governments' dedication to raising money within their own communities and that the net effects of intergovernmental assistance are few. Evidence is, however, that much state and federal aid has a *stimulating effect* on local revenues.[17] Many grant-in-aid programs seem to stimulate local governments to spend more than they otherwise would.

TAX, DEBT, AND EXPENDITURE LIMITS   Although, to our knowledge, no study has ever directly confronted the question and satisfactorily resolved it, it seems reasonable to expect that cities whose fiscal capacities are under stringent state limitations spend less than do cities in states where such restrictions are looser.

PREVIOUS EXPENDITURE LEVELS AND INCREMENTALISM   Studies of state expenditure levels have identified the level of previous expenditures as the most significant single predictor of state budgets. Ira Sharkansky found correlations between previous and current expenditure levels for different categories of state-government expenditures ranging from .70 to .96.[18] A similar stable pattern probably prevails in cities. The correlations of expenditures in several budget categories over time suggest that stable *incrementalism* is characteristic of local expenditures. Such findings also suggest "a conservative element in the political systems of American states and cities. The conservatism may reflect the influence of habit and routine, the practices of incremental budgeting, the problems involved in program expansion and/ or the processes of an administration's maturation."[19] We will return later to the importance of incremental budgeting.

GOVERNMENTAL REFORMISM   Much of the rhetorical thunder in support of municipal reforms (manager governments, nonpartisan elections, and at-large constituencies) claims that lower taxes—and by implication lower expenditures—will follow their adoption. But Lineberry and Fowler's study of taxes and expenditures in cities of over 50,000 population found slight differences between reformed and unreformed cities' spending levels.[20]

LOCAL PARTICIPATION AND PARTY COMPETITION   A well-known hypothesis in political science holds that more vigorous interparty competition and more participation by working-class groups will produce public policies more attuned to working-class interests.[21] The argument is that single-party systems with low voting turnouts probably tend to favor status quo politics beneficial to upper-income interests.

The more competition there is, the more parties seek support among wider circles of the electorate. Participation by lower-income groups increases, and their representatives obtain more benefits for them. Yet there are two difficulties with this argument. First, some careful studies of state spending have concluded that neither the level of voter participation nor the degree of interparty competition makes much difference in state expenditure levels.[22] Voter participation and turnout levels in local elections bear little relationship to tax or expenditure levels.[23] Although competition may have a bearing on local finance, the proposition can hardly be assumed out of hand. Second, it is not at all clear that more effective working-class representation operates to raise or lower public expenditures. Higher government expenditures may aid working-class groups who benefit from numerous local government programs. The evidence suggests, however, that lower-income people are the most dissatisfied with governments and their policies.[24] Some research also suggests that numerous working-class voters are alienated and tend to vote against both public expenditures and candidates who advocate increases in public expenditures.[25] Without any direct evidence we cannot assess the impact of turnout, participation, and party competition on local spending levels.

OTHER POLITICAL VARIABLES   The seven governmental and political factors that we have described do not, of course, exhaust the wide range of political variables that may influence a community's budget decisions. Besides, all the relations that we have identified are only *tendencies*, which mask numbers of deviant cases. Among other political factors of likely significance are the attitudes of community residents, the nature of the local power structure, and the risk-taking propensities of the local officials called on to propose budget and tax increases. A community dominated by public-regarding people may spend more than one dominated by private-regarding people. A monolithic power structure, ruling in the interests of the upper class, may be less supportive of tax and expenditure increases than would a pluralistic structure.

Community Characteristics, Political Factors, and Spending

In principle it should be possible to examine any particular city, note its relative standings on scales of the major determinants of municipal spending levels, and make some educated guesses about its level of expenditures. Two caveats are necessary, however. First, as already noted, we have so far discussed a collection of mere *tendencies*. Factors unique to a particular community or its political system may account for marked deviation from the patterns predicted by larger studies of numerous communities. Cities may expand or contract their budgets in response to sudden changes in local economic conditions; they may respond to the urgings of strong and powerful political leaders to whittle down or drastically increase local budgets; or they may face particular service problems during single budget periods. A sudden change from a tight-fisted conservative administration to a free-spending liberal one may increase a city's budget expenditures significantly.

Second, we have described factors in isolation from one another. Conceivably, of course, a community could be found to score high on all factors contributing to higher municipal expenditures. More likely, however, any single community will be characterized by some factors that impel it toward lower budgets and others that impel it toward higher ones. In some communities, one factor might take on greater importance than the same factor would in other communities. The particular mix of influences on spending may be more important than the mere presence or absence of individual elements.

These caveats are important, but they should not obscure the general findings that local budgets respond to community socioeconomic and political characteristics. Budget makers do not simply enter the "fiscal restaurant" and order what they want. The macroeconomic structure of the community provides them with certain kinds of resources and denies them others, and the political structure furnishes additional opportunities and constraints. No amount of zeal on the part of urban officials can eliminate all the strictures imposed by limited resources, political opposition to property taxes, and state spending and taxing limitations. Imagination can be only a partial substitute for resources. Given the macro context of financial decision making that we have described, we can now examine the micro context of budgeting: the process, the actors, and their strategies in the budgeting game.

THE BUDGETARY PROCESS IN URBAN GOVERNMENT: A MICRO PERSPECTIVE

A budget may be viewed from several angles. "In its most literal sense," according to Aaron Wildavsky, "a budget is a document, containing words and figures, which proposes expenditures for certain items and purposes." From a larger social perspective, budgeting is "the translation of financial resources into human purposes . . . [or] a series of goals with price tags attached."[26] Budgets itemize public revenues and divide public expenditures into categories by programs or expenditure items. Federal, state, and local budgets are imposing to behold. Some municipal budgets rival local telephone directories in sheer bulk (and unreadability).

How the Urban Budgetary Process Works
and Why It Is Important to Understand It

Ordinarily people find public budgets simply dull. It is certainly true that public urban budgets do not make exciting reading. Budgets are detailed, are labyrinthine, and seem to combine the worst manifestations of both lawyers and accountants. The Chicago municipal budget for 1976, for example, contained appropriations like the following:

Department of Purchases, Contracts, and Supplies, for reclamation and salvage	$214,087
Fire Department, for fire prevention in hotels, night clubs, large restaurants, and public assemblies	$1,066,367
Department of Streets and Sanitation, for weed control	$182,740
Animal Care and Control Commission, for animal care	$986,989
Department of Health, for sickle cell detection	$63,583

These items—and literally thousands like them in every city—constitute the real outputs of municipal governments. Whatever city governments are doing to solve urban problems or provide services will appear ultimately as a budget item. If it is not in the budget, it may be assumed that urban governments are not doing it.

There are three major characteristics of the municipal budget. First, the budget process is typically *fragmented*. Numerous actors each have particular interests in their own goals and strategies. Chief executives are interested in holding the line on costs without decreasing services; municipal employees and unions are interested in keeping up with—and preferably ahead of—the cost of living; agency heads seek higher expenditures for their own agencies. Frederick Wirt examined budgetary politics in San Francisco and found a highly fragmented, free-enterprise process. Generally it was "every agency for himself." He concluded that "such a budgetary process strengthens the separation of governmental domains. . . . Each agency constructs over time its own scenario, complete with supporting esthetic theory, emotional appeals, intricate choreography and stage movements, and a cast of characters. While these differ among the agencies, each scenario is primarily designed to present the best possible claim on the pool of city resources."[27] Typically police chiefs stress the significant crime problem and ask for more police officers; parks departments stress the importance of recreation in preventing juvenile delinquency and seek more recreation services; fire chiefs stress fire losses and want more equipment and personnel. Every agency has its interest, and every agency possesses a constituency for its appeal.

Second, the budgetary process is often *uncontrollable*. A substantial share of any city's budget is simply beyond the reach of manipulation. When New York Mayor Abe Beame began searching for ways of reducing the city's $850 million deficit, he quickly discovered how much of the budget was uncuttable.[28] More than one-third of its budget is fixed by law or by contractual commitments. Among the items that no city administration could pare are matching funds for federal and state aid, pension payments to retired workers, payments to bond-holders, and earmarked programs. Items that are not *legally* uncontrollable may be politically off limits. Wages and salaries cannot be cut without incurring the wrath of municipal employees. At a time when crime rates are rising everywhere, it is difficult to cut law enforcement expenditures. Neighborhoods would oppose the closing of parks or libraries. Uncontrollability contributes to inflexibility in the budget process.

The third attribute of the urban budget process is its *incremental* character. We can understand the incremental budgeting process better if we examine the way in which most urban budgets are prepared.

Budget Strategies and Decisions

There is such a wide variety of organization in local governments that it is difficult to describe a typical budgetary process, but the general patterns and major actors identified in studies of national and state budgeting also seem to hold at local levels.[29] The major actors include *agencies, chief executives* (in local governments, either mayors or managers), and *legislative bodies*. Some cities employ such variations as legislative budget systems, special budgeting boards, or joint committees. In a legislative budget system, the review of agency requests occurs within a committee of the city council before the full council votes on the appropriations. When there is a city budget board, a group of administrative officers, which may include the treasurer and controller, as well as the mayor or manager, reviews agency requests. A joint-committee budget is reviewed by a group that includes both legislators and administrators. But for purposes of simplicity and because the patterns we describe seem to prevail generally, we will assume that agencies, chief executives, and municipal councils are the major decision makers.

A fairly typical sequence of steps in the budgetary process is presented graphically in Figure 9.2. Although this diagram is only an aid to understanding a complex process, it identifies the major steps and their interrelations. Of enormous importance for actual outcomes is the fact that *revenue decisions are made before expenditure deci-*

sions. One way to construct a public budget might be to identify all the public needs on which money could be spent, add up their probable costs to the government, draw up a budget, and then establish tax rates. But governments do not work this way any more than families

Figure 9.2   An Overview of the Municipal Budgetary Process

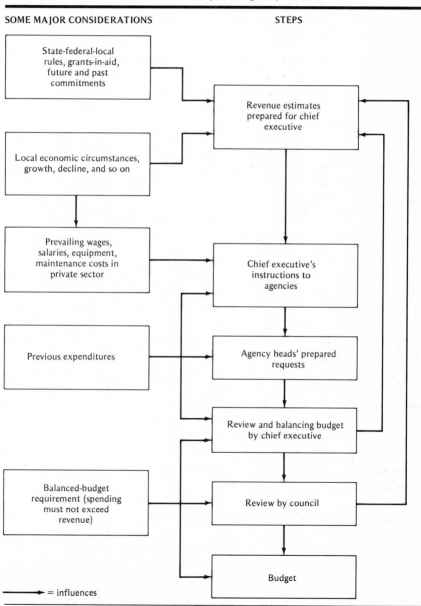

SOME MAJOR CONSIDERATIONS   STEPS

State-federal-local rules, grants-in-aid, future and past commitments

Local economic circumstances, growth, decline, and so on

Prevailing wages, salaries, equipment, maintenance costs in private sector

Previous expenditures

Balanced-budget requirement (spending must not exceed revenue)

Revenue estimates prepared for chief executive

Chief executive's instructions to agencies

Agency heads' prepared requests

Review and balancing budget by chief executive

Review by council

Budget

= influences

decide their needs first and then arrange for their incomes to meet their needs. Rather, revenue estimates for the coming year are made first, and to a large degree they determine the expenditure decisions that are made.[30] Estimates of anticipated revenues are submitted to the office of the chief executive and constitute the first significant input in the budgetary process.

In most large cities it is the legal responsibility of the chief executives to present budgets to the municipal councils. In weak-mayor cities, councils may themselves play more direct roles, whereas other officials or even agencies themselves may be charged with budget preparation. In strong-mayor and manager cities, however, the responsibility normally belongs to chief executives, either mayors or managers. According to John P. Crecine, the problem confronting the executive is

largely one of recommending a budget which (1) is balanced, (2) at least maintains existing service levels, (3) provides for increases in city employees' wages if at all possible, and (4) avoids tax increases (especially property-tax increases in the belief that increased property taxes cause business and industry to move from the city, reducing its tax base).[31]

Of these four requirements, the most stringent is that of a balanced budget. The constitutions of most states do not permit local governments to engage in deficit spending. Revenues and expenditures must match.

On receipt of revenue estimates the mayor or manager issues to his department heads a set of budget instructions. He may include guidelines on service increases, levels of salary and wage increments that he proposes to grant, and other matters. His instructions are shaped by the revenue estimates, and they guide actions by agency heads.

One of the most significant items included in the mayor's fiscal program and his budgetary instructions is wages and salaries. In an inflationary economy, municipal employees expect wage and salary increases that help them keep up with the cost of living; over the long run they also expect to better their relative positions. Moreover, the public sector competes with the private sector for skilled personnel. The municipal government cannot afford to lose large numbers of employees to the private sector as wages become more attractive in business and industry. Thus the prevailing wage rates in the private sector, plus any inflation that has occurred since the last budget, will almost certainly force increases in the budget.

It is common to expect that public (and private) bureaucracies will seek to expand their own programs by means of increased appropriations. But acquisitive strategies can be pushed too far and backfire. Agencies that consistently ask for much—or for more than their fair shares—will come to be viewed by executives and the council as too

aggressive or irresponsible. Such agencies may find their appropriations cut to levels below what they would have received if they had
been more reasonable. Many agency heads walk a delicate line between expansion and political feasibility. Their major question, How
much shall we ask for? is answered in part by the question, How much
are we likely to get?[32]

Agency requests are returned to the chief executive, who then
prepares the budget proposal. At this point, "the decision process in
the (chief executive's) office can usefully be thought of as a search for
a solution to the balanced-budget problem."[33] The mayor's or manager's office is not likely to inquire very deeply into an agency's budget
if no increase is requested and if the total city budget is close to being
in balance. When cuts or increases are necessary, however, there is a
well-defined list of priorities:

1. administrative salaries
2. nonadministrative salaries and wages
3. operating expenses, supplies, and materials
4. equipment
5. maintenance

Budget reviewers will cut agencies' requests in maintenance and
equipment before cutting supplies and salaries, and they will distribute surplus funds to salaries and wages ahead of other categories. It is
only after all other categories have been cut that reductions of salaries
and wages are ordered, and it is only after all higher categories have
received their rewards that any surplus is spent on equipment and
supplies. Part of the reasoning behind this hierarchy of priorities is, no
doubt, that supplies and equipment do not vote, whereas municipal
employees do. The result of all this juggling, adding, subtracting, and
dividing is a balanced budget, which is mimeographed or printed and
forwarded to the council. The council has — within the limits of state
law — the legal power either to approve, to disapprove, or to change
any allocation of municipal funds or the tax rate.

At the federal level, Congress is generally a budget cutter.[34] The
House Appropriations Committee in particular views its major role as
"guardian of the public treasury" and takes a jaundiced view of most
requests for increased appropriations.[35] The typical city council, on
the other hand, operates more as a rubber stamp for decisions made by
the executive.[36] Councils usually make few changes in the budgets
submitted by mayors or managers. The budget is a very complex document, the product of a network of delicate compromises, and to intervene at the final stage would certainly upset this delicate financial balance, for a change in one item would require a compensating change
in another, and so on. Moreover, the city council, in contrast to a congressional committee, lacks a staff to assist it in its budgetary review.

There are exceptions to the rule of minimum interference, and an unpopular chief executive or one from an opposing political party may find the council in a mood to tinker. Most of the time, however, the executive's budget emerges from the council unscathed.

Incremental Budgeting

One way of constructing a municipal budget would be to follow the tenets of rational problem solving that we described in Chapter 7 (pp. 203–204). Each possible goal of an agency's program might be identified, the goals ranked in a preference hierarchy, and then a series of comparisons made among budget alternatives. The end product would, at some level of abstraction, account for all policy goals served by the government and represent a weighing of every possible budgetary strategy to meet these goals. But for reasons that we explained in Chapter 6 — and for additional reasons that we will discuss shortly — rational budgeting is virtually impossible to achieve. The more common budgeting model is *incremental:* Past experience — and especially past expenditures — is used as a guide to future spending. Bastable, the nineteenth-century Irish student of public finance, wrote:

Fortunately the question of expenditure in all its forms does not present itself as a single problem. It would be quite hopeless to prepare a budget of outlay for any country without the aid of the material collected during previous experience. The great mass of expenditure is taken as settled, and it is only the particular changes that have to be anxiously weighed in order to estimate their probable advantage. This method of treatment simplifies issues very much.[37]

Because "the great mass of expenditure is taken as settled," incrementalism focuses attention mainly on deviations from past behavior. Each agency has an expenditure base below which it is not likely to be cut.[38] It is the increments that are subject to close examination. Agency expenditures, as well as total city expenditures, will be very highly correlated with previous expenditures. The tendency toward incremental decisions is not the only factor that produces high correlations between present and past expenditures. The stability of local-revenue sources and the availability of continuing grants-in-aid for specific programs are two additional factors.

Meltsner emphasizes the incremental character of budgeting in Oakland. "Previous decisions," he says, "determine present allocations. . . . If one allows for slight increases in the cost of Oakland's employees and expenses, then last year's budget is this year's budget."[39] One of the costs of incrementalism is that changes are slow in coming. The new mayor who campaigned for more police expenditures or neighborhood services will quickly discover how little money he or she has to implement these programs.

Budgeting and the Policy Process

Students of budgeting have generally used one of three basic perspectives. Crecine has described them as: (1) the "optimizing process," (2) "budgeting as an externally determined event," and (3) "budgeting as an internal bureaucratic process."[40] The notion that budgets *optimize* community values reflects the idea that public budgets are a function of public needs and represent decision makers' efforts to bring public resources into line with overall community goals. The *externally determined* view is that budgets result from economic and political forces. Citizens' demands for service, the power of community elites, the demands of various groups, and responses to economic pressures are some explanations for a budget's final shape. Business groups are said to seek lower taxes; proponents of law and order demand more money for law enforcement; and PTAs want more money for schools. These demands or requests for services and expenditures are channeled through mayors, councils, and agencies, and the sum of these pressures determines the level of public expenditures. In the third model, that of budgeting as an internal bureaucratic process, external forces are viewed as unimportant, and instead the budget is explained as the outcome of rules and strategies for decision making employed by agencies, chief executives, and legislative bodies.

The data presented by Crecine suggest that neither optimization of community values nor externally determined events offer realistic explanations of the budgetary outcomes. "It is quite clear (from interviews) that the decision-makers *do not* see the problem as one of optimally balancing community resources, allocating funds among functions to achieve overall community goals, and the like."[41] Nor was there much evidence that decision makers perceived great pressures for higher or lower expenditures from groups. When pressures did occur, the common response was, "We just have so much money and we can't do everything."[42]

According to Crecine's findings, budgeting is primarily a bureaucratic process, operating—once revenue estimates are made—as a relatively closed system. The dominant decision-making method is incrementalism. As we have seen above, however, the local budget maker operates in a context that is determined partly by the macro-level factors of the community's economic resources, social composition, and local government structure, and the constraints imposed on the city by its state government.

Two things stand out about the budgetary process. First, it is remarkably *insulated* from local politics and political action. In Chapter 5, we described various interest groups in local arenas and detailed many of their demands on urban decision makers. *But to the degree that those demands cost money,* they may not get translated into policy. The poor who want neighborhood revival, groups who want crime prevention, and parents who want better schools may receive more sympathy than budget outlays. The second matter pertains to the one exception to the general insulation of the budget process: *Economic factors affect the budget largely through the revenue side.* Most cities cannot legally engage in deficit financing, so revenues have to match expenditures. A depressed political economy will be felt in declining revenues, and alternatives will have to be located or budget cuts made. This sets in motion the coping process of local budget politics, including a press for new intergovernmental aids and the constant additions of nickel and dime taxes.

THE URBAN FISCAL CRISIS: NEW YORK AND ELSEWHERE

The Roots of Fiscal Crisis

The fiscal crisis of the American city has many roots. It brings into focus a number of elements that we have discussed. In Chapter 3 we described the great migrations associated with the political sociology of metropolitan areas; in Chapter 4 the political economy of the city was related to industrial and commercial decisions; in Chapter 5 we showed how many citizens respond to tax increases and service declines by exiting; in Chapter 7 the demands of municipal workers for higher wages and benefits were emphasized; and in this chapter we showed how the urban revenue and spending process worked. These factors combine to produce a fiscal crisis of astounding proportions in numerous cities.

We suggest that there are five major roots of the urban fiscal crisis. Shortly we will show how New York City confronted threats of municipal bankruptcy. But the nation's largest city and many other cities confront a set of factors promoting fiscal instability. Among them are:

FRAGMENTATION OF METROPOLITAN GOVERNMENT AND THE EXIT OF PEOPLE AND PRODUCTION TO THE PERIPHERY   The fragmentation of metropolitan government contributes to the "irony of urban wealth," where resources may be walled off from needs. Exit has become a common response both by families and by firms to the problems they encounter in bigger cities. When they exit to suburban areas, the fiscal strain in central cities is increased. Between 1953 and 1973, New York City lost manufacturing employment—and the industries that employ people and pay taxes—while gaining in government employment. Many of those losses were to suburban areas.

THE MOVEMENT TO THE "SUNBELT" AND THE DECLINE OF THE NORTHEAST GENERALLY   Sternlieb and Hughes note that "the New York malaise is too commonly viewed within the narrow framework of central city versus suburb. In appraising New York City and its neighbors in the Northeast, we must be concerned with the broad patterns of regional shifts, the growing dominance of the South and Southwest at the expense of old areas."[43] Federal policy (discussed in Chapter 4, pp. 61–62) has consistently given more support to "sunbelt" than "frostbelt" states.

INFLATION   Families are hurt by inflation, as real incomes decline even while dollar incomes increase. So, too, with municipal governments. The costs of services that cities must buy has actually increased faster than the costs of services that families buy. Chicago is a city in generally good shape fiscally, but inflation has eroded its purchasing power. Figure 9.3 shows the eroding effects of inflation on the urban budget of Chicago.

EXHAUSTION OF THE PROPERTY TAX AND OTHER LOCAL REVENUES
Earlier we showed how the property tax has often reached its prac-

Figure 9.3   Inflation Impact on the Chicago Budget

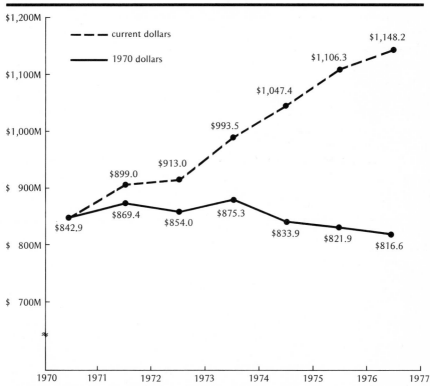

Source: Budgetary Division, City of Chicago, November 14, 1975.

tical political limit. Even if it is politically possible to increase property tax collections, an increase that causes more exit of families and
firms yields no net increase in revenues.

INCREASE IN DEMANDS FOR SERVICES AND PAYROLLS EVEN IN THE
FACE OF DECLINING REVENUES   While revenues have lagged, citizen
demands have not. Indeed, demands often increase in response to
problems of deterioration. Nor have the demands of municipal
workers slacked off. Hit by inflation and erosion of their own purchasing power, unionized and nonunionized workers demand a fair share
of urban budgets.

  Almost all of these problems — plus some others — culminated in the
great near-bankruptcy of New York City.

Fiscal Crisis in New York

The fiscal crisis in New York City that came to a head in 1975 illustrates in all-too-startling fashion that urban taxing and spending is not
all routine.[44] In this case the Big Apple itself faced the implications of
having exceeded financial prudence over a number of preceding years
and was left with only distasteful alternatives: to make unprecedented
reductions in public services and civil-service payrolls; to go into
bankruptcy with its unknown implications for creditors, government
employees, and service recipients; or to engineer some unique combination of measures, with their details very dependent on actions taken
by New York State and the national government. Even if New York's
problem was entirely its own, it would be a case worthy of consideration. New York is by far the largest and most prominent American
city, with expenditures totaling about 25 percent of all cities' expenditures. By the end of 1975 its finances were so tangled with those of
New York State that a city bankruptcy would probably have meant a
state bankruptcy. Even the threat of a New York City bankruptcy sent
shock waves through the bond markets. Other cities and states — even
those with sound balances — found it impossible to sell bonds at reasonable rates of interest. European governments brought pressure to
bear on the White House to help out the City and suggested that international financial confidence in the United States could falter — with
the possible consequence of a deeper world depression — if the nation's most prominent city was allowed to go under. On the other side
there were arguments against special federal aid by those who feared
dire consequences for the proper balance of the federal system, and
even for the sanctity of American capitalism (as if that had not already
undergone irreversible changes). By all accounts the New York fiscal
crisis has been a monumental event. Not only has it had direct and indirect implications far beyond the borders of the city itself, but it also

reveals—albeit in a somewhat more extreme form that exists in other cities—the variety of economic, social, and political features that can impose severe constraints on current policy making.

On the surface the problem of the city was insufficient tax revenues to meet required payments, and a deteriorating credit rating that made it impossible to borrow additional money to pay its bills. It was pressed to reduce expenditures partly to save the actual money involved and thus to have that much lower obligations the next month and partly to convince wary lenders that it was moving toward fiscal responsibility. Various announcements during the latter part of the year told of $1 billion worth of construction being stopped; closing of certain city hospitals; elimination of subsidies to museums and other cultural activities; postponement of paying bills and bondholders; wage freezes or postponed increases in employee salaries; and reduction of the civil-service staff by some 37,000. There was a contorted series of proposals for aid by New York State and various state and city pension funds, complicated by some apparent changes of heart after certain officials had committed themselves publicly to aiding the city, as well as court suits designed to block extraordinary procedures to keep the city from bankruptcy. At an early point the state committed itself to lend money to the city and pledge its own credit behind new bonds designed to help the city through its cash shortage. The state got in so deep that its own bonds were tainted by their identification with New York City. Despite its recently strong credit rating, the state could not sell bonds without paying an intolerably high rate of interest. (The less comfortable a lender feels about a borrower's certainty to pay on time, the more he hedges his bet with a higher rate of interest. At a certain point, as in this case with New York State, it is possible to borrow money but at interest rates so high as to make it not worthwhile).

The Ford Administration showed no great enthusiasm for giving the city special help. Despite generous sentiments coming out of the liberal Democrats in Congress, the President relied on his veto power to control the actual federal response. Throughout much of the year the city received only dour lectures from the executive branch. The front page of New York's *Daily News* for 30 October 1975 was half-covered with the headline: "FORD TO CITY: DROP DEAD." Treasury Secretary William Simon reinforced the President's message to the effect that the city and state governments had primary responsibility for the city's plight, that fiscal responsibility was in order, and that special federal help would threaten unhealthy changes in the character of federalism and the bond markets. Critics of the Administration were quick to compare this rhetoric with that used by President Hoover in the early days of the Great Depression. The Administration recognized that numerous banks held large sums of New York

City's debt. One survey revealed that 53 national banks held New York City bonds equal to 40 percent of their capital; and another survey found 62 state-chartered banks with New York City bonds equal to 50 percent of their capital. At the point when Washington was chary of aiding the city directly, Chairman Arthur Burns of the Federal Reserve Board assured the banks of special help from the Federal Deposit Insurance Corporation should New York's impending default threaten their solvency. By year's end, special federal assistance had passed Congress and the White House, consisting of special loans, plus changes in the bankruptcy laws enabling the city to alter the terms of the bonds it had sold its creditors — in effect postponing the repayment of principal but extending the payment of interest — without first obtaining the creditors' consent. This brought howls of protest from some creditors and the initiation of lawsuits likely to reach the Supreme Court.

It may take years for the city's plight to be resolved and for its reverberations to cease. This is hardly the place to indicate how the crisis has altered established patterns of municipal finance. It is possible, however, to identify some of the causes of the city's problem and to gauge the extent of these problems in other cities.

The analysis of New York City's problems suggests that they were not typical of numerous other cities. The key factors seem to be exceptionally generous public services, civil-service salaries, and fringe benefits, including pension commitments whose burdens on the city continue for years to come. These features, in turn, reflect New York's demanding electorate, its role as a magnet for streams of needy migrants from the rural South and the Caribbean, and its position in the forefront of public-employee unionization. Aggressive labor leaders worked throughout the 1960s and early 1970s to boost New York's public workforce and to fatten its compensation. Added to all these special characteristics was the general national experience of economic decline in 1974 and 1975, which increased demands for city welfare services at the same time that it cut into the city's revenues from income, sales, and property taxes.

Examples of New York's generosity to citizens and employees are not hard to find. Coin changers in the subway received $229 per week while bank clerks were being paid $164; policemen on the job three years earned $17,458; a 1974 survey of the U.S. Bureau of the Census found the average monthly earnings of New York City employees to be $1,156, while those of employees in 74 major metropolitan areas was only $1,005; many employees hired before 1974 could retire after 20 years on the job with pensions of one-half their last year's earnings. This last provision made it possible for a worker to retire in his early forties with a $15,000 pension, plus the opportunity to work at another job for the remaining years of his prime. When students at public universities around the country were paying an average $552 per year for tuition and fees, those enrolled at the City University of New York were getting by with only $110.

Administrative control was not a strong point for the city. At various times in the crisis journalists reported that no one knew exactly how many people worked for the city: Estimates ranged from 295,500 to 400,000. And while it cost the city some $40 per ton to collect garbage, the same task was done by private contractors for $22 a ton in San Francisco, $19 a ton in Boston, and $18 a ton in Minneapolis.

Partly in an effort to stem the contagion of New York's problems to their own credit ratings, the officials of numerous cities pointed to the uniqueness of New York's crisis. *Time* magazine reported in October that 8 of the 10 other largest cities finished 1974 with budget surpluses, and expected further surpluses for 1975. Wichita, Kansas – hardly a community that could claim to face the social problems of New York – launched a National Alliance of Financially Responsible Local Governments. Other qualified charter members were Sacramento, Indianapolis, Cedar Rapids, St. Paul, Albuquerque, and Dallas.

No amount of urban self-righteousness could contain the New York crisis entirely. Interest rates on municipal and state bonds increased across the board, reflecting investors' desire for more reward commensurate with what they claimed was greater risk no matter which city or state was borrowing their money. Numerous "solvent" cities and states withdrew bond offerings rather than pay historically high rates of interest. It is yet to be determined just how much the city's crisis will alter established procedures of municipal finance. Other factors to be considered in evaluating this include any continued worsening in the economy that will push additional cities into required borrowing; the package of assurances coming from Washington that will either quiet or alarm the fears of investors about the security of funds loaned to local governments; and – assuming a continued increase in interest rates – the decisions taken in various localities about the pros and cons of further borrowing; tax increases; or cuts in spending, services, and the workforce.

New York is not merely living from hand-to-mouth. It still teeters on the brink of bankruptcy. A state court late in 1976 declared the intricate arrangements to delay paying bondholders unconstitutional, and the city once again faced the unpleasant prospect of insolvency. A series of articles in *Society* magazine heralded the gloomy theme. Among the titles were "Stagnant Metropolis," "New York: Future without a Future?" "Aging Metropolis in Decline," and – perhaps most painful to New Yorkers – "What New York Can Learn from Texas."[45]

Is New York Atypical or Merely a Foretaste of the Urban Future?

Some observers consider New York City an atypical case. In some ways it is. The city has responsibilities no other city undertakes, including expensive health and hospital programs, a vast city university system, and welfare programs handled elsewhere by other layers of government. Yet others believe that New York, though first to reach

Table 9.5   Fiscal Strain Index

	Municipal fiscal strain		Municipal fiscal strain
Extra high		26. Milwaukee, Mis.	44.28
1. New York, N.Y.	169.59	27. Palo Alto, Cal.	42.82
2. Boston, Mass.	138.82	28. Minneapolis, Minn.	42.57
		29. Tyler, Texas	42.27
High		30. Waco, Texas	42.00
3. San Francisco, Cal.	104.65	31. Charlotte, N.C.	40.78
4. Newark, N.J.	103.51	32. South Bend, Ind.	39.91
5. Albany, N.Y.	100.69	33. Indianapolis, Ind.	37.65
6. Cambridge, Mass.	91.44	34. Fort Worth, Texas	38.77
7. Malden, Mass.	90.19	35. Euclid, Ohio	36.72
		36. Phoenix, Ariz.	35.61
Medium		37. Bloomington, Minn.	34.41
8. Buffalo, N.Y.	88.65	38. Duluth, Minn.	33.43
9. Atlanta, Ga.	82.59	39. Gary, Ind.	33.24
10. Waterbury, Conn.	80.97	40. Irvington, N.J.	32.31
11. Utica, N.Y.	74.97	41. Santa Monica, Cal.	30.68
12. Seattle, Wash.	73.64	42. Schenectady, N.Y.	29.19
13. Jacksonville, Fla.	72.79	43. Clifton, N.J.	28.56
14. Manchester, N.H.	66.94	44. Hamilton, Ohio	27.84
15. Los Angeles, Cal.	63.70	45. Berkeley, Cal.	27.32
16. Akron, Ohio	62.61	45. Hammond, Ind.	27.29
17. Birmingham, Ala.	60.50	47. San Jose, Cal.	26.61
18. St. Louis, Mo.	58.74	48. St. Petersburg, Fla.	24.78
19. Chicago, Ill.	57.08	49. Warren, Mich.	22.73
20. Memphis, Tenn.	56.00		
21. Pasadena, Cal.	55.46	**Extra low**	
22. St. Paul, Minn.	52.61	50. Salt Lake City, Utah	20.71
23. Tampa, Fla.	48.88	51. Amarillo, Texas	18.72
24. Pittsburgh, Penna.	48.61	52. Waukegan, Ill.	15.99
		53. Fullerton, Cal.	8.80
Low		54. Santa Ana, Cal.	8.00
25. Long Beach, Cal.	46.28		

Source: Terry N. Clark, Department of Sociology, University of Chicago.

an advanced stage of fiscal decay, is a harbinger of things to come. One effort to set New York City in context is Terry N. Clark's assessment of "fiscal strain" in 54 American cities.[46] Clark used a combined index of factors promoting fiscal instability and scored each city on fiscal strain. His rankings of the 54 cities are presented in Table 9.5. In some ways, New York *is* unique: Only Boston also scores as "extra high" on Clark's rankings. But other cities score as "high" on fiscal strain, including San Francisco, and several northeastern cities. At the other extreme are cities such as Fullerton and Santa Ana, California, Waukegan, Illinois, and Amarillo, Texas. Clearly some cities are able to manage their financial affairs better than others.

SUMMARY

In this chapter we have identified the fiscal-policy options available to local governmental officials and have explained the choices that officials make. Our subject has been one of the most vital resources in urban politics: money. We have identified the major revenue sources of local governments and the major elements of local expenditures. We have found that most revenues come from property taxes, state aids, service charges, and borrowing. The single most important category of local expenditure is education; public utilities, highways, welfare, health, hospitals, police, interest on debt, and other such items take what is left.

We have tried to do more than simply to identify fiscal intake and outgo. We have examined critical differences in the expenditure and revenue patterns of local governments and traced these differences to community social, economic, and political characteristics. From a macro perspective, these patterns suggest a lack of individuality or innovation in budgeting. Our discussion of budget-making procedures reinforces this conclusion. Officials do not make budget policy after a thorough review of all the relevant conditions. They rely instead on mechanical procedures that boil down the potential criteria to very few. Although this tendency is not so strong as to preclude all possibility of innovation, budgeting is a conservative force that militates against introduction of new programs through the local government financial system. Innovations must first be accepted by other officials and must be presented to budget makers only after they have achieved such wide acceptance to be considered commitments to be honored by the financial officers.

One result of the budget and revenue process is a fiscal crisis in many cities. Movement of people and production, fragmentation of metropolitan government, inflation, rise of the "sunbelt," and demands for services and higher payrolls all combine to heighten fiscal strain. In New York City, fiscal malaise is most advanced, but other cities increasingly confront a revenue-expenditure squeeze.

Notes

1. One exception to this rule is Pennsylvania's so-called "tax-anything" law, in which cities may, in general, tax anything not already taxed by the state.
2. James A. Maxwell, *Financing State and Local Government* (Washington, D.C.: Brookings Institution, 1965), p. 143.
3. Rarely, if ever, are local property assessments actually based on market value. Properties are typically undervalued, and the limited staffs of assessment offices often permit valuations to remain unchanged over decades. Properties in areas with rapidly rising land values thus may still be assessed at much less than their true values. It may also be noted that in local governments not characterized by pristine integrity, assessments have sometimes been manipulated by local officials.
4. Real property most commonly subject to property taxes includes land, dwelling units, office buildings, factories, and the like.
5. Joseph A. Pechman and Benjamin Okner, *Who Bears the Tax Burden?* (Washington, D.C.: Brookings Institution, 1974).
6. Advisory Commission on Intergovernmental Relations, *Local Revenue Diversification* (Washington, D.C.: Government Printing Office, 1974), pp. 18–19.
7. Walter Heller, *New Dimensions of Political Economy* (New York: Norton, 1967), p. 153.
8. George Sternlieb and R. W. Burchall, "Neighborhood Change and Housing Abandonment," in James W. Hughes, ed., *Suburbanization Dynamics and the Future of the City* (New Brunswick, N.J.: Rutgers University, Center for Urban Policy Research, 1974), p. 96.
9. Arnold J. Meltsner, *The Politics of City Revenue* (Berkeley: University of California Press, 1961), p. 104.
10. See, for example, John F. Due, "Studies of State–Local Tax Influences on Industrial Location," *National Tax Journal, 14* (1961), 163–173.
11. L. L. Ecker-Racz, quoted in Heller, op. cit., p. 126.
12. Charles A. Beard, *American Government and Politics,* 4th ed. (New York: Macmillan, 1924), p. 727.
13. Louis H. Masotti and Don R. Bowen, "Communities and Budgets: The Sociology of Municipal Expenditures," *Urban Affairs Quarterly, 1* (1965), 39.
14. For a summary see Brett Hawkins, *Politics and Urban Policies* (Indianapolis: Bobbs-Merrill, 1971).
15. Robert L. Lineberry and Edmund P. Fowler, III, "Reformism and Public Policies in American Cities," *American Political Science Review, 61* (September 1967), 712.
16. Alan Campbell and Seymour Sacks, *Metropolitan America* (New York: Free Press, 1967), chap. 2.
17. Ibid., p. 173.
18. Ira Sharkansky, "Economic and Political Correlates of State Government Expenditures: General Tendencies and Deviant Cases," *Midwest Journal of Political Science, 11* (May 1967), 173–192.
19. Ibid., p. 191.
20. Lineberry and Fowler, op. cit., pp. 707–708.
21. V. O. Key, Jr., *Southern Politics* (New York: Knopf, 1951), pp. 298–314; and Duane Lockard, *New England State Politics* (Princeton, N.J.: Princeton University Press, 1959), pp. 320–340.

22. Ira Sharkansky, *Spending in the American States* (Skokie, Ill.: Rand McNally, 1968).

23. Edmund P. Fowler, III, and Robert L. Lineberry, "The Comparative Analysis of Urban Policy: Canada and the United States," in Harlan Hahn, ed., *People and Politics in Urban Society* (Beverly Hills, Calif.: Sage, 1972), pp. 345–368.

24. John C. Bollens, et al., *Exploring the Metropolitan Community* (Berkeley: University of California Press, 1961), pp. 258–268.

25. John E. Horton and Wayne E. Thompson, "Powerlessness and Political Negativism," *American Journal of Sociology*, 67 (March 1962), 485–493.

26. Aaron Wildavsky, *The Politics of the Budgetary Process* (Boston: Little, Brown, 1964), pp. 1–3.

27. Frederick M. Wirt, *Politics in the City* (Berkeley: University of California Press, 1974), p. 136.

28. New York *Times*, 25 May 1975, p. 40.

29. On national budgetary politics, see Wildavsky, op. cit. Studies of budget making at the state level include Thomas Anton, *The Politics of State Expenditure in Illinois* (Urbana: University of Illinois Press, 1966); and Ira Sharkansky, *The Politics of Taxing and Spending* (Indianapolis: Bobbs-Merrill, 1969), chap. 4. The most sophisticated study of budgetary policy making in urban government is John P. Crecine, *Governmental Problem Solving: A Computer Simulation of Municipal Budgeting* (Skokie, Ill.: Rand McNally, 1969). Our discussion of the process of determining municipal expenditures has benefited from Crecine's penetrating treatments of Detroit, Pittsburgh, and Cleveland.

30. Crecine, op. cit., pp. 32–34, 192.

31. Ibid., p. 39.

32. Wildavsky, op. cit., pp. 18–31.

33. Crecine, op. cit., p. 67.

34. Wildavsky, op. cit., pp. 47–48.

35. Richard Fenno, "The House Appropriations Committee as a Political System: The Problem of Integration," *American Political Science Review*, 56 (June 1962), 310–324.

36. Crecine, op. cit., p. 207.

37. Charles Francis Bastable, quoted in Mabel Walker, *Municipal Expenditures* (Baltimore: Johns Hopkins, 1930), p. 37.

38. Wildavsky, op. cit., pp. 16–18.

39. Meltsner, op. cit., pp. 162–163.

40. Crecine, op. cit., pp. 9 ff.

41. Ibid., p. 38.

42. Ibid., p. 189.

43. George Sternlieb and James W. Hughes, "New York: Future Without a Future?" *Society*, May/June 1976, p. 19.

44. On New York's problems, see Donald H. Haider, "Fiscal Scarcity: A New Urban Perspective," in Louis H. Masotti and Robert L. Lineberry, eds., *The New Urban Politics* (Cambridge, Mass.: Ballinger, 1976), chap. 8.

45. *Society*, op. cit.

46. Terry N. Clark and Lorna Ferguson, "Fiscal Strain and Fiscal Health in American Cities," paper presented to the Annual Meeting of the American Sociological Association, Chicago, September 6, 1977.

10
PUBLIC POLICY AND URBAN SERVICES

Urban governments are service machines. How well they produce services becomes a critical question in a time of fiscal crisis. Who benefits from services is always a critical question in urban politics. In this chapter we emphasize that:

- Cities faced with the end of an expanding budget in an inflationary era become more concerned with improved productivity and delivery.
- There is a widespread belief that the overall quality of urban services has declined recently, that neighborhoods are dirtier, that parks are deteriorating, and that services in general are worsening.
- Citizens and officials have become sensitive to issues of equity in service allocation, and courts have become involved in scrutinizing the distribution of municipal services.

There may be little drama in streets, sewers, swings, open spaces, fire protection, housing codes, and garbage pickup and disposal. Policing the city seems colorful and exciting, more no doubt because television makes it interesting than because the routines of the police officer's day-to-day life are so exciting. Education seems less dramatic but is felt to have a profound impact as an avenue to upward mobility. But most urban services lack the color and drama that make a good story. Most service decisions are invisible.

People assume that service decisions get "handled" somewhere in government, but it is clear that they are not always handled well or in an even-handed manner. Douglas Yates remarks that,

After a decade of protest and demands for participation and community control, urban government appears to be entering a new era. Now that the "urban crisis" has been discovered, debated and in some quarters dismissed, government officials and academic analysts alike have increasingly come to focus on "service delivery" as the central issue and problem of urban policy-making.

This shift from "crisis" rhetoric and dramatic solutions to the discussion of service delivery is itself highly interesting. . . . For one thing, it is difficult to see how a government can solve its dramatic problems if it cannot solve its routine ones.

Viewed from this perspective, the problem of urban management today is that, instead of asserting, as we used to, that there is no Democratic or Republican way to clean the streets, we are now asking whether government is capable of cleaning the streets at all.[1]

The costs of urban services are high. Even so elemental a service as brush removal can consume a half million dollars in a medium-sized city. Some urban services literally may be matters of life and death. Sanitation, fire protection, and water quality are as intimately connected to physical survival as police protection, and more so than schooling. The loss of life and property from urban fires rivals the loss from crime.

SERVICING THE CITY

Virtually all of the city's rawest nerves touch the delivery of urban services. As we have noted above, the city represents a mosaic of races, classes, and groups living in a densely settled space. The acquisition of quality public services (parks, schools, libraries, clean streets) and avoidance of a negatively valued municipal output (a sewerage treatment plant, an unwanted public housing project) define the gamut of urban conflict. The belief of the affluent that the service grass is greener on the other side of the municipal fence has contributed to their exodus from the cities.[2] We discussed earlier the "exit" and "voice" options open to those dissatisfied, and nothing better illustrates these choices than public services. If better services can be secured along with an even lower tax rate, it is rational to move to the suburbs. For many it is easier to switch than fight.

Others who cannot, or will not, switch may stay to fight. Neighborhoods organize to pressure municipal governments into upgrading police protection, street maintenance, and other services to prevent decay. In lower-income neighborhoods, the quality of services becomes a visible manifestation of their standing in local politics. Claude Brown, describing his childhood in Harlem, says that "Harlem was [slighted] by everybody, the politicians, the police, the businessman, everybody. . . . We'd laugh about when the big snowstorms came, they'd have the snowplows out downtown as soon as it stopped, but they'd let it pile up for weeks in Harlem."[3]

The urban poor are more dependent on the public sector than the more affluent. Groups that do not have ample yards and private pools must rely on public parks and pools; those without means to seek private medical care must rely on public facilities; those who cannot pay for private schooling must take whatever the public schools have to offer; those who cannot purchase books must rely on the public libraries. When the quality of services declines, the poor suffer most.

There is some suspicion that the quality of service in American cities has slipped in recent years. Data bearing on this question appear in Table 10.1. They are the combined responses of the Urban Observatory's 10-city study of citizen attitudes toward public services. Of interest is both the distribution by social class and citizen statements

Table 10.1   Responses by Socioeconomic Status to Questions Concerning Whether You Get Your Money's Worth in City Services

| Money's worth | Socioeconomic status | | | | | |
	Upper	Upper middle	Lower middle	Upper lower	Lower	Total
Yes	54.3% (134)	51.7% (289)	43.9% (282)	36.4% (500)	27.7% (148)	40.2% (1402)
No	45.7% (113)	48.3% (270)	56.1% (360)	63.6% (959)	72.3% (386)	59.8% (2088)
						100.0% (3480)

Source: Pooled data from Urban Observatories' 10-city survey of citizen evaluations of city taxes and services.

about getting their "money's worth" from city services. In the aggregate, those responding negatively outnumber the yea-sayers by a 3–2 margin. As one might expect, there are some differences by social class. Even among the higher-status class, however, only a bare majority (54 to 46 percent) think they are getting what they pay for. Because these data come from a single point in time, they do not provide any evidence on the deterioration of services. However, citizens were queried on their perceptions of changes in city government over the past half decade. The results appear in Table 10.2. Unfortunately the question was not service-specific (it did not ask in what way government was worse) nor did it permit the respondents to say that services had become "worse." Even with those limitations, we can assume some perception of stagnation (if not deterioration), since the ratio of persons picking "the same" to those who chose "better" is just about 3–2 regardless of social class. During this period, moreover, city governments were increasing their expenditures faster than inflation. These increases in costs (and taxes) help to explain citizens' feeling of not getting their money's worth.

It is entirely possible that citizen assessments of public services are simply wrong. People may be chafing about their own cares of inflation, unemployment, or family problems and merely find a convenient scapegoat in city government. People may mistake a high crime rate for poor police protection, as if better police protection could somehow deter every mugger and rapist. They may blame city sanitation departments for dirty neighborhoods caused by the sloppiness of their friends and neighbors. They may blame the schools for failures that

Table 10.2   Response by Socioeconomic Status to Questions Concerning Whether City Government in the Last Five Years Has Improved or Stayed the Same

Evaluation of city government	Socioeconomic status					
	Upper	Upper middle	Lower middle	Upper lower	Lower	Total
Improved	42.8 (92)	43.4 (193)	39.3 (193)	38.3 (426)	39.4 (146)	39.8 (1050)
Same	57.2 (123)	56.6 (252)	60.7 (298)	61.7 (687)	60.6 (225)	60.2 (1585)
						100.00 (2635)

Source: Pooled data from Urban Observatories' 10-city survey of citizen evaluations of city taxes and services.

the schools could never have reversed. In short, what people *think* about services is important, but subjective and objective assessments of service quality may diverge. It would be sobering indeed to learn that objective indexes of service quality had declined. If municipal governments are now investing two or three times as much in their outputs as they did only a decade ago, one certainly hopes that the production of services has improved, along with costs. Yet, as we shall see in the next section, very little is known about whether this vast expansion in spending has brought improvements in the quantity and quality of services delivered.

PRODUCING PUBLIC SERVICES

Public Goods and the Rise of the Productivity Issue

Is government "productive"? Whether it is or isn't, should it be? If it should be, how can we decide whether we are getting our money's worth? Surely, if more than one of every four dollars is spent by government, we should be as attentive to questions of cost and quality as we are with cars, hair dryers, or other gadgetry of the marketplace. Some years ago, economist William Baumol drew a distinction between two sectors of the economy, the "productive" one and the other where productivity was either undesirable or difficult to ensure.[4] We may want more productivity in the manufacture of automobiles, so

that output per man-hour is improved, thereby offering a better product, hopefully, at the same or lower price. In the other sector — the arts
are the most conspicuous example — we may not actually desire to
improve productivity; and even if we did, we may not be able to. One
could, in Baumol's famous example, improve musical "productivity"
by playing the "Minute Waltz" in 30 seconds. But we do not want that
sort of improvement. In education we could improve the "productivity" of teachers by having each teacher teach 100 pupils instead of 30,
or, even better, by having each teacher convey more information, understanding, or appreciation about the material at hand.

The problem of productivity is considerably more complex in the
public sector than in the private sector. In the private sector the pricing system of the market may spur improvements in productivity. In
the public sector we often do not know what we are buying, how to
measure it, or how to improve the ratio of inputs (money, personnel) to
outputs (services rendered and problems ameliorated). Harry Hatry of
the Urban Institute has remarked that "citizen concern about the quality of public services . . . is nothing new. Surprisingly, however, until
very recently governments themselves and others have done little to
measure the quality of these services."[5] The point of the productivity
argument is a simple one: Knowing what the public sector does well,
or does badly, reduces the chance of throwing good money after bad
and helps to direct public investments toward those activities that
yield maximal results.

Firefighting — an essential urban service.

The Misleading Metric of Money

Money spent is a commonplace, but not a very good, index of service quality and productivity. Per-pupil expenditures, per-capita police protection expenditures, and per-capita investments in roads and highways tell only how much government spends, not what services it gets from expenditures. "The more money, the more impact" is a standard assumption of groups demanding higher expenditures on their favorite service. Sharkansky has called such an assumption the "spending-service cliche"; it typically unites agency heads and client-constituents in asserting that higher outputs will come with more resources.[6] Only the naive citizen, like the naive consumer, believes that the best test of a policy's net worth is its price tag. One who buys by price risks getting what he or she pays for. So, too, with policy. Economist Dick Netzer put it bluntly in contending that "money does not really matter, except as a device to facilitate transactions (and measurements); what does matter is the use of human and material resources."[7] Money, it is said, does not buy happiness (though the rich say that more often than the poor). Neither does it guarantee a high level of service outputs.

A very high level of public spending on a particular service, whether parks, or police, or schools, or whatever, may indicate many things. For example, it could mean that:

1. Labor costs are very high. Because two-thirds to three-fourths of all public service expenditures are in salaries and wages, high labor costs push spending upwards. New York City looks like a municipal spendthrift compared with most other places largely because it pays unionized municipal employees so highly.
2. Services are produced very inefficiently, necessitating high costs when even better services could be produced at lower costs.
3. Services are actually first-rate. Good public services, like good private services, cost money.

Nor do low per-capita spending levels necessarily prove that productivity or service quality is inferior. It is best to measure expenditures in relation to what is being purchased, not in simple dollar amounts.

Two policy areas where the relationship between money and outputs has been most carefully examined are schools and policing. High educational expenditures reflect many things, including high teacher salaries, the cost of land and construction, vandalism, insurance costs, and maintenance. They may reflect the fact that the community is purchasing the "best" education that money and professional know-how can produce. Or they may reflect the facts that unionized teachers are able to secure higher salaries, that maintenance costs are very high in older facilities, or vandalism necessitates heavy repair bills. All things considered, it is difficult to demonstrate a strong relationship between the per-pupil level of expenditures and the "quality" of schooling. Christopher Jencks and his associates reviewed the evidence on school spending and *pupil performance on standard tests* (a limitation that should be emphasized) and concluded that "the evidence we have examined does not suggest that doubling expenditures would raise students' performance on standard tests . . . no measurable school resource or policy shows a consistent relationship to schools' effectiveness in boosting achievement."[8] Yet such sobering discoveries do not justify a lack of concern for school finance. What these findings about money and schools' productivity *do* suggest is still important: One who would improve school performance is well-advised to be *at least as interested* in the *content* of school policy and the *utilization* of its resources as in the dollars actually spent.

A similar story can be told about the relationship between money and police productivity. Although we have been spending far more money recently on law enforcement, crime rates have soared. Between 1950 and 1970, law-enforcement expenditures increased by 145 percent; yet the amount of crime measured by the Federal Bureau of Investigation *also increased* by almost exactly the same amount, 144 percent. Table 10.3 provides some averages and trends for selected measures of productivity in law enforcement. While expenditures were increasing, and police forces were expanding, crime rates were

Table 10.3 Some Indicators of Productivity in Law Enforcement; Cities over 250,000, 1965–1970

	1970	Percent change, 1965–1970
I. Increase in police resources		
1. Police officers/1000 population	326	+23
2. Police expenditures per police officer (constant dollars)	$14,500	+11
II. Productivity indicators		
1. Reported FBI "index crimes"[a] per 100,000 population	5,340	+117
2. "Index crimes" per police officer	16.4	+76
3. Clearance rate	.218	−20

[a] "Index crimes" refers to the "index" of the most serious crimes (murder, robbery, rape, and so on) developed by the Federal Bureau of Investigation and reported in its *Uniform Crime Reports.*
Source: George P. Barbour, Jr., "Measuring Local Government Productivity," *Municipal Yearbook 1973* (Washington, D.C.: International City Management Association, 1973), p. 40.

increasing. The clearance rate (a measure police departments use to show when an individual crime has been "cleared" by an arrest) declined during the period, despite the additional investment in police resources. If these are good measures of police "productivity," then additional spending has not brought much improvement in service.[9]

Getting More Bang for the Buck

But what should we make of data such as that contained in Table 10.3? The bull-headed critic of police departments contends that more police have no effect on crime, and that police departments are a "rat hole" down which more public money should not be poured. The bull-headed "law and order" type could argue that if police resources had not been substantially increased, crime rates might have escalated much more than they did. (In fact, more police officers *discover* more crime.) Police departments, often all, do a great deal more than merely fight crime in television-detective tradition (see discussion in Chapter 11, pp. 285–289). Most measures of productivity of public services, including student test scores and FBI crime indexes, are crude at best. Surely we want schools to do more than improve test scores; surely we want police departments to do more than produce a high clearance rate, which is easy enough to do simply by arresting someone. At least one virtue of the productivity emphasis is that it requires us to decide *what* we want public services to accomplish and to develop indexes that assess progress toward such ends.

One interesting opportunity to test the impact of personnel on productivity followed the layoffs of service personnel in the wake of New York's financial crisis. A November 1975 report on street cleanliness concluded that, despite layoffs of 1500 sanitation workers and a money-saving reduction in garbage collection, the city's neighborhoods were about as clean as they were a year previous. Despite similar layoffs and cuts in the parks department, productivity did not decline.[10] Productivity experiments in other cities have shown that it is possible to improve service output with equivalent resource inputs or even with reduced inputs. Detroit and other communities have experimented with schemes to tie employee incentives to improvements in productivity.

Efforts to improve service production will not advance much ahead of methods of measure productivity. Agencies that lumber along incrementally, measuring their effectiveness solely in terms of dollars spent or routines accomplished, are not likely candidates for productivity improvement. But we are beginning to ask new questions and seek new data on productivity. One study identifies more than 80 measures of service quality indicators, all of which can be measured in most cities.[11] As budgets get tighter, and as neighborhood groups become more demanding in the services that they expect, it seems likely that local governments will undertake such measurements more regularly.

PRIVATIZING PUBLIC SERVICES: DEMONOPOLIZING AND COMPETITION

Municipal services are *public* services, performed by *public* personnel, paid through *public* tax dollars, supposedly responsible to *publicly* elected officials. Public-service agencies are more or less monopolies. At least, as their critics are fond of saying, they act as if they are. Surprisingly it was not always this way. The economic theory of public goods implies that certain functions—police and fire protection, road building, garbage pickup, transit systems, street lights, libraries, parks—become public responsibilities precisely because they are not capable of being produced by the private sector. Historically, though, almost every service now performed by the public sector was once provided by the private sector. It is now forgotten that one of the major efforts of the municipal-reform movement was to make governmental responsibilities what was normally provided by private competitors. Whether to create public agencies for "public" services was once a very hotly contested issue. In 1899 Edward Bemis edited *Municipal Monopolies: A Collection of Papers by Eminent Economists and Specialists,* in which he and his collaborators argued —successfully, as it turned out—that it was more efficient to provide transit services, street lights, fire protection, and other services through the public sector.[12]

Actually municipal-service bureaucracies are not monopolies in a strict sense. There are competing private providers of almost every public service: private hospitals, sanitation services, security services, schools, and even postal systems. Private security personnel actually outnumber public police officers by a 2-to-1 ratio. The monopolistic character of public-service bureaucracies stems, not from their role as the *sole* provider, but from two other considerations. First, they do not respond seriously to competition (they *behave* monopolistically, according to critics) in the quality, cost, or quantity of services that they produce. Second, for lower-income groups, unable to afford private alternatives, public service bureaucracies *are* the only service provider. People who cannot afford private schools must depend on public schools; people who cannot afford time and money for private recreational opportunities must depend on public parks; people who cannot afford private medical care must depend on whatever service they get from public-health facilities.

E. S. Savas has been the most forceful opponent of the monopoly position of public service providors. He remarks that:

The inefficiency of municipal services is not due to bad commissions, mayors, managers, workers, unions, or labor leaders; it is a natural consequence of a monopoly system. *The public has created the monopoly, the monopoly behaves in predictable fashion, and there are no culprits, only scape-goats.*[13]

The image of a monopoly is typically very different than one conjured up by urban-service bureaucracies. Usually it entails powerful, clever, ruthless owners and managers relentlessly squeezing out competitors and maximizing profits. Economist Albert Hirschman, though, asks this question about monopolies:

But what if we have to worry, not only about the profit maximizing exertion and exactions of the monopolist, but about his proneness to inefficiency, decay, and flabbiness? This may be, in the end, the more frequent danger: the monopolist sets a high price for his product not to amass super-profits, but because he is unable to keep his costs down, or more typically, he allows the quality of his product to deteriorate without gaining any pecuniary advantage in the process.

In view of the spectacular nature of such phenomena as exploitation and profiteering, the nearly opposite failings which monopoly and market power allow, namely, laziness, flabbiness and decay have come in for much less scrutiny.[14]

This characterization of monopoly is precisely Savas's fear, namely, that urban public service monopolies have allowed "the quality of their product to deteriorate."

Savas and others provide evidence to support the "flabby monopoly" hypothesis. The evidence, fragmentary though it is, suggests that public monopolies often provide lower-quality services at higher costs than private competitors. It costs New York City $39.71 per ton to collect garbage; private firms spend only $17.28. Specifically, in Douglastown, an area of New York City with single-family dwelling units, the city picks up garbage twice a week at curbside for an annual unit cost of $207. In nearby Bellerose, similar but outside the city, a private firm provides thrice-weekly pickups from backyards at an annual unit cost of $79. There is some irony, Savas notes, in the fact that capitalist Wall Street uses public garbage collection, while socialist Belgrade contracts out garbage collection to private entrepreneurs. In a national survey of the efficiency of private versus public sanitation services, Savas discovered that private firms contracting with city governments do no worse and usually do better at providing higher service levels at lower cost.[15] A similar pattern has been found by other investigators in other service areas. The city of Scottsdale, Arizona, for example, contracts out its fire protection to a private corporation, and its costs and quality are higher than those of similar public fire protection operations. It costs the city of Chicago $1.23 to read one water meter, but Indianapolis pays a private firm only 27.5¢ per meter to do the same thing (but, then, political machines such as Chicago's have an incentive to be labor-intensive).[16]

The advocates of more competition, contracting, and demonopolizing argue that competition will improve productivity and lower costs, being subjected to a sort of marketplace economy. Standards can be regulated by public authorities, and nondiscrimination regulations can be written. Quality and cost advantages are spurred by the virtues of competition. Such arrangements are not often popular with municipal bureaucracies or municipal unions, which view them as devices to replace well-paid civil servants with cheap labor and reduced work forces.

Important debates about privatizing have occurred in education, as well as in labor-intensive services like garbage collection. Long ago, conservative economist Milton Friedman advocated a "voucher system" for schooling. Each family would receive a sum of money with which to "purchase" education for the children. The school authorities could insist on certain standards (nondiscrimination, certain teaching requirements, and so forth), but the choice of school would be left to parents. That way, schools not responsive to parental wishes would simply fold, giving a quasi-market character to schooling.[17] One school system, Alum Rock Union Elementary School District in San Jose, California, has inaugurated a voucher experiment, whose results are being monitored by both proponents and opponents of the idea. Other educational experiments have been tried with "performance contracting," where private firms are given contracts to improve reading scores and are paid in proportion to the improvements that students show. Though widely touted, most performance contracting experiments have been found rather ineffective,

The notion of setting competition against monopoly and the private sector against the public is an idea whose time may have come. There is scattered evidence that private purveyance of certain services may improve productivity. As yet there is no evidence that a headlong rush to privatize will produce more efficiency than public sector monopolies. As cities face revenue squeezes, though, they will increasingly look to productivity improvements where they can find them. We may even have come full circle from the municipal reformers, who successfully advocated that public services must be provided by public funds spent by public agencies.

DELIVERING URBAN SERVICES

"Administration Is Politics": The Unseen Hand in the Service Delivery System

Who gets what how from urban government is a central issue of urban services. Urban governments are gigantic machines that produce services—police and fire protection, sanitation, road repairs, parks, libraries, and so forth. Countless decisions about service allocations are made annually. Of the many problems of public safety, which will be addressed first? Of the many miles of streets needing repair, which will be done? Of the dozen or so branch libraries, which ones will get the most new books? Which neighborhoods will receive a new park, school, or fire house? The accumulation of all these decisions, little and big, affects the distribution of urban services.

Most of these allocations come from the bureaucracies of local governments. Power structures, private-interest groups, and even elected officials have little to do with seemingly routine decisions.[18] Service delivery is a bureaucratic game, played out in the departments and agencies of local government. The decision rules of service agencies, though designed to make agency decision making easier or more efficient, result in patterns of benefits and burdens to local neighborhoods.

Consider the case of police departments. Expected by the public and charged by law with an incredible battery of tasks (directing traffic, preventing crimes, answering complaints about rowdy gangs, investigating accidents, deterring speedsters), departments cannot do everything at once. Police officers cannot be sent out willy-nilly with the admonition merely to "go ye and police." Long ago, Eliot Ness, the fabled "untouchable" who was also police chief of Cincinnati, observed that "every police department believes that it suffers from insufficient manpower. Every police executive, wishing to meet his complex problems, has been faced with the difficult job of most effectively allocating his personnel. The need for making this decision according to a plan or system is obvious."[19] Out of such plans or systems emerge *decision rules* about how to allocate scarce bureaucratic resources. How to carve up the city into patrol beats, how to answer calls within the limits of time and personnel constraints, and where to cluster resources are decisions made almost entirely by departmental officers.

Or consider libraries. To accomplish their goals, library departments must seek optimal combinations of three resources: personnel, facilities, and collections. The library department that assigns new books and personnel to branches with the highest circulation rates will almost certainly have its best collections in the most educated and affluent neighborhoods. Such allocations become self-fulfilling prophecies. If collections remain small and inadequate in some neighborhoods, its residents will not patronzie the library, circulation rates will remain low, and collections will remain undernourished.

These bureaucratic decision rules have distributive consequences. Why one decision rule rather than another is chosen is never entirely clear, but usually decision rules derive from one or more of the following criteria:

1. *Demand.* Service levels are based on previous patterns of demand or consumption. Levy and his associates call these "Adam Smith" decision rules, where some consumption measure (traffic counts, library books checked out) determines allocation.[20]
2. *Professional norms.* Service levels are determined on the basis of what professional standards dictate, for example, the "proper" ratio of park space to population, the "recommended" ratio of library books to population served, or the "seriousness" of a police call.
3. *Pressure.* Bureaucracies yield to political pressures, whether from elected officials or interest groups. Put simply, squeaky wheels receive grease.
4. *Need.* Services are allocated on the basis of some conception of "need," as when police resources are concentrated in high-crime areas or when fire departments cluster resources in high-density areas.
5. *Equality.* Service allocations treat every neighborhood or household as equally as possible, regardless of demand or need.

Table 10.4 illustrates bureaucratic decision rules in the allocation of public services. A problem for administrators is that *these contending criteria are typically in conflict with one another.* It is the central dictum of modern economics that one cannot maximize two values at once. Police patrols cannot be allocated simultaneously to meet citizen *pressures*, the *need* to cluster resources in high crime areas, and *equality* all at once. If new library books are allocated to branches according to past consumption and demand, they will not be allocated on the basis of equality. What criteria will be maximized, and thus what allocations will result, is often an "administrative" decision removed from the light of legislative debate or public controversy.

Who Gets What: The Emerging Issue of Equity in Urban Services

The outcomes of these bureaucratic decision rules are the allocations of services to population groups and neighborhoods. The most common hypothesis is that urban service delivery is not equal and discriminates against the poor and minorities. It is said that poor or nonwhite neighborhoods receive the poorest streets, the slowest police response, the most inadequate and poorly maintained parks, and the most crowded schools. A pattern that gears the quantity and quality of services to the socioeconomic status of neighborhoods may be *discriminatory*, reflecting the biblical dictum that

For to everyone who has will more be given, and he will have abundance, but from him who has not, even what he has will be taken away (Matthew, 28:29, RSV).

Those citizens living in neighborhoods disadvantaged by the private sector are disadvantaged by the public sector as well.

In fact, neighborhood-to-neighborhood variations in service quality

Table 10.4   Some Decision Rules in the Allocation of Urban Services

1. Allocate new books to libraries on the basis of circulation rates during previous years (demand).
2. Resurface and repair streets that cause the most complaints to the city council (pressure).
3. Develop a hierarchy of police calls by "seriousness," where "officer in trouble" and "armed robbery in progress" are high priority and "family disturbances" are low priority (professional norms).
4. Give every household twice-weekly garbage pickup (equality).
5. Locate fire stations so that no call takes longer than three minutes to answer (professional norms).
6. Allocate police patrol beats to put more police officers in high-crime areas (need).
7. Install traffic signals in response to traffic counts (and accident rates) at intersections (professional norms).
8. Install traffic lights in response to neighborhood requests (pressure).
9. Resurface and repair streets that have the highest traffic counts and show the greatest wear (professional norms).

may follow several patterns. They may be *equal*, where neighborhoods regardless of their economic or racial status, receive equivalent shares of public services. Schools over the whole city may be good or bad, but in an equal distribution, in all neighborhoods sharing alike in the excellence or inadequacy. A redistributive or *compensatory* pattern may exist, where disadvantaged neighborhoods secure higher-quality or -quantity services. A compensatory pattern helps to overcome disadvantages of the private sector. Such public services as inoculations and other public-health services, and public-assistance payments, do go disproportionately to the neediest neighborhoods. It is also possible for services to be related to neighborhood traits in a *curvilinear* fashion, advantaging perhaps the middle-income neighborhoods more than the rich or the poor, or the rich and poor more than the middle. Municipal colleges may attract mostly middle-income people, with the poor tending to avoid higher education altogether and well-to-do seeking more attractive opportunities elsewhere. Figure 10.1 represents graphically these four possible allocation patterns with respect to neighborhood characteristics.

Few cities represent pure cases, distributing all their services according to one or another of these patterns. One exception is surely the tiny town of Shaw, Mississippi, whose pattern of service delivery reminds one of the Jim Crow era of public drinking fountains for whites and none for blacks. In *Hawkins* v. *Town of Shaw*, the Fifth Circuit Court of Appeals found a pattern of racially motivated denials of equal protection in the provision of street lighting and paving, water mains, storm and sanitary sewers and other services. Nearly 98

Figure 10.1   Four Possible Relationships Between Social Status of Neighborhoods and Their Urban Service Quality

1. Equal: All neighborhoods enjoy roughly equivalent service levels

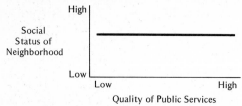

2. Compensatory: Poorer neighborhoods get better services

3. Discrimnatory: Poorer neighborhoods get worse services

4. Curvilinear: Middle-class neighborhoods get better (or worse) services than either rich or poor neighborhoods

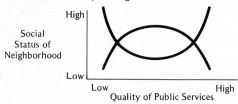

percent of homes fronting on unpaved streets were black-occupied, and 97 percent of the homes not served by sanitary sewers were in black neighborhoods.[21] These patterns of blatant discrimination are unlikely to appear in larger cities. There minorities are more active politically, and service delivery and discrimination are more complex.

Services in Two Cities

Levy, Meltsner, and Wildavsky have examined "who got what" in Oakland, California. With respect to the service areas of schools, streets, and sewers, in particular, they concluded:

There is an adage that the rich get richer and the poor get poorer, but in our work we found a distribution pattern that favored both extremes. Some mechanisms were biased toward the rich. Other mechanisms favored the poor. We discovered no examples of mechanisms that favor the middle.[22]

School resources in Oakland were allocated in a fashion that favored both rich and poor against the middle-income neighborhoods. Street maintenance expenditures tended to advantage the upper-income neighborhoods. Library allocations were more complex. The decisions of the library administration in Oakland resulted in overinvestment in the main library compared with its circulation (it got 60 percent of the resources, but had only 25 percent of the circulation). Users in the branch libraries were at a disadvantage, with those in the poor neighborhoods having the smallest collections. As with most allocation patterns, those in Oakland were the result of complex bureaucratic decision rules. Well-to-do neighborhoods had more money spent on street maintenance, because the street department did not make repairs where utility companies would soon be digging up streets for underground work. Because the utility systems in older, poorer neighborhoods were often in need of repair, the streets department delayed repeatedly its repair work in those areas.

A similar story can be told about the distribution of services in San Antonio, Texas. Lineberry examined the interneighborhood variations in parks, police, libraries, fire, and other public services. Proximity to service facilities (nearness to a park, a library, or a fire station) was greatest in the poorer, more heavily minority neighborhoods. The quality of service facilities from neighborhood to neighborhood could best be described as "unpatterned inequality." One particularly outstanding branch library might serve a lower-middle-class neighborhood, while a mediocre library might serve a well-to-do neighborhood. In fact, the poorest services in San Antonio are probably in those upper-middle-class areas of new subdivisions on the outskirts of the city, where population growth has moved ahead of service facilities.[23]

Various cities present different patterns. Few will have such open-and-shut cases of service discrimination as the tiny town of Shaw, Mississippi. Most will resemble the more complex patterns of Oakland or San Antonio. The variability of urban services, however, is no longer simply a matter for grumbling. Citizens in many locales have organized to secure better police protection, to prevent the deterioration or closing of a school or library, and to fight for more and better services. Such groups increasingly want the court on their side. The Fifth Circuit Court majority, writing in *Hawkins* v. *Shaw*, remarked that

Referring to a portion of a town or a segment of society as being "on the other side of the tracks" has for too long been a familiar expression to most Americans. . . . While there may be many reasons why such areas exist in nearly all our cities, one reason that cannot be accepted is the discriminatory provision of municipal services based on race.[24]

If a racial connection exists, *Hawkins* and other decisions indicate that discrimination against neighborhoods in service provision violates the equal-protection clause of the 14th Amendment. The Ford Foundation has entered this arena, with a grant to the Lawyers' Committee on Civil Rights under Law. Its purpose is to challenge the distribution of urban services in American cities. The challenge to urban service allocations may begin as a quiet revolution, but it may become an important one.

CONCLUSIONS

No longer do urbanites simply assume that public services will be provided efficiently and equitably. Rather, they have become increasingly dissatisfied with both the quality and the cost of parks, police and fire protection, sanitation, and other services. Evidence indicates that urbanites think their public services are not always worth the tax dollars they cost. Cities hit by a fiscal squeeze have frequently responded by reducing even further the outputs of city services, which merely fuels citizen unhappiness. The last few years have also seen an increased attention to the problem of productivity in municipal government. While we cannot expect city governments to be productive in the same way that a corporation is productive, we may nonetheless hope that increases in spending and personnel are positively related to service improvements. Hopefully, more inputs will buy more outputs. But things do not always work that way.

One reason why increases in costs fail to register productivity improvements is that city bureaucracies are relatively monopolistic enterprises. We borrowed Hirschman's term "flabby monopoly" to describe the way many critics see the municipal bureaucracy. Some of these critics have even argued that public services might be more efficiently produced through private contracting under public regulation.

Recently, too, urbanites have been more concerned about the distribution of public services from neighborhood to neighborhood. The bureaucracies that produce public services may use a variety of decision-rules, including demands, pressure, need, professional norms, and equality. When these decision-rules result in unequal services to particular neighborhoods, citizens are likely to complain and even take their complaints to court. In one notable case, *Hawkins v. Shaw*, a federal appeals court held that discriminatory provisions of services violated the Constitution's equal protection guarantees.

All of these issues—the problem of productivity, the role of the massive service bureaucracies, their decision-rules, and the resulting distributions of services—combine to make urban public services an important aspect of urban public policy.

Notes

1. "Service Delivery and the Urban Political Order," in Willis D. Hawley and David Rogers, eds., *Improving the Quality of Urban Management* (Beverly Hills, Calif.: Sage Publications, 1974), pp. 213–214.
2. The well-known Tiebout hypothesis suggests that urbanites move about the city in rational search for the optimal mix of services and taxes. See Charles M. Tiebout, "A Pure Theory of Local Expenditures," *Journal of Political Economy, 64* (October 1956), 416–424.
3. Claude Brown, *Manchild in the Promised Land* (New York: Macmillan, 1965), p. 193.
4. William Baumol, "The Macroeconomics of Unbalanced Growth," *American Economic Review, 57* (June 1967), 415–426.
5. Harry Hatry, "Measuring the Quality of Public Services," in Hawley and Rogers op. cit., p. 39. For a general overview of the public-sector productivity problem, see the reports of the National Commission on Productivity, specifically those dealing with productivity in state and local government. On local government and productivity, see John P. Ross and Jesse Burkhead, *Productivity in the Local Government Sector* (Lexington, Mass.: Heath, 1974).
6. Ira Sharkansky, *The Routines of Politics* (New York: Van Nostrand Reinhold, 1970), pp. 106–123.
7. Dick Netzer, *Economics and Urban Problems* (New York: Basic Books, 1970), p. 7.
8. Christopher Jencks et al., *Inequality: A Reassessment of the Role of Family and Schooling in America* (New York: Basic Books, 1972), pp. 93 and 96.
9. On productivity in law enforcement, see J. L. Wolfe and J. E. Heaphy, eds., *Readings on Productivity in Policing* (Washington, D.C.: The Police Foundation, 1975).
10. *The New York Times,* 30 November 1975, p. 1; and 2 February 1975, p. 1.
11. Robert L. Lineberry and Robert C. Welch, "Who Gets What: Measuring the Distribution of Urban Public Services," *Social Science Quarterly, 54* (March 1974), Table 1, 706–708. See also Hatry, op. cit., as well as various publications of The Urban Institute, Washington, D.C., on measuring particular local services.
12. (New York: Crowell, 1899).
13. E. S. Savas, "Municipal Monopoly," *Harper's* Magazine, December 1971, p. 55.

14. Albert O. Hirschman, *Exit, Voice and Loyalty: Responses to Decline in Firms, Organizations, and States* (Cambridge: Harvard University Press, 1970), p. 57.
15. E. S. Savas, "Municipal Monopolies versus Competition in Delivering Urban Services," in Hawley and Rogers, op. cit.; and "Evaluating the Organization of Service Delivery: Solid Waste Collection and Disposal," a report to the National Science Foundation, October 1975.
16. On the fire-protection example, see Roger Allbrandt, "Efficiency in the Provision of Fire Services," *Public Choice, 16* (Fall 1973), 1–15; on the meter reading evidence, see Chicago *Daily News,* 25 November 1974, p. 13.
17. On educational vouchers, see George LaNoue, *Educational Vouchers: Concepts and Controversies* (New York: Columbia University Press, 1972).
18. On the role of the service bureaucracies and their decision roles, see Frank S. Levy, Arnold J. Meltsner, and Aaron Wildavsky, *Urban Outcomes: Schools, Streets, Libraries* (Berkeley: University of California Press, 1974); Bryan D. Jones, et al., "Bureaucratic Response to Citizen-Initiated Contacts: Environmental Enforcement in Detroit," *American Political Science Review, 71* (March 1977), 148–165; and Robert L. Lineberry, *Equality and Urban Policy: The Distribution of Urban Services* (Beverly Hills, Calif.: Sage, 1977), chap. 5.
19. Eliot Ness, "Foreword" to O. W. Wilson, *Distribution of Police Patrol Force* (Chicago: Public Administration Service, 1941).
20. Levy et al., op. cit.
21. 437 F. 2d at 1286 (5th Cir. 1971).
22. Levy et al., op. cit, p. 219.
23. Lineberry, op. cit.
24. 437 F. 2d at 1287. For a discussion of the legal issues in service discrimination, see Robert L. Lineberry, "Mandating Urban Equality: The Distribution of Urban Public Services," *Texas Law Review, 53* (December 1974), 26–59.

11

URBAN CRIME AND THE PROBLEMATIC IMPACT OF LAW ENFORCEMENT

Crime ranks high on everyone's list of urban problems. While official crime rates rise faster than the population, victimization surveys conclude that true crime rates are higher even than official data suggest. In this chapter we focus on three principal issues:

- What is the scope and nature of urban crime as a policy problem?
- What are the principal policies and institutions designed to cope with problems of crime?
- What evidence is available concerning the policy impact of law enforcement?

Finally they simply hanged themselves. Hans and Emma Kabel had lived in the same Bronx apartment for 40 years, but the neighborhood itself had changed. Before he retired, he had been a factory worker. After retirement, their routines were simple and their needs minimal. Both Mr. and Mrs. Kabel had been victims on several occasions of assaults and thefts. The crime, or the fear of it, was severe enough to produce a double suicide in October 1976.

The example is both real and extreme. Few resort to suicide as a result of crime and the fear of crime. One's chances of falling victim to a homicide are not really very great. The chance of dying by another's hand is about the same as death from fires or drowning, and only half as great as falls (and only half as great as death by one's own hand). It may even be true that the *fear of crime* is a more serious urban problem than crime itself. To use terms we discussed in Chapter 5, some citizens have responded to crime by *exiting*. The safety and security of a new neighborhood is an important factor in choosing a locale. Others have responded by *voice*, organizing neighborhood associations to demand more police protection or to provide self-protection. Urban vigilante groups are found in many cities. Other citizens have turned to private security systems for protection, threatening to literalize the old cliché about "a man's home is his castle." Neighborhoods and businesses (hit by an estimated $20–40 billion annual crime loss) have hired private security guards in such numbers that they outnumber public police officers by 2 to 1.

The local police department has been the major institution for handling the crime problem. Yet as we shall see in this chapter, there is much debate about the policy impact of law-enforcement institutions. Urban law enforcement is under attack, and urban justice systems are a source of concern to friends and critics.

THE CRIME PROBLEM

How Much Crime in the City?

A distinction is commonly drawn between *crimes against the person* and *crimes against property*. Included in the first are murder, rape, robbery, and assault, and in the second are burglary, auto theft, and larceny of more than $50. Both have steadily escalated since the FBI first began compiling the index in 1933. Crimes against property have multiplied much faster than crimes against persons. The fear of crime, however, is more closely tied to the latter. Violent crimes have escalated from fewer than 150 to more than 400 per 100,000 population between 1940 and the 1970s.

These statistics are sometimes used to show an alarming increase in the "criminality" of the American population. Actually, once appropriate cautions have been drawn, it is very difficult to draw such inferences. Using crime statistics to make generalizations about changes over time requires satisfactory answers to two questions:

1. Do official crime statistics accurately reflect the total amount of crime in the United States?
2. Are there systematic differences in their accuracy over time?

Even if statistics *today* were off considerably, but the *ratio* of reported to unreported crime were constant over time, we could nonetheless make good guesses about changes in the crime rate. There is reason to suspect that these ratios have changed markedly, however. People seem more inclined to report crimes to the police, especially property crimes where insurance companies insist on a police report before paying off. Police departments also do a much better job of tabulating crime data than they did in years past. So even if the amount of crime today were exactly the same as it was in 1933, but twice as many crimes are reported, a purely statistical crime wave would have occurred.

There are two principal sources of error in official crime statistics: (1) underreporting by citizens and (2) inaccurate reporting by police departments to the FBI.[1] Citizens often do not report crimes committed against them. Among the reasons are fear of retaliation, the belief that "the police couldn't help anyway," and just not wanting to "get involved." Some crimes are more often than not unreported (less than one-third of all personal thefts are reported), and others are usually reported (two-thirds of all auto thefts are reported). Even when citizens report crimes, police do not always register them officially or report them to the FBI. American police departments have never been very good at statistics. Some cities such as Washington and St. Louis keep meticulous records; others, such as Philadelphia and Milwaukee, produce notoriously unreliable reports.

In a word, there are powerful arguments for being suspicious of crime-rate data, especially back beyond the last few years. Noted criminologist Hans Zeisel remarks, "If, as I believe, our ultimate task is to cooperate in bringing about the reduction of a crime rate that far exceeds other developed countries, then the presently available crime and law enforcement statistics are almost useless."[2]

Toward a Sounder Indicator of Crime Rates: The Victim Survey

The development of the "victimization survey" has made it possible to estimate "true" crime rates more exactly. A public-opinion survey is able to predict election outcomes with considerable accuracy. The same principle is used in the victim survey. Samples of households are asked whether, during the past year, a family member has been victimized by a crime. Results of these surveys enable students of crime to understand both the level and the nature of criminal incidents. Today the Census Bureau regularly collects victim survey data in numerous cities.[3]

The principal finding of these surveys may be stated simply: official crime statistics substantially *underestimate* true crime rates. In most cities, three times as much crime occurs as is reported to the police. Table 11.1 provides data on the surveys in 26 cities in 1972–1973. Several important inferences can be drawn from those data:

1. There is considerable variation in the ratio of police crime data to victim-reported crime data. In Newark and Miami, most crime is reflected in the official data; in Milwaukee, at the other extreme, almost five and a half crimes occur for every one reported. Obviously these discrepancies make places such as New York, Miami, Washington, and Newark look more crime-ridden than they are.
2. Cities that are well-known, even notorious, for their crime problems (e.g., Washington, Chicago, and Newark) actually have *lower* crime rates than places such as Minneapolis, Denver, and San Diego. There is a very weak relationship between a city's rank on official crime rate and victim-reported rates.

Table 11.1   Victimization Data versus Official Crime Statistics for 26 Cities, 1972–73

City	Victimization-derived crime rate per 1000 (rank)	Official crime rate per 1000 (rank)	Ratio survey police rates
Minneapolis, Minnesota	384 (1)	104 (23)	3.7
Denver, Colorado	318 (2)	118 (7)	3.2
San Diego, California	359 (3)	84 (19.5)	4.3
Portland, Oregon	346 (4)	121 (5)	2.6
Houston, Texas	341 (5)	89 (17)	3.8
Boston, Massachusetts	339 (6)	116 (6)	2.8
Oakland, California	326 (7)	162 (1)	2.0
San Francisco, California	326 (8)	105 (12)	3.1
Los Angeles, California	312 (9)	110 (9)	2.8
Detroit, Michigan	309 (10)	88 (18)	3.5
Cincinnati, Ohio	307 (11)	90 (16)	3.4
Milwaukee, Wisconsin	304 (12)	57 (25)	5.4
Dallas, Texas	285 (13)	106 (10.5)	2.7
Atlanta, Georgia	282 (14)	123 (4)	2.3
Philadelphia, Pennsylvania	264 (15)	54 (26)	4.9
New Orleans, Louisiana	262 (16)	82 (21)	3.2
Cleveland, Ohio	251 (17)	96 (15)	2.6
Chicago, Illinois	245 (18)	80 (12)	3.1
Baltimore, Maryland	242 (19)	106 (10.5)	2.4
Pittsburgh, Pennsylvania	234 (20)	68 (24)	3.4
St. Louis, Missouri	233 (21)	153 (2)	1.5
Buffalo, New York	224 (22)	70 (23)	3.2
Newark, New Jersey	185 (23)	150 (3)	1.2
Washington, D.C.	169 (24)	99 (14)	1.7
New York, New York	147 (25)	84 (19.5)	1.8
Miami, Florida	146 (26)	114 (8)	1.3
Average	278	101	2.9

Source: Comparison of Census Bureau victimization survey data, 1972 or 1973, for 26 cities, with Uniform Crime Report data for the corresponding year, compiled by Paul D. Reynolds, Department of Sociology, University of Minnesota.

The development of sophisticated victimization surveys has demonstrated that the annual Federal Bureau of Investigation's Uniform Crime Reports should be taken with some caution. When the FBI announced that 1975 rates were 10 percent greater than in 1974, the careful observer would note that crime rates reflect reporting deficiencies on the parts of citizens and of police departments.

Variation in Crime Rates

Not everyone has an equal probability of falling victim to a crime. Nor does everyone have an equal probability of becoming a perpetrator of a crime.[4] The average American in larger cities has a one-in-four chance of being victimized in any given year. Some people are on the high side of that average, and others are very much on the low side. Crime rates vary both socially and spatially.

First, *crime rates are higher in cities than in suburbs.* It is sometimes noted that the increase in crime *rates* is faster in suburbs than cities. In fact, in 1975, cities of 250,000 or more people reported increases of 7 percent in serious crime, suburbs reported 10 percent, and rural areas 8 percent increases. These figures fail, however, to distinguish between *rate* and *base.* The base is so much higher in cities that it would take decades for rates in the suburbs to catch up. The 32 largest cities contain only 16 percent of the nation's population, but account for two-thirds of the robberies. Crime is essentially a big-city phenomenon.

Second, *blacks are the most frequent victims of crime.* Black men and women are 6 to 8 times more likely to fall victim to a crime than whites. Homicide in New York is the largest killer of young black males.

Just as certain kinds of people are likely to fall victim to crime, certain groups are overrepresented in the offender class. *Crime is basically a young man's game.* Though women are catching up with men here as in other sectors of society, crime remains a male business and one dominated by the young. Table 11.2 shows that crime rates are increasing much more rapidly among the young than the adult populations. More 15-year-olds are arrested than any other age, and 16-year-olds are close behind. Youth now constitute a larger proportion of the population than ever before, making an increase in the crime rate partly an artifact of an increasingly youthful population. One out of

Table 11.2   Increases in Arrests Among Juveniles and Adults, 1960–1973

	Juveniles (under 18)	Adults (over 18)
Murder	201%	86%
Rape	132	95
Burglary	104	59
Prostitution	286	62
Narcotics violations	4673	174
Drunken driving	401	188

every 6 males under the age of 18 will be hauled into court at some point in his life, and the figure for young black males is considerably higher.

Participation in crime is also dependent on past participation in crime. *Recidivism*—the probability of ending up as a two- (or more) time loser—is high. Some estimates place it at 60 percent. Critics of the criminal-justice system argue that correctional institutions constitute schools for crime and may do more to increase than decrease the crime rate. In any case, the patterns of repeated criminal activity suggest that crime—like urban budgets—is an incremental phenomenon.

Crime and Politics

Whatever its reality as an urban problem, crime is a political growth stock. Whether "crime pays" or not, it seems to pay off as a political issue campaign target. Richard Nixon (somewhat ironically) and George Wallace both campaigned in 1968 and 1972 on "law and order" platforms. Three big-city mayors—Charles Stenvig in Minneapolis, Frank Rizzo in Philadelphia, and Thomas Bradley in Los Angeles—have been former police officers. Rizzo was the tough ex-chief of Philadelphia's department, a man who would make Kojak look like a patsy. Stenvig was a white former captain in Minneapolis and Bradley a black captain in Los Angeles. These three and other mayoral candidates have touted their own abilities to do something

about urban crime rates. Police themselves have also become an issue. The power of police in local politics has been enhanced by unionization.[5] The first major police strike in the United States was Boston's 1919 walkout, which was met by Governor Calvin Coolidge's firing of most of the department.[6] Recently police strikes have become more frequent. On 23 October 1975 almost 400 Oklahoma City officers tossed down their badges on city hall steps. The strike was settled three days later after the council promised a 9 percent raise.

Numerous issues about crime are highly emotional and symbolic political questions. One of these is gun control. About 40 million handguns are in circulation in American cities. More than 2.5 million new ones are either imported or produced annually. "Saturday night specials" are a major weapon in homicides and armed robberies. A few states and cities have passed handgun registration laws, but these are vigorously opposed by such organizations as the National Rifle Association. The possibility of a federal registration law seems remote, and its policy impact problematic in any case.

If gun control is a contentious political issue, the relation between drug abuse and crime is just as contentious. Some criminologists argue that there is a strong causal connection between heroin use and participation in crime. Wilson, for example, estimates that the proportion of property crime committed by addicts ranges between 25 and 67 percent, a more precise estimate being virtually impossible to make.[7] Richard Nixon called it "public enemy number one." Yet a 1976 report by the National Institute on Drug Abuse suggested that the tie between heroin and crime was much weaker than previously thought. Heroin users appear to get most of their purchase price from ordinary jobs or from peddling to others, rather than from property crime.[8] Even if crime were clearly attributable to addicts, it does not follow that eliminating addiction would abolish the criminal habits of former addicts.

Gun control and the drug problem both illustrate that crime politics is often symbolic politics. There is much heat (some would say, too, that there is little light) on both sides of those questions. Still, the most common single policy response to the problem of crime is to *strengthen police forces*. Let us examine, therefore, the thin blue line, the city's primary policy institution responsible for crime control.

THE POLICE

Police and their Roles

We begin our discussion of the police by reproducing a description, recorded by the President's Commission on Law Enforcement and the Administration of Justice, of an actual tour of duty by two officers, whom the Commission called Jones and Smith:

After receiving routine instructions . . . Officers Jones and Smith located the car to which they were assigned and started out for the area in which they would spend their tour of duty. While en route, they received instructions from the dispatcher to handle a fight in an alley. Upon arrival, they found a group of young men surrounded by their parents, wives, and children.

The mother of B was the complainant. She claimed that C had attacked her son with a knife and she demanded that C be arrested and jailed. C readily admitted that he had been fighting with B, but he claimed that he had just tried to protect A. C had been drinking and was very belligerent. He indicated a readiness to take on anyone and everyone, including the police. . . .

A attempted to explain the situation. . . . A's mother-in-law interrupted at this time to explain that A was innocent; that the fight was B's fault. B's mother did not stand for this accusation and entered the fray.

The confusion spread . . . Officers Jones and Smith decided to take the participants to the station where conditions would make possible a more orderly inquiry. [Finally, at the station] C was formally arrested and charged with disorderly conduct. By charging C with disorderly conduct rather than a more serious crime, the officers felt that they were saving themselves some paperwork. They felt that their action in letting the mother sign a complaint against the "loudmouthed" C had served to pacify her.

[After filling out arrest reports on C, Jones and Smith were dispatched to two successive domestic quarrels, in which wives complained that their husbands had beaten them up and then left the houses. After advising each to obtain a warrant or peace bond, they were then dispatched to two noisy parties, advised each host to "hold it down," and stopped for cokes before placing themselves back in service. After breaking up a rowdy crowd at a hotdog stand, arresting a drunk, and warning instead of ticketing a Vietnam veteran for a traffic violation, the officers requested permission from the dispatcher to eat. Instead, he sent them back to the first party they had quieted. Again denying their request to eat, the dispatcher sent them to a public pool, the scene of a stabbing.]

There were three persons present—two lifeguards and a watchman. One of the lifeguards had been knifed. He was placed in a police car and the officers started off to the nearest hospital. . . . [They] later returned to the scene but found no additional information. . . . The reports were turned in for attention by the detectives.

The officers then, without asking, took their meal break, after which they reported that they had completed their work on the stabbing. They were dispatched to a party disturbance. . . .[9]

If there is anything atypical about Jones and Smith's tour, it is probably more active and exciting than most. Contrary to popularized images generated by movies and television, an enormous proportion of police work is simply dullsville. To get an idea of the nature of police work, consider Table 11.3, which lists calls to a Chicago police precinct during two hours of a typical day. "Illegal parking," "disturbance loud music," and "man drinking and throwing garbage" are not the materials on which "Police Story" can be based. Probably half an officer's time on patrol is spent in handling routine calls for service, filling out reports, and other activities. But driving around in a car for hours on end can be a dull business, so that a large percentage of time is spent eating, resting, girl watching, and the like. Based on Jones and Smith's tour and on the precinct calls in Table 11.3, we can also suggest that there is often a large amount of *ambiguity* and *discretion* involved in policing. Ambiguity and discretion are mutually reinforcing. Both situations and legal codes (e.g., those dealing with disturbing the peace) are ambiguous, and the more ambiguous the law and the immediate situation are, the greater is the discretion open to the officer.[10]

Social scientists and experienced police officers seem to agree that the police play three important roles in urban society. One New York City police commander enumerated them: "One [role] is law enforce-

---

Table 11.3   Calling the Police: Two Hours of Calls to Chicago's 15th Precinct, 13 July 1976

3:00 P.M. to 4:00 P.M.

15:30—open fire hydrant	15:33—burglary alarm
15:05—disturbance loud music	15:44—theft of saw
15:06—illegal parking	15:50—threats
15:09—robbery	15:52—drug overdose victim
15:13—teen-age disturbance	15:55—fire call
15:33—burglary alarm	16:00—injured woman

8:00 P.M. to 9:00 P.M.

20:05—disturbance with neighbors	20:37—threatening phone calls
20:05—traffic control	20:39—fight
20:06—illegal parking	20:41—information on stolen
20:06—illegal parking	bike
20:08—man hanging out of	20:45—youth firing gun
second-floor window	20:48—injured person
20:11—disturbance at gas station	20:48—person breaking furniture
20:12—teen-agers on roof	20:50—domestic dispute
20:13—illegal parking	20:51—man with gun
20:15—illegal parking	20:53—vicious dog report
20:20—illegal parking	20:53—dispute over child
20:24—illegal parking	20:54—fight on street
20:29—wagon (prisoner)	20:55—missing person
20:33—domestic disturbance	20:57—disturbance loud music
20:36—report of man drinking and	20:58—damage to property
throwing garbage	
20:37—domestic disturbance	

Source: Chicago *Tribune,* 5 September 1976, p. 29.

ment. Another is keeping the peace. The third is furnishing services."[11] James Q. Wilson, one of the leading academic observers of police officers and their departments, has emphasized the same three functions and has provided some systematic data on the relative frequency with which they are performed.[12]

The most common public image of the police officer is that of law enforcer, but only about 10 percent of police calls require exercise of the law-enforcement function. Very few of the calls appear to represent opportunities for officers to make dramatic "pinches" of hardened criminals, and, in fact, the International Association of Chiefs of Police estimates that only about 10 percent of total police work is related to the traditional enforcement of criminal law.[13]

The role of providing service is far more common. Some police departments, according to Wilson, even emphasize service. For example, those in Nassau County, New York, and Brighton, Massachusetts, provide courteous and efficient, though perhaps low-keyed, law enforcement but also spend enormous amounts of energy and money on community relations. The Nassau County Police Department stands ready to provide articulate speakers at civic or school affairs and maintains a full-time staff of 24 officers to operate the department's boys' club program. Departments emphasizing services recruit well-educated men, pay them well, and demand scrupulous honesty from them. This emphasis is most common in homogeneous, upper-middle-class suburban communities. But regardless of whether the department emphasizes service, a considerable part of any police officer's time and energy is devoted to providing it to citizens.

The police role that Wilson has called "order maintenance" and others call "keeping the peace" is both the least recognized and also the most controversial. Situations requiring maintenance of order sometimes involve transgressions of the law — especially if the law is sufficiently ambiguous — but more often they involve breaches of public serenity. In most such situations, at least two parties (bickering spouses, feuding neighbors, and people in and outside bars) are involved in disputes in which the fault is not self-evident and is possibly shared equally. (The confrontation of A, B, and C by officers Jones and Smith is a classic example of the exercise of this function, one that happened to lead to an arrest.) These cases involve maximum ambiguity and therefore maximum discretion on the part of the officer. According to Wilson, the policeman "approaches incidents that threaten order *not in terms of enforcing the law but in terms of 'handling the situation.'* "[14] Although it might be possible to turn every such case into a law-enforcement case, strong reasons militate against it: Tempers cool quickly, participants are reluctant to file charges, blame is difficult to determine, and law enforcement involves detailed reports and tedious court appearances. Officers thus tend to handle

such incidents informally. When a clear violation of written law occurs — burglary, vandalism, or dope pushing — the police have little
discretion, especially if they regard it as a "serious" crime. But the
discretion that officers have in maintaining public peace is their greatest opportunity both to inject a personal element into the abstract
business of law enforcement *and* to exert their personal idiosyn-
cracies, whims, and prejudices. In Wilson's words, maintenance of
order involves "sub-professionals, working alone, [exercising] wide
discretion in matters of utmost importance (life and death, honor and
dishonor) in an environment that is apprehensive and hostile."[15]

BACKGROUND AND ATTITUDES   After the John Birch Society introduced the "Support Your Local Police" bumper sticker (the phrase
appeared recently on Alabama's state license plates), New Left critics
countered with a bumper sticker of their own, reading "Control Your
Local Pigs." Heroes to conservatives, who view them as the last bastions of law and order, police officers are depicted as bent on violence,
authoritarian, and bigoted by the Left and by many blacks. Perhaps
the police self-image is equally stereotyped: Most police officers see
themselves as performing tough, poorly paid, and unpleasant jobs,
risking their lives and receiving either hostility or, at best, grudging
tolerance from the public at large. Wilson found from surveys of
Chicago police sergeants that they believed that: (1) most Chicagoans
did not respect them or their work, (2) most people gave only minimum cooperation, (3) most people obeyed the law only for fear of getting caught, and (4) even their civilian friends were likely to criticize
the department.[16] This image is, however, contradicted by countless
studies of public attitudes toward the police indicating that overwhelming proportions of Americans (especially white Americans)
think that the police in their communities are doing "excellent" or
"pretty good" jobs. Although police see themselves as downwardly
mobile in the occupational structure, studies of occupational prestige
indicate that their relative position has improved over the years.[17]
There is, therefore, a wide gap between *actual* public acclaim for the
police and *perceived* public support by the police.

Why, when the general public so widely supports police work, do
police officers sense hostility? Part of the answer is provided by Wilson, who has observed that "most police contacts are not with the general public and thus general public opinion is not most relevant."[18]
Rather than interacting with a random cross section of the public, the
police see much of the worst kind of people and the best people only
at their worst. Police work involves antagonistic contact with a very
atypical segment of the public in situations of maximum hostility. The
police officer's lot — the necessity for physical violence, personal
danger, low pay, verbal abuse from self-proclaimed good citizens — is

hardly conducive to an optimistic, tender-minded view of human nature. Most police officers, moreover, are recruited from working-class
backgrounds; only a handful come from the middle class. "Working
class background, high-school education or less, average intelligence,
cautious personality—these are the typical features of the modern
police recruit," Niederhoffer has observed.[19] It thus happens that
police officers are recruited from that segment of the population most
inclined toward intolerance of unpopular views, racial prejudice, and
authoritarian conceptions of family life and public policy.

Recruits bring with them the attitudes and behavior patterns of
their backgrounds, including a preference for things physical rather
than intellectual, a predisposition toward toughness, and high regard
for established authority and ways. But there is little evidence to
suggest that police recruits are any more authoritarian than are other
members of the working class.[20] It seems to be the occupational milieu
of the force that engenders extremes of authoritarianism, cynicism,
and political conservatism among experienced officers. Although police authoritarianism has probably been overemphasized, the police
system itself tends to heighten this image by promoting the better-
educated and least-authoritarian officers, leaving behind for patrol
work and public contact those with the strongest predisposition
toward authoritarianism.

Cynicism about both life in general and the department in particular appears shortly after the rookie has left the police academy, with its
social-scientific emphasis on professionalism and has entered the
grimy world of the precinct station. General cynicism was expressed
by the late Chief William H. Parker of Los Angeles, who claimed that
"this civilization will destroy itself, as others have before it." Cynicism about the force itself is indicated by the widespread belief that
getting ahead is a result of whom you know rather than what you do.
Political conservatism is also a typical police attitude. Chief Parker
described the political ideology of the nation's peace officers as "conservative, ultraconservative, and very right-wing." The dominant political philosophy on the police force is a Goldwater-type conservatism, and such organizations as the John Birch Society harbor
generous sprinklings of the "men in blue."[21]

The Police and the Public

The police officer is the prototypical example of the "street-level bureaucrat" (see discussion on pp. 202–203). Writing about the street-
level functions of the officer, David Perry observes that "the heart of
the police function is found in the activities of the patrolman on the
street. The police officer is, in a real sense, a 'man in the middle'—an
agent of government employed, in part, to manage the 'dirty work' of

society."[22] The police officer on patrol sees the seamiest side of urban life and encounters the worst segments of urban society, and even the best people in their worst moments. The law-enforcement role is tension generating because the police have such limited resources with which to prevent crime. But it is the order-maintenance role that generates most hostility between police and their constituents. Order-maintenance situations have all the attributes — from the officer's perspective — of "heads I win, tails you lose" problems. Operating under the thinnest possible veneer of "law," cops are expected to handle problems that neighbors by definition cannot. Those whose peace is disturbed often find the police too slow and too unwilling to "do something," whereas those accused of disturbances see the police as "harassing" them.

The most obvious manifestation of these police–community tensions is found in the relations between police and minority neighborhoods in the city. In some respects, the police themselves may be viewed as a minority group — they are physically distinguished from the rest of us by uniforms, they exhibit high in-group loyalty, they view the outside world as hostile, and they interact heavily among themselves. Conflict among minority groups is a commonplace in American political annals. Moreover, as the police in some cities are recruited primarily from ethnic groups (e.g., the Irish), existing ethnic hostilities spill over into police–citizen relations. In any event, the National Advisory Commission on Civil Disorders' report on ghetto violence in the 1960s observed that "the policeman in the ghetto is the most visible symbol of a society from which many ghetto dwellers are increasingly alienated."[23] It has not been demonstrated that the police are more prejudiced against blacks than are other whites.[24] Yet the commission's surveys indicated that police relations were the leading grievance of ghetto residents, even more significant than housing deficiencies, inadequate schools, and unemployment. Incidents involving the police precipitated most of the major race riots of the 1960s, including those in Los Angeles, Detroit, and Newark.

Three major ingredients characterize the hostility between the police and ghetto residents. First is the familiar charge of *police brutality*. Whether or not and how much brutality exists depends, of course, on definitions. But fully half the residents of Watts in Los Angeles believed that some brutality had occurred there. Perhaps more important, more than four-fifths complained of instances not of overt physical force but of *harassment*, including "insulting language," "stop and search for no good reason," and the like. In Denver similar proportions of both police and minority-group members (about one-fourth in each case) claimed to have witnessed either harassment or excessive use of police force. The problem of harassment appears to be far more common than that of brutality. The President's Commis-

Table 11.4   Race and Attitudes toward Police, Crime, and Law Enforcement

	White	Spanish	Black	Total[a]
I. Comparison of police crimefighting in respondent's neighborhood and rest of city				
Better	21.9%	10.9%	10.9%	19.1%
Same	71.3	75.5	61.0	66.7
Not as good	6.8	13.6	28.2	21.7
II. Police response time				
Police "come right away"	75.9%	60.6%	44.4%	68.1%
Police "take a while"	24.1	39.1	55.6	31.9
III. Rating of police–neighborhood relations				
Very good	53.5%	39.1%	23.2%	46.3%
Good enough	39.6	45.3	46.7	41.5
Not so good	4.7	9.5	20.4	8.3
Not good at all	2.1	6.1	9.7	3.9

Source: Pooled data from Urban Observatories' 10-city survey of citizen attitudes toward local government.

[a] Totals includes a very small number of "other" races.

sion on Law Enforcement and the Administration of Justice investigated 5339 police–citizen contacts and found that only a minuscule proportion had involved excessive force, but that a much larger proportion had involved rude, discriminatory, or abusive verbal behavior.[25] Even though the proportion of police–citizen contacts involving roughness or rudeness may be small, the continual nature of police work enhances the probability that an individual ghetto dweller will at some time experience a hostile confrontation with the police.

The second source of police–ghetto tensions lies in what the ghetto sees as *inadequate police protection.* Regardless of class or income level, blacks are far more likely than are whites to see the police as ineffectual law enforcers. Ghetto leaders and residents are painfully aware of the crime and delinquency in the ghetto: Black men are six times and black women eight times as likely to be victims of crime as are white men and women, respectively.

Third, minority neighborhoods condemn the *inadequacy of grievance mechanisms.* Police departments like to handle internally complaints against their members (though note that police departments are not much different than other bureaucracies and even professions such as law, medicine, and teaching). When complaints are lodged but no disciplinary actions follow, charges of "whitewash" are made. Efforts to create civilian review boards — offical citizen commissions to investigate and recommend disciplinary actions against errant police officers — were widespread in the 1960s. Though rarely adopted, the campaigns evoked bitter charges and countercharges by police and their antagonists. No city rivaled New York in the intensity of its conflict over police "accountability."[26]

Given both the inherent tensions in the police role and the particularly abrasive relationship between police and minority groups, it is perhaps surprising to find as much support for the police as citizen attitude surveys reveal. Table 11.4 reports citizen impressions in 10 cities concerning the effectiveness of neighborhood crime-fighting efforts, police response time, and police–neighborhood relations. Decisive majorities of white, Spanish, and black respondents report favorable responses to each question, with a single exception, black perceptions that police are slow to respond to calls from their neighborhoods.[27] All survey questions that prompt a "good" or "bad" evaluation are subject to interpretation. But in the light of the strident criticism of departments and the inherent conflicts in street-level bureaucracies, these attitudes strike us as more supportive than one might reasonably expect.

THE POLICY IMPACT OF POLICING

Patrol and Detectives: The Two Strategies

Police, as we have seen, do *not* spend most of their time fighting crime. But they have used two principal strategies to hold down crime. These are *preventive patrol* and *detective work*. The object in both cases is similar. Potential criminals are said to be *deterred* by a visible police presence and by the probability of *apprehension*. The patrol function consumes more than half of the average department's budget.[28] The cost of operating and manning a round-the-clock patrol car runs from $100,000 to $200,000. Most patrol work is — like Jones's and Smith's tour of duty — routine, even grubby, business. Detective work is supposedly more dramatic. Television has popularized the detective (such as Cannon or Kojak), whose hard-boiled persistence and ability to handle himself under fire are the presumed keystones of successful police work. The evidence, however, is that image and real policy impact diverge considerably.

The Kansas City Patrol Experiment

One important effort to test the policy impact of policing was conducted by the Kansas City, Missouri, police department in 1972–1973. At the time of the experiment, Clarence Kelly, later FBI Director, was the police chief. His department recognized that it had little knowledge about the most effective utilization of an increased number of officers. So, in consultation with the Police Foundation, they conducted a most revealing experiment on the effectiveness of preventive patrol.[29] Routine or preventive patrol has long stood at the core of police crime-prevention activities. The policy assumption is that a visible, continued police presence patrolling the city will: (1) deter crime by the threat of immediate discovery and apprehension, (2) reduce response time to emergency calls, and (3) enable police to witness some crime in progress. Additionally, of course, it plays a role in assumptions about traffic enforcement, as potential speedsters always risk detection by roving patrol cars.

The police department in Kansas City divided one section of the city into three kinds of beats. In each case, beats were matched by socioeconomic profiles. *Reactive* beats were those where *no routine patrol* activities took place. Police came in response to calls, but were instructed not to engage in random patrol operations. In *proactive beats,* neighborhoods were saturated with patrol cars—three to four times as many as normal. And in *control beats,* patrol was carried on just as it had been in the past. After a year of the experiment, the experimentors concluded that:

1. There were very few significant differences in crime rates among the three neighborhoods.
2. Citizen surveys of victimization revealed few differences among the three neighborhoods.
3. Traffic death and accident rates did not vary much from one type of beat to the other.

Initially the Assistant Chief of the Kansas City police department told a *New York Times* reporter after the study was completed that "we went out and proved that the liberal cliché is correct: crime is caused by social conditions which very frequently are beyond the control of the police." Later the new Chief of Police in Kansas City was more circumspect, restrained, and filled with double negatives: "A great deal of caution must be used to avoid the error of believing that the experiment proved more than it did. One thing the experiment did not show is that a visible police presence can have no impact on crime in selected circumstances."[30]

Not surprisingly the Kansas City experiment provoked some debate in police circles and some sharp criticism of it soon emerged.[31] Even if its answers were not definitive, it asked perhaps the most significant question ever asked about urban policing: Just what impact does policing have on crime rates anyway? It was a question that criminologists, econometricians, and—reluctantly—even police officials were beginning to raise.[32]

At about the same time that the Kansas City department was experimenting with police patrol, the RAND Corporation's report on detective work produced other surprises. According to the RAND study, detective work in resolving crime is much more limited than usually depicted. In fact, the principal determinants of whether a crime is cleared by arrest is whether a witness was present and willing to testify. This indicates that both of the major police strategies to deter and apprehend crime and criminals have very uncertain policy impacts.

We should emphasize that the police are only one part of the criminal justice system. Limitations of policing are significant. As the President's Commission on Law Enforcement and the Administration of Justice observed:

> The fact is, of course, that even under the most favorable circumstances the ability of the police to act against crime is limited. The police did not create and cannot resolve the social conditions that stimulate crime. They did not start and cannot stop the convulsive social changes that are taking place in America. They do not enact the laws that they are trying to enforce, nor do they dispose of the criminals that they arrest. The police are only one part of the criminal justice system; and the criminal justice system is only one part of the government; and the government is only one part of society. Insofar as crime is a social phenomenon, crime prevention is the responsibility of every part of society. . . Some "handcuffs" on the police are irremovable.[33]

Let us therefore examine the criminal justice system in the American city, of which the police are only a small part.

DISPENSING JUSTICE

An Overview of the Criminal Justice System

Criminal-justice policy does not end with the police. In some ways it only begins there. From the police department's perspective, their job is done when a crime is "cleared" by an arrest. Clearance is quite different from conviction. Most crimes do *not* get cleared, and most arrestees do not ultimately get convicted. One simplified "flow model" of the criminal justice system is presented in Figure 11.1. There are no exact figures there, but the size of the arrows is roughly consistent with the filtration effects of the criminal-justice system. Clearly only a minority of crimes (about one in five) are cleared by arrest. Very few of the arrestees ever end up in an adult correctional institution.

Figure 11.1   Flow of People Through the Criminal–Justice System

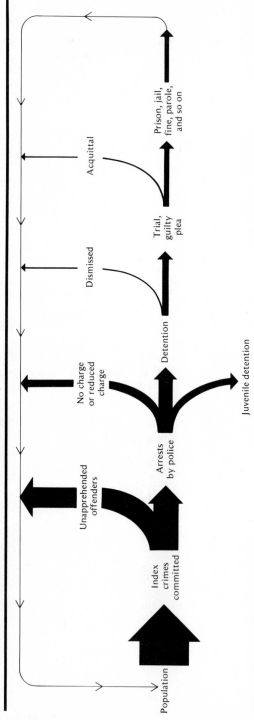

Source: Simplified from the President's Commission on Law Enforcement and the Administration of Justice, *The Challenge of Crime in a Free Society* (Washington, D.C.: Government Printing Office, 1967), pp. 262–263.

After the police department, trial courts are the next way-station in the criminal-justice system. A typical trial court is pressed for time, so justice is often more speedy than careful. Jacob emphasizes that "the principal driving force of the justice system . . . is the impulse to tame the workload. Considerations of due process or of other requirements of the adversarial process have become secondary."[34] Just as police have television shows that emphasize the dramatic, so do lawyers have episodes of the flashy courtroom performance by a trial lawyer. The facts are otherwise. More than 90 percent of criminal cases in urban courts begin and end with a guilty plea.[35] Frequently the defendent pleads guilty to a lesser charge — trading a murder charge, for example, for a manslaugher charge — in the process known as *plea bargaining*. The reason for plea bargaining system is simple. It saves time for prosecutors, judges, and defense attorneys. If all cases actually went to trial, the delay in meeting the constitutional mandate for a "speedy trial" would be measured in decades. Now it is measured only in months or (in a few big cities) years. In urban justice the dramatic case, fought out by flamboyant attorneys for the prosecution and the defense, is the exception and not the rule.

Only a minority of crimes results in arrest; only a minority of arrests results in an actual trial; and only a minority of persons convicted in a trial actually are sentenced to a prison. Some conservatives have argued that the criminal-justice system is a giant sieve, letting thousands of hardened offenders slip through gaping holes. Liberals have agreed in part but emphasize that the criminal-justice system is itself a major part of the crime problem. What is needed to resolve those debates is some clear evidence about the *policy impact of sanctions*. Is there, in other words, a strong probability that the application of sanctions does anything to deter crime?

Sanctions and the Policy Impact of the Criminal-Justice System

We are concerned in this book with *policy impact* — what happens to a policy problem on the application of a particular policy. We saw a few pages back that the policy impact of policing on crime rates is quite problematic and uncertain.

Clearly, after the police dispose of a case to their satisfaction, the lawyers take over. Judges, prosecutors, defense attorneys, and public defenders dominate the rest of the criminal-justice system, and a complex, overburdened, and slow system it is. Our popular stereotypes of the dispensation of justice are formed pretty much like our stereotypes of police work, from motion pictures, novels, and television. The glamor of the trial attorney's work and the artistry of a Percy Foreman or an F. Lee Bailey are somehow not very congruent with the actualities of most urban courtrooms. The legal precision characterizing the cases of Patty Hearst, Joan Little, and other controversial defendants do not reflect the fact that most urban justice is plea-bargained, that prosecutors and defense attorneys often spend only minutes, rather than months, preparing a case, and that delays from arrest to trial are typically measured in months and years. And, of course, urban justice is increasingly juvenile justice, where the usual rules of criminal procedure are more lax.

The other end of the criminal-justice funnel is the prison and correctional system. More than 200,000 adults are held in state and federal prisons, more than 50,000 "adjudicated delinquents" are held in juvenile facilities, and other adults and juveniles are housed in municipal and county jails. These institutions vary in the amenities that they provide, ranging from the relatively comfortable "correctional facility" where several Watergate convicts were housed to the rather less desirable accommodations offered by city and county jails and state prisons.

When we venture into the correctional system, we venture out of urban policy. Most correctional programs are part of state and federal systems of prisons. Ignoring them altogether, however, would leave our account of the criminal-justice system incomplete. Incarcerating (a rather technical term for putting offenders into prison) people can be hypothesized to have three impacts on the crime rate: *deterrence,* which arises because people thinking about committing crimes fear imprisonment; *incapacitation,* meaning that people held in prison cannot commit crime while there; and *rehabilitation,* meaning that people in prison can be socialized into noncriminal behavioral and attitudinal patterns, thus lessening the possibility of recidivism.

Only one of these hypotheses is self-evidently true. There is no doubt that incapacitating potential criminals reduces the crime rate. Putting people who would otherwise be criminals on the streets in prison will certainly "work."

Unfortunately evidence on the other two hypotheses—those about deterrence and rehabilitation—is skimpy. There is a fair body of evidence from criminologists suggesting that the *swiftness* and *certainty* of punishment—but not the severity of punishment—is associated with lower crime rates.[36] It is, of course, extraordinarily difficult to manipulate the certainty of punishment through public policy. If, as we noted above, most culprits pay little attention to the presence of police in the neighborhood, they may be unmoved by efforts to beef up policing to apprehend more criminals. Severity is much easier to manipulate. Convicted felons can be sentenced to longer periods of time in prison. This has the effect of increasing their incapacitation, but juries may be less likely to convict in the first place if sentences seem too severe for the crime.

What is most remarkable about the criminal-justice system is how little is known with confidence about the rehabilitative effects of corrections. It has long been a curious tenet of American penology that one could simultaneously punish an offender and reform him while he was behind bars. Today a multitude of schemes, both in and after prison, are touted as rehabilitating. Innovations in parole, work-release programs, halfway houses, and dozens of other reforms vie with one another for support. Yet there is little evidence on the policy impact of these schemes. One sociologist reviewing 100 studies of the effects of rehabilitative programs on recidivism, concluded that only one offered clear evidence on the impact of the program evaluated.[37] As Schnur remarks:

No research has been done to date that enables us to say that one treatment program is better than another or that enables us to examine a man and specify the treatment he needs. There is no evidence that probation is better than institutions, that institutions are better than probation, or that being given a parole is better than escaping. So much of what is now being done about crime may be so wrong that the net effect of the actions is to increase rather than to decrease crime.[38]

CONCLUSION

The observations just quoted have a gloomy ring to them. Unfortunately the same uncertainties can be expressed about almost every element of the criminal-justice system, from the nature of crime itself, to policing, to the impact of sanctions on criminal propensities. All this should reflect a theme that has permeated this chapter: *The criminal-justice system, perhaps more than any urban policy examined in this book, operates under a veil of ignorance.* All policy making is shrouded in uncertainty; the criminal-justice system more so. What has happened in police and law-enforcement policy is the gradual erosion of a once-certain policy paradigm. For generations a few simple assumptions pervaded law enforcement policy: A visible police presence can deter crime, effective detective work can apprehend criminals, more police deter more crime, and stern punishment reduces crime rates. The accumulated evidence has gradually chipped away at many of these once-cherished assumptions. One reason that Gilbert and Sullivan's aphorism about "the policeman's unhappy lot" is particularly apt today is simply that police departments are less confident that their paradigm works. For decades departments have defended their existence and demanded more resources, justifying themselves as "crime fighters."

Perhaps the only thing we can say with certainty is that crime rates are high — everyone thinks that they are much too high — in the American city. The major institution for crime-fighting policy has been the police department, which has relied on the twin strategies of patrol and detective work. Yet evidence has not accumulated to make us certain about the policy impact of policing. Further evidence on the policy impact of sanctions raises issues about the efficacy of the larger criminal-justice system. These conclusions may be sobering, but they may also emphasize that a careful analysis of policy impact is important in understanding the role of urban government in crime prevention.

Notes

1. On the problems with crime data, see Wesley G. Skogan, "Crime and Crime Rates," chapter 6 in Skogan, ed., *Sample Surveys of the Victims of Crime* (Cambridge, Mass.: Ballinger, 1976).
2. "The Future of Law Enforcement Statistics: A Summary View," in President's Commission on Federal Statistics, *Report,* Vol. 2 (Washington, D.C.: Government Printing Office, 1971), p. 531.
3. For an assessment of these data, see the papers in Skogan, op. cit.
4. President's Commission on Law Enforcement and the Administration of Justice, *Task Force Report: Crime* (Washington, D.C.: Government Printing Office, 1967).
5. See Hervey A. Juris and Peter Feuille, *Police Unionism* (Lexington, Mass.: Lexington Books, 1973).
6. Francis Russell, *A City in Terror: 1919, The Boston Police Strike* (New York: Viking, 1975).
7. James Q. Wilson et al., "The Problem of Heroin," *The Public Interest, 29* (Fall 1972), 3–28.
8. See the preliminary report in the Pittsburgh *Press,* 2 September 1976, p. 25.
9. President's Commission on Law Enforcement and the Administration of Justice, *Task Force Report: The Police* (Washington, D.C.: Government Printing Office, 1967), pp. 14–16.
10. Police discretion is discussed in James Q. Wilson, *Varieties of Police Behavior* (Cambridge, Mass.: Harvard University Press, 1968), chap. 4; and in Albert J. Reiss, Jr., *The Police and the Public* (New Haven, Conn.: Yale University Press, 1971).
11. Saul Braun, "The Cop as Social Scientist," *The New York Times Magazine,* 24 August 1969, p. 69.
12. Wilson, *Varieties,* op. cit.
13. Cited by Arthur Niederhoffer, *Behind the Shield* (Garden City, N.Y.: Doubleday, 1967), p. 71.
14. Wilson, *Varieties,* p. 31.
15. Ibid., p. 30.
16. James Q. Wilson, "Police Morale, Reform, and Citizen Respect: The Chicago Case," in David Bordua, ed., *The Police* (New York: Wiley, 1967), pp. 137–162.
17. Among 90 occupational groups, the ranking of policemen by the general public went from fifty-fifth in 1947 to forty-seventh (just a notch below the median) in 1963. If anything, the police are upwardly mobile. See Robert W. Hodge et al., "Occupational Prestige in the United States, 1925–1963," in Reinhard Bendix and Seymour Martin Lipset, eds., *Class, Status and Power* (New York: Free Press, 1966), p. 324, Table 1.

18. Wilson, *Varieties*, p. 28.

19. Niederhoffer, p. 38.

20. A Denver survey found that policemen were no more "authoritarian" on the "F scale," a common measure of authoritarian attitudes, than were the rest of the working class. See David H. Bayley and Harold Mendelsohn, *Minorities and the Police* (New York: Free Press, 1969), pp. 17–18.

21. Jerome Skolnick, *Justice Without Trial* (New York: Wiley, 1966), p. 61.

22. David C. Perry, *Police in the Metropolis* (Columbus, Ohio: Merrill, 1975), p. 164. See also David C. Perry and Paula Sornoff, *Politics at the Street Level: The Select Case of Police Administration and the Community* (Beverly Hills, Calif.: Sage, 1973).

23. National Advisory Commission on Civil Disorders, *Report* (Washington, D.C.: Government Printing Office, 1968), p. 157.

24. Evidence on police prejudice varies. Skolnick (pp. 80–88) has argued that prejudice is commonplace on the police force. But the Denver data reported in Bayley and Mendelsohn (p. 144) found police no more prejudiced than the rest of the white population.

25. President's Commission, *Task Force Report*, p. 147.

26. See Ronald Kahn, "Urban Reform and Police Accountability in New York City: 1950–1974," in Robert L. Lineberry and Louis H. Masotti, eds., *Urban Problems and Public Policy* (Lexington, Mass.: Heath, 1975), chap. 10.

27. One study of response time to white versus black neighborhoods finds that the actual promptness in Houston did not vary with the race of the neighborhood. See Kenneth Mladenka, *Servicing the City: The Distribution of Municipal Services*, unpublished Ph.D. dissert., Rice University, 1975, chap. 3.

28. Richard C. Larson, *Urban Police Patrol Analysis* (Cambridge, Mass.: MIT Press, 1976), p. 5.

29. George Kelling et al., *The Kansas City Preventive Patrol Experiment: Summary Report* (Washington: Police Foundation, 1974).

30. Joseph McNamara, "Preface" to ibid., pp. v–vi.

31. Edward M. Davis and Lyle Knowles, "An Evaluation of the Kansas City Patrol Experiment," *The Police Chief* (June 1975), 22–27; Richard C. Larson. "What Happened to Patrol Operations in Kansas City?" *Journal of Criminal Justice, 3* (1975), 267–297.

32. There are now emerging a number of econometric studies of the connection between factors such as police manpower and expenditures and their impacts on crime rates. They usually find only the faintest connnections. One example is Thomas Pogue, "Effect of Police Expenditures on Crime Rates," *Public Finance Quarterly, 3* (January 1975), 14–44.

33. *Task Force Report: The Police*, p. 1.

34. Herbert Jacob, *Urban Justice* (Englewood Cliffs, N.J.: Prentice-Hall, 1973), p. 100.

35. Ibid., p. 98.

36. See, for example, Charles R. Tittle and Charles H. Logan, "Sanctions and Deviance: Evidence and Remaining Questions," *Law and Society Review, 7* (Spring 1973), 371–392.

37. Charles Logan, "Evaluation Research in Crime and Delinquency," *Journal of Criminal Law, Criminology, and Police Science, 63* (1972), 378–387.

38. Quoted in ibid.

12

THE CITY
AND INEQUALITY

Historically the city has been seen as an equalizer. Millions of immigrants certainly saw it as such. Even today the poor in cities are typically better off than the poor in rural areas. Whether they are more *equal* — in terms of incomes, life chances, schooling, and so on — to other urbanites may be another matter. That is what we explore in this chapter. Our focus is on urban policy and the problem of inequality. Some of the most enduring issues of urban policy factor out as problems of how equal people are and how equal they should be. Thus we focus on:

- why several issues of urban policy can best be seen as manifestations of an old American debate about inequality
- how Americans have long seen the school as the principal equalizing device and why there is now much dispute about the impact of education in equality
- how poverty persists in the urban community, despite major policy efforts to reduce it

Just before the celebration of the 1976 bicentennial, the Supreme Court of New Jersey did something quite unusual: It ordered the entire public school system of that state shut down.[1] On 30 June 1976 the court ruled that no public monies could be spent on the schools because the legislature had failed to comply with a court order to fund schools more equitably. The case was styled *Robinson* v. *Cahill* and was first filed in February 1970. Citizens in Jersey City had filed the original suit. They charged that the state had unconstitutionally tied the funding of schools to a local community's tax base, so that rich school districts could support much higher expenditures than poor ones. Poorer districts such as Jersey City had to use much higher tax rates than wealthier (often suburban) districts, yet got less tax money because this base was so much smaller. This situation, the state Supreme Court held, was inequitable and unconstitutional. Between its original ruling in April 1973 and in August 1976 — after the court took its drastic step of closing the schools — the legislature, governor, education-interest groups, and school boards were constantly battling about the school finance problem. Finally, after a four-day marathon session late in the summer of 1976, the legislature passed a new school finance law. Jersey City, incidentally, ended up collecting $4 million less under the new formula than the old one.

The tangled story of school finance (which we examine later in this chapter) illustrates how questions of equality and equity crop up repeatedly in urban politics. Americans have historically believed that schools were important equalizing agencies. But as the New Jersey case points up, some have challenged the inegalitarian traits of the schools. Not only in school finance, but also in school integration, equality has been an important symbol. Court decisions favoring integration, even requiring school busing to achieve it, have stirred major controversies. We discuss those policies and their impacts in this chapter.

Ultimately, though, equality deals with resources and opportunities to secure resources. The city has important effects on income and its distribution. Income remains a test of one's status in this life. The presence of large cadres of poor and near-poor urbanites remains a policy problem despite the affluence of American cities. David Harvey argues that the " 'hidden mechanisms' of income redistribution in a complex city system usually increase inequalities rather than reduce them."[2] Certain urban policies, though, have been ostensibly designed to reduce, eliminate, or contain poverty. We also explore those policies and their impacts.

THE NEW POLITICS
OF URBAN SCHOOLS

Education has come a long way since Sir William Berkeley, governor of the Virginia colony, observed in 1677 that "Thank God there are no free schools or printing; . . . for learning has brought disobedience and heresy into the world, and printing has divulged them. . . . God keep us from both."[3] Today education is an important part of the American dream. Schooling contributes to the nation's economic growth, providing millions with skills ranging from simple literacy to occupational training. Historically Americans have had a high regard for their public schools. A survey conducted in the early 1960s found almost 90 percent of urban residents satisfied with their schools.[4] But support has been slipping for the schools, as for other major social institutions. Recently Louis Harris polled Americans about their confidence in major institutions, including schools. Only 40 percent expressed a "great deal" of confidence in the local public schools.[5] Schools were held in higher esteem than many other institutions (such as Congress, the courts, state and local governments) but still got less support than they once did.

One reason, we suggest, that schools have slipped in public estimation is because education has recently become embroiled in more and more political conflicts. Once nonpartisan in spirit and often in fact, the educational system is now a bubbling cauldron of conflict. Teachers' unions have changed the image of the poorly paid, toiling teach-

ers to that of—in some citizen's minds—the overpaid and un-
derworked teacher, willing to strike at the breakdown of a contract
talk. School desegregation and school finance issues have crowded
the courts and resulted in controversial decisions unpopular with
many urbanites. The costs of education have greatly increased, even
though the number of children has been declining and despite scholarly evidence disputing the link between resources and learning. All
of these impressions have shaken the historic assumption that schools
should somehow be "above politics." Instead, school politics is
among the most conflict-ridden forms of urban politics.

From the "Nonpartisan School"
to the Time of Turbulence

The apolitical and nonpartisan character of American education is a
fundamental part of the national credo. But the notion of citizen control of schools, an equally pervasive precept, makes education an object of citizen concern and, inevitably, of political conflict.[6] The structure and organization of local school districts reflect the tensions
between the conflicting goals of citizen accountability and educational autonomy. In important respects, the organization of school districts parallels the council-manager system of municipal government.
A lay school board has the responsibility to make policy, establish
budgets, and hire and fire the superintendent. Like the city manager,
the superintendent is thought of as a professional, mobile, and nonpolitical administrator.

Most professional educators believe that education is too important
to be left to amateurs like parents and school-board members. Board
members find themselves caught between their statutory obligations to
govern the schools and educators' demands for noninterference.
Given their limited time and lack of expertise in educational questions, boards typically defer to the superintendent on all matters not
plainly political. Educators like it that way. The school superintendent has the same kinds of political resources as does the city manager: time, control of technical information, training, experience, and
a near-monopoly of administrative routine.

Citizens, like school boards, ordinarily defer to the professional
judgment of school administrators. As long as the issues are "reading,
writing, and arithmetic," citizens are delighted to let administrators
and teachers run the school. Parents may grumble about "new math,"
but math is rarely a political issue. But several new items are hot
issues.

Schools have entered a new time of turbulence over five issues,
many of which we will be examining in this chapter: (1) the new social
role of the schools; (2) the hard realities of demography and costs; (3)

the focal issue of race; (4) the debate about school finance; and (5) some disquieting evidence on school performance.

THE NEW SOCIAL ROLE OF THE SCHOOLS   A social mission has been added to the educational mission of the schools. Once the sole purpose of the school was conventional teaching in conventional branches of knowledge, plus a heavy dose of moral authority and religious values. Today the school is increasingly saddled with social problems that other institutions have seemed unable to handle. If illegitimate births and venereal disease are increasing, then the schools should teach sex education; if racial conflict stems from racial prejudice, then schools should nurture racial understanding; if drugs are a problem, the schools should do more about drug education; and if the police cannot reduce crime, then perhaps the schools should do more. Increasingly, schools have been expected to handle society's social problems. How well they do this job is much disputed. But conflict over sex education is much sharper than conflict over fourth-grade math.[7]

SOME HARD REALITIES OF DEMOGRAPHY AND COST   Enrollments shrink while expenditures continue to climb. Since 1971 each year's enrollments have been smaller than the year before. Enrollment declines by about 1 percent annually, or about 400,000 to 500,000 children. Schools close while teachers want to hold their jobs and while parents protest closing "their" school. Downey, California, has recently closed 5 schools. By 1981 the school population will require 8000 fewer schools. State-aid formulas, though, are tied to enrollments, and cities and suburbs alike find budgets squeezed. But costs keep escalating. Unionized teachers have succeeded in getting better wage settlements and have resisted layoffs from declining enrollments. Taxpayers have become more recalcitrant. The year 1971 marked the first year that a majority of bond referenda were disapproved by school taxpayers. Today some school boards do not even bother with referenda certain to be disapproved. Instead they try "economizing." "Frills" go first, then French. (Athletics usually remains sacrosanct, as some cities discovered when they tried to reduce costs by cutting high-school athletic programs.)

THE FOCAL ISSUE OF RACE   Ever since the Supreme Court's 1954 decision in *Brown v. Board of Education of Topeka* holding that legally endorsed segregation is unconstitutional, the issue of desegregation has been foremost among school problems. Annually new Supreme Court decisions clarify or complicate integration policies. Boston, Detroit, Louisville, and other cities have experienced major conflicts, even violent protest, over school busing. Southern school districts – partly because they were specifically covered by the *Brown* ruling—have made for more vigorous movement toward desegregation than northern schools. Today the North is the focal point of conflict over school desegregation. Much debated, though, is whether one externality of school integration is an increase in white "exit" from desegregating districts. This is the "white-flight" hypothesis, which we discuss below (pp. 309–310).

THE DEBATE ABOUT SCHOOL FINANCE   We began this chapter with a story about what happened in New Jersey about the issue of school finance and inequity. In several states residents of tax-poor (often central-city) districts went to court to challenge inequities in school resources from district to district. The California Supreme Court ordered a reallocation of funds to favor poorer districts. But the United States Supreme Court, in *Rodriguez* v. *San Antonio Independent School District* (1973) held that differences in tax base from rich to poor districts were not unconstitutional. Yet the plight of poor districts is an issue—as it was in New Jersey—in many states.

SOME DISQUIETING EVIDENCE ON SCHOOL PERFORMANCE   At the same time that school budgets were increasing by leaps and bounds, schools were the subject of some very disquieting evidence about their performance. James S. Coleman, for example, was commissioned by the Office of Education to study achievement and motivation in American schools.[8] He collected data on 600,000 students, their

Poverty and unemployment were viewed by many as reasons for arson and looting in New York City's 1977 blackout.

parents, and their schools, and concluded that school resources made less difference than parental environment or the class composition of the school itself. In a massive review of evidence on school's impact, Christopher Jencks bluntly concluded that even doubling school expenditures would probably have very little impact on learning and pupil performance.[9] These sobering conclusions reinforced a public skepticism that schools might not be very certain of their educational role, nor doing a very good job in performing it.

RACE AND THE SCHOOLS

The Segregation Problem

Robert Dentler has argued that "the most urgent urban educational challenge of the day is not curriculum or instruction. It is the challenge of changing race relations."[10] From Washington to the local community, race is the most controversial of all educational issues. The problem has numerous dimensions, including: (1) the demands for *community control* of ghetto schools; (2) the great debate, associated with Berkeley psychologist Arthur Jensen, about racial differences in learning capacity; (3) differences in school quality from black to white neighborhoods; and (4) the old school desegragation issue and its contemporary manifestation — busing. For other minority groups, these as well as other issues — the problem of bilingualism in the education of Spanish-heritage children, for example — are also crucial.

Segregation by race in public schools is of two types: *de jure* (required by law) and *de facto* (resulting from socioeconomic circumstances). *De jure* segregation was declared a violation of the "equal protection" clause of the Fourteenth Amendment in the Supreme Court's 1954 decision in *Brown* v. *Board of Education of Topeka*, which theoretically put an end to legally sanctioned segregation in seventeen southern and border states. The Court ordered school systems in those states to desegregate their schools with "all deliberate speed." But seven years after the *Brown* decision the percentage of southern black children in schools with whites ranged from 0 in Mississippi, Alabama, and South Carolina to 1.5 in Texas. Observers calculated that at the rate of integration in 1954–1961, it would take 3180 years to desegregate southern schools.[11] The pace quickened, however, with the passage of the Civil Rights Act of 1964. This required the U.S. Office of Education to cut off funds to schools that failed to establish and execute desegregation plans. It also authorized the U.S. Attorney General to initiate legal proceedings to hasten desegregation. A few of these plans involved the mandatory busing of black children to previously white schools (and, infrequently, vice versa). Quickly, *forced busing* became the hottest political issue on the domestic scene. The outcry against busing extended from one end of Pennsylvania Avenue to the other, and from Washington to the local school board. The Supreme Court upheld the busing alternative in *Swann* v. *Charlotte-Mecklenberg County Schools* (1971) as a remedy for the vestiges of *de jure* segregation. The school bus, after all, is a familiar American institution. Two-fifths of the nation's school children were bused to school before *Swann*, including countless black children transported miles past white schools to attend a segregated one.

De facto segregation is a straightforward function of neighborhood segregation in housing and of geographical attendance zones. *Neighborhood schools* means that students living in black neighborhoods go to black schools and students living in white neighborhoods go to white schools. As we saw in Chapter 3, residential segregation has continued unchanged in cities since blacks first arrived in the city. Although *de facto* segregation is not technically a product of public policy, local boards have often intensified school segregation by deliberate manipulation of policy. Careful drawing of attendance zones, teacher assignments, construction of new schools in the heart of segregated neighborhoods rather than on the periphery, and other subtle practices reinforced black-and-white school patterns. If segregation has negative effects on pupils, *de facto* segregation is no less serious than *de jure* segregation. According to the Civil Rights Commission, "racial isolation, whether or not sanctioned by law, damages Negro students by adversely affecting both their attitudes and achievement."[12] Nonetheless, both Congress and the courts have been reluctant to hold *de facto* segregation based on the neighborhood-school concept in violation of the Constitution.

Today, the South—the historic bastion of *de jure* segregation—is considerably more desegregated than the North, where *de facto* patterns prevail. After a decade of vigorous legal and political pressure, states such as Mississippi and Alabama have taken the lead in the percentages of black children in formerly all-white schools. Table 12.1 provides some evidence on desegregation in the North and the South. Clearly, desegregating southern schools has not been easy. But compared with school desegregation in the North, the South has moved at a rapid pace. While southern schools were being slowly, almost imperceptibly, integrated, the percentage of black children in black schools actually increased in the North.[13]

Metropolitan Solutions, Busing, and the "White-Flight" Hypothesis

The yellow bus has almost become like the red flag waved in front of the bull. Although millions of children are regularly bused to school daily, busing for purposes of "racial balance" has provoked violence in the streets. In October 1976 Boston's white parents protested *en masse*, spat on the usually popular Senator Edward Kennedy, and kept children home from school in defiance of federal Judge Garrity's integration orders. To say that racially motivated busing was unpopular was to risk massive understatement. Thousands of parents in Boston and elsewhere, *resorted to voice.*

Others, however, may resort to "exit." If white parents, motivated by fear of, or opposition to, school integration, move to suburban areas, they may be able to escape entirely the onus of integration. (The reason is obvious, and suggested by our repeated arguments in this book that suburbs remain nearly all-white). This is the so-called "white-flight" hypothesis. It suggests that the higher the percentage of blacks in urban schools, the more exit options used by whites. "For sale" signs come with school integration. Some observers noticed an increased level of real-estate sales in Boston and other cities with court-ordered busing. James S. Coleman, author of the important Coleman Report, became a proponent of the "white-flight" hypothesis. Analyzing demographic patterns, he concluded that, "There is a segregating process occurring through individual movement, primarily of white families, from schools in which there is greater integration or a greater proportion of blacks, to schools and districts in which there is less integration or a smaller proportion of blacks."[14] This argument has been much disputed (as with most arguments in

Table 12.1   School Desegregation, North and South

U.S. Averages	
Percent of black pupils in 50% to 100% black schools	63.7
Percent of black pupils in 95% to 100% black schools	34.8

Percent of black pupils in 95% to 100% black schools: Five Northern States	
California	43.9
Connecticut	21.7
Michigan	49.9
New York	40.1
New Jersey	37.6

Percent of black pupils in 95% to 100% black schools: Five Southern States	
Alabama	33.5
Arkansas	2.3
Georgia	22.5
Mississippi	26.4
South Carolina	13.8

Source: U.S. Bureau of the Census, *Statistical Abstract, 1975* (Washington: Government Printing Office, 1975), p. 125.

the area of school desegregation). Christine Rossell maintains that Coleman greatly overstated the amount of desegregation taking place in the school systems that he studied and therefore attributed "natural" losses of white populations to exit for racial reasons. Her more careful analysis concludes that, "School desegregation causes little or no significant white flight," beyond what occurs as a result of suburbanization itself.[15] "White flight" is thus a myth, she suggests.

Yet it is often the *fear* of white flight that motivates school policy making. City officials may react more to suspicions than to well-founded knowledge, just as a homeowner panics if he sees housing values threatened. Thus, in many cities the goal of superintendents, mayors, and school boards has been *racial stabilization*. That term may mean many things to different people, but at a minimum it means that whites should be given no incentive to exit the city. Indeed in cities like Washington, Newark, Atlanta, and Detroit, there are not enough *white* city pupils to permit real integration. The spectre of an all-black public school system (such as that in Washington, D.C.) haunts white, and many black, school officials. The Chicago school board member who cast the deciding vote for a largely segregated attendance plan explained his vote by emphasizing that, "In my mind [it] is the only way that we can prevent the exodus from the city."[16]

As long as the suburban schools remain almost entirely white, exit will remain an option. One solution widely advocated is a metropolitanwide policy toward desegregation. A federal judge in Richmond ordered the consolidation of Richmond city and suburban districts to achieve metropolitan integration, but the Court of Appeals struck down his decision. Another judge in Michigan ordered Detroit suburbs to participate in school integration plans with Detroit schools. But, in a notable decision, the Supreme Court struck down his decision, holding that suburban districts were not responsible for Detroit's segregation and could not be required to participate in its resolution. Whites and blacks in city schools could be integrated, but whites in suburban schools need not be integrated. Exit, whether a minor or a major consequence of school desegregation in the cities, remains an escape valve.

Compensation and Integration:
The Policy Impacts

Barring deliberate alteration via public policy (e.g., massive school busing), school segregation follows inevitably from two factors: neighborhood housing segregation and the neighborhood school. One long-run solution to the segregated school, of course, is housing desegregation. But progress on this front, as we will show, has been nil. Short-run policy alternatives for equalizing educational opportunity to minority children are of two kinds, *desegregation* and *compensatory education*. Only Massachusetts has enacted legislation specifically limiting the proportion of black students in any school (50 percent), although other states have undertaken policies to discourage racial concentration.[17] Because of slow progress on the desegregation front, some have sworn off that battle in favor of a program of compensatory education for minority children. Compensatory programs accept the reality of segregated schools but demand enrichment and special services to disadvantaged children.

Unfortunately the evidence on the policy impact of both compensatory education and integration via busing is very mixed. Let us consider each in turn. Compensatory programs, it appears, have fallen short of uplifting the motivation and achievement of minority children. The most highly touted compensatory program of them all was designed to give disadvantaged children a "head start" with intensive preschool nurturing. Evidence on the impact of the Head Start program, however, indicates some short-term, but few long-term, effects in motivating disadvantaged children.[18]

Evidence on integration is also mixed. It is a canon of integrationist belief that minority children placed in integrated environments will evidence improved motivation and achievement. Some research suggests these results. The Coleman Report, commissioned by the Civil Rights Act of 1964 and representing the most thorough study of school performance ever conducted, found that performance of minority children in integrated schools was better than those in segregated schools, and that integration did not adversely affect middle-class children. If correct, this represents the optimal solution to racial equality, with minority performance elevated without diminution of middle-class performance. On the other hand, David Armor, himself a strong advocate of integrated education, reviewed "The Evidence on Busing,"[19] and found it mostly negative. Minority children who were bused showed no appreciable improvement on five dimensions of educational performance (achievement, aspiration, self-concept, race relations, and educational attainment). Control groups of unbused children did as well as bused groups on each dimension. Armor's evidence on busing, however, has been vigorously attacked as biased and selective. His own mentor and Harvard sociologist Thomas Pettigrew, in a rebuttal to Armor's "Evidence on Busing," contended that Armor's evidence ignored studies that showed busing successful, failed to meet scholarly standards for documentation, and established unrealistic standards for success.[20] The evidence must, therefore, be read as inconclusive. Perhaps the most careful assessment of the accumulated evidence on integrated education (which is not the same as "busing") is that educational gains are small and positive and losses rare or nonexistent.[21]

What, then, if anything, works? The evidence is clear on one point at least: No one should expect spectacular changes from a little cross-town transportation or from extra dollars dumped into ghetto schools. Overcoming the disabilities of generations of racial inequality does not yield easily to educational reforms. As with many policy issues, the problem is as much one of goal identification than goal attainment. If an integrated society is a policy goal, then integrated schools are to be preferred in their own right, regardless of the educational consequences. If segregation is either desired or unalterable, then a policy of compensatory education, mixed perhaps with a strong dose of community control, might be preferred. Schools are not autonomous institutions but are part of society itself. Outside the family they are the dominant social institutions for millions of children and teachers. Schools are important not only for what they *produce* in learning, but for what they *are*.

INEQUALITY IN EDUCATION

Americans have always thought of public education as the great equalizer. The tradition of education as a guarantor of social mobility is as old as Horace Mann's establishment of common schools in Massachusetts and as contemporary as the demand for equal educational opportunity for minority children. The road from rags to riches almost always leads through the schoolhouse. Some suspect, however, that the schools do not equalize opportunity but rather perpetuate existing social inequality. If middle-class communities generally provide the best schools and the best teachers, schools cannot do much equalizing. Educational inequality can be seen at both macro and micro levels. At the macro level, there are inequalities of resources among the states, among districts within states, and among schools within particular districts. Micro-level inequality appears as differences in the backgrounds and intellects of individual students and the impact of education on equalizing those inequalities.

Macro Inequalities

Some schools, especially those in affluent suburbs, contain superior teachers, working in modern educational "modules," operating fully equipped science and language laboratories, well-stocked libraries, and diverse extracurricular programs. Other schools, especially those in rural and core-city areas, operate in ramshackle facilities with harassed and overworked teachers, where every special program hangs by a fiscal thread. In the Detroit metropolitan area, for example, 25 suburban school districts spend an average of $500 per pupil per year more than does the city of Detroit. In the core city of Detroit, almost one-third of the school buildings in use today were constructed during the administration of President Ulysses S. Grant. James B. Conant, former president of Harvard University and a long-time observer of the public schools, notes that "the contrast in money available to the schools in a wealthy suburb and to the schools in a large city jolts one's notion of the meaning of educational opportunity."[22]

One explanation of resource inequality lies in state-to-state differences in wealth. Substantial inequalities also exist among districts within states and within particular districts. These differences are often associated with resource and income differences of states, districts, and neighborhoods. If one believes that high expenditures produce quality education, then one should, if at all possible, locate one's family in an affluent area of an affluent district in an affluent state, and then take care that his fellow citizens support school taxes and bond referenda. Only a handful of families, of course, can make such decisions.

DIFFERENCES AMONG STATES   Of the $61.5 billion spent on elementary and secondary public education in 1975, the federal government contributed less than 10 percent. Per-pupil expenditure for education was $2005 in New York while per-pupil outlays in Mississippi and Arkansas were only $834 and $896, respectively. The wealth of a state is commonly used to explain these differences in spending. Although there are exceptions, poor states typically rank at the bottom of the spending heap with wealthy states at the top. This remains true, even though poor states tax their residents heavily for education. Heavy tax burdens and low tax yields are the chronic plight of poor states and poor districts. Although almost all states have equalization programs to even out differences between their poor and rich districts, very few such programs actually equalize educational finance. A typical equalization formula will weigh state aid to poorer districts and districts that make greater tax effort, but many formulas are riddled with exceptions and confusions. The result is that wealthy districts typically outspend their poorer counterparts within the state, and state aid sometimes favors the already favored.

DIFFERENCES AMONG DISTRICTS   On 23 December 1971 a federal court in Texas handed the Texas legislature a novel Christmas present by declaring the state's educational finance system unconstitutional. It ordered the legislature to develop a new scheme that would not discriminate against children in poor school districts. The decision in *Rodriguez* v. *San Antonio Independent School District* paralleled an earlier decision by the California Supreme Court in the case of *Serrano* v. *Priest* (1971). Dimitrio Rodriguez, a parent in San Antonio's impoverished Edgewood district, contended that his tax rates were higher than those of taxpayers in affluent districts, and that Edge-

Table 12.2   Relationship Among Market Value of Taxable Property, Tax Rates, and Tax Yield in Texas School Districts, 1970

Market value of taxable property per pupil	Tax rate per $100	Tax yield per pupil
Above $100,000 (10 districts)	$0.31	$585
$100,000–$50,000 (26 districts)	0.38	262
$50,000–$30,000 (30 districts)	0.55	213
$30,000–$10,000 (40 districts)	0.72	162
Below $10,000 (4 districts)	0.70	60

Source: Joel Berke, affidavit submitted in behalf of plaintiff, *Rodriguez* v. *San Antonio Independent School District,* United States District Court, Western District of Texas, San Antonio Division, 1 October 1971, p. 13.

wood's per-pupil expenditures were still shockingly inferior to those in affluent districts. Table 12.2 presents some data submitted in behalf of Rodriguez's position. The pattern of poor district–high tax burdens–low tax yields versus rich district–low tax burden–high tax yields is readily apparent in the San Antonio area. Such variations in taxable wealth from district to district make education a function of wealth. As the *Wall Street Journal* observed:

In America, "free" public education is for sale. You buy a good or bad school for your child when you buy a house. You pay the bill when you pay the annual property taxes on your home.

Not only is public schooling for sale. It is also priced more erratically than perhaps any other product. You may pay a lot and get an inferior school. Or, you may pay relatively little and come away with a first-class institution. Generally, the poor pay more and get less.[23]

The issue raised by Dimitrio Rodriguez, John Anthony Serrano, and plaintiffs in several other states is whether the states, forbidden by the Fourteenth Amendment of the U.S. Constitution to deny "equal protection of the laws," can permit educational resources to be a function of the wealth of parents and their neighbors. In recent years state and lower federal courts have rejected finance systems based on local property taxes and ordered new systems that did not discriminate against lower-income school districts. Yet the cases raised as many questions as they solved: Did per-pupil expenditures have to be equalized from the neighborhood to the state line? Must states assume the entire burden of school finance? Would impoverished big-city districts or impoverished rural districts be the beneficiaries? Did money have anything to do with the quality of education in any case? In March 1973 the United States Supreme Court overturned by the narrowest of margins (a 5 to 4 decision) the lower court decision in *Rodriguez,* arguing that the decision on school finance belonged to legislatures rather than to the courts. The narrowness of the decision as well as the political activities of educational-interest groups at the state level suggest, however, that the issue of interdistrict inequality has not been laid to rest.

DIFFERENCES WITHIN DISTRICTS   Within a school district itself, there are often marked differences among schools, programs, and teachers serving various neighborhoods. Patricia Cayo Sexton examined elementary and secondary schools in Detroit and discovered strong correlations between income levels of neighborhoods and the quality of their schools. She measured educational quality in several ways, including class size, teacher training, availability of extracurricular programs, and age and nature of facilities. Schools in upper-income neighborhoods had: (1) newer buildings; (2) more libraries, labs, and other special facilities; (3) smaller classes; (4) better-trained teachers; (5) more extensive extracurricular offerings; and, incredibly enough, (6) more frequent provision of free lunch and free milk programs.[24] These differences were more closely related to the social class than to the racial characteristics of various neighborhoods. Such patterns of intradistrict inequalities are repeated in city after city, although they are not so universal and seldom so extreme as interstate and interdistrict differences.

The issue of intradistrict differences in school quality has become a lively legal topic, most notably in the District of Columbia. Even though 90 percent of the school population of the nation's capital is black, white neighborhoods still received the lion's share of school services. Julius Hobson, a black parent and member of the D.C. Board of Education, challenged this racially imbalanced pattern in the courts. In *Hobson* v. *Hansen* (1967), Judge Skelly Wright ordered an equalization of instructional expenditures in the district's schools to ensure that white and well-off schools were not so favored.

THE PROBLEMATIC IMPACT OF MONEY   Even a brief review of educational finance should convince the reader that school taxation and expenditures are riddled with inequalities. If the pattern of resource inequality is as commonplace as it appears, and *if school resources are translated into learning differences,* then educational inequalities would parallel and reinforce socioeconomic inequalities. The problem, however, is contained in the *if* clause. The link between the amount of money spent on schools and their educational effectiveness has never been established. The controversial Coleman Report found that per-pupil expenditures, facilities, and even teacher quality were far less important in explaining pupil achievement and motivation than were characteristics of the students themselves and their family backgrounds.[25] Christopher Jencks and his associates summed up the impact of expenditures by bluntly arguing that "the evidence we have examined does not suggest that doubling expenditures would raise students' performance on standardized tests."[26] To be sure, improving test scores is not the only goal of the public schools, but it may be the only measure of educational output comparable from school to school.

The evidence on school resources is not yet conclusive. It does not prove that expenditures make *no* difference in learning, but neither does it prove that they make any appreciable difference. The level of school spending may be a trivial influence on school quality when compared with other considerations. One whose goal is to improve the schools is better advised to concern himself with the content of school services rather than the amount of money spent on them. This view, of course, does not make inequities in school finance equitable. Indeed, one view of school spending holds that low-income students deserve *higher*-than-average spending in order to buy the services and facilities that compensate for the advantages that middle- and upper-income children receive in their homes. Or, as John Coons, the legal eagle of school-finance cases, observed, "If money is inadequate to improve education, the residents of poor districts should at least have an equal opportunity to be disappointed by it."[27]

Micro Inequalities

The macro sources of inequalities in the schools — financial variations among states, districts, and neighborhoods — look abstract and remote when compared with differences among individual students. The explanation of individual performance and achievement is as confused and unresolved as the debates over finance. The discussion about individual performance concerns *innate differences, cognitive abilities,* and *environmental differences* derived from the family.

INNATE DIFFERENCES: THE IQ CONTROVERSY   Few of the normally arcane issues of social science research have sparked such public controversy as the assertion by genetic psychologists that IQ is inherited and largely determines success. Although millions of IQ tests are given annually, and thousands of scholarly articles have described, attacked, and defended them, very little about IQ is settled. A few psychologists like Richard Herrnstein have insisted that as much as 80 percent of variation in IQ is explained by genes and that IQ predicts occupational success as neatly as it predicts school performance.[28] Jencks and his associates show, however, that this figure is greatly exaggerated and that IQ is positively, but not very strongly, associated with school performance.[29] Still, those who hold that IQ is a strong correlate of success in school will be skeptical of policy options designed to upgrade performance of disadvantaged children.

FAMILY, RACE, AND CLASS   By the time children enter grade school, they have already had important experiences. Attitudes toward authority and toward the political system — even their political party affiliations — are products of their family environment. Research on political socialization points to the family as the "foremost" or "dominant" agency of political learning.[30] The family's major role in socialization results from its near-monopoly of two critical resources — time and emotional attachment — during the formative years.

The role of the family in student achievement and motivation has been documented by the most extensive analysis of American education ever undertaken. This is the Equal Educational Opportunity survey, usually called the Coleman Report after its principal author, Professor James S. Coleman of Johns Hopkins University.[31] The study was commissioned by Congress under the Civil Rights Act of 1964 and was designed to investigate educational opportunities and race. The level of achievement, as Coleman discovered, differs markedly according to race. As Table 12.3 shows, whites generally scored higher on achievement tests in both the first and twelfth grades. In addition to differences between races in educational achievement, there

Table 12.3   Median Test Scores for Pupils in First and Twelfth Grades

Grade	Racial or ethnic group					
	Puerto Rican	American Indian	Mexican-American	Oriental American	Black	White
First grade						
Verbal	45.8	53.0	50.0	56.6	43.4	54.1
Nonverbal	44.9	47.8	46.5	51.6	45.4	53.2
Twelfth grade						
Average of five tests	43.1	45.1	44.4	50.1	41.1	52.0

Source: James S. Coleman et al., Equality of Educational Opportunity (Washington, D.C.: Government Printing Office, 1966), p. 20.

were also regional differences. Pupils in the metropolitan North were the highest achievers, whereas pupils in the nonmetropolitan South were the lowest achievers, regardless of race.

The single most important factor that Coleman found to explain educational achievement and motivation was the family background of the student. Whatever the school's impact, therefore, it is constrained by family circumstances. Coleman also investigated the effects of several other factors. Consistent with most other evidence, he found that differences in facilities, finances, and curriculum were of scant importance, although teacher competence was not insignificant. Other than family background, however, the most important single predictor of pupil performance was the *composition of the student body.* Particularly for students from minority groups, accomplishment is stimulated by being in school with motivated and able peers. In the words of the report, "attributes of other students account for far more variation in the achievement of minority group children than do any attributes of school facilities and slightly more than do attributes of staff."[32] Elsewhere Coleman summarized his results by concluding that, "The educational resources provided by a child's fellow students are more important for his achievement than are the resources provided by the school board."[33]

ASSESSING THE IMPACT OF EDUCATION

Assessing the impact of the schools is an old, tricky, and controversial business. As far back as 1895, Dr. Joseph Mayer Rice, a pediatrician with an interest in the budding field of psychology, attempted to gauge the impact of the schools on spelling competence. He persuaded school officials to administer a spelling test that he concocted to 16,000 students. The depressing results showed no relationship between the amount of time spent on spelling lessons and scores on Rice's tests. Dr. Rice soon became *persona non grata* in educational circles.[34] As with all measures of policy impact, the effectiveness of schools depends jointly on the goals specified and the measures selected. (See the discussion of the measurement of policy impact on pp. 220–222.) People differ, of course, about both goals and measures. One Boston administrator viewed it this way: "How does one know whether a school is effective? Any teacher can tell just by walking through the halls. He sees whether the students are wearing coats and ties, whether they are orderly in the corridors, whether they are respectful of authority."[35] Others prefer standards more closely related to learning than orderliness.

Conventional wisdom about the impact of schools has received serious challenges in recent years. The controversy comes from three sources: (1) the discovery that resources are not very consistently related to pupil performance; (2) the emphasis on family background and IQ as the primary determinants of achievement; and (3) the uncertainty attached to both compensatory education and mandatory busing as agents of racial integration. Some of the most sobering conclusions of all regarding the impact of the schools are those of Christopher Jencks and his associates. Their findings about equality, family background, cognitive traits, and the schools may be summarized as follows:

1. Family background and IQ are the most important determinants of school achievement, although they are not sufficient by themselves to explain differences in performance.
2. However measured (by teacher quality, money, facilities, programs, etc.) the equality of schools is far from a reality.
3. But, regardless of inequalities in the schools, school-related factors are trivial in accounting for differential pupil achievement.
4. And, whatever minor effects schools have on pupils are further vitiated by the miniscule correlations between education and later success, measured by occupational status, income, and job satisfaction.[36]

To the degree that equality is a desirable social goal, Jencks argues that there are more direct and effective ways of achieving it than through school reform. In the last analysis, though, all hitherto existing studies bear only on the schools as they are, not as they might be.[37] Whether some dramatic changes in them will make schools the equalizers some think they should be, can only be speculative. The challenge to educational policy is to establish (or reestablish) a link between the quality of the schools and the quality of life in an urban society.

THE CITY, INCOMES, AND POVERTY

Income, Poverty, and Policy

Most Americans think of themselves as "middle class." One survey reported that 82 percent of all Americans see themselves as middle or upper middle class.[38] Economist Robert Heilbroner estimates that a more realistic definition would include those making $15,000 to $32,000, which is no more than 35 percent of American families. As he remarks, "Eighty-two percent of Americans may *think* of themselves as middle-class or higher, but more than half of these families are kidding themselves."[39] For most middle-class Americans, indeed for most Americans whatever their economic status, real incomes (discounting inflation) have been going up consistently. Steelworkers, real-estate salespersons, teachers, postal workers, and others have more disposable income than ever before. The 1977 median family income of about $14,960 goes farther than it ever did, even after taxes and inflation.

The metropolis includes a wide range of income groups. Normally urbanites are spatially clustered by income levels. The *economic* facts of income distribution parallel the *social* facts of spatial distribution. In the U.S. as a whole, the distribution of income has changed very little since the end of World War II. Although there were substantial reductions in income inequality brought about by the war, income patterns settled thereafter into a rather steady pattern, so that the shape of the income distribution looks pretty much today like it did in the late 1940s. "Income shares" by each fourth or fifth of the population remain essentially unchanged. To the degree that any change has been perceptible, income distribution has, as one economist says, "inched a tiny bit toward equality."[40] Everyone, of course, is absolutely better off because the real incomes (that is, earnings taking account of inflation, measured in "constant dollars") have gone up steadily. But the relative shares have remained relatively stable. The share of the top 5 percent of income earners has declined somewhat over the years, but the *absolute gap* in dollars between rich and poor has widened. In 1947 the gap between the median income for the top fifth and for the bottom fifth was $20,995. Today it is almost twice that amount.

Public policy has important effects on the distribution of income. Who gets rich and who becomes poor is partly a result of marketplace decisions. But it is also a result of federal, state, and local policies. There are several ways in which public policy can affect incomes, specifically:

1. *Policies determine how much and what to tax.* On balance, national taxes are progressive, whereas state and local taxes are regressive (see pp. 230–231). Thus local governments tend to enrich the rich, while federal taxes take more of the rich family's income than the poor family's income. When all kinds of taxes are balanced, the net effect of taxes on income redistribution is minimal. Rich, average, and poor alike pay about one-third of their incomes in taxes.[41]
2. *Policies distribute direct cash transfers to various groups.* The welfare system, aid to small businessmen, and farm subsidies are all examples of direct aids to social groups. We will shortly examine the public-welfare system and show its impact on the problem of poverty.
3. *Policies distribute "in-kind" transfer payments to various groups.* Food stamps and Medicaid services go mostly to the poor, but health services and other indirect aids are widely available.
4. *Policies may manipulate the opportunity structure of society, so that people can improve their earning capacities.* Civil-rights legislation, obviously, is designed to eliminate barriers to jobs and promotion, so that white and black workers have similar opportunities in the job market. The "war on poverty" was intended to improve opportunities for poor families (through job-training

programs, community organization, and other programs) to enter the economic mainstream.

The Problem of Poverty

Poverty, of course, is a matter of definition. If we adopt a relative approach, and the American poor are compared with average Haitians or Ethiopians, then one can virtually eradicate poverty in America with a flip of the definitional wrist. If, on the other hand, one emphasizes a standard of relative deprivation, or inequality of income, then there is plenty of poverty in the United States. Whether poverty is increasing or decreasing is a matter of the initial definition. The Census Bureau has developed a standard of living for an urban family of four and used it as a means to establish a *poverty level*. Using the Census Bureau standard, Table 12.4 provides data on poverty in the United States from 1967 to 1975. While the proportion of Americans poor by constant standards had been declining throughout the decade of the 1960s, the early years of the 1970s saw mostly vacillations.

It is an interesting question in sociology of knowledge to ask when exactly Americans began to discover their poor. During the 1950s, both popular and scholarly writers discussed the *affluent society* and a *people of plenty* and debated the meaning of leisure time. Although economists such as John Kenneth Galbraith emphasized the presence of pockets of poverty in an otherwise well-off society, their emphasis on affluence captured more attention in that comfortable Republican decade. In many ways, it was the 1963 publication of Michael Harrington's *The Other America* that brought home the persistence of poverty in the affluent society.[42] President John F. Kennedy himself

Table 12.4   Changes in the Number of Poor Persons, 1967–1976

	Number	Change from previous year
1967	27.8 million	*down* .7 million
1968	25.4 million	*down* 2.4 million
1969	24.3 million	*down* 1.1 million
1970	25.5 million	*up* 1.2 million
1971	25.6 million	*up* .1 million
1972	24.5 million	*down* 1.1 million
1973	23.0 million	*down* 1.5 million
1974	23.4 million	*down* .4 million
1975	25.8 million	*up* 2.5 million
1976	25.1 million	*down* .9 million

Source: U.S. Bureau of the Census, annual estimates.

was influenced by Harrington's account of how the other America lived—the day after the assassination, an adviser found a dog-eared copy of the book in the White House Oval Office—and had proposed a major legislative program addressed to poverty just before his death. President Johnson made the program a major ingredient in his Great Society package of legislation, adopted by the Eighty-Sixth Congress. But before we embark on a discussion of poverty and urban policy, it may be useful to describe the nature and structure of American poverty, from both community and individual perspectives.

Macro and Micro Distribution of Poverty

Sometimes we think of the poor as concentrated mainly in the racial ghettos of our biggest cities or in the most rural backwoods of Appalachia. The pattern, however, is somewhat more complex. Statistically speaking, there is *proportionately* more poverty in rural areas than in metropolitan areas, but, *in absolute terms*, there is more poverty in metropolitan than in rural areas, simply because such a large proportion of the nation's population (about two-thirds) lives in metropolitan areas. Moreover, there is proportionately less poverty in the largest than in the smallest cities. The percentage of poor people is, for example, twice as high in Bryan, Texas, as in Dallas; in East St. Louis, Illinois, as in Chicago; and in Newburgh, New York, as in New York City. But again, because so many more people live in cities such as Chicago, New York, and Dallas than in smaller ones, the absolute number—and the concentration—of poor people in major metropolitan areas is greater and offers greater challenges.

Within the metropolitan area itself there are also important differences in the distribution of poverty. It is common to view metropolitan central cities as havens of the poor and downtrodden and the suburbs as homes of the white well-to-do. This image is, however, so oversimplified as to be seriously misleading. The size of the metropolitan area is a crucial variable in understanding the distribution of poverty within the metropolis. In the largest metropolitan areas there is indeed a clear tendency for poorer people to reside in the central cities and for wealthier ones to live in the suburbs, but this pattern reverses itself in the smaller metropolitan areas. In those with populations of less than 250,000, there are proportionately more poor people in the fringe areas than in the central cities. Within each central city, of course, there is a marked tendency for the poor to live in the oldest parts of town, where housing is cheapest. But the poor are not always separated by great physical distances from the wealthy. Some of the poorest neighborhoods in Washington, D.C., are within a short walk of affluent Georgetown. The socioeconomic distance between New

York's Park Avenue and its slum dwellers is great, but the physical distance is surprisingly short.

Just as poverty is distributed on a macro scale, that is, among and within communities, it is also distributed on a micro scale. The probability of being poor varies from group to group and from person to person. Certain types of families and individuals are especially likely to fall below this poverty line. Poverty is particularly concentrated among the aged, families headed by females, members of minority groups, and those with mental, emotional, physical, or occupational handicaps.

But the poor are not a homogeneous group (except in the obvious sense that they all have low incomes). The one safe generalization about poverty is that *very, very few families headed by a white, nonaged, employable male fall below the poverty line*. It follows that families that do not share these attributes run a much higher risk of being poor. Specifically, possession of each of the following attributes statistically increases the probabilities of falling victim to the ruthless mathematics of poverty:

- being aged
- living in a female-headed household
- living in a large family
- being nonwhite
- having a mental, emotional, or physical affliction

None of these predicts perfectly to poverty. In fact, a majority of the people in each category are nonpoor — most of the aged are not poor, most people in female-headed households are not poor, and so on. The cumulative effect is critical.

One useful profile of the poor is provided by the University of Michigan's panel study of a sample of American families over six years.[43] The Michigan survey divided American families into five basic groups: (1) *stable nonpoor*, a group consistently above the poverty line; (2) *chronic poor*, consistently below it; (3) *upwardly mobile*, families that had been below the poverty line but had steadily risen above it; (4) *downwardly mobile*, above the poverty line but now sinking into poverty, and (5) *unstable poor*, who may rise and fall irregularly. *The overwhelming majority of American families are either stable nonpoor or chronic poor*. Only about 1 in 20 families was upwardly or downwardly mobile. The Michigan researchers found only two factors that systematically explained why people move in or out of the poverty cadre. First (and not surprisingly) was a change in labor-force participation — getting a job, losing one, getting a better one, a wife working or stopping work, and so on. The second factor was change in the composition of the family itself. Divorce, separation, death, birth, and a child leaving home all operated to raise or lower a family's status.

What was not important in explaining changes in a family's status is just as interesting. One factor of trivial importance in explaining why some families rise out of or fall into poverty was their economic and social attitudes. Many have hypothesized a "culture of poverty" among the poor. Edward C. Banfield, for example, described the poor as "present oriented" in contrast to the more "future-oriented" middle classes.[44] Yet there is very little evidence to support the view that the poor have attitudes toward work, toward moral behavior, and toward other values that are fundamentally different from other Americans.[45] The Michigan panel studies of income recipients support the same conclusions.

Americans have long exhibited hostility toward their poor. As sympathetic as they have been toward the "deserving poor" — presumably widows, orphans, and the physically disabled — they have also singled out another segment of the poor, the "despised poor." Feagin found that most Americans cherish a simplistic view of poverty and tend to blame poverty on individual derelictions and failures. "Americans," he says, "still believe that God helps those who help themselves."[46] He asked a sample of the American population to list the major reasons why "there are poor people in this country." Their explanations, ranked by frequency of mention, included:

1. lack of thrift and proper money management
2. lack of effort by the poor themselves
3. lack of ability and talent among poor people
4. loose morals and drunkenness
5. sickness and physical handicaps
6. low wages in some businesses and industries
7. failure of society to provide good schools for many Americans
8. prejudice and discrimination against blacks
9. failure of private industry to provide enough jobs
10. being taken advantage of by rich people
11. just bad luck

Clearly, Americans adhere to an individualistic, micro-level, explanation for poverty. Loose morals, drunkenness, laziness, and improper management, constitute the dominant explanations.

Individualistic explanations, however, overlook some significant structural or macro-level explanations for poverty. For the poor who are concentrated on farms, the mechanization of agriculture has helped to create their plight, even forcing some to flee to cities, where they are scarcely equipped for urban existence.[47] For those in core cities a deteriorating economy reduces economic opportunities even for the most energetic and well educated of the poor. To the degree that there are limited housing opportunities outside the central city for persons of low income, the poor suffer the worst schools and services in the metropolitan area and face the most stagnant economic circumstances. It is also true that practices of many businessmen add to the poverty of the poor. David Caplovitz, for example, studied consumer practices in poor neighborhoods and uncovered a consistent pattern of high prices, poor quality, high interest rates, and unethical merchandising.[48] Finally, as both liberals and conservatives alike concede, the welfare system works to perpetuate poverty through a series of selected disincentives (see discussion below). As these considerations indicate, structural explanations for poverty should compete with individualistic explanations.

Being Poor

So far poverty has been treated as if it were entirely a matter of having a low income. Being poor, however, means much more than having too little money to buy what others consider essential. Some years ago, several U.S. senators and their families simulated poverty for a week by living on a welfare-budget diet. The results, dutifully reported to the press, were persistent hunger, constant exhaustion, chronic irritability, and general malaise. However much this noble experiment dramatizes and personalizes poverty, it still fails to capture the multidimensional nature of being poor, especially because the poor cannot look forward to the weekend.

Research has identified numerous variables on which the poor differ from the rest of the population.[49] They are more likely to be victims of crime. They also are more likely to be victims of disease, mental illness, and malnutrition. The psychological costs of being poor are indicated by the much larger proportions of poor people who report being generally unhappy, by the higher incidence of mental illness among them, and by their feelings that they can do little to manipulate their own environment. This last feeling of social ineffectiveness is paralleled by a low sense of political efficacy and a high sense of political futility. The poor see the political world as alien, complicated, distant, and impervious to them. Poor neighborhoods have very weak systems of social ties and organizations; most socializing takes place within the extended families and immediate neighborhoods. Very few poor neighborhoods have produced indigenous community or group leaders, which makes all efforts to organize the poor very difficult. Leaders claiming to represent the poor have usually gained their status by reference to race, rather than to poverty alone. Family life among the poor often tends toward instability, sometimes fostered by welfare dependency. Family instability in turn produces higher levels of insecurity and occasionally deviant behavior among youth.[50]

Nonetheless, we should avoid the image of a nearly complete homogeneity of attitudes and behavior among the poor. No more than we would assume that every person whose income is over $10,000 thinks and behaves as does every other should we assume that all the poor are stamped from the same mold. Perhaps the most significant factor dividing the poor is race; conflict between whites and blacks overshadows whatever common interests are engendered by economic circumstances. The variety of belief and behavior patterns among the poor is particularly evident in political life. Political alienation, for example, is found more often among low-income groups than among the more affluent, but not all the poor are alienated. Even among the alienated, some express their hostility and isolation by withdrawal and nonparticipation, whereas others actively participate in ways that sedate members of the middle class would call deviant. The intensity of this *negative participation* may be expressed by voting against both incumbent office holders and referenda propositions. For some black Americans, participating in racial disorders is protest aginst the system. Authoritarian political attitudes, characterized by intolerance of dissenting views and hostility toward out-groups, also characterize many lower-class people, although the better educated of the poor are no more authoritarian than other Americans.

Some writers feel that these attitudes cluster together in a "culture of poverty," which is passed on from generation to generation, making it difficult to break a cycle of poverty. The notion of a poverty culture has become a common explanation for the difficulties in ending poverty.[51] One frequently cited application of the culture of poverty hypothesis is Edward C. Banfield's theory of the "present-oriented" lower class. Lower-class people, he says, "live from moment to moment ... Impulse governs their behavior...."[52] Work is only a means of staying alive, and lower-class people have little conception of, or interest in, the future. On the other hand, middle-class people take account of the future, expecting that efforts will make their lives, and their children's lives, better. Jobs are held steadily; plans are made; children are pushed to do well and succeed. The real problem of poverty, Banfield contends, is not financial but cultural.

There is, however, very little evidence to support the hypothesis that middle- and lower-class people differ sharply in their value orientations. Rainwater, Goodwin, the Michigan researchers, and others have regularly found that poor and nonpoor people have generally similar attitudes.[53] Greenberg explicitly tested Banfield's theory in several poor neighborhoods by asking people whether "the wise person lives for today and lets tomorrow take care of itself."[54] Decisive majorities of the poor (about 2 to 1) rejected the "present-oriented" response. Interestingly, however, Greenberg singled out one group not usually included in social-science surveys, a group he called the "street-corner society." These young men were often unemployed, spent time "hanging around" bars and street corners, and were normally single. Alone among the poor—no one knows how large the "street-corner" segment is—there may be some truth to the culture of poverty hypothesis or the present-orientation theory. But for most of the poor, values and attitudes duplicate those of nonpoor Americans. If the poor do not work, it is more likely to be because they cannot find it than because they are psychologically disinclined to work.

Poverty and Race:
An Overworked Assumption

One sometimes feels, from the frequency with which questions of "poverty" and those of "race" are linked, that poverty is mainly a black problem and that most black Americans are poor. Both assumptions are plainly wrong: most poor Americans are white, and most black families are not poor. The majority of black Americans live in families with husband and wife and children, where fathers (and increasingly mothers) work. Outside the South, the incomes of young black families in which both parents work—increasingly the norm for both races—are almost exactly identical to those of equivalent white families. Only a small minority of urban blacks live in ghettos, where row after row of crowded tenements are owned by absentee landlords. Black fertility rates remain higher than white, but fewer children are being born annually to both races. Nearly three-fourths of black youth complete high school (up from less than two-thirds as recently as 1970), and more and more go to college.

Black families are still less affluent than white families. Consequently they are disproportionately represented in the poverty class. One in three poor people is nonwhite, a proportion much greater than their one-in-eight share of the total population. For a while during the 1960s, blacks seemed to be closing the "affluence gap." In 1960 the average black family made only 50 percent as much money as the average white family. But by 1970 this ratio had increased to 61 percent. Some scholars were confidently predicting in the late 1960s that differences between white and black income would be negligible by 1978. Those hopes were probably exaggerated, although the gains of the 1960s made by blacks persisted into the less-prosperous 1970s.[55]

There is one overarching factor that separates white from black families in explaining their position in the income structure. That is the large share of female-headed black families. More than 1 million black females are family heads. These families have a better-than-even chance of falling below the poverty line and now account for two-thirds of poverty among black families. Here, then, is an important dimension of the black–white differences: *Black families headed by males continue to rise above the poverty line, but an increasing proportion of black families are female headed.* Youth in these families risk abnormally high unemployment in a labor market where teen-age unemployment rates run to 35 percent. In a word, intact black families tend to stay at least moderately above the poverty line, with a few falling below when times are bad. Split black families are prime candidates for the chronic poor that we described above. It is almost appropriate to say that there are not one but two black Americas, one where the white–black gap shows signs of closing (albeit no faster than the pace of economic growth permits) and the other where white–black gaps give no signs of altering in the near future.

We stress that there are strong ties between poverty and race, but they are not two ways of stating the same problem. Most blacks are not poor (some are very rich, in fact); most poor people are not black. Blacks, however, are disproportionately poor, a condition exacerbated by a recent widening in the black–white affluence gap. Black poverty is particularly acute among those families headed by females. A majority of such family units are poor, and their numbers are increasing.

POLICY AND POVERTY:
THE WELFARE SYSTEM

What Is the Welfare System, and Why Are People Saying Those Awful Things About It?

Welfare must surely rank as the most unpopular public policy in America. Despised by middle-class taxpayers who see welfare payments as subsidizing the shiftless, it is equally unpopular with recipients. Governors and mayors try annually to unload more welfare costs on the federal government. Congress has not been an eager recipient of this intergovernmental generosity.

The $17 billion spent on public welfare in fiscal 1976 consists primarily of three major programs:

- *Aid to Families with Dependent Children* (AFDC), the most controversial welfare program, amounting to almost $4.5 million; a mixed federal-state program
- *General Assistance,* entirely a state and local program, costing about $1.2 million
- *Supplemental Security Income* (SSI) programs, whose $6 billion cost was largely paid by the federal government and which provided assistance for the aged, blind, and disabled.

Other programs make up the balance, but these three cover the lion's share of the welfare budget.

To the public, welfare symbolizes social support for the indolent, paid for by taxing the hard-working. To social workers charged with

Table 12.5   Public Perceptions of Welfare Programs

	Agree	Disagree	Uncertain	Total
There are too many people receiving welfare money who should be working.	84	11	5	100
Many people getting welfare are *not* honest about their need.	71	17	12	100
A lot of people are moving to this state from other states just to get welfare money here.	41	31	28	100

Source: Joe R. Feagin, "America's Welfare Stereotypes," *Social Science Quarterly,* 52 (March 1972), Table 1, 923.

day-to-day operation of the system, it is riddled with red tape, complex rules, and regulation, and it often fails to deal with the most pressing cases. Recipients feel the degradation attached to the "dole," dislike the surveillance of the system, and deplore the built-in disincentives to work. Among the public, social workers, and even recipients themselves, there remains the nagging suspicion that many people who prefer doles to work are being subsidized by the welfare system. Feagin asked his respondents for their attitudes about welfare recipients. Some of his results are indicated in Table 12.5. To say that welfare recipients are not popular with their fellow citizens would be an understatement. Most pointedly, overwhelming majorities of Americans suspect that hordes of able-bodied men are mooching out of the welfare trough instead of working. In fact, only about 1 percent of the nation's welfare recipients are able-bodied males, and state laws universally require that such persons actively seek work.[57] The actual breakdown of welfare recipients indicates that most of the other 99 percent are children without fathers, elderly, or physically and emotionally disabled. Very little evidence indicates that vast numbers of recipients are cheating the states and cities. Occasional purges of the welfare rolls usually reveal only 3 to 5 percent of ineligible recipients, and the costs of such investigations are often greater than the payments saved. The small proportion of ineligible recipients actually receiving aid is offset by the repeated discovery that many eligibles are not receiving payments at all.

Some of the bluntest criticism of the welfare system was leveled by the National Advisory Commission on Civil Disorders:

The Commission believes that our present system of public assistance contributes materially to the tensions and social disorganization that have led to civil disorders. The failures of the system alienate the taxpayers who support it, the social workers who administer it, and the poor who depend upon it. As one critic told the Commission, "The welfare system is designed to save money instead of people and tragically ends up doing neither."[58]

Among specific criticisms of the welfare strategy of attacking poverty are, first, that it contains built-in discouragement to advancement. Until recently all payments received from work were deducted from welfare payments that the individual or family could otherwise receive. If the mother of dependent children undertook to improve her economic lot by working part time, she would thus lose an amount of welfare aid equal to her wages.

Some recent changes have lessened this equivalent of a 100-percent tax on earned income; but welfare payments have long produced disincentives for advancement. Liberals, conservatives, welfare officials, and recipients have all deplored the system of "welfare dependency."[59]

Second, there is wide variation in payments both within and among states. Even with greater federal financing and standard setting, states still show staggering variations that cannot be explained only by interstate differences in wealth or cost of living. The most generous state (Massachusetts) paid nearly *eight times* more per family in AFDC payments than the most frugal state (Mississippi). In Massachusetts an AFDC family could receive nearly $400 in assistance in September, 1975; the same family in Mississippi would have collected less than $50. (Though Massachusetts is wealthier than Mississippi, it is hardly eight times wealthier.) Even within states, standards for eligibility may be differently applied by different local authorities. People eligible at one welfare office may not be at another.

Third, the public-welfare system is institutionalized charity and has the usual social stigma attached to such doles. Because eligibility requirements are complex and usually rigid, there is considerable personal investigation and long-term surveillance of recipients. The most extreme form is the *midnight raid,* in which a welfare agent checks to see if there is a man around the house of a mother receiving aid to dependent children, an agency practice the Supreme Court recently outlawed.

Fourth, the relations between social-welfare workers and clients are commonly "abrasive" and "brittle," in the Kerner Commission's words. The caseworker is forced into antagonisitc relations with clients whom he is supposed to be assisting. Although the worker is expected to establish a high level of personal rapport so that he may be able to influence client behavior, he also plays the antagonistic role of investigator and "snoop."

The Welfare Explosion and Why

The 1960s witnessed what can only be called a "welfare explosion." Even though the number of poor persons actually declined between 1960 and 1970, the number of persons receiving welfare aid more than doubled. By 1976 more than 16 million Americans received aid under AFDC, General Assistance, or SSI provisions. Big cities saw the proportion of welfare recipients escalate dramatically. In February 1976 St. Louis had 17 percent of its population on welfare, Baltimore had 16 percent, Boston and Washington had 14 percent, New Orleans, New York and Chicago each 11 percent.

What explains this paradox of declining poverty and rising welfare costs? One interesting and provocative theory is offered by Francis Fox Piven and Richard Cloward in *Regulating the Poor*.[60] *Welfare payments*, they contend, *bear little relation to poverty but are rather associated with high levels of civil unrest*. The 1960s, of course, was a period of great racial and social turmoil in American cities, and government responded with more welfare. Welfare payments, according to Piven and Cloward, always come with "strings attached." Rules about "proper" behavior and requirements that recipients must actively seek work mean that government can enforce social control over potentially dissident groups. Thus welfare payments do not reflect a noble spirit of generosity but enable government to regulate the disruptive behavior of the poor. Government, according to their theory, *responds not to the numbers of poor people but to the troubles they cause*.

There were, of course, other factors operating to expand the welfare rolls in the 1960s. Court rulings expanded eligibility and reduced agency capriciousness in cutting off assistance. In 1969, for example, the Supreme Court struck down residency requirements as a condition for aid; in 1970, it held that residents were entitled to a trial-like hearing before an agency could terminate their assistance. In addition, the emergence of legal-assistance programs through the war on poverty provided both information and legal aid for the poor in doing battle with welfare agencies. The National Welfare Rights Organization pressured local and state agencies to process applications expeditiously and to treat claimants more civilly.

If the Welfare System is So Unpopular, Why Do We Still Have It?

Popularity is necessary to enact a new policy, but unpopularity is no guarantee that an old one will be abandoned. Piecemeal reforms of old policies may be politically easier than adoption of wholly new policies. Such has been the case with welfare. Mayors and governors were horrified by escalating costs (which nearly bankrupted the state of Michigan, for example) but encouraged the federal government to create the SSI program in 1972 and take over state costs. Welfare recipients and civil-rights groups succeeded in eliminating some of the most arbitrary policies (such as midnight raids and residency requirements) through the courts.

Efforts to substitute new poverty and incomes policies for welfare have so far been unsuccessful. Throughout the 1960s, economists and politicians, both conservative and liberal, began to advocate some form of *guaranteed annual income*. Others called for a *negative income tax,* which would amount to virtually the same thing. Democratic presidential candidate George McGovern crawled out on a political limb in the 1972 campaign with his advocacy of a guaranteed income scheme. But it was his victorious opponent who had first proposed the idea to Congress. Back in 1968 Nixon had proposed a "Family Assistance Plan" (FAP), which would have replaced the existing welfare system with a modest minimum income, peaking at $1600 per family.[61] But the FAP became impaled on the horns of a classic political dilemma: The program was too generous for most conservatives, yet too stingy for most liberals. The program never got through Congress. Welfare remains America's policy for the poor. The only other major alternative to it in recent decades was the much-touted but ill-fated war on poverty.

MAKING WAR ON POVERTY

Who Started the War on Poverty?

Disregarding the biblical warning that "the poor shall never cease out of this land," President Lyndon B. Johnson, on 20 August 1964, signed the Economic Opportunity Act. [62] Speaking at the signing ceremony in the White House Rose Garden, the President declared this nation's commitment to "eradicate poverty among its people." Armed with the metaphor, if not the money, of the military, the government inaugurated the "war on poverty." The enemy, poverty, would prove to be as elusive and difficult to define as the Vietcong, and the debate over strategies would be only slightly less furious than that over Southeast Asia.

During the Kennedy administration, a group of Washington, D.C., bureaucrats, mostly in sub-Cabinet positions, came together informally to prepare legislation aimed at the problem of poverty in the United States. Although members of the group were divided among themselves on specific strategies, they universally held to a structural, as opposed to an individualistic, view of the causes of poverty. Such a perspective contained within it the seeds of a critique of traditional welfare policies, which they viewed as aimed at amelioration of individual problems rather than at institutional change. In the eyes of some members of the inner circle of poverty planners, public-welfare bureaucracies actually impeded antipoverty action, for they are more concerned with maintenance of their own organization than with major social change. In June 1963, President Kennedy gave Walter Heller, who as chairman of the Council of Economic Advisers had been a major figure in the planning, his support for the antipoverty legislation. Those plans were nearly complete when Kennedy's death placed Lyndon Johnson in the White House.

Despite some planners' fears, Johnson evinced immediate interest in the legislation then being prepared for Congress: "That's my kind of program. It will help people. I want you to move full speed ahead," he told Heller. Once the commitment to do something had been made, jockeying for support among elements of the federal bureaucracy followed. The Labor Department favored a major program of job retraining under its own administration. The Department of Health, Education, and Welfare favored major educational and health programs, though it was willing to provide some money to Labor for summer work programs. The Commerce Department favored loans to small entrepreneurs among the poor, whereas the Agriculture Department argued that there were surely as many poor farming entrepreneurs as there were poor businessmen. The Interior Department mentioned poverty among the Indians but did not formulate a program. These conflicts among the departments, as well as between the departments collectively and the Bureau of the Budget, became severe enough to threaten a delay in the legislative program. President Johnson appointed Sargent Shriver chairman of a task force to come up with a presentable program. After eight weeks of balancing, negotiating, and compromising, the task force drafted the legislation.

The result was a hastily forged compromise. The task force's most important contribution to the legislative package was the idea of an independent agency in the Executive Office of the President to administer the program. The Office of Economic Opportunity (OEO) thus became the nation's antipoverty agency. In both draft and final legislation the OEO was given the responsibility for administering several specific components of the war on poverty. The Job Corps was designed to provide education, vocational training, and work experience for youth. The Volunteers in Service to America (VISTA) program was envisioned as the domestic analogue of the Peace Corps, a group of volunteers who were to work in public projects or with community-action programs. The Head Start program, the least controversial of the programs, was to provide preschool training for disadvantaged youngsters. The Neighborhood Youth Corps would provide work experience and vocational training for youths living at home. The OEO was also charged with administrative responsibility for community-action programs.

There was a general belief among the poverty planners that local choice and flexibility should be maximal. As the circumstances of poverty varied from community to community, it was necessary to include a *decentralizing element* in the legislation. The planners differed in their views about the Community Action Agency, but most favored its inclusion. Local agencies would be directed by boards broadly representative of the communities and would tailor specific projects to meet local needs, even though they would be funded mainly by the federal government.

Three little words, however—"maximum feasible participation"—threw the whole community-action concept into intense controversy once the warriors headed for the battlefield. The phrase appeared, innocently enough, in the definition of a community-action project in Title II, Section 202(b) of the Economic Opportunity Act. Specifically a CAP was defined as an agency that: (1) would mobilize community resources for an attack on poverty; (2) provide services to eliminate poverty by improving human performance and the like; and (3) would be "developed, conducted, and administered with the maximum feasible participation of residents of the areas and members of the groups served." Even participants in the original planning disagree about the source of the phrase, for at first no one paid much attention to it. In congressional hearings on the bill, only Robert F. Kennedy made even incidental reference to maximum feasible participation. Moynihan has claimed that the intent of the framers was merely to ensure that the poor were, in fact, the beneficiaries of the programs. If the poor, particularly blacks in the South, were "not sharing—that is, participating—in the benefits of the new program, Washington could intervene on the grounds that the requirements of the legislation were not being met."[63] In any event, no one, not even the most radical of the planners, intended the phrase to mean that the poor should be given control of the local programs. That some people, especially militant poverty workers, interpreted maximum feasible participation to mean policy control by the poor came to be the major political albatross of the war on poverty.

The draft legislation, maximum feasible participation and all, sailed through Congress with the minimum imaginable debate. Only a handful of changes was made in committee, and the bill passed both houses of Congress with comfortable majorities. Most of the opposition rhetoric was ideological, but even conservatives were cautious in their criticisms for fear of appearing to support poverty in an election year. Nearly all Democrats outside the South supported the legislation, and they were joined by most liberal Republicans. Opposition came mainly from southern Democrats and conservative Republicans, not an uncommon lineup against domestic social-welfare legislation.

Warring on Poverty —
or on City Governments?

The controversial cornerstone of the war on poverty was the local Community Action Agencies. The governing boards of the CAAs were to consist of representatives of three groups: public agencies, including the city government, school systems, and social-welfare agencies; private groups, including business, labor, and religious groups, and leaders of established minority groups such as the NAACP; and representatives of the neighborhoods to be served by the programs. Local agencies could choose among a variety of programs authorized by the Economic Opportunity Act, including: (1) remedial or supplementary educational programs such as preschool day-care centers; (2) employment development, job training, and counseling; (3) health and vocational-rehabilitation programs, like health examinations and family-planning advice; (4) home management and improvement; (5) improving welfare services; (6) consumer-information projects; (7) legal aid; (8) creation of neighborhood centers and organizations; (9) VISTA and Job Corps activities; and (10) encouraging resident participation in the policy making of both the CAA itself and of such other public and private institutions as the traditional welfare programs.

For the most part, these CAAs were dominated by establishment forces within local communities, typically operated *for* the poor (at least some of the time) but rarely *by* the poor. Some local agencies, however, were soon engulfed in conflict over the implementation of the "maximum feasible participation" requirement. Spokesmen for the poor emphasized the need for *maximum* participation; city officials countered with emphasis on *feasible* participation. In San Francisco, for example, "the fight for maximum feasible participation evolved from a contest between the mayor and minority group spokesmen for control of the program into a succession of power struggles within the target areas and between them and the central administration."[64] The overwhelming proportions of the budgets and energies of the OEO nationally and the CAAs locally went to such programs as child development, Head Start, health services, and social services, but OEO activities in legal aid and neighborhood organization made the headlines. Many observers, including some congressmen, a few journalists, a number of mayors, and former Vice-President Agnew, were certain that the OEO was dominated by radicals intent on redistributing political power from elected officials to self-appointed spokesmen for the poor. The subsequent trials and tribulations of the war on poverty could fill (and have filled) volumes.

Many mayors and local officials thought the war on poverty was really a war on municipal governments waged by Washington. Local antipoverty activists, funded by OEO, sometimes led picketing, sit-ins, and demonstrations against city policies. Welfare-rights organizations sued welfare bureaucracies. Mayors wanted control of antipoverty agencies and pressed Washington for a weakening of the "maximum feasible participation" requirements. Yet the political activities of the war-on-poverty activists made more headlines than they merited. One definitive study of community action agencies in five large cities concluded that the political influence and ideology of the mayor was the major factor shaping participation in the poverty program. New York Mayor John Lindsay was sympathetic to participation and engineered a highly participatory program there. Chicago Mayor Daley had little interest in activating the poor and promoted a services-only poverty program.[65]

The Impact of the War on Poverty — A Failure or Not?

President Nixon was not fond of the war on poverty. After his second inaugural, he set out to dismantle it. He appointed Howard Phillips the new director, who promptly announced that the OEO was "a failure." Unfortunately the evidence on the policy impact of the war on poverty is difficult to assess. More than a decade later it is difficult to see lasting effects on local politics, social conditions of the poor, or poverty itself. Poverty as officially defined declined after the war on poverty was launched, but it had been declining before then, too. The incidence of poverty began creeping up again in the early 1970s, but that was related as much to a recession as to a winding down of the war on poverty.

There is some evidence to suggest that the impact was variable from community to community. Clark and Hopkins evaluated a dozen community-action programs and divided them into three categories of effectiveness. Five were relatively effective (New Haven, Syracuse, Newark, Paterson, and Minneapolis), four were mixed (New York, Washington, San Francisco, and Los Angeles), and three were relatively ineffective (Chicago, Cleveland, and Boston).[66] The more effective programs were relatively autonomous and free from political intervention by local officials; they were program, rather than patronage, oriented; and they were led by sophisticated boards with real political power. James Vanecko studied 50 local antipoverty programs and concluded that the most effective ones emphasized community organization and mobilization of the poor.[67] Both of these studies indicate that politically independent and activist-oriented boards coexist with the most effective kinds of local agencies. Obviously these are also the most controversial politically.

URBAN POLICY AND INEQUALITY: SOME CONCLUDING NOTES

We cannot really describe urban inequality and policy responses to it in this chapter alone. Indeed, we have met the issue at many places in this book. For example:

- In Chapter 2 we showed how migration of rural peoples to cities in most nations added to pressures on local employment markets.
- In Chapters 3 and 4 we showed how the political economy and the political sociology of metropolitan areas distributed jobs and economic opportunities, leaving fewer jobs in core cities where poorer people are clustered.
- In Chapter 5 we showed how participation in urban politics was related to social class characteristics and to race, and how participation often paralleled social inequalities.
- In Chapter 10 we showed how urban services may serve needs of poor and rich differentially.
- In Chapter 11 we emphasized that the poor were more often victimized by crime than the rich.

All these factors contribute to inequality. In Chapter 14 we will examine problems related to growth and decay, showing that the problems of decay often coincide with problems of the poor.

But in this chapter we have focused more generally on the relation between public policy and the problem of inequality. Americans have long believed that education was a great equalizer, and school policies were examined. Schools have become a major political issue for several reasons, including their assumption of more social and more controversial roles, declining enrollments and rising costs, problems of race, problems of school finance, and questions of school performance. Issues of equality and education are most often joined in the debates over school integration, but the inequalities in school finance have also been a much-disputed policy problem.

In the last decade the problem of poverty has been a focus for several policies related to urban inequality. The traditional welfare system has many opponents and few supporters. But no lasting policy alternative to welfare has yet been adopted. Despite widely agreed-on negative policy impacts of the welfare system, efforts to replace it through some income maintenance scheme have come to naught. The highly touted war on poverty represented the Johnson Administration's effort to attack poverty. But its impacts were difficult to measure. Thus far at least, urban policy seems to have verified the biblical warning that, "The poor shall never cease out of this land."

Notes

1. Our account of the New Jersey school story relies on Richard Lehne, "Complex Justice: Courts, Agenda Setting and School Finance," paper presented at the Annual Meeting of the American Political Science Association, Chicago, 2–5 September 1976.

2. David Harvey, *Social Justice and the City* (Baltimore: John Hopkins University Press, 1973), p. 52.

3. Quoted from the frontispiece of Neil Postman and Charles Weingartner, *Teaching as a Subversive Activity* (New York: Delacorte Press, 1969).

4. Basil G. Zimmer and Amos H. Hawley, *Metropolitan Area Schools* (Beverly Hills, Calif.: Sage, 1968), p. 86.

5. United States Senate, Subcommittee on Intergovernmental Relations, *Confidence and Concern* (Washington, D.C.: Government Printing Office, 1973), pp. 37–38.

6. An excellent overview of school politics is contained in Frederick M. Wirt and Michael Kirst, *The Political Web of American Schools* (Boston: Little, Brown, 1972).

7. See, for example, James Hottois and Neal A. Milner, *The Sex Education Controversy* (Lexington, Mass.: Heath, 1975).

8. James S. Coleman et al., *Equality of Educational Opportunity* (Washington, D.C.: Government Printing Office, 1966).

9. Christopher Jencks et al., *Inequality* (New York: Basic Books, 1972).

10. Robert A. Dentler et al., eds., *The Urban R's* (New York: Praeger, 1967), p. x.

11. Donald R. Matthews and James W. Prothro, "Stateways vs. Folkways: Critical Factors in Southern Reactions to *Brown* v. *Board of Education.*" in G. Dietze, ed., *Essays on the American Constitution* (Englewood Cliffs, N.J.: Prentice-Hall, 1964), p. 144.

12. U.S. Commission on Civil Rights, *Racial Isolation in the Public Schools,* Vol. 1 (Washington, D.C.: Government Printing Office, 1967), p. 190.

13. Paul Peterson, *School Politics — Chicago Style* (Chicago: University of Chicago Press, 1976), p. 145.

14. James S. Coleman, Sara D. Kelly, and John H. Moore, *Trends in School Segregation, 1968–73* (Washington, D.C.: The Urban Institute, 1975), p. 53.

15. Christine H. Rossell, "School Desegregation and White Flight." *Political Science Quarterly, 90* (Winter 1975–76), p. 688.

16. Peterson, op. cit., p. 175.

17. For a discussion of the Massachusetts Racial Imbalance Act, see Frank Levy, *Northern Schools and Civil Rights* (Chicago: Markham, 1971).

18. Jencks, op. cit., p. 88.

19. David Armor, "The Evidence on Busing," *The Public Interest, 28* (Summer 1972), 90–126.

20. Thomas Pettigrew et al., "Busing: A Review of 'The Evidence,' " *The Public Interest, 30* (Winter 1973), 88–118.

21. Nancy St. John, *School Desegregation: Outcomes for Children* (New York: Wiley-Interscience, 1975).

22. James B. Conant, *Slums and Suburbs* (New York: McGraw-Hill, 1961), p. 3.

23. *Wall Street Journal,* 2 March 1972, p. 1. Some of the best scholarly material on the inequality of resources problem can be found in Arthur Wise, *Rich Schools, Poor Schools* (Chicago: University of Chicago Press, 1967) and John

E. Coons et al., *Private Wealth and Public Education* (Cambridge, Mass.: Harvard University Press, 1970).

24. Patricia Cayo Sexton, *Education and Income* (New York: Viking, 1961), pp. 16–17. See also Martin T. Katzman, *The Political Economy of Urban Schools* (Cambridge: Harvard University Press, 1971), chap. 3; Richard A. Berk and Alice Hartman, "Race and District Differences in Per Pupil Staffing Expenditures in Chicago Elementary Schools, 1970–1971," Center for Urban Affairs, Northwestern University, 1971; and James W. Guthrie et al., "Educational Inequality, School Finance, and a Plan for the '70's," in Senate Select Committee on Equal Educational Opportunity, *Hearings*, Vol. 7 (Washington, D.C.: Government Printing Office, 1970), pp. 3457–3458.

25. Coleman, *Equality*, op. cit.

26. Jencks, p. 93.

27. Quoted in *Wall Street Journal*, op. cit.

28. Richard Herrnstein, *IQ in the Meritocracy* (Boston: Little, Brown, 1973).

29. Jencks, op. cit., pp. 57–58.

30. These descriptions are used, respectively, by Herbert Hyman, *Political Socialization* (New York: Free Press, 1958), p. 69; and Richard E. Dawson and Kenneth Prewitt, *Political Socialization* (Boston: Little, Brown, 1969) p. 122.

31. Coleman, op. cit.

32. Ibid., p. 302.

33. James S. Coleman, "Toward Open Schools," *The Public Interest*, No. 9 (Fall 1967), 21.

34. Dr. Rice's story is told by Edward Wynne, *The Politics of School Accountability* (Berkeley, Calif.: McCutchan, 1972), p. 33.

35. Cited in Katzman, p. 19.

36. Jencks, op. cit.

37. For some critiques of the schools as they are, see Ivan Illich, *De-Schooling Society* (New York: Harper & Row, 1971); Mario Fantini et al., *Community Control and the Urban School* (New York: Praeger, 1970); and Charles E. Silberman, *Crisis in the Classroom* (New York: Random House, 1970).

38. Robert Heilbroner, "Middle-Class Myths, Middle-Class Realities," *Atlantic*, October 1976, p. 37.

39. Ibid, p. 40.

40. Arthur Okun, *Equality and Efficiency: The Big Tradeoff* (Washington, D.C.: Brookings, 1975), p. 68.

41. Joseph Pechman and Benjamin A. Okner, *Who Bears the Tax Burden?* (Washington, D.C.: Brookings, 1974).

42. Michael Harrington, *The Other America* (New York: Macmillan, 1963).

43. James N. Morgan et al., *Five Thousand American Families: Patterns of Economic Progress* (Ann Arbor: University of Michigan, Institute for Social Research, 1974).

44. Edward C. Banfield, *The Unheavenly City Revisited* (Boston: Little, Brown, 1974), chap. 3.

45. On the attitudes of the poor toward life in general, work and family in particular, see Lee Rainwater, "The Problem of Lower-Class Culture and Poverty-War Strategy," in Daniel Patrick Moynihan, ed., *On Understanding Poverty* (New York: Basic Books, 1969), chap. 9; Leonard Goodwin, *Do the Poor Want to Work?* (Washington, D.C.: Brookings 1972); and Stanley B. Greenberg, *Politics and Poverty* (New York: Wiley-Interscience, 1974).

46. Joe R. Feagin, "Poverty: We Still Believe That God Helps Those Who Help Themselves," *Psychology Today* (November 1972), 101–110 ff. See the book-length report in *Subordinating the Poor: Welfare and American Beliefs* (Englewood Cliffs, N.J.: Prentice-Hall, 1975).

47. Niles Hansen, *Rural Poverty and the Urban Crisis* (Bloomington: Indiana University Press, 1970).

48. David Caplovitz, *The Poor Pay More* (New York: Free Press, 1963).

49. An excellent summary of research on the poor is in the bibliographical essay by Zahava D. Blum and Peter H. Rossi, "Social Class Research and Images of the Poor: A Bibliographical Review," in Moynihan, op. cit., pp. 343–398.

50. Notable for its emphasis on the importance of family structure among blacks is the controversial Moynihan Report, reprinted in Lee Rainwater and William Yancey, eds., *The Moynihan Report and the Politics of Controversy* (Cambridge, Mass.: MIT Press, 1967).

51. For a critique of culture-of-poverty theories, see Charles A. Valentine, *Culture and Poverty* (Chicago: University of Chicago Press, 1968).

52. Banfield, op. cit., p. 61.

53. See Rainwater, op. cit.; Goodwin, op. cit.; and Morgan, op. cit.

54. Greenberg, op. cit., pp. 94–96.

55. Reynolds Farley, "Trends in Racial Inequalities: Have the Gains of the 1960s Disappeared in the 1970s? *American Sociological Review, 42* (April 1977), 189–208.

56. For a very useful compilation data on blacks and whites, see U.S. Bureau of the Census, *The Social and Economic Status of the Black Population of the United States* (Washington, D.C.: Government Printing Office, annual).

57. Joe R. Feagin, "America's Welfare Stereotypes," *Social Science Quarterly, 52* (March 1972), 924.

58. National Advisory Commission on Civil Disorders, *Report* (Washington, D.C.: Government Printing Office, 1968), p. 252.

59. A very useful treatment of the welfare dependence issue is found in Daniel P. Moynihan, *The Politics of a Guaranteed Income* (New York: Random House, 1973), chap. 1.

60. (New York: Pantheon, 1971).

61. On the politics of the FAP, see Moynihan, *Politics,* op. cit.

62. There are numerous accounts of the origins of the war on poverty. Among others, see Sar A. Leviten, *The Great Society's Poor Law* (Baltimore: Johns Hopkins University Press, 1969); John C. Donovon, *The Politics of Poverty* (New York: Pegasus, 1967); and Daniel P. Moynihan, *Maximum Feasible Misunderstanding* (New York: Free Press, 1969).

63. Moynihan, *Maximum Feasible Misunderstanding,* p. 87.

64. Richard Kraemer, *Participation of the Poor* (Englewood Cliffs, N.J.: Prentice-Hall, 1969), p. 66.

65. J. David Greenstone and Paul E. Peterson, *Race and Authority in Urban Politics* (New York: Russell Sage Foundation, 1973).

66. Kenneth B. Clark and Jeanette Hopkins, *A Relevant War on Poverty* (New York: Harper & Row, 1968), chap. 5.

67. James Vanecko, "Community Mobilization and Institutional Charge: The Influence of the Community Action Program in Large Cities," *Social Science Quarterly, 50* (December 1969), 609–630.

13

TRANSPORTATION AND URBAN POLICY

Both the political sociology and the political economy of the city are shaped crucially by its modes of transportation. The American city has become dominated by the automobile. Often the political conflict over transportation is framed as a "roads versus rails" battle. In that battle, roads interests held the edge for decades. Federal support for highways long exceeded the paltry sums given to mass-transit systems, which decayed and declined. Only recently have there been signs of a revival of mass transit. BART, the Bay Area Rapid Transit system, is the principal expression of the renewed attention to mass transit. Yet both the opportunities and the problems of mass transit are typified by BART.

In San Francisco they were busily digging the tunnels, building the tracks, designing the cars, and constructing the stations for BART, the Bay Area Rapid Transit system. At the same time, Massachusetts was designing a major segment of Highway I-95 around Boston. When completed, I-95 would go from Houlton, Maine, to South Miami, Florida, without a single traffic light. One neighborhood through which I-95 would go was Jamaica Plain. A group called Urban Planning Aid, under the leadership of James Morey, was battling the transportation planners in Boston. The state and federal highway departments favored it and pressed to complete the planning. The residents of Jamaica Plain opposed it. The planners wanted to move quickly from plans to construction. Morey and the Jamaica Plain residents wanted a restudy. People in Jamaica Plain, Cambridge, and other areas through which the road would pass organized a "People Before Highways Day" and assembled on historic Boston Common.[1]

In this chapter we are concerned with transportation policy. The politics of transportation is a complex story, one about neighborhoods, about energy, about access to good jobs and schools, but it is also one about people. More and better systems of transportation represent the lifeblood of an industrial civilization. People who are immobile lack access to factors that could improve their life quality. Mobile people have the access that accompanies ease of movement throughout the metropolis. The American city has become an automobile-based economy. In other cities (e.g., London, Toronto, Mexico City, Moscow, Paris) a low-cost, efficient system of mass transportation facilitates intraurban movement. Trains in Europe compete with airlines and automobiles for interurban mobility. The situation in the United States is very different. The automobile accounts for the lion's share of intraurban movement, and mass transit's share is actually declining. The automobile and the airplane account for almost all interurban movement. Some wish it were otherwise. Noting that the car is the most energy-inefficient form of transportation, they want a mass-transit system rivaling those of other urban centers.

TRANSPORTATION: THE URBAN CONNECTION

Transportation is the urban connection, a mode of mobility in time and space. In the battle between the automobile and the rail-based system, there was never really much contest. The "roads versus rails" conflict was long ago won by roads interests.

Among other appellations, the twentieth century has been described as the "age of the automobile." Eighty percent of American families—all but a few of the very rich and a number of the very poor—own cars. Many a family owns two, and increasing numbers own three.

If Detroit is the city of the automobile from the point of view of production, Los Angeles is the city of the automobile in consumption terms. In Los Angeles, one-third of the total land area—two-thirds of the downtown area—is devoted to uses related to motor vehicles: principally streets, freeways, parking lots, and facilities to sell, service, and destroy automobiles. In Los Angeles and elsewhere, there is a reciprocal relationship between the decentralization of the metropolitan population and the ubiquity of the car. (*Reciprocal relationship* is a social scientist's term for what laymen might describe as a chicken-and-egg problem.) The automobile has made metropolitan deconcentration possible; deconcentration has made the car essential. Of course, the automobile alone did not cause the suburbanization of the American urban population. Other factors such as central-city land values and deterioration, affluence, and the sheer demand for space abetted population decentralization. Ownership of automobiles by urbanites may not be a *sufficient* condition for suburbanization, but it is almost surely a *necessary* one.

In Chapters 3 and 4 we described the political sociology and the political economy of metropolitan areas. The political sociology of the city results from five major migrations—urbanization, the ethnic migration, the blackening of the central cities, suburbanization, and the westward movement. The nature of transportation systems affected all of these. Indeed, the history of the city can be written in terms of transportation technology. Early cities (such as Boston, Charleston, New York, and Baltimore) were located on waterways. St. Louis grew because of its proximity to two major rivers; Chicago mushroomed from a tiny village of several hundred families in the 1830s to 1 million people by the 1860s because it was the shortest portage from the Great Lakes to the Mississippi. The invention of the steam engine made it no longer necessary to locate on waterways, and the invention of the automobile revolutionized the city economy and society. Today the economics of transportation helps to feed suburbanization of families and firms. In a rail-based economy it was necessary for industry to concentrate near rail intersections, and these were typically in the core of the city. In a truck-based economy it is economically unfeasible to locate at the core, because congestion there is greatest. When trucks ship the vast majority of all commodities, it is wisest to locate on the periphery of the metropolitan area to facilitate interurban movement of goods.

Public Policy and the Victory of Roads over Rails

One defender of the automobile, B. Bruce-Briggs, remarks that, "America has the best mass transportation system in the world. This mass transit system moves people with a speed, convenience, comfort, and flexibility quite beyond comparison with other systems."[2] The American "mass transit" system is, of course, the car. The automobile moves 94 percent of all intracity trips, 80 percent of all trips to work, and 85 percent of all intercity trips. The victory of the car over other forms of transportation has not been entirely accidental, because public policies have consistently favored roads over rails.

Transportation policies, like most other policies affecting urban America, are intertwined with the federal system. At the federal level the first assistance-to-highways program was inaugurated in 1916, but it was not until 1944 that the present direction of federal highway policy was made clear. In that year Congress created the skeleton of the now-familiar interstate transportation system, authorizing 41,000 miles of federally assisted interstate highways; no significant funding appeared in the federal budget until the mid-1950s, however. In 1956, Congress (1) established the dominance of the federal government in interstate road financing by providing federal funding for 90 percent of the cost, (2) reoriented the interstate system from a principally rural pattern of roads to an interurban system, (3) gave the Bureau of Public Roads effective power to determine the routes to be taken by the interstate system. When the system is complete, 41,000 miles of highways will link the nation's major cities.

Along with education and welfare, the highway program has long been one of the "big three" items in state finance. But for many years states have tended to use highway-financing formulas that favor rural over urban areas. This pattern has been common among the states, regardless of the equity of their legislative apportionments. Urban governments have thus been compelled to undertake a larger share of the burden of providing traffic arteries than have their rural counterparts. Within metropolitan areas, the fragmentation of local governments has further complicated the planning of balanced transportation systems to serve the needs of both suburbanites and central-city interests. Central cities have often made heavy expenditures for transportation facilities used by suburbanites, who, in most cases, pay no taxes to the central cities.

At all levels—federal, state, and local—transportation politics has centered on the conflict between advocates of roads and equally ardent advocates of rail, or mass-transit, systems.[3] At least in the larger metropolitan areas, the essential elements of the *road coalition* have been officials of state and federal highway departments, truckers, automobile associations, construction and materials companies, petroleum interests, bus companies, and a number of business interests that would benefit from the expansion of the road network. Their commitment of political resources has been high.

In contrast to the politically potent road coalition, the *rail coalition* is a shaky alliance at best. Central-city commercial, political, and newspaper interests; commuters; and the railroads themselves have been the main spokesmen for balanced transportation, but there is considerable disharmony among them. Railroads themselves have often been eager to divest themselves of unprofitable commuter runs, and commuters are often at odds with the railroads over inadequate service.

Highways and Politics: A Case Study

Few large American cities have been free from controversy over the location and construction of highways. In Boston, antiroads forces combined to battle a loop of I-95 around the city.[4] Elsewhere opponents of highways have argued that the economic, human, and environmental cost of continued highway building is simply too high and have pressed for a moratorium on freeway construction. The San Antonio, Texas, North Expressway controversy offers a useful insight into the politics of highways. San Antonio environmentalists waged a long and complicated battle with the City of San Antonio and the Texas State Highway Department to prevent construction of the North Expressway, which would have sent—in order to dodge some expensive homes in the suburb of Olmos Park—the highway through the

center of a college campus, within a stone's throw of the bear pits at
the city zoo, and through the city's historic Brackenridge Park.[5] Although planning for the expressway began in 1956, not until 1959 did
the State Highway Department and city officials pick a route that
would have taken the highway through the zoo and park. Subsequently the San Antonio Conservation Society got wind of the routing
and opposed the passage of a 1960 bond election financing the project.
By the slimmest of margins (331 votes) the money to finance the local
share of the North Expressway's costs was disapproved. Following the
defeat, however, City Hall and the San Antonio civic leadership
mobilized all their resources. The city council constituted itself as the
Parks and Expressways Committee and determined to "wake the
public up" to the need for the road. The second bond election held on
10 January 1961 passed decisively.

Conservationists took the issue to the courts and were joined by Incarnate Word College, whose campus would be severed by the routing. While the issue bounced around state and federal courts, the
Highway Department proceeded with planning, negotiation of rights-
of-way, and contract awarding. After several years of contesting, the
City of San Antonio finally offered the Sisters of Incarnate Word $1.2
million, which placated their objections sufficiently so that they
settled out of court. The conservationists persisted in their legal and
political battles and were rewarded with a partial victory when
Congress in 1966 passed legislation forbidding construction of high-

New subway in Washington, D.C.

ways through public parks unless there was no other feasible alternative. The Department of Transportation in Washington tentatively
approved the state's plans for the North Expressway, pending revisions to preserve the park. The state responded by splitting the
expressway project into three sections. Since it could not secure federal approval for the middle one, it wanted to proceed with the two
noncontroversial parts. By 1970 the environmentalists' suit had
worked its way up to the U.S. Supreme Court, which rejected their
demand for injunctions against the construction by a narrow decision.
But on 2 March 1971 the Supreme Court upheld a conservationist suit
challenging a federal highway project through Overton Park in Memphis. While environmentalists led a protest march of 800 people along
the proposed route of the North Expressway, the San Antonio controversy went back to federal court, this time armed by the precedent
of *Citizens to Preserve Overton Park, Inc.* v. *Volpe*. A series of court
decisions in 1971 appeared to kill off the project once and for all. But
there was still life in the proponents. The state announced in 1972 that
it had withdrawn its request for federal funds (thus putting it outside
the control of the 1966 congressional legislation against destroying
parks) and would go it alone. The issue went back to the courts, where
it had been for much of its life.

Finally, environmentalists lost and the highway won. Ground
clearing had taken some while, to say the least. But another link was
forged in the urban highway system, making it easier for commuters
and others to bypass residential streets and move at higher speeds to
jobs, relaxation, or homes. Whether the price was too high is still in
dispute.

THE DEMISE OF MASS TRANSIT
AND EFFORTS TO REVIVE IT

The Demise

As the role of cars has grown, the role of their principal competitors —
rail-based transit systems — has diminished. Table 13.1 provides some
sobering evidence to those who prefer mass transit over the automobile. Passenger ridership is down sharply, operating costs are up,
and fares are escalating. Perhaps most sobering is the fact that transit
systems now operate in the red. A 31-percent excess of costs over revenues is not a sign of an economically vital enterprise. Mass-transit
systems spent $3.5 billion in 1975, while receiving revenues of only
$2 billion. New York City is a case in point. The Metropolitan Transit
Authority's data on ridership show that passengers have declined almost every year since 1945. The only important exception — during
the energy crisis of 1974 — was short-lived. Nationally 23 billion pas-

Table 13.1   Some Facts About Mass Transit Systems, 1950–1973

	1950	1960	1970	1973
Revenue passengers (millions)	13,845	7,521	5,932	5,345
Average fare (1967 dollars)	14¢	21¢	23¢	24¢
Operating expenses as a percentage of operating revenue	89%	92%	111%	131%

Source: American Transit Association data, appearing in B. Bruce-Briggs, "Mass Transportation and Minority Transportation," *The Public Interest* (Summer 1975), 62.

sengers were carried in 1945. By 1975, only 7 billion took mass-transit rides.[6]

The Attempted Revival

Mass transit has always been a major element in programs to cure the "urban crisis." Its defenders point to several advantages of rail systems over automobiles:

1. Mass transit is far more energy-efficient than automobiles. An important reason in the United States, where 6 percent of the world's population consumes a third of the world's energy, is the high energy consumption of an automobile-based ecomony.
2. Mass transit is safer than automobiles, which account for 50,000 deaths annually.
3. Mass transit would put poor, inner-city workers within easier reach of jobs in the suburbs.
4. Mass-transit systems produce far less pollution than cars.
5. Mass-transit systems are individually cheaper to operate per unit mile, costing only one-third as much as a private automobile.

However impressive these arguments are to defenders of mass-transit systems, they have yet to produce a major revolution in urban transportation policy. There are clear signs, however, of greater support of mass transit by federal policy. The Urban Mass Transit Administration (UMTA) was first created in 1961 but began to grow substantially only a decade later. In 1974 Congress passed the Urban Mass Transportation Assistance Act. In that law Congress declared that, "In recent years the maintenance of even minimal mass transportation service in urban areas has become so financially burdensome as to threaten the continuation of this essential public service," and that, "Immediate substantial federal assistance is needed to enable many mass-transportation systems to continue to provide vital service." The Mass Transportation Act essentially provides subsidies to operating revenues of rail-based lines and bus service in urban areas. It also encourages "demonstration projects," particularly in "fare-free" systems. Cities such as Dayton, Seattle, Nashville, and Duluth have experimented with free bus service in downtown areas. Today the federal budget for mass-transit assistance totals about $12 billion annually.

Twelve billion sounds like a lot of money. But compared with the cost of building *new* mass-transit systems, it is only a drop in the bucket. No experiment in mass transportation better illustrates the spiralling costs and mounting problems that does BART—the Bay Area Rapid Transit system.

BART: The Hope That Failed, or Did It?

BART, serving San Francisco, Oakland, and surrounding suburbs, represents the space age in urban transportation.[7] It was even designed and built by aerospace engineers, presumably because people who could get a man to the moon could also move people around a city. BART was the first major mass-transit system built in an American city since the construction of the old systems in New York, Boston, and Chicago. Since BART was built, Atlanta voters approved a transit network supposed to cost $1.3 billion, and Congress approved a system for Washington, D.C., at a projected cost of $2.5 billion. Both systems were plagued by "cost overrun." Washington's is estimated to cost upwards of $5 billion by its competition. The same problem plagued BART. When it was first passed in a 1962 referendum, the bill was estimated at $800 million. When it was substantially completed by the early 1970s, the cost was greater than $1.5 billion. Clearly, even if the $12 billion in mass-transit funds were to go entirely to constructing new transit systems (instead of subsidizing existing ones), it would be quickly spent in only a few cities.

BART opened to more problems than its designers had hoped. Doors sometimes flew open unexpectedly; computers tracked "phantom" cars but ignored real ones; less than a month after the system opened, a train ran off the end of a track. Though most BART riders report comfortable experiences, some more important questions are raised about the policy goals of mass-transit advocates. It is not at all clear that the availability of BART has reduced car ridership. There is even some evidence that the principal effect of mass-transit systems is to shift riders from other forms of mass transit (mainly busses) to rail systems.[8] Transit systems cannot very well reduce pollution or energy consumption if they have no net effect on automobile ridership. BART was designed to handle 200,000 riders a day; yet by 1975 ridership was only 125,000.

BART illustrates one other source of conflict in the mass-transit debate: whether mass transit systems can operate efficiently only in high density cities. The lower the density, the larger the number of stations required, the longer the individual lines, and the less "rapid" is rapid transit. Some fear that the fares in high-density cities would be so high that they would deter ridership. Cities with old mass-transit systems (e.g., Boston and Chicago) are high-density cities, as is San Francisco. Whether low-density places (e.g., Sacramento, Phoenix, Dallas, and Denver) could profitably operate mass-transit systems without massive public subsidies is quite uncertain.

How much should one expect from the first mass-transit system constructed in over 50 years? If one expected it to reverse major problems of the cities, surely BART was a disappointment. If one is willing to call it an experiment, albeit a costly one, which may point the way to new directions in transportation planning, one will not be so disappointed.

CONCLUSIONS

Transportation is the urban lifeblood. The transportation problem is not merely a matter of congestion and inconvenience. Transportation represents *access*, to good schools, good jobs, and a high quality of life. The major division in transportation policy has been the conflict between "roads" and "rails." So far the car has had the edge. Transit systems have decayed and declined and now operate in the red. Recent federal policy has shifted somewhat to accommodate mass-transit interests. But the relatively meager resources available for urban mass transit are quite modest to support a major change in transportation systems. A new era in urban mass transit is yet to dawn, despite efforts in San Francisco, Washington, Atlanta, and elsewhere. Whether the policy objectives of mass-transit systems are likely to be realized is still uncertain.

Notes

1. Alan Lupo, Frank Colcord, and Edmund P. Fowler, *Rites of Way* (Boston: Little, Brown, 1971), especially chaps. 1–3.
2. "Mass Transportation and Minority Transportation," *The Public Interest, 40* (Summer 1975), 43.
3. See the discussion of road-versus-rail interests in Jameson W. Doig, *Metropolitan Transportation Politics in the New York Region,* (New York: Columbia University Press, 1966), chap. 2; and Frank C. Colcord, Jr., "Decision-making and Transportation Policies: A Comparative Analysis," *Social Science Quarterly, 48* (December 1967), 383–398.
4. Lupo et al., op. cit.

5. Our account of the North Expressway controversy is based on Susan Knight, "The North Expressway" (unpublished manuscript, Lyndon B. Johnson School of Public Affairs, University of Texas, 1972).

6. American Public Transit Association, *Transit Fact Book, 1975–1976* (Washington, D.C.: APTA, 1976), Figure III, p. 31.

7. On BART, see Robert Lindsey, "Mass Transit, Little Mass," *New York Times Magazine,* 19 October 1974, pp. 17 ff.; and Melvin M. Webber, "San Francisco Area Rapid Transit—A 'Disappointing' Model," *New York Times,* 13 November 1976, p. 23.

8. Bruce-Briggs, op. cit., p. 66.

14

GROWTH AND DECAY AS POLICY PROBLEMS

Earlier, particularly in Chapters 3 and 4, we described the sociology and economics of urban growth. There we saw some of the policy problems that growth presented, but we did not address the policy responses to that growth. In this chapter we focus on growth and decay as mutually reinforcing policy problems. The latest American frontier is its cities. The urban frontier can be seen at the city's rim, where strategies for managing growth create policy conflict. But it can also be seen at the city's central core, where policies to retard deterioration and spur economic growth are frequently debated. In this chapter we:

- describe the principal strategies (particularly zoning and planning) for manipulating growth
- show how growth often leaves decay in its wake and prompts demands for policies to cope with the social and economic costs of deterioration
- show how housing policies epitomize the twin policy problems of growth and decay
- discuss federal policies that have fostered growth in one place while permitting — even encouraging — decay elsewhere
- emphasize that the city in a society of scarcity may face fundamental tradeoffs about future growth.

An atom smasher (technically called an "atomic accelerator") seems initially to have little bearing on urban politics. Yet the village of Weston, Illinois, on the periphery of the Chicago metropolitan area, owed its eventual extinction to the location of a billion-dollar atom smasher in its midst.[1] A fierce competition had emerged among the states when the Atomic Energy Commission announced plans to build the nation's third (and largest) atom smasher. Forty-six states submitted elaborate bids for the project, each outbidding others in an attempt to secure the prestigious accelerator, sure to be a boon to the local economy of its eventual location. Politically there was not much doubt that the Midwest would win the competition. The East Coast and the West Coast had accelerators in their backyards (at Brookhaven, New York and Berkeley, California), and midwestern governors, congressmen, universities, and scientists had pressed hard for the new accelerator. Illinois in particular launched an aggressive campaign. Governor Otto Kerner, his state Department of Business and Economic Development, Mayor Daley of Chicago, universities in the entire midwestern area, and the Chicago financial community provided the leadership in the quest for one of the biggest federal projects anywhere.

The state had to find the land — several thousand acres — which could be given to the Atomic Energy Commission. It picked Weston, Illinois, in DuPage County. DuPage, one of the wealthiest counties in the nation, was in the urbanizing periphery of the Chicago metropolitan area. The county board had used stringent zoning and land-use restrictions to minimize growth and to ensure that what growth took place would be of upper-status families. But Weston had slipped through the DuPage County Board's net. A community of 100 "tract" homes, it had been developed by real-estate interests eager to make a quick profit. After years of political conflict with the DuPage Board, the developers finally went bankrupt, the homes' landlord became the federal government, and further development of Weston was finally stopped. The state of Illinois and the Atomic Energy Commission, however, finally accomplished what DuPage County could never quite do: obliterate Weston. On receiving the nod for the atomic accelerator in December 1966, the state proceeded to procure the land under its power of eminent domain. Villagers and farmers of Weston moved on, hopeful at least that their town would be memorialized in the very name of the accelerator. But it was not. The accelerator has a postal address at nearby Batavia, for Weston had simply ceased to exist.

The Weston story weaves several threads about urban growth into a whole cloth. It demonstrates that growth involves a multiplicity of actors in both the private sector and the public sector. City and county authorities, state governments, and the federal government all play critical roles in growth policies. Second, it shows that growth policies are much disputed. The DuPage Board favored slow growth in keeping with the "character" of the area. Weston's developers and residents had different motives. The developers pursued profits wherever they could be found, and residents wanted low-cost development of housing units, their little piece of the suburban dream. Growth may be a "natural" process associated with cities, but public policy shapes it profoundly. And in shaping and manipulating growth, urban policies have impacts on deterioration as well.

THE TWO URBAN FRONTIERS

Anthony Downs has distinguished between two urban frontiers, the *frontier of growth* and the *frontier of deterioration*.[2] The first takes place mostly in the periphery of the metropolitan area, in an area that might be called the "urban rim." We showed in Chapters 3 and 4 how a migration of persons and production had shifted both to the suburban areas.

Decentralization of production and population is the fundamental feature of metropolitan America. Millions of urbanites have moved to the suburbs. Industries, department stores, and commercial establishments have also found their places in the suburbs. On almost every indicator of economic activity, central cities have experienced a relative decline in comparison with fringe areas, and some central cities have experienced absolute declines as well. The cost of relocation within the central city may be many times greater than a move to the suburbs. The same economic patterns appear to affect both families and firms: The most prosperous of both are the most mobile, with the result that the poor, whether firms or families, are left behind to add to the human and economic problems in the city. This area becomes the frontier of deterioration.

Edward C. Banfield has described the "logic of metropolitan growth" as follows:

Much of what has happened — as well as what is happening — in the typical city or metropolitan area can be understood in terms of three imperatives. The first is demographic: if the population of a city increases, the city must expand in one direction or another — up, down, or from the center outward. The second is technological: if it is feasible to transport large numbers of people outward (by train, bus, and automobile) but not upward or downward (by elevator), the city must expand outward. The third is economic: if the distribution of wealth and income is such that some can afford new housing and the time and money to commute considerable distances to work while others cannot, the expanding periphery of the city must be occupied by the first group (the "well-off") while the older, inner parts of the city, where most of the jobs are, must be occupied by the second group (the "not well-off").[3]

While true enough as *tendencies*, these fall short of being *imperatives*. Banfield's view understates the importance of government and public policy in shaping urban growth. Demographic changes are not merely the accidental by-products of market forces but are intentionally manipulated by public policy. Zoning policy is the most notable way in which local government attempts to shape its social and economic environment, but it is not the only way. The selection of highway sites, the use of urban renewal and housing, the quality and quantity of urban public services, and many other factors affect the location choices of persons and production.[4]

The Costs and Politics of Growth

Americans have long believed that growth is good and more growth is better. The Chamber of Commerce may be the most outspoken local proponent of growth, but it is hardly a lone voice. Harvey Molotch argues that, "The political and economic essence of virtually any American locality, in the present American context, is *growth*. . . . The city, for those who count, is a growth machine."[5] Cities and states conduct expensive industrial promotion campaigns. Tulsa, Oklahoma, which scored second on Arthur Louis's ranking of the quality of American cities (see pp. 6–7) took out magazine advertisements boasting that it was (like a rental-car company with headquarters in Tulsa) "only number two but trying harder." Growth is defended because it creates jobs, bolsters the local tax base, and turns a minor city into a major one. Growth is clearly in the economic interests of some groups. Real-estate developers and realtors, newspapers, locally owned firms (national firms care little whether growth takes place here or there), and other economic interests favor growth policies. Politicians may often favor it, if for no other reason than that it is more rewarding to have power in a big pond than a small pond. These pro-growth forces, of course, coalesce in the urban rim, where farmland is converted to urban land at the rate of thousands of acres per year. The new residents of that land are not likely to oppose growth (at least until they have arrived and want to keep others out), for it enabled them to move out and away from problems elsewhere. For those who can "exit," the virtues of growth are very real.

Yet growth has recently fallen on hard times as a valued goal. New growth produces new demands on services and schools. Growth does

not come cheaply. Hundreds of communities have virtually sold their economic souls to economic development, hoping that it will expand tax bases, only to discover that costs in services outweigh gains in taxes. In fact, per-capita costs of services rise as population expands.[6] Nor is there much evidence that growth really creates jobs in the private sector. Molotch analyzed the unemployment rates of the fastest-growing and the slowest-growing metropolitan areas and found little difference.[7] Table 14.1 is based on the data which Molotch uses in his analysis. Clearly, the rapidly growing metropolitan regions and the ones losing population have similar unemployment rates. Growth does not create jobs. Emerging coalitions of "no-growth" advocates have achieved political power in cities such as Boulder and Aspen, Colorado, and in the state of Oregon. These antigrowth groups have a natural ally in upper-class suburban areas (such as DuPage County in the Weston story) who want to prevent an influx of central-city people. Zoning, of course, is the principal weapon of those who want to minimize growth. In many respects the politics of growth is a politics of zoning. *What purposes* land is zoned for and *what groups* can afford to live here or there are the major questions we ask about the policy impacts of zoning (see pp. 359–361).

Table 14.1   Growth and Unemployment: Rates of Unemployment in 5 Fastest-Growing and 5 Slowest-Growing SMSAs (1960–1970)

	Percent growth rate, 1960–1970	Percent unemployment, 1970
Five fastest-growing SMSAs		
Las Vegas, Nevada	115.2	5.2
Anaheim-Santa Ana-Garden Grove, California	101.8	5.4
Oxnard-Ventura, California	89.0	5.9
Fort Lauderdale-Hollywood, Florida	85.7	3.4
San Jose, California	68.8	5.8
U.S. Average		4.3
Five slowest-growing SMSAs		
Charleston, West Virginia	−9.3	4.1
Brownsville-Harlingen-San Benito, Texas	−7.1	6.6
Johnstown, Pennsylvania	−6.4	4.9
Duluth, Minnesota-Superior, Wisconsin	−4.1	7.3
St. Joseph, Missouri	−4.0	3.9

Source: From U.S. Bureau of the Census data reported in Harvey Molotch, "The City as a Growth Machine," *American Journal of Sociology,* 82 (1976), Tables 2 and 3.

The Problem of Decay

Decay, at least in the United States, seems to be a natural corollary of growth. Urbanities have long assumed a direct relation between residential mobility and social-class mobility. In the American city *outward meant upward.*[8] The dominant theory of housing is often called the "trickle-down" theory. Houses are said to be "filtered" as they move through successive occupancies. As a family becomes more secure financially, it moves outward to newer housing, vacating the unit for another family just below it on the economic ladder. Subsequently, further outward movement vacates the housing again as houses are "filtered" from richer to poorer. The upshot of filtering or trickling down, of course, is that old housing will be occupied by the poor. The extreme stage of filtration is housing abandonment. In older core cities, the paradox of housing shortages with housing abandonment constitutes a policy problem of enormous magnitude.

To some degree the problem of decay results from "natural" forces like the trickle-down effect. As long as growth continues at the periphery, decay follows at the core. We will show later, though, that decay is not always a benign, accidental by-product of economic forces. Decay can be hastened by public policies and by private-sector decisions. Among these are the levels of municipal taxes and services, which may hasten the exit of people who can afford to do so, the availability of mortgage money in decaying neighborhoods, and policies of city and federal governments. It will be useful, therefore, to think about citizen responses to the problems of neighborhood decay in terms of the "exit" and "voice" model that was introduced in Chapter 5. Faced with deterioration, some may exit. Others, for one reason or another, may not switch, but may stay, using the voice option. Still others may simply resign themselves to decay and deterioration, seeing exit as too costly and voice as inefficacious.

MANAGING GROWTH

Urban growth consists of increases in population or in production, or both. It therefore has both a social face and an economic face. Note that this distinction parallels the distinctions that we made in Chapters 3 and 4 between the political sociology and the political economy of metropolitan areas. Not all types of growth are considered equally desirable by community policy makers. Generally an increase in people alone without a corresponding increase in productive capacity will be thought undesirable. The reason is not hard to understand. People consume services, send children to schools, need police protection, and demand other goods from local governments. While they do pay taxes, sometimes taxes paid do not match the amount of dollars spent on servicing them. City officials often distinguish between apartments and their residents, who (they believe) cost more in services than they pay in taxes, and owners of single family houses, who are believed to "pay their own way." On the other hand, commercial growth generally adds more to the local tax base than new economic enterprises consume in services (or so local officials believe). For this reason, city governments often work closely with chambers of commerce and local business groups in economic promotion campaigns. But communities do differ in their stance toward growth. Some communities want no part of industrial activity or even shopping centers, and want to maintain an image of a pristine residential greenbelt. Such places are typically upper-middle-class suburbs, where culturally suburban values are found in demographically suburban cities. Typically they use what we call "social zoning" to secure and maintain crucial life-style values.

Zoning and planning are the principal policy vehicles for managing urban growth. Without doubt, zoning is the most important public policy that is almost solely in the hands of local governments. Schools, policing, housing, and transportation are domains where local authority is shared with state and federal authorities. But very few states have state zoning controls, and there is no general national land-use policy. Thus the use of zoning and other land-use powers is the most important policy through which urban growth is manipulated by government.

Planners and Their Plans

If we take *planning* to mean identifying goals and the resources and constraints involved in attaining them, then it is clear that we all plan to some degree all the time. Most such planning, however, covers only some of the available alternatives. The same is true of city politics, in which all actors (voters, mayors, agency heads, party leaders) attempt to match scarce resources to general goals. More narrowly, though somewhat tautologically, the term *city planning* refers to the activities undertaken by the city planning department and its professional staff. Like city managers, planners are professional employees of the municipal government; in principle they are hired on the basis of their professional competence, rather than because of their personal contacts. Organizationally, the planning staff is a part either of a quasi-independent agency, usually called the planning commission, or of a staff agency assisting the mayor or city manager. Directors of most planning agencies are appointed by the chief executives, although a minority is still appointed by city councils or by the planning commissions themselves.[9]

Regardless of the professional backgrounds or organizational milieus of planning agencies, several activities form a common denominator for almost all such staffs. All necessarily must *gather information* and *process data*. Although all municipal agencies gather and analyze data, cities with large and effective planning staffs are increasingly centralizing some of these activities in their planning departments. The information available to the planner is his most important resource. One of the most visible products of planning activities is the *land-use plan*, which reflects technical studies of existing land use, trends and projections of economic growth, municipal policies toward economic development, and planners' conceptions of community goals. Whatever the plan, once it is formulated the planner is usually involved in its implementation.

Zoning, the principal tool for enforcing use of private property as prescribed by the municipality, is designed to restrict what planners call "nonconforming uses," use of land in contradiction to the plans proposed by the professionals and adopted by the council. Ordinarily, after the adoption of a plan, nonconforming uses (e.g., building a service station on a quiet residential street) may not be undertaken, and already existing ones may not be expanded. Land-use plans also include rules and regulations for subdivisions, specifying such details as sizes of lots, setbacks from streets, and sidewalk and street construction. Building codes containing standards for industrial, commercial, and residential construction are usually included in plans formulated and implemented by the planning office.

Their education, their occupational milieu, and the intellectual origins of the planning movement itself incline planners toward the view that physical and spatial relations strongly determine social interaction. David C. Ranney has described this attitude as a philosophy of "environmental determinism."[10] To planners, land and its uses, spatial relations, and aesthetics are critical components in any formula for the good life.

Environmental determinism is rooted in the origins of the planning movement. One of the founding fathers of city planning was Ebenezer Howard, whose book *Tomorrow*[11] stressed that most urban problems arise from the sheer size and density of the urban population. Howard argued that smaller, less dense settlements would solve the social and economic ills of the cities and advocated the creation of new towns of limited size (32,000) and severely limited density. Altering people's spatial relations, he argued, could eliminate social and economic problems attributable to high densities. Although new towns have been developed extensively in Great Britain and the rest of Europe and advocated vigorously in the United States, there are few important examples on this side of the Atlantic. Reston, Virginia, and Greenbelt and Columbia, Maryland, are perhaps the most important.

The urban-planning movement began with the reformism of the

Progressive era, with which it shares an important affinity. Like the reformers, planners are interested in the community as a whole, which they believe transcends narrow and private-regarding interests of community segments. Accordingly the public interest appears to them both different from and morally superior to transitory individual and group interests. "The view," according to Alan Altshuler, "that clashes of interest are only apparent has always appealed to one element of the American intellect. It is assumed by most conservative defenders of the status quo no less than by progressive attackers of 'politics.' "[12]

Many planners share with both the Progressives and the contemporary reform groups a bias against things political. Ranney has suggested that "planners have traditionally distrusted local government, viewing it as the pawn of special interest groups. This distrust is at least partly the result of the relationship between the planning movement and the municipal reform movement."[13] Rightly or wrongly, many planners see the municipal political process as sacrificing community-regarding goals in favor of rewards to self-seeking individuals and groups. Politicans, as we saw in Chaper 7, cannot often claim to behave rationally because of the myriad constraints on rational choice. Planners, however, are likely to believe that rational choice, though never easy, is in principle an attainable goal.

Zoning as Public Policy

Probably the greatest single impact of planning on the socioeconomic environment of American cities has been through zoning policy. Typical regulations, which consist of the zoning ordinance itself, subdivision regulations, and building codes, divide the city's space into various categories. The most common classifications are industrial, commercial, and residential, although each may contain gradations within. The residential category, for example, may be further divided into land for single-family dwellings and multiple-family dwellings. In the industrial classification distinctions may be made between areas for industries with noxious effects (smoke, noise, congestion) and those without. Requests to alter the zoning classification of a particular piece of property are usually considered by the municipal planning commission, whose decisions are ordinarily subject to review by the city council. Some planning commissions take a jaundiced view of any modifications in a zoning classification laid down in the ordinance and reject all requests for change. Others are sometimes eager to permit numerous exceptions in the form of *spot zoning,* granting exceptions for a few pieces of property in a larger area of homogeneous land use. Zoning ordinances, housing codes, and subdivision regulations typically prescribe land use and other matters as well. For residential areas, minimum lot sizes, the buildings' distance from streets, and certain other regulations may be invoked. Requirements also may be established for commercial and industrial property. The latter may also be regulated to minimize smoke, pollution, and noise.

Because zoning represents a government's efforts to control the uses of private property, the rights of municipalities to enact and enforce zoning have been repeatedly challenged in the courts. But despite arguments that zoning is socialistic and an infringement on private property rights, the late Justice George Sutherland, usually considered a very conservative member of the Supreme Court, wrote a crucial opinion supporting zoning in *Village of Euclid* v. *Ambler Realty Co.* (1927).

Zoning as public policy accomplishes a number of purposes. It contributes to the aesthetic appeal of neighborhoods and communities, rids residential areas of noxious commercial enterprises, and secures property values from deterioration by forces beyond the homeowner's control. Yet it also has significant policy impacts in shaping metropolitan growth, in determining where children go to school, where families can purchase homes, what tax bases communities and school districts possess, and the quality of services that can be provided. Zoning is important because it has economic and social impacts. We call these two functions of zoning *fiscal* and *social* zoning.

FISCAL ZONING AND PROMOTION   Zoning alone does not lead to the kind of economic development that residents desire. It merely classifies land for use. If industry is wanted, a hospitable zoning policy must be combined with the willingness of city planners to gather data for prospective firms, with special promotional efforts, and, in many communities, with tax incentives. Where the desire to keep taxes low is a major objective, communities usually try to attract industry. Industries, it is widely believed, are generous taxpayers. Moreover, their operations spill over into the macro and micro sectors of the local economy. Yet industries are not only taxpayers but also very heavy service consumers. In the Philadelphia region, for example, the highest municipal expenditures were found in the industrial suburbs, largely because of service consumption by industries.[14] Industries also bring workers and managers who consume municipal services, particularly education. Some industries impose higher service costs than they contribute in taxes to the public coffers. The trick is thus to secure industries whose input into the public and private sectors is high and whose outtake from the public sector is low. Firms specializing in research and development employ highly trained and well-paid personnel and are preferred to noisy, sooty factories that contribute to congestion. The problem is that there are not enough such firms and their equivalents to go around.

Municipalities are thus compelled to play a fiscal zoning game in an effort to attract—or pirate from other communities—industries that pay more in taxes than they consume in municipal services.[15] The nature of communities will restrict strategies in the fiscal zoning game. Although some residents may settle for any industry that pays its way, others draw the line at noisy ones, smoky ones, or ones that bring congestion. Whatever the limitations, most communities, large and small, play the game through promotional policies, free or inexpensive services to new business, and favorable land-use policies.

SOCIAL ZONING   Some communities want no part of zoning and related policies to attract industry. These communities are typically high-income, upper-class residential suburbs, which prefer to accept the increasing costs of local government in order to retain the character of a residential greenbelt. These cities play the game of social zoning rather than fiscal zoning. Zoning industry out is easy enough; all land can be reserved for residential and retail development. It is more challenging to manipulate land-use regulation to secure a particular class (and, by accident or design, racial) composition. It may be accomplished by requiring, for example, minimum lot sizes from one-half acre to four acres or by establishing such stringent building-code requirements that housing costs become prohibitive except for the wealthy. Greenwich, Connecticut, and Scarsdale, New York, and other upper-middle-class communities have used tight zoning restrictions to maintain homogeneous residential communities amid creeping industrialization. Such practices, when carried to extremes, produce what Whitney Young called "gilded ghettos." *Restrictive covenants*, devices by which deed restrictions are used to prevent the sale of housing to members of minority groups, were declared unenforceable by the Supreme Court in 1948,[16] and Congress has forbidden racial discrimination in the sale or rental of housing since 1968. But zoning policies that substitute class for racial premises may have consequences similar to racial ones.

PLANNING, ZONING, AND
THE BATTLE OF THE SUBURBS

Zoning is both more popular and more effective in newer suburbs than in older central cities. The reasons are not obscure. As the physical development of older cities took place before zoning had been developed to a fine art, land use there has been determined by the often haphazard decisions of the marketplace. Today nearly all large cities have zoning ordinances (Houston, Texas, is the only significant exception). In most, however, zoning affects choices only at the margins. Most land-use decisions are already "given" by earlier market considerations. But many suburbs, whose development has postdated the zoning revolution, began their growth with rigid land-use restrictions already in force. Zoning has quite literally shaped those communities. One disgruntled property owner in Greenwich, Connecticut, has grumbled that "in Greenwich, no one can get elected unless he swears on the Bible, under a tree at midnight, and with a blood oath, to uphold zoning."[17]

It is not difficult for a suburban community, if it passes an effective zoning ordinance before land development is really under way, to guarantee a simon-pure residential haven. To the affluent suburb, an influx of lower-income neighbors means larger school enrollments, more service demands, higher tax rates, and—to many residents—a deterioration in the "quality" of the community. There are ample techniques of social zoning available to ensure a quality community. Building codes can be designated for half-acre or larger lots, or multifamily structures can be prohibited. These practices, variously called *snob zoning* or *Cadillac zoning*, have the effect of inflating housing costs. This can put suburban housing in attractive areas well beyond the financial reach of younger, larger, or middle-income families. Zoning and land-use policy thus constitutes an effort to manipulate the social and economic environment of a community. Robert Wood, in his study of the New York metropolitan region, noted that, "planning, zoning, and promotion . . . represent ways by which [local governments] can keep 'undesirables' out and encourage 'desirables' to come in, if they choose. And, of course, the definition of desirables and undesirables varies from place to place."[18]

The principal effect of such zoning practices, of course, is to raise the cost of housing. Upward residential mobility out of the central city is thus retarded, because housing is out of the reach of vast numbers of middle-income people. Anthony Downs emphasizes that the "suburban sanctuary of the middle class has been created at the expense of the urban poor by compelling them to live in areas of concentrated poverty."[19] Half of all residentially zoned vacant land in the New York metropolitan area is zoned for lots of one-half acre or more. Some suburban communities have zoned parcels of land for industry—thus securing an industrial tax base—but little or no land for working-class residents. Workers may work there, but at night must return to older—and often poorer—cities. In such cases fiscal and social zoning games merge into a single zoning game. The overall object is to secure the blessings of urban development (e.g., tax bases) for one's own community but to consign the problems (e.g., crime, higher school enrollments, and service demands) to another community. The Advisory Commission on Intergovernmental Relations has argued that "under present zoning law, the affluent suburbs are able to exclude low income families and minimize tax burdens which are then transferred to the overburdened central city."[20] Robert Wood calls such strategies "beggar thy neighbor" policies.[21]

The Strange Politics
of Exclusionary Zoning

Politics, it is sometimes said, makes strange bedfellows. Nowhere is this dictum more evident than in the strange politics of exclusionary zoning. Two groups—leaders of central-city minority groups and suburban real-estate interests—have both sought to break the zoning walls that some suburbs erect. The battle of the suburbs has been waged by spokesmen for poor and minority groups, intent on breaking down the barriers of suburban exclusivity.[22] To them, zoning is like Jehovah's advice to Ezekiel, to "put seigeworks against it, and build up a seige wall against it, and cast up a mound against it; set camps also against it, and plant battering rams against it round about. And take an iron plate, and place it as an iron wall between you and the city (Ezekiel 4:2–3)." The "iron plates" of suburban zoning have been under legal attack in Blackjack, Missouri, New Canaan, Connecticut, Troy, Michigan, Mahwah, New Jersey, and Arlington Heights, Illinois. Arlington Heights, for example, is a Chicago suburb with a population of 70,000 people, but only 200 blacks. The city was sued by the Metropolitan Housing Development Corporation, which wanted to build 190 townhouses for low- and moderate-income families there. The village, however, refused to rezone any land for the proposed development.

But another significant element in the attack on exclusionary zoning is the real-estate community. Clearly more money is to be made on large-scale complexes than on single-family dwelling units. The same 10-acre tract that could support 20 expensive single-family dwelling units could support scores of apartments. Consequently, John Hart, president of the National Association of Home Builders, has emphasized his opposition to selective zoning in affluent suburbs. Attacking "economic discrimination," he emphasized that the majority of Americans are being priced out of the housing market.

The case of Weston, Illinois, with which we began this chapter, suggests some elements of the strange politics of exclusionary zoning. Developers of Weston and its middle-income residents were aligned against a county board hostile to tract development. One of the developers' strategies was to have the area incorporated as a village, which would permit it to develop its own housing code. Officers of the development company who lived in Weston, in fact, led the battle for incorporation.

Not until 1977 did the Supreme Court finally reach a definitive decision on exclusionary zoning, and even then the decision would likely be tossed around the lower courts for decades. The case involved the suburb of Arlington Heights, Illinois. Nearly 70,000 people live in Arlington Heights, but only 200 of them were black. When the Metropolitan Housing Development Corporation, a private group interested in building low-cost housing for the poor, tried to get 190 townhouses built in Arlington Heights, the city pointed out that no land was zoned for such purposes. The opponents and proponents battled in the city, but eventually the advocates of the project took the city to court. The plaintiffs charged that Arlington Heights' zoning code had the discrimnatory effect of denying equal protection of the laws in violation of the Fourteenth Amendment. They also charged that city was violating the federal Fair Housing Act. Eventually, the case reached the United States Supreme Court (which itself sits in a city that is 84 percent black).

The Court held that zoning codes cannot be challenged as constitutionally discrimnatory unless it can be shown that *intent* to discriminate was present. The mere demonstration of differential *effects*, as in Arlington Heights, does not make a zoning ordinance unconstitutional. Even with that holding, the Court still left the door open to further challenges to exclusionary zoning. While it refused to uphold the plaintiffs' contention of unconstitutional behavior, it sent back to the lower courts the issue of whether the Fair Housing Act had been violated. The years ahead will surely see further challenges to suburban zoning in the courts.

The Other Frontier:
How Neighborhoods Decay

Unlike cities in most other developed nations, American cities find that old neighborhoods are typically deteriorating neighborhoods. Americans so often link "aged" with "decaying" when they think of city areas that it is worth emphasizing that no other nation finds the link to be very strong. Yet Americans have long associated outward mobility with upward mobility. Hence groups and families that "make it" move on to new housing further out. This sets in motion the trickle-down or "filtering" process, in which housing units turn over from one family to another just below it on the socioeconomic ladder. The frontier of growth gradually shades into the frontier of deterioration. The reasons for this outward movement are many (some were discussed in Chapter 3 when we described the suburbanization process). Many of the choices ("exits") made by individuals are free and unfettered. They move to be closer to work or to secure a more satisfactory living space. But these choices are shaped by important private-sector forces and public-policy choices that help to explain the process of deterioration.

In the private sector, a process of "disinvestment" and "decapitalization" of older neighborhoods is now operating. Neighborhoods cannot long survive without capital. They need capital for two purposes, housing investment and production. In a profit-maximizing system, capital naturally flows where profits can be maximized. Old neighborhoods are often seen as places where capital is poorly invested. The principal source of capital for private housing has been savings and loan associations. They finance about one-half of all single-family dwelling units.[23] Typically they rely on savings accounts to supply money for home loans. Banks are a less significant source of capital for homes, but more important for multi-unit dwellings. Increasingly, insurance companies have invested in large-scale developments of suburban tracts or apartment complexes. These three big lending institutions — savings and loan associations, banks, and insurance companies — finance most urban housing.

Until recently, lending institutions would often "redline" particular neighborhoods and refuse loans in such areas. The term comes from a thin red line said to be drawn on city maps in lending offices, inside which loans were considered too risky. Typically such areas were racially transitional. Transformation of an area from white to black was believed to insure declining property values,[24] and lenders protected their investments by concentrating loans only in "racially stable" (i.e., segregated) neighborhoods. Today it is unlikely that even the most careful search of lending institutions would turn up a single map with red lines on it. But disinvestment remains. Suburban savings and loan associations invest almost all their mortgage money in suburban housing. And central-city savings and loan associations invest larger and larger shares of their money in suburban loans. Residents of central-city areas thus complain that they are funding the decay of their own neighborhood and the enrichment of other neighborhoods. Bradford and Rubinovitz emphasize that, "In short, both in single-family and multifamily housing, older neighborhoods are at a serious disadvantage compared to newly developing suburban areas."[25] Decapitalization of the housing market, of course, parallels decapitalization of the business sector. Christian and Bennett, for example, show how the two-year period from 1969 to 1971 saw Chicago's black neighborhoods lose 7000 jobs and several million dollars in capital from industrial relocations.[26]

A large number of homes in older neighborhoods was funded through mortgage money guaranteed by the Federal Housing Administration (FHA). Lending institutions, of course, had nothing to lose when their loans were backed by the federal government. The FHA fell heir to properties whose mortgages had not been paid and has now become the nation's largest real-estate agent as well as its largest landlord. Consequently FHA has unloaded hundreds of thousands of properties, some in disrepair, others to risky buyers, still others to speculators who buy up batches of houses and then unload them quickly. These practices have not encouraged neighborhood stability.

The frontier of deterioration presents different policy problems than the frontier of growth does. "Revitalizing neighborhoods" is a

common cry in political campaigns. Yet neighborhoods are not revitalized by campaign rhetoric. Deterioration is simultaneously a process
of social transition and economic transformation. People opt for exit
when neighborhoods seem to begin a deteriorating spiral. The presence of "for sale" signs is widely taken to be an indication of a neighborhood gone bad. Housing abandonment is a sure sign. Small businesses tend to go first on the economic side and are followed by larger
firms seeking expansion and new markets. There is no reason to think
that decay is irreversible, but stemming the tide of deterioration
demands major alterations in urban policy.

HOUSING, GROWTH, AND DECAY

Contrasting new tract homes or apartment dwellings in a fast-growing
suburb with an entire block of abandoned housing in the core city
gives an extreme, but vivid, sense of the relationship between housing and urban growth. No public policy area we examine is so
complicated, yet none so important to urbanites as housing. Housing
is important, not only in its own right, but also because it ensures or
deters access to public and private advantages. One may live in a rapidly developing area, where jobs are plentiful, or in an economically
stagnant area where even low-skilled work is scarce. Where one lives
affects his taxes, schools, and the quality of other urban services. Of all
the public policies we discuss in this book, housing policy probably
has more implications for more people than any other. No personal
choice (except perhaps marriage and divorce) is more carefully
weighed than housing, at least among persons whose income permits
them a choice. Public policy, principally through federal resources,
has had a significant impact on housing choices for Americans of all income levels. Almost all housing programs have their roots in the New
Deal. Not only is the federal government (through local authorities)
the nation's largest landlord for poor families, it is also the impetus for
millions of middle-income families' housing investments.

Explaining urban housing policy will not be easy in this short
space. Yet we can simplify matters somewhat if we focus on four elements: (1) the increasing problems of housing for the middle classes;
(2) the perennial problems of housing for the poor; (3) the special connection between housing and race; and (4) the two faces of federal
housing policy.

Housing and the Middle Classes

The American dream house is typically a detached, single-family
dwelling unit with a lawn (free of crabgrass, of course), and a bedroom
for each child. Whether they include a split-level in the suburbs or an

older, roomier house in the city, housing goals have not changed much in recent decades. What has changed sharply, though, is the price of housing. Like other items of the family budget, housing has been subject to considerable inflation. A survey by *Professional Builder*, a trade magazine for the housing industry, found that 92.7 percent of home shoppers wanted a detached house, but that 61 percent cannot pay more than $35,000.[27] By those standards the dream house is quite literally a dream. By 1977 the price of a new home was $51,600, nearly 40 percent more than three years before. The usual rule of thumb is that people can afford a house priced at twice their income. Yet the median family income in 1977 was only $14,900. The Congressional Joint Economic Committee estimates that new houses are priced beyond the reach of 85 percent of American families and used homes beyond the reach of 80 percent.[28] The annual number of new housing starts exceeded 2 million in the early 1970s, but had fallen to 1.4 million by 1976. Part of the reason was simply that the price of a new home had increased rapidly in the past decade. Many middle-class families have simply abandoned any realistic hope of home ownership, a luxury available increasingly only to the upper middle classes. The types of housing construction showing increases are, therefore, apartments and mobile homes. In fact, mobile homes are the fastest-growing segment of the housing market.

It was not always that way. In the post-World War II years, two federal programs greatly expanded home ownership. One was the Federal Housing Administration, which guaranteed loans mostly for new homes in the suburbs. The other was the Veteran's Administration, which did the same things but confined its efforts to World War II and Korean war veterans. Between the two programs a suburban revolution was assured. Millions of families exited to the periphery, finding their ivy-covered, tree-shaded dream homes a reality. Once there, they could take advantage of federal tax writeoffs on interest payments, which made home ownership an even better bargain. We explore below the policy impacts of these federal programs.

Housing and the Poor

If affordable housing is scarce for the middle classes, it must be even tighter for the lower classes.[29] To be sure, there is ample evidence to suggest that the American housing situation has improved significantly since Franklin D. Roosevelt announced that "one-third of a nation [is] . . . ill-housed, ill-clad, ill-nourished" in his 1937 inaugural address. The data in Table 14.2 detail the current housing picture in the United States and clearly suggest that the overwhelming majority of housing units are structurally sound and sanitary. Most inadequate housing is found in rural areas, rather than in cities. At least half of the substandard housing units in the United States are in rural areas, and

Table 14.2   Housing Conditions, 1960 and 1970

	1960	1970
Total occupied units	53,024,000	63,417,000
Percentage with all plumbing facilities	84	95
Percentage lacking some facilities	16	5

Source: Statistical Abstract of the United States (Washington, D.C.: Government Printing Office, 1972), p. 690.

fewer than one-fourth are in large cities. Still, most middle-class Americans would not consider only such facilities as hot and cold running water and private baths to be very reliable criteria of creature comforts. The higher one's standards for good housing, the larger is the number of units that must be described as substandard.

These objective indicators, however, mask some underlying problems of housing for the poor. One estimate is that 2 million families in the three-state New York metropolitan region occupy deteriorating housing.[30] Poor housing is not merely unpleasant or crowded. Housing, as we emphasized, is a key element of social and economic access in the urban community. Four specific problems with poor housing should be stressed. First, poor housing is often expensive housing. The poor typically pay a larger share of their incomes for housing than do the affluent. Welfield used some very simple calculations from government data to show what percent the poor pay for housing. Table 14.3 indicates the range in selected cities. The poor in Newark, Chicago, and San Francisco pay an incredible two-thirds of their income in rent. Yet the poor in Oklahoma City, San Antonio, Denver, and New York (partly because much housing in New York City is rent-controlled) pay one-third or less.[31] Second, poor housing is typically found in neighborhoods (and cities) that offer the poorest municipal services at the highest tax rates. Schools, fire protection, parks, and other urban amenities are often worse in older neighborhoods, but taxes are often higher. Third, poor housing often separates residents from jobs. The decapitalization of urban neighborhoods means that economic resources and job opportunities have moved elsewhere. There is very little housing available for the poor in the dynamic sectors of the urban community. Finally, poor housing and high crime are located together nearly everywhere. Old persons and females in deteriorated housing are often helpless victims of street crime. Poor housing may not create crime, but it coexists with it. But of all the aspects of poor housing that pose policy problems, none may be more significant than that poor housing is typically segregated housing.

Housing and the Special Problems of Race

Although the housing circumstances of all Americans have improved, minority groups still occupy the worst of it. We showed in Chapter 3 that racial segregation is the dominant pattern in most American cities, with little variation by size of city or region (see pp. 53–56). Perhaps the most important single observation about race and housing is this: *Most nonpoor white Americans live in nonpoor neighborhoods, but most nonpoor black Americans live in neighborhoods where a majority of the population falls below the poverty line.* Separated from the economically vibrant sectors of the local economy, segregated neighborhoods also produce segregated schools. If black and white residents were scattered randomly around the city, there would be little dispute over school busing policies.

The expansion of black neighborhoods has been a constant source

Table 14.3 Percent of Income Paid for Housing by Poor Families in Selected Cities

City	Rent/income ratio
Very high	
Chicago, Illinois	69
San Francisco, California	69
Newark, New Jersey	65
Portland, Oregon	54
Akron, Ohio	53
High	
Miami, Florida	49
Baltimore, Maryland	45
St. Paul, Minnesota	44
Medium	
New York City	35
Houston, Texas	32
Denver, Colorado	31
Low	
Oklahoma City, Oklahoma	18
San Antonio, Texas	13

Source: Irving H. Welfeld, *America's Housing Problem* (Washington, D.C.: American Enterprise Institute for Public Policy Research, 1973), Table 1, pp. 7–8.

of tension between minority groups and white urbanites. "Blockbusting" strategies by realtors encourage white fears that neighborhoods will suddenly blacken and housing values will plummet. Actually there is strong evidence that housing values have little to do with racial transition.[32] But realtors make money from high-volume turnover, and fears feed on fears. Realtors have sometimes used "steering" to direct blacks only to black neighborhoods. These practices make the integration of urban neighborhoods exceedingly unlikely. Consequently the number of stable, integrated neighborhoods in American cities is miniscule.

Recently, to be sure, there has been a significant expansion in the absolute numbers of black urbanites living in the suburbs. Sometimes it is assumed that these residential patterns are "salt and pepper" living, with black and white families intermingled in a particular block. In fact, black suburbanization typically arises either from (1) the spilling over of all-black city neighborhoods into inner-ring suburbs, thereby crossing the Census-defined boundary between central-city and outside-central-city areas or (2) movement to black suburbs. There has been no net growth in the share of black suburban populations. In both 1960 and 1970, the suburban percentage of blacks remained exactly constant at 4.8 percent. Indeed, suburban areas are *more* residentially segregated than central cities.[33]

The Federal Housing Role:
The Early Years

The federal government has now become the nation's largest landlord and, according to some, the largest slumlord as well; it is also the largest impetus to middle-income housing opportunities, both through its FHA loan program and its generous provision for tax writeoffs of interest on home loans. In this section and the next, we trace the origins of federal housing policy. Then we will examine the "two faces" of that policy.

There are at least four possible governmental responses to the housing problem of the poor. First, government can do nothing at all. It can assume that the private sector will handle the problem,[34] that its own efforts would be ineffective, or that the spillover costs would outweigh the benefits. Second, government can adopt an indirect strategy of general assistance to the poor but not for housing per se. The underlying premise of this strategy is that poor housing is merely symptomatic of deeper and more pervasive poverty, which should be attacked through welfare payments or a form of guaranteed annual income. Third, the government can, in Lawrence Friedman's words, "attempt to get rid of bad housing by forbidding it."[35] This approach includes enforcing housing codes for new construction and maintenance codes to which landlords must conform. Fourth, the government can try to provide good housing. In practice, of course, these four strategies are not mutually exclusive, and federal and city governments actually use combinations of them.

The problem of inadequate housing did not begin with the Depression of the 1930s, but the first significant housing legislation was the National Housing Act of 1934, which recognized housing as a subject of national concern and created the still-thriving Federal Housing Administration. The FHA's principal activity through the years has been to guarantee home mortgages. In the third of a century of its existence, it has insured billions of dollars of single-family housing. The FHA, however, has consistently benefited families with medium incomes, rather than the poor.

Another Depression agency, the Public Works Administration, undertook some slum clearance during the 1930s and constructed a few units of public housing, but it was the Housing Act of 1937 that laid the real basis for public housing, slum clearance, and later urban renewal. That act created the U.S. Housing Agency, funded it with a half billion dollars, and authorized it to lend money to local public-housing authorities to clear slum land and provide public housing. Once minimum federal standards had been met and the loan provided, a local public agency (LPA) was responsible for land acquisition, clearance, planning, construction, and operation.

The Housing Act of 1937 was the first in a series of laws tying public housing to slum clearance, but with the Housing Act of 1949, and especially its 1954 amendments, public housing began to take a back seat to *urban renewal*. Title I of the 1949 act authorized the purchase of slum land by local public authorities. The land would then be sold to private developers, who in turn were required to use the land for "predominantly residential" construction. Local housing or redevelopment authorities could use the power of eminent domain to acquire land and sell it to private development corporations.[36] The difference between the high price paid for the land and the lower price received for it would be made up largely by federal grants. The federal government would absorb two-thirds (in certain cases, three-fourths) of the "net project cost," that is, the difference between purchase and sale prices. The local government was required to make up the other one-third (or one-fourth) in cash, kind, or services. Not surprisingly, some groups, real-estate interests, for example, that had vocally opposed public-housing legislation gave wholehearted support to Title I.

The 1949 act linked the concept of urban redevelopment to public housing. The public-housing provisions of the act were not popular with either Congress or business interests, but federal subsidizing of land transfers was attractive to city officials and commercial interests.

Cities could shore up sagging tax bases with revenues from more-valuable property, and developers could enjoy federal subsidies instead of small profits and possible losses. Urban renewal thus became a popular vehicle for redressing the urban financial imbalance, while public housing continued to eke out narrow victories or heavy losses.

The Two Faces of Federal Housing Policy

The federal government's housing policy has historically had two faces, one turned toward the middle class and the other toward the poor. The dominant policies of the middle-class face have been the FHA and VA home loan guarantees and the capacity of home buyers to write off interest charges on their mortgages. FHA and VA loans contributed significantly to suburbanizing an urban nation. Tax writeoffs (the biggest tax "loophole" of all) provided powerful incentives to become buyers rather than renters.

Created by the National Housing Act of 1934, the FHA (together with later parallel programs administered by the Veteran's Administration) made a possible significant expansion in the number of single-family homes. Because the FHA guaranteed home loans mainly for *new* homes, it became profitable for developers to locate tracts of land and create "subdivisions." Economies of scale would permit the simultaneous construction of large tracts of houses, and scores of FHA-backed buyers would move in on completion. These large tracts of vacant land were naturally more available, and at lower cost, in peripheral areas of the city—the suburbs—than the older part of the city. FHA thus contributed significantly to the suburban population explosion.

FHA also had an important impact on racial segregation. Established at a time when racial segregation was not merely the norm, but the law, it was assumed that property values were unstable in integrated neighborhoods. And FHA by law could insure only sound mortgages. Mortgages in integrated areas were, by common knowledge, simply unsound. Orfield observes that:

The FHA shaped the housing market through policies spelled out in successive revisions of its *Underwriting Manual*. The manual was one of those decisive but little-known bureaucratic documents which helped form American civilization. It compelled FHA officials to prevent fiscal risk by requiring effective guarantees against "inharmonious racial groups." Appraisers were told to look for physical barriers between racial groups or restrictive covenants. "Incompatible racial elements" was officially listed as a valid reason for rejecting a mortgage.[37]

FHA unabashedly gave its assistance to families buying into new, typically all-white, neighborhoods. These restrictions were subsequently abandoned, but not until after millions of American families had secured coverage under FHA mortgage guarantees. Indeed, even after the Supreme Court had outlawed racial covenants (contracts forbidding sales to minority groups) in 1948, the FHA refused for years to change its insuring policies.

The Rise and Demise of Public Housing — and of Pruitt-Igoe

Housing for the poor has typically been in public-housing projects. Public housing originated in the housing legislation of the New Deal. Such housing had its proponents, but it also had a formidable array of opponents, including the National Association of Real Estate Boards, the construction industry, banks, and savings and loan institutions.[38] Public housing has also challenged some fundamental precepts of American ideology, including laissez-faire and faith in private ownership. To conservatives the program smacks of socialism because it rewards those who are least "deserving." One congressman, in debate on New Deal housing legislation, declared, "The poor are living in shacks and hovels because God made them unable to earn more."[39] James Fuerst describes public housing as "a type of twentieth century poor-house" and emphasizes that *public housing had to be built for poor people and had to look like it.*"[40]

Public housing had a very different clientele than those who could partake of FHA and VA loans, write off their interest charges, and move to the suburbs. While the recipients of FHA and VA loans have been disproportionately middle-class, a majority of public-housing residents have been drawn from lower-income groups. In fact, most are black poor rather than white poor. Even though a majority of the poor — and thus the "pool" of prospective tenants — are white, public-housing projects are overwhelmingly black. In Chicago, for example, 82 percent of the 145,000 public-housing tenants are black, 17 percent are white, and 1 percent are Latino. Public housing also differs from FHA and VA programs in another significant way. Whereas middle-income housing schemes have been directed toward the suburbs, public-housing projects were built not only in the central cities but typically in all-black areas of the cities.

Perhaps the most notorious of all public housing projects was Pruitt-Igoe in St. Louis. Ten thousand people lived in what Lee Rainwater called a "federally built and supported slum."[41] The project contained 33 eleven-story buildings near downtown St. Louis. Originally the developers had planned to create two housing projects, one called Pruitt for blacks and another, across the street, called Igoe for whites. But the Supreme Court ruled that scheme unconstitutional and the project soon became a black-only venture. Though the project was touted as a national showpiece of what public housing could do, it was a failure almost from its dedication. Elevators stopped only at the fourth, seventh, and tenth floors; children were impossible to supervise outdoors; crime and vandalism was as high as anywhere in the country; one in four units remained vacant. Finally, the project was simply demolished. Almost no one regretted its demise. In some ways, what happened to Pruitt-Igoe is symbolic of American public housing. Never popular with political conservatives and a disillusionment to liberals, public-housing starts declined regularly throughout the 1960s and 1970s. From 44,000 new public-housing starts in 1960, only 15,000 were begun in 1974.

Public housing was being squeezed on another front during the 1960s through legal challenges to its segregating character. In the 1974 case of *Gautreaux* v. *Hills,* a decade of litigation (so long that Gautreaux had by then died) resulted in a Supreme Court decision ordering the Chicago Housing Authority to build public housing in white neighborhoods. The order specifically required construction in suburbs as well as the city itself. Yet suburbs did not welcome public housing with open arms. However symbolic the decision, public housing by then was clearly on the way out. Little public housing would be built *anywhere* in the future.

The New Fragmented Housing System

The near-universal dissatisfaction with public housing, which led to its demise, has also prompted new initiatives in federal housing policy.[42] There is now more emphasis on housing subsidies and less on federally supported construction. Several of these initiatives were undertaken during the Johnson Administration's Great Society period. The creation of the Department of Housing and Urban Development in 1965 coincided with a new rent-supplement program. The poor could pay part of the rent (up to 25 percent of their income), and supplements would assist them with the rest. A 1968 Housing Act in two provisions (sections 235 and 236) stimulated private investment for home ownership and rental at reduced costs for the poor. Subsequent legislation expanded the involvement of the private sector, operating with government incentives and subsidies. More than a million units have been constructed or rehabilitated under the 235 and 236 provisions above.

Yet overall, most assessments of federal housing policy impacts remain skeptical. Allbrandt reviews 40 years of housing legislation and concludes that "governmental intervention into the field of housing and community development has not been a resounding success."[43] Downs emphasizes that federal-housing programs have

been very effective in stimulating the frontier of growth but very ineffective in reducing the frontier of deterioration.[44] Many of the policy
issues in housing—segregated versus integrated, concentration in
growth or decay areas, middle class versus poor orientation, and
private versus public involvement—are likely to be with us for years
to come.

FEDERAL POLICY FOR GROWTH AND DECAY

The Paradox of Federal Policy

We have had numerous opportunities to describe federal impact on
cities. Here we can bring several of these strands together by focusing
on the net policy impact of federal urban policies, particularly as they
affect growth and decay. Among the major policies would be:

- the FHA and VA schemes that encouraged suburbanization, especially of
  middle-income, white families (see above)
- public-housing programs directed at central cities and housing predominantly
  black populations (see above)
- federal transportation policies favoring roads over rails and producing an automobile-based urban environment (see Chapter 13)
- federal grants, aid, defense projects and other programs that have facilitated
  growth in the "sunbelt," financed in part by disproportionate taxes in the
  "frostbelt" (see pp. 60–62)
- federal urban renewal programs that have been designed to improve tax bases
  and to spur economic growth (see below at pp. 376–380).

The paradox of federal policy is that one side of it is intended to
reverse the decay exacerbated by the other side. If federal transportation and housing policies encourage central-city decapitalization
and depopulation, then urban-renewal programs can revitalize the
central city. If disproportionate aid to the sunbelt spurs population
and production to migrate southward, then major efforts can be inaugurated to save older, industrial (and, hence, northeastern) cities. If
urban renewal displaces low-income residents from their neighborhoods, they could live in federal housing projects. Some years ago
James Q. Wilson remarked on the contradictory nature of federal
urban policies as exemplified by the Department of Housing and
Urban Development (HUD).

Under its previous name (the Housing and House Finance Agency), it subsidized
the flight to the suburbs with FHA mortgage insurance, while trying to lure back
suburbanites to the central city with subsidies provided by the Urban Renewal
Administration. The Public Housing Administration built low-rent units for the
poor while urban renewal was tearing them down.[45]

Although these and other contradictions occur in federal urban policy, some of them are the inevitable by-products of politics itself or of politics in a relatively democratic system. There are, after all, multiple constituencies in each field of policy, and efforts to provide at least some "goodies" for all seem bound to produce inconsistencies in terms of some abstract ideal. Moreover, it is not clear that urban policy is any more fragmented and inconsistent than are other federal policies. Policy making in other areas shows elements of logrolling and "every man for himself" instead of well-ordered consistency. Farm policy shows inconsistent mixtures designed to benefit both commercial enterprises and less-profitable family farms. Federal urban policy may be fragmented and inconsistent. But fragmented policies arise from the fragmented structure of urban interests. Pluralistic politics at the national level produces fragmented, piecemeal — and often contradictory — urban policies.

Some efforts by the national government to foster coordination have produced further confusion. The regional offices of federal agencies are designed to smooth intergovernmental relations. Yet the regional offices have become the target of further competition among states and localities. Cities view the offices as economic prizes that offer steady payrolls, plus attractions for visiting officials who patronize hotels and restaurants. Until recently, Congress and the administration have spread these benefits to a large number of cities. Local governments in Kentucky, for example, have been served by the regional office of HUD in Atlanta, Georgia; HEW in Charlottesville, Virginia; the Bureau of Employment Security in Cleveland, Ohio; the Bureau of Work Programs and OEO in Washington, D.C.; and the Economic Development Administration in Huntington, West Virginia.

The result, we suggest, is not merely lack of coordination or confusion. Federal policies have been paradoxical. Policies stimulating growth here have promoted decay there. Nowhere are such paradoxes better illustrated than in urban renewal. Creating generous tax bases and spurring economic growth, urban renewal schemes have also created externalities that promote decay.

The Origins and Structure of Urban Renewal

Urban renewal, as we have seen was originally tied to public housing in the 1949 and 1954 Housing Acts.[46] The 1949 legislation established the principle of federal subsidies for land sold to private developers through the slum-clearance program. Between 1934 and 1954, slum clearance in its various forms eliminated an estimated 400,000 substandard housing units, but they constituted only 7 percent of the 5.6 million substandard units counted in the 1950 Census. There was no net increase in the availability of low-cost housing; in fact, more slum dwellings were demolished than public-housing units were constructed. Moreover, there was an inevitable lag between demolition and construction, and, as long as the program continued to expand, more units were taken out of the market than were replaced. The 1954 Housing Act was partly designed to rectify these flaws, by providing what some called "an alternative to the bulldozer." The 1954 provisions, which added the term *urban renewal* to our vocabulary, emphasized rehabilitation rather than demolition and wholesale reconstruction of an area. Structures that are deteriorating but salvageable can be renewed rather than demolished. The act also broke earlier precedents that had insisted on the predominantly residential requirement for all new construction. It permitted 10 percent of federal grants to be used for nonresidential construction, a figure that was increased to 20 percent in 1959 and to 30 percent in 1961. Urban renewal became, through a series of incremental changes, more and more remote from the notion of improved housing. Increasingly it became a program to revitalize the private marketplace and the city treasury. To city officials faced with crushing demands for services and limited resources, urban renewal was a blessing in disguise. The disguise was public housing.

Like the social-security system and the interstate-highway program, urban renewal is an example of cooperative federalism. The key ingredients are congressional definition of standards and sharing of costs and administrative responsibilities by federal and local agencies. The program was administered through the Department of Housing and Urban Development, while operation at the local level was the responsibility of local public authorities.

The financial picture, or budget, of a fairly typical urban-renewal project is given in Table 14.4. The figures in this table do not represent average costs but are used rather for simplicity of calculation and

Table 14.4   A Sample Urban-Renewal Project: The Financial Structure

Gross project cost	
Land acquisition	$ 8 million
Demolition, relocation	1 million
Provision of public facilities by city	1 million
Total	$10 million
Proceeds from sale of land	$ 4 million
Net project cost: Gross cost less proceeds from land	$ 6 million
Grants	
Federal grant for two-thirds (sometimes three-quarters) net project cost	$ 4 million
Local grant of cash, kind, or services	2 million
Total	$ 6 million

presentation. Assuming the total or gross cost of the project is $10 million and that proceeds from the sale of land are $4 million, there is a deficit, or "net project cost," of $6 million. Two-thirds (or three-fourths) of this sum is supplied by federal grants and one-third (or one-fourth) by local contributions in cash, kind, or services.

The Impact of Urban Renewal

We tread on difficult terrain when we attempt to assess the impact of urban-renewal programs. Many of their most-important dimensions are not susceptible to measurement. Although several excellent studies have attempted to apply cost–benefit analysis to urban renewal, many variables have had to be either measured indirectly or ignored altogether.[47] The costs and benefits of a project, from the perspective of the municipal budget, are relatively easy to measure but the costs and benefits to those relocated cannot be measured without making some capricious assumptions.

ECONOMIC AND FISCAL IMPACT   The most universally accepted claim for urban renewal, and probably the most valid one, is that it has expanded the tax base and improved the economic vitality of the city. The Urban Renewal Administration liked to emphasize the "before" and "after" tax effects of renewal.[48] For 768 projects on which land acquisition had been completed by 1971 the estimated increase in property values was from $464 million to $1.7 billion; from this increase the cities could reap generous tax revenues. In economic terms, each of these projects also had a potential *multiplier effect*, stimulating more jobs and production in service industries. Given evidence of this sort, it is small wonder that some city officials have considered renewal a godsend. Nevertheless, Martin Anderson has cautioned that such lavish assessments of the economic productivity of renewal projects should be discounted somewhat.[49] He has noted that: (1) some of the new construction would have been undertaken in any case; (2) cities lose tax revenues between the times when structures are demolished and new construction is completed—often a period of 5 to 10 years; and (3) even without renewal projects, land would increase somewhat in value over the years. Anderson investigated the tax gains from Boston's West End project and concluded that it would not begin to "break even" and make up the revenues lost after demolition until 1980 or later, even though the city had taken title to the land as early as 1958. Although Anderson's case may be overstated,[50] it is a useful corrective to unqualified enthusiasm over renewal's contribution to city tax coffers. On balance, and despite Anderson's reservations, most of the evidence from specific cities indicates that both direct and multiplier effects enhance municipal revenues and stimulate economic growth.

The success of renewal in raising municipal tax receipts has led to the somewhat paradoxical pattern of a public project that must turn a *profit* in order to be successful. The necessity for profit from urban renewal is registered in two ways. In the private sector each project must be profitable enough to attract private developers to whom land can be sold. In the public sector, the city government seeks profit for its own treasury from increased tax receipts.

The Newark Housing Authority (NHA), for example, found its first renewal project a financial disaster because no developer would buy the cleared site. Thereafter, the city's renewal officials remodeled their development schemes on the principle, "Find a redeveloper first, and then see what interests him."[51] The responsibility for site selection, planning, and decisions about land reuse is thus defined in terms of profit for the redeveloper, as well as of professional criteria.

Renewal must also be attractive to city government. Its net effect should be to produce, rather than to consume, tax revenues. What kinds of projects are likely to be profitable to both developers and city governments?

A negative answer is easiest. The least-profitable use of cleared land is for public housing, simply because the latter yields neither city taxes nor private profit. Perhaps the next least profitable use is low-cost private housing, for it produces relatively little in taxes and attracts people with low incomes, who have minimum "multiplier effects" on the economy. The most productive residential use, of course, is for middle- or high-income housing. Equally productive — sometimes more productive, depending upon the kind of business attracted — is commercial or industrial use. In some respects, the net effect of urban renewal is thus to *redistribute land to higher- and higher-cost enterprises*. Newark is again a case in point. As one Newark redevelopment official said, NHA's goal was "middle income housing on cleared slum sites."[52] Because of the profit incentive in urban renewal, the initial choice of land for clearance is important. The key questions become whether the private developer can make a profit from middle-income housing (or other justifiable use under the law) and whether the city can improve its fiscal situation. Local renewal authorities and prospective redevelopers thus "tend to pick the best possible area that could still be justified as a slum to meet the requirements of the Title I law."[53] In Newark, at least, there appeared to be "an inverse correlation between the degree of blight in the area and its acceptability to [federal renewal officials] and the redevelopers"[54] The upshot of the public and private profit requirements is that few of the very worst slums are renewed.

One of the more significant consequences of renewal legislation has been to shift land use from residential to nonresidential purposes. As such, it has taken a toll of housing opportunities available to lower-income families. The 1949 renewal law required that renewal land was to be used for *predominantly residential* purposes. The term *predominantly* was usually interpreted to mean that *over half* of the new land use would be residential. In a succession of amendments, however, the requirement for reuse in residential purposes was relaxed. The effect of such amendments was to reduce the pressure on local authorities to replace the housing stock razed by the federal bulldozer. The data in Table 14.5 indicate the pattern of changes in housing stock. Between 1967 and 1971, 538,000 housing units were razed, but only 201,000 replaced.[55] This gap represents about 0.3 percent of the nation's housing stock. The burdens of the housing gap associated with urban renewal have typically fallen hardest on the poor.

The economic effects of urban renewal are not limited to land use and financial gains to real-estate interests and municipal governments. Charles Abrams has described "some blessings of urban renewal":

1. increased capacity of cities to attract and maintain industries and commercial establishments
2. ability of universities, hospitals, and other public institutions to expand facilities
3. impetus to cultural improvements such as New York City's Lincoln Center
4. expanded middle-income housing
5. revitalization of downtown and central-city areas
6. greater aesthetic appeal[56]

Table 14.5   Housing Stock Changes Associated with Urban Renewal

| | | New housing units planned | | New housing units completed | |
Fiscal year	Housing units razed	Total	Public, low and moderate income	Total	Public, low and moderate income
1967	383,449	195,999	76,363	106,961	42,601
1968	422,817	226,031	97,573	124,781	52,399
1969	460,482	256,978	113,485	144,317	63,021
1970	499,407	286,707	133,199	169,224	80,696
1971	538,044	324,615	162,587	200,687	101,461

Note: All data are cumulative.
Source: John A. Weicher, *Urban Renewal: National Program for Local Problems* (Washington, D.C.: American Enterprise Institute, 1972), p. 6.

The Spillover Effects

We have emphasized that all public policies have *spillover effects,* or *latent impacts,* unintended by-products of the manifest (or intended) impacts of the policies. Perhaps the spillover effects of no other public policy have been so much investigated as have those of urban renewal; perhaps these impacts have been decried by critics more loudly than have those of any other policy. Many, though not all, of the spillover effects of urban renewal are related to relocation and displacement of people.

Since the passage of the New Deal public-housing acts and the urban-renewal provisions of the 1949 and 1954 acts, hundreds of thousands of Americans have received letters similar to the following:

The building in which you now live is located in an area which has been taken by the Boston Redevelopment Authority according to law as part of the Government Center Project. The buildings will be demolished after the families have been relocated and the land will be sold to developers for public and commercial uses, according to the Land Assembly and Redevelopment plan presently being prepared.[57]

A congressional study estimated that, between 1964 and 1972, no fewer than 825,000 families and 136,000 businesses would be required to vacate their present structures because of urban-renewal and federal highway programs.[58] If we estimate that each of these families has 3 people (possibly an underestimation), then in 8 years about 2.5 million people, equivalent to the population of Los Angeles, would be displaced. Some people have moved into areas slated for later clearance, thus becoming "two-time losers."

Needless to say, the vast majority of families and individuals who have to relocate are the poor and the nearly poor. More than 60 percent of the displaced are nonwhite, leading to charges that the urban-renewal program is really black removal. Many families and unrelated individuals in renewal areas are elderly, both white and black.

Urban-renewal legislation requires authorities to establish that adequate housing is available for all people to be displaced by renewal projects. They are also required to assist in relocation and to provide relocation payments, but the average relocation payment per family is less than $100, principally for moving expenses. Most critics and many supporters of urban renewal consider the relocation problem its most serious defect. The critics doubt that local authorities can in practice guarantee suitable accommodations at reasonable costs to the displaced. They argue, reasonably enough, that, if suitable housing were available at rents that the relocated could afford, they would be living there already, instead of in slums. Urban-renewal officials claim that more than 90 percent of relocated families have moved to standard housing, but most private studies dispute such claims.[59] Not only do these urban displaced persons often move into substandard housing, but their rents typically increase as well. John Weicher concluded that "all things considered, the typical relocatee is probably worse off. To claim that he is 'really' better off is to substitute the judgment of the government for a person's own judgment of what is best for himself."[60]

Small businessmen are especially vulnerable to relocation. Most businesses in renewal areas are small, employing only handsful of people and depending on carefully nurtured neighborhood clienteles. A Boston study indicated that almost 40 percent of the businessmen who were forced to evacuate renewal areas went out of business,[61] and the Renewal Assistance Administration's own national studies indicate that about one-third of dislocated businesses have discontinued operations altogether.[62] The disappearance of the small businessman, partly because he seems an anachronism in our age of mass production and mass marketing, is particularly likely to be a spillover effect of urban renewal.

Finally, relocation has exacted a psychological cost as well. People's reactions differ, of course, when they are displaced from their homes and forced to seek other habitation, but for a good many, according to Marc Fried, "It seems quite precise to speak of their reactions as grief."[63] Some of the relocated from Boston's West End, whom Fried studied, expressed intense emotion at separation from old-neighborhood social patterns: "I felt like my heart was taken out of me"; "What's the use of thinking about it?"; Even now I feel like crying when I pass by." To middle-class Americans, these strong emotional responses may be surprising. But the social networks and spatial relations within a neighborhood are much more salient to lower-class than to middle- and upper-class people because almost all the socializing of lower-class Americans takes place in the immediate neighborhood, whereas middle-class contacts and interactions are much wider. For this reason, the disruption of neighborhood social ties can foster deep feelings of alienation and frustration among low-income residents.

CONSOLIDATION AND DECENTRALIZATION: COMMUNITY DEVELOPMENT BLOCK GRANTS

The Nixon administration often spoke fondly of "decentralizing" urban policy to the states and cities. "Let us put the money where the needs are," Nixon said in his 1971 State of the Union message. "And let us put the power to spend it where the people are." That rhetoric justified several new policy directions. Revenue sharing was one policy resulting from this decentralist orientation. The other policy manifestation was the creation of the Community Development

Block Grant (CDBG) program. In August 1974, President Ford signed the Housing and Community Act, which included the "special revenue sharing" monies for the CDBG. It consolidated seven existing categorical grants-in-aid programs to cities, including urban renewal and model cities grants. A so-called "hold harmless" provision insured that cities would receive no less money under the CDBG program than they had been receiving under the previous categorical programs.

As with revenue sharing, CDBG funds have been popular with local politicians and administrators. Monies are allocated by an automatic formula to nearly 2500 local governments and the chief executives have considerable discretion in establishing priorities for its use. The amount involved is substantial — $3.2 billion in fiscal year 1977 — almost half as much as General Revenue Sharing is allocating to cities *and* states. But unlike General Revenue Sharing, city governments are required by the law to give "maximum feasible priority" to activities that will benefit low- or moderate-income families. Recipients of CDBG dollars are supposed to use the grants to expand public services, to enhance housing opportunities, and to eliminate slums. In doing so, the bulk of their efforts are to be benefiting poorer neighborhoods. But the federal government has maintained a very loose rein on local authorities and does very little monitoring of CDBG funds.

The result of this wide local discretion is that cities have not taken very seriously the requirement to aid their low-income neighborhoods. A staff report to a House Subcommittee bluntly observed that "all of the monitoring studies of the [CDBG] program reviewed by the staff conclude that the low and moderate income objectives of the Act are not being met."[64] A study by the Brookings Institution, for example, examined 62 cities' use of Community Development grants. It found that only 29 percent of the monies were used in neighborhoods with lower-than-average incomes. Weak federal monitoring has combined with limited political power of low-income neighborhoods to reduce pressures for compliance with the statute. Streets have been paved, police officers hired, sidewalks built, traffic lights installed, water filtration plants modernized, and open spaces preserved — but not necessarily in and for low-income neighborhoods. It has been easier to make helping the poor a political objective than a political reality.

The Community Development program, however, has been popular with local officials, with Congress, and even with President Carter (who promised to expand funding for the program). Local governments liked it because it brought major chunks of money with few strings and little monitoring attached. Members of Congress have always liked programs that give benefits to every constituency. So in fall 1977, the Congress passed an expanded version of the CDBG program, which by 1980 would spread $4.3 billion annually to cities. The revised CDBG statute would give additional benefits to older cities in the northeast by including a measure of age of housing in the allocation formula. What it did not guarantee was that spending would live up to the mandate of aiding low- and moderate-income neighborhoods.

The Impacts of Federal Policy:
Toward a Balance Sheet

Assessing the impact of any policy or set of policies is almost like asking, "What would things have been like in the absence of policy?" Consequently it is rarely possible to specify exactly policy impact, for we can never fully imagine what might have been. If the Federal gov-

Table 14.6   The Impact of Federal Policies on Urban Growth and Decay: A Balance Sheet

	Impacts	Some externalities
1. Transportation A. Building the interstate highway system	Facilitated both intra- and interurban movement of firms and families	Probably made both commercial and family exit to periphery easier
2. Housing A. FHA and VA	Spurred new home construction; enabled middle-class families to buy houses	Increased exit to suburbs by whites; in early days explicitly required racial segregation
B. Public housing	Provided housing for poor, mostly black, families	Increased segregation by clustering in black neighborhoods
C. Urban renewal	Bolstered tax base; encouraged "redevelopment" of cities	Displaced neighborhood, especially black residents; eliminated small businesses
D. Federal grants, contracts	Advantaged "sunbelt" over "frostbelt"	Facilitated growth in South; encouraged decay in North
E. Community development block grants	Subsidized basic city services, but not particularly those in poor neighborhoods	Increased authority of chief executives in allocating federal moneys; reduced direct federal control

ernment had *not* encouraged a massive interurban highway system, or had *not* built public housing, or had *not* given millions of families FHA and VA loans, the landscape of the city would probably be very different. How different it would be is hard to say.

Our argument, however, is that federal urban policy *has* profoundly reshaped the urban landscape. In that process some neighborhoods and communities have grown while others have deteriorated; even entire regions have grown or declined, partly in response to federal governmental decisions. The kinds of people who live in particular places has also been shaped by federal policy. How, then, can we construct a balance sheet?

Table 14.5 provides our very rough assessment of principal impacts of federal urban policies. We briefly indicate there some impacts and externalities of policies in several areas. Externalities are inherent in all policies. In Table 14.6 we do not suggest all possible externalities stemming from federal policies. We could, for example, add numerous energy and environmental externalities of each policy. But we do offer some hypothesized externalities particularly on the phenomenon of "exit," that is, mobility of populations. People and firms move, we said, for many reasons, some very idiosyncratic and private. But they also make choices, responding in part to events set in motion by federal urban policies. Even if our impact assessments are wrong, few will dispute the profound impact of federal policies on the life quality of urban residents.

THE CITY AND THE EMERGENCE OF SCARCITY

Accustomed to growth, cities have now begun to experience scarcity. To be sure, scarcity has been, and still is, far more commonplace in human society than is abundance. But in the American city, growth is often linked with abundance. In part, this is because Americans have always assumed that more growth in the future would bring a bigger economic pie to divide up. Confronting inequalities directly was a painful process. But they could be indirectly handled by promising that more could be had by all. Zbigniew Brzezinski, national security adviser to President Carter, remarks that, "What has made inequality bearable is that in the American tradition (as well as myth) it is balanced by opportunity. Growth makes it possible for an individual to rise or at least entertain the dream of rising."[65] Banfield's theory of urban growth explicitly links growth with the equalizing function of the city, so that outward movement accompanies upward mobility.[66] These are not merely academic theories but are beliefs about growth, equality, and abundance which are widely shared. Growth and the quality of life have gone hand in hand.

Yet growth brings problems — as we have already suggested — and also scarcity. The natural and fiscal resources needed to grow are in short supply and may often be secured only at someone else's expense. Americans, most of whom are urbanities, consume about one-third of all the world's energy. Urbanites account for a disproportionate share of this disproportionate share. Only recently have Americans come to question seriously their consumption of the world's goods to enhance their own growth. Louis Harris asked a sample of the American population in 1975 whether our big share of energy consumption "is morally wrong." More than 6 in 10 Americans agreed.[67] Three-fourths also agreed that the United States also was too dependent on foreign resources such as oil. If growth brings scarcity, it also brings interdependence. We showed in Chapter 2 how one American city, Columbus, Ohio, was deeply enmeshed in the world economy and how decisions made elsewhere shaped the quality of life that urbanites enjoyed.

Consequently in this section we emphasize the two faces of the problem of resources — exploitation and despoilation. We then show how urban-policy problems increasingly are shaped by issues of scarcity.

The Two Faces of
the Environmental Problem

Architect Percival Goodman once observed that "the time has been reached when society's basic institution, capitalism, has begun to consume irreplaceably its basic resource, the environment."[68] The environmental problem has two faces, both inextricably linked to growth. One derives from the *exploitation* of natural resources faster than resources are discovered or replenished. The other stems from the *despoilation* of the environment by ever-present effluents from the affluent society. To be sure, the twin problems began when primitive man slew his first meal and dumped the bones into a river. No one was much troubled, however, until population growth reached such a point as to threaten the exhaustion and intolerable degradation of the natural bounty. In this sense, exploitation and despoilation are the inevitable by-products of population and economic growth. An MIT team of scientists have dramatically and forcefully emphasized the linkage among population, resource usage, pollution, and economic growth in a controversial book, *The Limits to Growth.*[69] In the absence of limits on growth, the inexorable march of the other elements in their model lead to dire global consequences.

In the American city, environmental problems range from minor annoyances like temporary brownouts and blackouts to serious challenges such as those arising from dangerous concentrations of lead, carbon monoxide, and other pollutants in the atmosphere. Because municipal (and state) governments either operate or regulate the major energy-producing utilities, the increasing consumption—and shortages—of fuels is a major concern of urban decision makers. Years of technological advances in home appliances, the development of bigger and faster cars, and the affluence needed to purchase them have combined to skyrocket the urbanite's consumption of energy. Americans, who constitute 6 percent of the world's population, consume one-third of its resources, and consumption patterns are increasing faster than the population.

Despoilation: The Pollution Problem

The resources of the natural environment—land, air, and water—constitute the raw materials for our affluent society. Yet the natural environment is also the receptacle of our economy's waste materials. What engineers call the *law of materials balance* holds that the total weight of materials taken from nature will equal the total weight of wastes discharged into the environment plus any materials recycled.[70] Air, land, and water from which the resources to build a civilization are extracted become the repository for that civilization's solid, liquid, and gaseous waste products. Viewed from the perspective of material balance, pollutants are the inevitable by-products of the economic system, but to most specialists in public health and environmental engineering, the problem of waste and pollution has become grim indeed.

Air pollution consists primarily of carbon monoxide, hydrocarbons, nitrogen oxides from automobiles and industrial uses, and sulphur dioxide from the burning of oil and coal. Also contained in city air are fragments of solid materials like lead, zinc, and asbestos. Automobiles are responsible for the largest proportion of air pollution—approximately 60 percent nationally but 88 percent in Los Angeles. In fact, the role of the automobile in producing pollution is one of the major arguments for developing mass-transit systems and a viable alternative to the gasoline-powered engine. It is now acknowledged that air pollution has become a serious health hazard. Roger Revelle, a specialist on pollution and public health, notes, however, that the effects are not fully understood: " . . . common sense suggests that pollutants capable of darkening house paint, disintegrating stone statues, corroding metals, dissolving nylon stockings, and embrittling rubber must also be injurious to delicate bronchial and lung tissues; but there is little hard evidence at present."[71]

It is clear that air pollution is a very serious problem in areas where thermal inversions occur regularly. Such meteorological phenomena, in which layers of warm air settle over layers of cool air and prevent the dispersion of pollutants, are said to have produced 4000 deaths in

London in 1952 and 200 in New York in 1953. Although there is some disagreement about the causal connection between pollution and various respiratory and pulmonary diseases, few, if any, scientists doubt that there is a threshold beyond which air pollution becomes a serious public-health problem. The difficulty has been in specifying that threshold.

Air pollution is a highly variable quality-of-life indicator from city to city. Concentration of nitrogen oxides, for example, range from 50 micrograms per cubic meter of air in Corpus Christi to 252 micrograms in Los Angeles.[72] The Council on Municipal Performance developed a rating system of air quality in 43 large cities. The rankings are reported in Table 14.7. It must be emphasized that these are *overall* rankings, and that different types of air pollutants may be strong or weak in particular cities. Birmingham, for example, was the eighth cleanest city in terms of nitrogen dioxide, but thirty-ninth in the concentration of particulate matter. Generally, as the Council concluded, "cities in warmer climates requiring lower fossil fuel consumption for heating, and with less heavy industry, are least polluted."[73] Sunbelt cities as a rule are cleaner. And residents of frost belt cities will testify that few urban scenes are less attractive than snow with soot on it.

Like air, water is also used as a receptacle for waste. Lake Erie, the main source of water for 10 million Americans from Detroit to Buffalo, is virtually closed to swimming and fishing; were it not for massive investments in treatment facilities, it would be undrinkable too. The Cuyahoga, Delaware, Potomac, and other rivers are at times unsafe even for boating. In fact, the Cuyahoga has caught fire several times. Although industrial pollution may be more serious than municipal pollution, municipalities have often dumped minimally treated sewage into rivers that are used as water sources by communities farther downstream.

Land is also a receptacle for urban wastes. Americans now produce 400 million tons of solid waste per year, or two tons per capita. More than eighty percent of it is hauled somewhere by local governments or private contractors, covering the annual equivalent of 80,000 acres 6 feet deep. The U.S. Public Health Service has declared 94 percent of all land fills unsanitary.[74]

According to Revelle, "solid wastes can be burned, buried, flushed, reused, or simply thrown away in more or less open country in the hope that they won't be noticed."[75] But each of these options implies certain costs. The first three methods produce air, land, and water pollution, respectively. Reusing wastes has so far not been found economical. Simply throwing trash away is a popular, but aesthetically unpleasant and increasingly expensive, method. In many areas, sanitary land fills are exhausted, and refuse must be either barged out to sea (in coastal areas) or hauled to rural areas, at ever-higher costs. Technological changes have complicated the problem of disposal of

Table 14.7   Pollution in Cities: Overall Ranking of 43 Cities' Air Cleanliness (1 = lowest pollution level; 43 = highest pollution level)

1. San Antonio, Texas	23. Salt Lake City, Utah
2. Corpus Christi, Texas	24. Indianapolis, Indiana
3. Sacramento, California	24. Bridgeport, Connecticut
4. New Orleans, Louisiana	26. Boston, Massachusetts
5. Dallas, Texas	27. Minneapolis, Minnesota
6. Miami, Florida	28. Newark, New Jersey
7. Buffalo, New York	29. Philadelphia, Pennsylvania
8. Houston, Texas	39. Milwaukee, Wisconsin
9. Kansas City, Missouri	31. Atlanta, Georgia
10. San Francisco, California	32. Phoenix, Arizona
11. Fresno, California	33. Washington, D.C.
12. Seattle, Washington	34. New York, New York
13. Portland, Oregon	35. Fairbanks, Alaska
14. New Haven, Connecticut	36. St. Louis, Missouri
15. El Paso, Texas	37. Cleveland, Ohio
16. Rochester, New York	38. Baltimore, Maryland,
17. Birmingham, Alabama	39. Los Angeles, California
18. Syracuse, New York	40. Chicago, Illinois
19. Cincinnati, Ohio	40. Springfield, Massachusetts
19. San Diego, California	42. Detroit, Michigan
21. Denver, Colorado	43. Pittsburgh, Pennsylvania
22. Toledo, Ohio	

Source: Council on Municipal Performance, *City Air,* 1 (1974), p. 22.

solid refuse. The aluminum can, for example, is much more difficult to get rid of than tin cans were, and some plastics are nearly indestructible.

The Politics of Pollution

Americans exhibit a high degree of abstract concern for the environmental plight. Urbanites, not surprisingly, are more worried than their rural counterparts, and better-educated citizens are more concerned than less well-educated ones.[76] Regardless of such differences, concern is general and not unique to particular population groupings. But, as we noted in Chapter 5 when we discussed environmental-interest groups, abstract commitment is often coupled with behavioral malaise. A fifth of the population, for example, is unwilling to pay any additional taxes for water-pollution abatement or for cars with emission-control devices. A majority is unwilling to pay more than an extra $50 for such improvements. When the fundamental issues are broached—such as the possibility of curtailing economic growth or

government-imposed curbs on population increases — the public is
sharply divided.

Matthew Crenson has written a penetrating study about the politics
of pollution in the city. He studied the issue (or nonissue) in 51 American communities.[77] The simplest hypothesis suggests that pollution-
control policy reflects a serious need for the policy, as measured by
the dirtiness of the air. It was true that there was a positive relationship between seriousness of the problem and the likelihood of antipollution activities, but the correlations were only modest. We must
consider factors other than the degree of need to explain why some
communities invoke pollution controls and others do not. Crenson
relies heavily on the concept of *nondecision* to explain pollution politics. Once the issue was raised and placed on the council's agenda, its
chances of passage were almost perfect. Thirty of the 50 health commissioners Crenson interviewed reported that antipollution ordinances had been introduced in their cities, and *not one ordinance was
defeated by council vote.* No local politician, presumably, wants to get
a reputation of being *for* pollution. If the pollution-control ordinance
is to be countered, the only way "is to prevent the issue from coming
up in the first place."[78] Opponents require a nondecision. Because
support for the pollution-control policy is diffuse and opposition is
concentrated in industrial corporations, it is sometimes easy for proponents to be deterred by the power they see in the corporations. In
such cases, the *reputation for power* may be effective in deterring proponents of control, even if the power is never exercised. Whatever the
particulars of local pollution politics, however, it is almost always elite
politics. The issue rarely energizes the masses, as school busing,
fluoridation, or taxes sometimes do. The battle is usually fought by
a limited number of protagonists, with the principal supporters of
air-pollution control being the city bureaucracies and its principal
opponents being the corporations. Citizens, for the most part, are
bystanders.

Pollution Policy and Its Impact

The most significant constraint on public officials who deal with the
pollution problem is that, quite literally, pollution cannot be eliminated. At best, public policy can only reduce the most serious forms of
pollution and then select among several alternatives for distributing
the remainder among land, water, and air. The dominance of a market
economy with weak central direction means that most decisions about
pollution are often really nondecisions, the product of accumulated
individual decisions of families and firms. As with many urban policies, much of the original impetus for pollution control came from
supralocal sources, particularly from a few states and the federal gov-

ernment. California passed the first air-pollution-control law in 1947, but even as recently as 1961 only 17 states spent as much as $5000 annually to fight air pollution. The more significant initiatives have come from the federal government.

During the 1960s and 1970s, Congress passed a series of policies intended to minimize environmental despoilation of the air and water. The Department of Transportation, for example, was charged with the responsibility for requiring antipollution devices on automobiles. The Clean Air Act of 1970, which contained these instructions, also required the Environmental Protection Administration to develop and enforce "ambient air quality" standards in various areas. In 37 especially severely polluted areas, the EPA was granted broad discretion to implement policies to reduce pollution. The implementation of the Clean Air Act has been a complicated case of politics in policy implementation, discretion, and delegation. At one point the EPA was developing policies that would have required the city of Boston to reduce parking spaces in the downtown area by one-fourth, hoping to cut commuting and reduce pollution. Boston's political leaders complained, however, that the externalities — reduced shopping in downtown, deteriorating tax base resulting from fewer dollars being spent, and fewer jobs from fewer dollars — would overwhelm the benefits of the program.

The Water Pollution Control Act of 1972 included similar efforts to reduce water pollution. Municipal, industrial, and other polluters were required to secure permits for discharging waste products into rivers and lakes. The Environmental Protection Administration was charged with developing water-quality guidelines and bringing states, cities, and private sources into compliance with those guidelines within fixed time periods. To help municipalities meet the costs of developing their own systems of water and sewerage treatment, legislation authorized $18 billion in assistance to cities striving to meet EPA requirements. It was this appropriation that President Nixon "impounded" — meaning that he refused to spend the money even though it had been officially "spent" by Congress — and thereby provoked a major confrontation between the legislative and executive branches of government.

Assessing the policy impact of antipollution policies is made difficult by the inadequacies of data collected over time. Data were largely nonexistent before the 1960s and much of that was not very sophisticated. Moreover, few of the pollution-control programs have been fully implemented. Water-control legislation has never been fully funded, and delays in developing standards have been commonplace. It is difficult to estimate the impacts of a program until it is implemented and operational. Nonetheless, there is considerable evidence to suggest that air and water quality have improved and reasonable grounds for tracing some of these improvements to the legislation itself. In Los Angeles, for example, 3.7 million cars in 1966 produced 10,485 tons per day of carbon monoxide. By 1975, 4.5 million cars produced only half as much carbon monoxide. Efforts to reduce pollution around the Great Lakes have slowed, if not reversed, the eutrophication of Lake Erie.[79]

Exploitation: The City and Scarcity

"City air," it has been said, "is free air." Yet air is about the only free resource needed for urban existence. The average urbanite consumes daily an estimated 46 pounds of coal, 9.5 gallons of oil products, 7 gallons of natural gas, and .5 pints of nuclear energy.[80] Energy consumption dipped slightly in the aftermath of the Arab oil embargo of 1974 but returned to its pre-embargo level by 1976. Consumption of energy has increased more rapidly than the population has increased. There is good reason to believe that many resources are finite and that practical limits of their availability will be shortly discovered. Coal is the single resource that the United States possesses in great abundance; our supplies of other resources such as oil, iron, copper, tungsten, and natural gas are diminishing or nonexistent.[81] Our one generously endowed resource, however, produces soot-blackened cities and very high levels of atmospheric pollution, as well as health hazards for miners. Coal also is increasingly strip-mined, which poses hazards for land and ecological systems.

Land itself is a resource that many people ignore. A very large quantity of land is converted each year from rural to urban uses, including much of the nation's best crop land. In introducing legislation for a national land-use policy, Senator Henry Jackson noted that 18 million acres of land will be required for urban growth over the next 30 years. Each decade urban growth will absorb an area as large as New Jersey. Each land-use choice will be preferred by some and opposed by others. An acre zoned for commercial use will not be used for residential purposes; an acre zoned for two single-family dwelling units will not do much to foster exit from central-city problems. Land, in other words, is a scarce resource, and political conflicts are provoked by scarcity.

Cities are almost the hapless victims of resource scarcity, dependent almost entirely on the federal government, private corporations, and (more and more) foreign powers to provide their resource needs. Obviously city populations have at their doorsteps few natural resources and city governments have no natural-resource policies besides hope. The emergence of a society of scarcity, however, may have more impact on the city of the future than any policy it pursues for itself.

Some Tradeoffs and
the Future of the City

In no area of public policy are costs, benefits, spillover effects, and tradeoffs so complex as in the energy-environment domain. Issues as basic as whether society should encourage or discourage population and economic growth have become entangled in the pollution problem. Tradeoffs and spillover effects pose painfully difficult choices for decision makers. In an effort to reduce pollution levels, it is sometimes necessary to increase resource exploitation. One example concerns federal air-pollution regulations, which require emission-control devices on automobiles. Such devices, however, increase gasoline consumption (1973 cars used 20 percent more gasoline than cars built prior to the regulations) and thus hasten exploitation of petroleum reserves. Sometimes tradeoffs must be made between different types of pollution. The banning of garbage burning reduces air pollution, but it increases the need for refuse dumps and aggravates land pollution.

The biggest tradeoff of all may be that between economic growth and policies to end despoilation and exploitation. Growth has brought affluence, but it has diminished the supply of resources needed to support more growth. Growth has brought enhanced opportunities to those at the bottom of the economic ladder, but it has also brought environmental despoilation to all. Some have advocated a "steady-state economy," where both population and economic growth goals are set at zero.[82] In a sense, some American cities have already arrived at a "steady state." The vast majority of older, industrialized central cities have now advanced into a "post-steady-state" economy, declining in population and economic resources. Few urban officials there would be persuaded that this is a desirable circumstance. But the "steady-state" argument does not envision the twin frontiers of decay and growth. Rather, it stresses a single frontier of stability. Cities adjusting to a genuine stable economy could expect no increases in tax base, jobs, or population—but no decreases either. At a minimum it would signal changes in policy responses to growth issues. If our argument that urban politics is often fought at the frontiers of growth and decay is correct, then an era of "steady-state" living would profoundly alter urban political patterns.

CONCLUSIONS

Much has been said in this chapter about the two urban frontiers, those of *growth* and of *deterioration*. Few policy issues touch on so many elements of urban life, including tax base, housing and residential patterns, land use, zoning, and other related problems. Urban politics is, to a large degree, concerned with manipulating growth and containing decay. Both private-sector choices and the policies of federal and state governments have constrained the policy options available to city governments. Private decisions made by banks, developers, realtors, businesses, and individual households combine with scores of federal urban policies to reshape the urban landscape. The most important policy tools available to local governments are planning and zoning. Through the careful drawing of zoning requirements, newer communities can have a major impact on their economic, social, and even racial composition.

Key federal policies contributed to the peripheralization of metropolitan areas. FHA and VA loan guarantees opened housing opportunities in the suburbs to new middle-class families. Public housing, on the other hand, was available to some of those left behind. Tensions between public housing and FHA housing illustrate the paradox of federal urban policy in shaping growth.

Increasingly, though, cities will face another tension, that between exploitation and despoilation of their natural environments. Growth, once a universally valued goal, has been more disputed in recent years. Part of the reason is that growth does not come free. Rather, it may impose high costs on the community by exploiting and despoiling nature's bounty. Exploitation may have been needed for more growth, but it reduces resources and exacerbates despoilation in the forms of air, land, and water pollution. Perhaps American cities are moving closer to "steady-state" economies. If so, conflict over scarce resources may not diminish; but it may take new forms.

Notes

1. The Weston story is told by Theodore Lowi et al., *Poliscide* (New York: Macmillan, 1976).
2. Anthony Downs, *Urban Problems and Prospects,* 2nd ed. (Chicago: Rand McNally, 1976), p. 11.
3. Edward C. Banfield, *The Unheavenly City Revisited* (Boston: Little, Brown, 1974), p. 25.
4. For a useful treatment of location choice as a critical variable in urban politics, see Oliver P. Williams, *Metropolitan Political Analysis* (New York: Free Press, 1971).
5. Harvey Molotch, "The City as a Growth Machine," *American Journal of Sociology, 82* (1976), 309–332. See also Richard P. Appelbaum, "City Size and Urban Life: An Inquiry into Some Consequences of Growth in American Cities," *Urban Affairs Quarterly, 12* (December 1976), 139–170, and the references cited therein.
6. George Sternlieb et al., *Housing Development and Municipal Costs* (New Brunswick, N.J.: Rutgers University Center for Urban Policy Research, n.d.), p. 34.

7. Molotch, op. cit., 320–325.

8. Banfield, op. cit., is an articulate proponent of this view.

9. Organization of the planning office under the chief executive or an independent commission seems to have little effect, however, on its political power. See Francine Rabinovitz, *City Politics and Planning* (New York: Atherton, 1969).

10. David C. Ranney, *Planning and Politics in the Metropolis* (Columbus: Merrill, 1969), p. 20.

11. Ebenezer Howard, *Garden Cities of Tomorrow* (Cambridge, Mass.: MIT Press, 1965; first published as *Tomorrow* in 1898).

12. Alan Altshuler, *The City Planning Process* (Ithaca, N.Y.: Cornell University Press, 1965), p. 315.

13. Ranney, pp. 28–35.

14. Oliver P. Williams et al., *Suburban Differences and Metropolitan Policies* (Philadelphia: University of Pennsylvania Press, 1965), pp. 91 ff.

15. Alan K. Campbell and Seymour Sacks, "The Fiscal Zoning Game," *Municipal Finance, 65* (1964), 140–149.

16. *Shelley v. Kraemer,* 334 U.S. 24 (1948).

17. *The New York Times,* May 29, 1967, p. 13.

18. Robert C. Wood, *1400 Governments* (Cambridge, Mass.: Harvard University Press, 1961), p. 79.

19. Anthony Downs, *Opening Up the Suburbs* (New Haven, Conn.: Yale University Press, 1973), p. 166.

20. Advisory Commission on Intergovernmental Relations, *Metropolitan Fiscal Disparities* (Washington, D.C.: Government Printing Office, 1967), p. 44.

21. Wood, op. cit., p. 85.

22. On the political issues and strategies in exclusionary zoning, see Daniel R. Mandelker, *The Zoning Dilemma: A Legal Strategy for Urban Change* (Indianapolis, Ind.: Bobbs-Merrill, 1971); Leonard Rubinovitz, "A Question of Choice: Access of the Poor and the Black to Suburban Housing," in Louis H. Masotti and Jeffrey Hadden, eds., *The Urbanization of the Suburbs* (Beverly Hills, Calif.: Sage, 1973), chap. 13; Michael N. Danielson, "The Politics of Exclusionary Zoning In Suburbs," *Political Science Quarterly, 91* (Spring 1976), 1–18; and Downs, *Opening Up the Suburbs,* op. cit.

23. Calvin P. Bradford and Leonard S. Rubinovitz, "The Urban–Suburban Investment–Disinvestment Process: Consequences for Older Neighborhoods," *Annals, 422* (November 1975), 77–86.

24. If there is one proposition about the city on which almost every piece of social science research on the city is agreed, it is that property values in transitional neighborhoods dip slightly during a period of "panic selling," then return to their previous levels of growth. See, for example, Luigi Laurenti, *Property Values and Race* (Berkeley: University of California Press, 1960); and Donald Phares, "Racial Change and Housing Values," *Social Science Quarterly, 52* (December 1971), 560–573.

25. Bradford and Rubinovitz, op. cit., p. 84.

26. Charles M. Christian and Sari Bennett, "Industrial Relocations from the Black Community of Chicago," in Michael R. Greenberg, ed., *Readings in Urban Economics and Spatial Patterns* (New Brunswick, N.J.: Rutgers University Center for Urban Policy Research, 1974), chap. 9.

27. *New York Times,* 27 April 1975, p. 4E.
28. *New York Times,* 11 May 1975, p. 9E. For a contrary argument, see B. Bruce-Briggs, "The Cost of Housing," *The Public Interest, 32* (Summer 1973), 34–42.
29. Arthur P. Solomon, *Housing and the Urban Poor* (Cambridge, Mass.: M.I.T. Press, 1974).
30. *New York Times,* 11 May 1975, p. 31.
31. Irving H. Welfeld, *America's Housing Problem* (Washington: American Enterprise Institute for Public Policy Research, 1973).
32. See the sources cited in note 24.
33. Karl E. Taueber, "Racial Segregation: The Persisting Dilemma," *Annals, 422* (Novenber 1975), 87–96.
34. Martin Anderson has argued that "there is not a physical shortage of decent housing units. The real problem is that there is a certain group of people who either cannot or will not spend enough money to rent or buy this housing." Martin Anderson, *The Federal Bulldozer* (Cambridge, Mass.: M.I.T. Press, 1964), p. 200.
35. Lawrence M. Friedman, *Government and Slum Housing* (Skokie, Ill.: Rand McNally, 1968), pp. 22–23.
36. Eminent domain is the power of government to take possession of property for public purposes, paying just compensation to the owner. There was little doubt of the constitutionality of slum clearance in its earlier form, in which property was taken and *retained* by local housing authorities. The constitutionality of the 1949 Title I provisions, which permitted local authorities to use eminent domain to obtain land and then *sell it to private developers* was a more serious question. The Supreme Court, however, upheld Title I in *Berman v. Parker,* 348 U.S. 26 (1954).
37. Gary Orfield, "Federal Policy, Local Power, and Metropolitan Segregation," *Political Science Quarterly, 89* (Winter 1974–1975), 786.
38. For an analysis of group politics and public housing, see Leonard Freedman, *Public Housing* (New York: Holt, Rinehart and Winston, 1969), chap. 2.
39. Quoted in Jewell Bellush and Murray Hausknecht, "Urban Renewal: A Historical Overview," in Bellush and Hausknecht, eds., *Urban Renewal: People, Politics and Planning* (Garden City, N.Y.: Doubleday, 1967), p. 9.
40. James S. Fuerst, "Class, Family and Housing," *Society, 12* (November–December 1974), 48.
41. Lee Rainwater, *Behind Ghetto Walls: Black Family Life in a Federal Slum* (Chicago: Aldine, 1970), p. 1.
42. A brief review of federal housing programs is found in Roger Allbrandt, "Governmentally Assisted Housing: Institutions and Incentives," in Elinor Ostrom, ed., *The Delivery of Urban Services* (Beverly Hills, Calif.: Sage, 1976), pp. 17–21.
43. Ibid., p. 15.
44. Downs, *Urban Problems and Prospects,* p. 104.
45. James Q. Wilson, The War on Cities," in Robert Goldwin, ed., *A Nation of Cities* (Skokie, Ill.: Rand McNally, 1966), p. 19.
46. On urban renewal, see James Q. Wilson, ed., *Urban Renewal* (Cambridge, Mass.: M.I.T. Press, 1966); Bellush and Hausknecht, op. cit., Anderson, op.

cit.; and Richard Bingham, *Public Housing and Urban Renewal* (New York: Praeger, 1976).

47. Stanley Rothenberg, *Economic Evaluation of Urban Renewal* (Washington, D.C.: Brookings, 1967); and John C. Weicher, *Urban Renewal: National Program for Local Problems* (Washington, D.C.: American Enterprise Institute, 1972).

48. *HUD Statistical Yearbook 1971,* p. 55.

49. Anderson, chap. 10.

50. See the critique of Anderson's book in Robert Groberg, "Urban Renewal Realistically Appraised," *Law and Contemporary Problems, 30* (Winter 1965), 212–229.

51. Harold Kaplan, *Urban Renewal Politics* (New York: Columbia University Press, 1963), p. 24.

52. Ibid., p. 15.

53. James C. Davies, *Neighborhood Groups and Urban Renewal* (New York: Columbia University Press, 1966), p. 15.

54. Kaplan, op. cit., p. 16.

55. Weicher, op. cit., p. 6.

56. Charles Abrams, *The City Is the Frontier* (New York: Harper & Row, 1965), chap. 9.

57. The quotation is from a letter sent on 25 October 1961 to residents of a Boston Area slated for renewal cited in Anderson, p. 1.

58. Cited in Advisory Commission on Intergovernmental Relations, *Metropolitan America* (Washington, D.C.: Government Printing Office, 1966), p. 57.

59. One widely quoted study is Chester Hartman, "The Housing of Relocated Families," *Journal of the American Institute of Planners, 30* (November 1964), 266–286.

60. Weicher, p. 47.

61. Basil G. Zimmer, "The Small Businessman and Relocation," in Wilson, ed., *Urban Renewal,* p. 382.

62. Cited in Advisory Commission on Intergovernmental Relations, *Metropolitan America,* p. 69.

63. Marc Fried, "Grieving for a Lost Home," in Leonard J. Duhl, ed., *The Urban Condition* (New York: Basic Books, 1965), p. 151.

64. For a useful summary of this and related evidence, see Carl E. Van Horn, "Decentralized Policy Delivery," a paper presented at the Workshop on Policy Analysis in State and Local Government, SUNY—Stony Brook, May 22–24: 1977.

65. Zbigniew Brzezinski, "The Politics of Zero Growth," *Newsweek, 27* March 1972, p. 54.

66. Banfield, op. cit.

67. *Chicago Tribune,* 1 December 1975, sec. 2, p. 4.

68. Percival Goodman, "Prologue," *Georgetown Law Journal, 58* (March–May 1970), p. 671.

69. Donella H. Meadows et al., *The Limits to Growth* (New York: Universe Books, 1971). See, for a critique of *Limits,* H. S. D. Cole et al., *Models of Doom: A Critique of the Limits to Growth* (New York: Universe Books, 1973).

70. Allen V. Kneese, Robert O. Ayres, and Ralph d'Arge, *Economics and the En-*

vironment: A Materials Balance Approach (Baltimore: Johns Hopkins University Press, 1971).

71. Roger Revelle, "Pollution and Cities," in James Q. Wilson, ed., *The Metropolitan Enigma* (Washington, D.C.: U.S. Chamber of Commerce, 1967), p. 84.

72. Council on Municipal Performance, *City Air* (New York: Council on Municipal Performance, 1974, vol. 1, no. 5), p. 12.

73. Ibid., p. 22.

74. Jorgen Randers and Dennis Meadows, "The Dynamics of Solid Waste Generation," in Dennis L. Meadows and Donella H. Meadows, eds., *Toward a Global Equilibrium: Collected Papers* (Cambridge, Mass.: Wright Allen, 1973), pp. 167–168.

75. Revelle, op. cit., p. 103.

76. For some survey evidence on public support for environmental policies, see William Watts and Lloyd A. Free, *The State of the Nation* (New York: Universe Books, 1972), pp. 147–154; Frederick H. Buttel and William L. Flynn, "Economic Growth vs. the Environment: Survey Evidence," *Social Science Quarterly,* 57 (September 1976), 410–420.

77. Matthew A. Crenson, *The Un-Politics of Air Pollution* (Baltimore: Johns Hopkins University Press, 1971).

78. Ibid., p. 90.

79. A most valuable source of estimates on policy impact is the annual report of the Council of Environmental Quality, (Washington: Government Printing Office).

80. *Newsweek,* 22 January 1973, p. 54.

81. On resources and energy, see Ford Foundation Energy Project, *A Time to Choose* (Cambridge, Mass.: Ballinger, 1974); Preston Cloud, "Mineral Resources in Fact and Fancy," in Herman E. Daly, ed., *Toward a Steady State Economy* (San Francisco: Freeman, 1973), pp. 51–75; and Meadows et al., *Limits to Growth.*

82. See Daly, op. cit.

PART FIVE
Epilogue

15
CITIES,
POLITICS,
AND POLICY:
AN OVERVIEW

15
CITIES, POLITICS, AND POLICY: AN OVERVIEW

We have tried in this book to show the relationship among three vital links: *urban politics, urban policy,* and *quality of urban life.* Politics is intrinsically interesting to many people (certainly to political scientists), but we have not assumed that politics is important for its own sake. Rather, we have argued that political conflict and political power produce policy choices. We then explored urban politics and policy to show their impacts on the quality of urban life. While Americans might not agree on what factors contribute positively to quality of life, there is near-universal agreement that some things — crime, deterioration, pollution, high energy costs, inadequate schools and services — contribute negatively to life quality.

At a minimum, we hope that you will better be able to explore for yourself the policy issues of the local community. Urban issues surround us daily. Here are a few examples, culled from some recent headlines:

"City Laying Off 1200 Today" (*Detroit Free Press*)
"Public Employees' Union Fever Rising" (*Chicago Tribune*)
"Sunbelt Region Leads Nation in Growth of Population" (*New York Times*)
"Council Budget Study Focuses on Cop Hiring" (*Pittsburgh Press*)
"Property Taxes Soar in Nation" (*New York Times*)
"Many Municipalities Lag Behind the Nation in Economic Recovery: Flight of People, Business Hurts, Obsolete Plants, Bad Housing Are Factors" (*Wall Street Journal*)
"Metro Transit Bill Weighed" (*San Antonio Light*)
"Support Grows for Federal Aid to Cities" (*Chicago Tribune*)
"Price of a New House Goes Through the Roof" (*Chicago Tribune*)
"Blacks Gain an Edge in Boston Enrollment" (*New York Times*)
"Court Backs Firing of Policeman" (*Omaha World-Herald*)
"6 Mississippi Cities Sued by Blacks: Impounding U.S. Aid Asked Pending Equality of Services" (*New York Times*)
"City Finances Tough All Over, Mayors Say" (*Chicago Tribune*)
"Study Dispels Popular Myths About Mass Transportation" (*Oklahoma City Times*)

All of these news items touch on issues that we have addressed in this book. Virtually every domestic problem finds expression in the concerns of urban policy makers. Sharp increases in crime were felt first on the streets of the central city, then more recently in the suburbs. The frontier of racial conflict moved from southern counties to the school-bus routes of northern cities. Problems of inflation in the cost of housing, rising mortgage rates, and changing life styles discouraged the construction of single-family suburban homes and turned the attention of city planners to burgeoning apartment complexes. Issues of educational quality and tax equity came together in concerns about the character of central-city and suburban schools and the equality of school tax burdens from one community to the next in metropolitan areas. Even agricultural policy has an urban component. Although agricultural policy is often felt to be primarily a interest of rural areas, urban-centered social critics are concerned with the quality and cost of the food on supermarket shelves, as well as the importance of food stamps in the calculations of urban welfare offices.

No one concerned with the quality of life in the United States or any other country can ignore the cities. Ours has been an urban nation since early in this century. Increasingly the world is an urban world. Not only does the majority of people live in or around large cities, but the cities also hold the centers of industry, commerce, and finance that make up the nuclei of modern economies. Urban policy makers must consider both the needs of their populations and the impact of social policies on the institutions that fuel urban economies. The mix of social and economic policies is especially close in the case of regulatory measures designed to improve the quality of urban life: via programs to maintain or upgrade the character of air and water; to assure various groups equal opportunities to obtain jobs, housing, or credit; or to help consumers get a fair deal from the purveyors of goods and services.

Urban policy making reflects not only the demands from social and economic interests but also the nature of political institutions. In the United States the location of jurisdictional boundaries between states, municipalities, counties, school districts, and special districts make their own contribution to the problems of policy makers. Metropolitan fragmentation produces policy fragmentation. Administrative coordination across governmental borders is a major problem in urban areas. The financial aids of state and federal governments make important contributions to the coffers of local policy makers. However, they also add to the problems of coordinating numerous participants in each policy arena. The character of local institutions also leave their mark. Whether a community has a strong- or weak-mayor office or a professional city manager is likely to affect the procedures and outcomes of policy making. The personal traits of key figures among the mayor, manager, members of the council or department heads may also be important. The weights of federal, state, and local bureaucracies make themselves felt. Local bureaucracies, ready to use strikes to secure wage and working-condition improvements, have become a potent urban actor. And through it all, there are powerful incremental procedures that honor past decisions and bias policy makers against radical departures. Budget makers are reluctant to grant increases that do more than cover the costs of inflation, and policy makers in substantive fields are conscious of the traditions, commitments, and precedents that usually keep their programs of one year in line with their programs of the past. All told, the multiple institutions of urban policy making do permit changes but not easily.

SOME GRIM VIEWS

That some cities—perhaps all cities—face a gloomy future is argued by scores of urban commentators. Some attribute the key problems to an inexorable logic of demographic and economic movements, such as those described in Chapters 3 and 4. Suburbanization denudes the central city of its people and productive capacity, and the rise of the "sunbelt" aggravates problems in older, northern cities. Testifying before the House Committee on Banking, Currency, and Housing on 1 October 1976, Richard P. Nathan and Paul R. Dommel argued that *"the preponderance of infected core cities in the United States are in the Northeast Quadrant.* In fact, we are increasingly coming to the view that the problems of old, declining, and isolated core cities is *the* domestic problem of the United States." Nathan and Dommel stress, as we did in Chapter 2, a comparative perspective on the American city. They argue that "a comparison between the United States and other industrial nations supports the point. European cities are centers of cultural, social, and economic activity. America's infected core cities offer a bleak contrast."

Others see problems of cities as a direct function of their political, rather than their economic, structures. Douglas Yates argued that cities' problems are not those of an empty cupboard "where resources are limited, but those of a 'leaky seive,' where policies are poorly targeted to problems they were supposed to solve. The truth of the matter is that city governments had no idea how to attack their problems, but nevertheless launched policy initiatives on many fronts in the hopes that something would work."[1] Yet, as we have argued in this book (and will stress again later), well-motivated policy is no substitute for knowledge. Policies made in ignorance of their potential impacts may likely be policies with little impact.

Perhaps the grimmest view of cities' futures is that of William C. Baer, who unabashedly writes of the "death" of cities. However unpleasant to contemplate, Baer maintains, the fact is simply that some cities—and many neighborhoods within them—will simply die.[2] He suggests the battlefield analogy of "triage," where wounded soldiers are separated into three groups, those who can survive with little or no immediate attention, those who are hopeless and must be left to die, in order to devote time to those who can be saved by immediate attention. Devoting resources to the first two groups will only lessen the survivability of the third. These are disquieting policy options, which no policy maker is likely to advocate publicly. American politics is geographical politics, and cities, neighborhoods, and regions cannot be publicly written off. But the resources required for neighborhoods or cities to survive may be more than the nation is willing to pay.

THE URBAN CRISIS:
A BRIGHTER VIEW

Edward Banfield is one of the most vocal proponents of the view that things are not so bad as they seem. In fact, he finds them better than ever before:

The plain fact is that the overwhelming majority of city dwellers live more comfortably and conveniently than ever before. They have more and better housing, more and better schools, more and better transportation, and so on. By any conceivable measure of material welfare the present generation of urban Americans is, on the whole, better off than any other large group of people has ever been anywhere. What is more, there is every reason to expect that the general level of comfort and convenience will continue to rise at an even more rapid rate through the foreseeable future.[3]

In *The Unheavenly City Revisited*, Banfield has not disputed the existence of an urban crisis, but he has defined it in terms of frustrated expectations rather than of objective deprivation. According to him, the problems of poverty, ignorance, disease, poor housing, and crime affect "only a rather small minority of the whole urban population."[4] Moreover, some of the problems are necessary accompaniments of the attractions of urban society. Congestion will not go away as long as many people find great benefits in living close to many other people and the jobs and commercial and cultural opportunities that exist in urban areas. Traffic snarls will remain as long as people resist staggered employment hours.

Banfield has not denied the presence of segregation, inadequate housing , and poverty in urban areas, but he has claimed that conditions are better than in poor rural areas. The vast majority of inadequate housing exists *outside* large cities and metropolitan areas. Education levels are, to be sure, lower in central cities than in the suburbs, but they are lower in rural areas than in central cities. The urban police may be intemperate in their dealings with blacks and other ethnic minorities but not to the extent of rural southern sheriffs.

Banfield has found some of the alleged problems in urban areas grossly exaggerated. Population growth in low-income neighborhoods was greater in earlier decades of urban history because of immigration of the European poor, he has said. And to those who argue that vast numbers of poor blacks will overburden the cities' capacity for economic and social accommodation, he has replied that earler decades of peasant immigration placed larger numerical strains on urban political systems.

There are urban problems that do concern Banfield. One is the unprecedented concentration in cities of urban blacks whose psychological alienation from the dominant society may be far greater than suggested by indexes of material deprivation. Young, unemployed black males have especially bleak economic prospects, and, though their condition may be no worse economically — and may even be better — than that of their rural forebears, their concentration in urban ghettos provides the human masses that can explode and threaten our basic social fabric. Second, there is a gap between anticipated social and economic gains and the benefits actually achieved. As long as aspirations rise faster than do accomplishments, this gap will continue to widen; no matter how much social progress is achieved, the tinder for a social revolution will remain. Third, government programs that are unable to solve basic social and personal problems nevertheless sometimes help to increase aspirations and thus pave the way for increased frustrations:

To a large extent . . . our urban problems are like the mechanical rabbit at the racetrack, which is set to keep just ahead of the dogs no matter how fast they may run. Our performance is better and better, but because we set our standards and expectations to keep ahead of performance, the problems are never any nearer to solution. . . .

The effect of too-high standards cannot be to spur us on to reach the prescribed level of performance sooner than we otherwise would, for that level is by definition impossible of attainment. At the same time, these standards may cause us to adopt measures that are wasteful and injurious and, in the long run, to conclude from the inevitable failure of these measures that there is something fundamentally wrong with our society.[5]

There is merit in both the negative view of the urban situation and in Banfield's brighter assessment of it. Banfield seems right in his claim that things have never been better; yet he concedes that achievements have not caught up with aspirations and may even be falling farther behind. Social progress is not measured only by what is but also by what could be.

Any treatment of Banfield's discussion of the urban crisis must take into account his critics. Some of his fellow political scientists have called his work "racism," "fascism," and "primitive conservatism." One reviewer likened his book to Jonathan Swift's "A Modest Proposal," a satirical proposal that the Irish deal with their combined problems of hunger and birthrate by cannibalism. The titles of several reviews indicate the flavor of Banfield's reception in certain quarters: "Patent Racism," "Survival of the Fattest," "The City as Purgatory," and "Class, Race, and Reaction: A Trivial but Dangerous Analysis." For our purposes, the indications of sharp differences between Edward Banfield and his critics are not so much evidence as who is wise or evil, as much as they are signs of the bitter controversy over the nature of facts and analysis in the urban setting. They reveal that the urban crisis is as much intellectual as political or economic. It is no less a hurdle to determine what are the crises and their root causes than to design a series of action plans to improve the lives of urban residents.

Indeed, there is reason to believe that the conditions of cities today are infinitely better than a century ago. American cities a century ago resembled in important features the third-world cities that we described in Chapter 2. Rapid growth, industrialization, primitive services, and poorly-organized administrative systems all characterized the early American city. Charles R. Adrian and Ernest Griffith conducted a major study of American city government from 1775 to 1870 and emphasized that most of today's urban problems were even worse then.[6] Crime and riots were widespread and perhaps even more serious because police forces were virtually nonexistent. Pollution, which we think of as a major problem, was far more severe when there was little or no sewerage. Whole cities (such as Chicago) could be virtually destroyed by fire. The "good old days" were not much better than the present—and were possibly a lot worse.

A CRISIS OF IGNORANCE

In our view, urban policy making is beset as much by ignorance as by disagreement on goals and ends. Policies made with the best of intentions may not have maximum impacts. Scottish poet Robert Burns penned a famous line that "the best laid plans of mice and men aft gang aglee [often go awry]." Some of the reasons for this crisis of ignorance are related to our assumptions that governments can solve problems by putting resources to bear on them and expanding the bureaucracies to deal with them. Urban governments may end up trying to do everything but not doing anything very well. The federal government, we might hasten to add, has been a willing partner—perhaps the senior partner—in this enterprise.

Among the policy fields beset with controversy and imperfect information are those dealing with demands for economic growth amid emerging scarcity. Demands for growth may appear in plans for industrial development, construction of electricity-generating facilities, a new highway or rail line, or a residential subdivision. Demands for conservation may seek to preserve or enhance the quality of water or air; protect scenic beauty, wildlife, or open space from the onset of new development; or pursue health and safety standards in industrial workplaces and consumer goods. Scarcity means fewer resources to solve problems. Few policy debates about the urban economy are without proponents of growth arguing with those who would sacrifice growth for conservationist values.

Policy problems involving values of growth and conservation have both political and technical sides. Often it is hard to separate the two, insofar as predispositions on behalf of economic growth or environmental conservation may not be admitted openly, but be apparent only in the use of adjectives amidst seemingly technical matters. The technical issues are themselves likely to be blurred and require political choices when "scientific" analysis does not produce clear answers. Those issues that appear to be technical divide themselves into two categories: those dealing with hardware and software. Hardware problems include issues of mechanical feasibility: Can various facilities actually accomplish their designated tasks? This is likely to be a problem in innovative fields, such as ambitious efforts ro rid the air of industrial and automobile wastes. One sign of the problem was a series of advertisements from the American Electric Power Corporation, asserting that stack scrubbers required by the U.S. Environmental Protection Agency would not accomplish their tasks under actual field conditions within reasonable maintenance expenditures.

The hardware problems might be the simplest to solve, given time and money, unless, that is, a culture capable of inventing industrial processes that pollute cannot also produce inventions to protect the environment. Software problems are another matter. These include the problems of analysis to determine which projects should be pursued. The problems are similar if the primary thrust of a project is economic growth—with a secondary concern for conservation. The task in both cases is to identify the pluses and minuses of the proposals, expressed in benefits and costs, advantages and disadvantages.

The larger the project, the more difficult to identify all the primary and secondary effects. More difficult than mere identification—but essential if the ultimate decision is to be made with a full understanding of its implications—is the *measurement* of benefits and costs in comparable units of analysis, and the weighting of benefits and costs associated with each competing proposal. Books and articles on behalf of conservation or economic growth that have appeared in recent years have demonstrated the capacity of project initiators—and more so their critics—to identify an astounding range of calculations that ought to be made before a project should proceed. One study of an extensive pollution-control project along the Delaware River identified an impressive list of factors *not* taken into account by project officials, despite a four-year official analysis involving a sophisticated team with considerable staff assistance. The critics charged that the official analysis was dangerously oversimplified.[7]

It is not only the local bits of ignorance that get in the way of thoroughly informed policy making. What will or will not occur along a particular river front as a result of certain characteristics of water quality may be resolved with sufficient time and expertise. In a larger sense, however, urban policy makers must take into account global events extending into the future life spans of projects currently on their drawing boards. Questions about future availability and costs of petroleum or natural gas rest on political events occurring far from city hall; yet they are relevant to current planning for nuclear or non-nuclear generating stations. More local, but equally unknowable, changes may occur in the local acceptance of nuclear stations; these changes can only be estimated across the long lead times between planning and site selection and the actual startup of a nuclear-fueled generator.

Insofar as this book has described differences between urban policy making in the United States and elsewhere, it is appropriate to reckon with the even greater problems of forecasting and making policy choices in cities of poor countries. Not only do they face greater shortages of technical skills, but they must cope with an environment that offers greater prospects of radical change. The flood of rural migrants to the cities complicates both the tasks of physical planning and projecting the political climate. The orderly development of water and sewer lines, roads and mass transportation may not be able to wait for the unplanned spread of squatter settlements or for entrepreneurs willing to invest in commercial or industrial projects. If American planners have trouble foreseeing the tastes of citizens over the life span of a project, consider the difficulties of urban planners in poor countries, where a city's population grows much more rapidly and where there is a more likely prospect of radical change in the political order.

Urban governments the world over are short on information. Although civil engineering has progressed to remarkable levels, social engineering is still in its infancy and represents — to some — a disquieting idea in any case. Civil-engineering projects usually work: Bridges rarely collapse; highways seldom crumble. But we rarely know whether social engineering might have its intended impact. Numerous findings of weak correlations between spending levels and actual policy impact suggest the frustration of many policy goals. Comparative policy analysis helps to explain why some city governments outspend others, but it has yet to enlighten us on the actual impacts of public policies on the resources of communities and individuals. Moynihan observed of the war on poverty that "the government did not know what it was doing," and we suspect that this observation is equally applicable to other policy areas.[8] The lack of technical knowledge about policy supports the concerted search for the determinants of policy outputs. It also emphasizes the need for greater knowledge of such dimensions of the policy process as performance, use, distribution, and impact. The dearth of information both on human wants and needs and on the impacts of policy on them impedes responsible urban policy making. The blame for imperfect information must be shared alike by citizens, policy makers, and social scientists.

As academic social scientists, we concentrate on the need for more and better information. Yet the practicing policy maker cannot usually afford the luxury of reflection. The academic can decry the imperfect state of our knowledge, but the policy maker must face public pressures for action. Solutions to urban problems do not wait upon the final and tidy theories of the social scientist. Nevertheless, some academic techniques of policy analysis (both macro and micro) will aid the specific concerns of the policy maker. The perspectives of this book provide, we hope, a sense of realism about urban problems and about the range of permissible change.

TWO PROBLEMS COMPLICATING
ALL ANALYSES OF
URBAN FUTURES

Cities, some would say, face an uncertain future both here and abroad. We do not necessarily align ourselves with those pessimists who speak of urban triage and the death of cities. We have no crystal balls available to us, nor are we bold enough to make definitive assertions about the urban future. Yet there seem to be two rather settled components of any urban scenario. On the one hand, it is clear that American cities have become increasingly *dependent* on elements of the economic order essentially beyond their control. Ira Katznelson has aptly noted that "urban politics, in short, is a politics of dependency."[9] In a narrow sense, cities are simply more dependent on higher levels of government than before. They secure more and more resources from state- and federal-aid programs, and their policies are increasingly shaped by inputs from those other layers. But in a larger sense, cities have become dependent on demographic and economic forces largely beyond their own making. Recall from Chapter 2 how Columbus, Ohio, was deeply enmeshed in an international social and political economy. Columbus may be taken as symbolic of almost all American cities. The Arab oil embargo of 1973–1974 and the bitter winter of 1976–1977 reminded Americans of how dependent they are on events very much beyond their capacity to manipulate (what Arab sheiks do, how much natural gas nature laid down in the United States). The term *dependency* is typically used to characterize relationships between so-called "underdeveloped" countries and advanced countries. But it seems equally apt to describe the relationship between American cities and their larger environments. More dependency means less control over problems and policies. The best efforts by urban citizens and policy makers may result only in frustrations and weak policy impact. Dependent relations are boxed-in relations.

A second problem complicating all guesses about the future of the city is evidence of growing disenchantment with policy-making institutions. Surveys by Louis Harris and the University of Michigan's Survey Research Center both report declining confidence in major American institutions from the presidency to schools, from corporations to local governments, from medicine to unions. An erosion of confidence means, at the minimum, that decision makers must spend more time nurturing support for their policies. At the worst it means that people no longer accept government as legitimate and effective. Many of our arguments here have raised questions about the effectiveness of certain policies. We doubted, for example, that vast resources thrown at crime would do much to solve the problem of crime; we frankly suggested that the relationship between school resources and learning was weak. In a sense, therefore, this book has contributed to a weakening of the confidence in institutional effectiveness. Yet we are not particularly troubled by our stone throwing at urban institutions. In fact, an uncritical acceptance of institutional effectiveness is unlikely to yield changes in policies whose impact is more symbolic than real. If a large part of the urban crisis is a crisis of ignorance, there is no substitute for critical evaluation of institutional effectiveness.

A PERSONAL POSTCRIPT

Predictions are hazardous, especially about the urban future. We indicated earlier in this chapter some sharp disagreements about the quality of life in the urban *present*. Disagreements about the urban future are even more likely to reflect the crisis of ignorance. We take very seriously—though we do not fully accept—the views of those who talk of the death of cities and even suggest an urban triage. Several of the processes that we have described—particularly the changing political economy and political sociology of cities, the new interdependence and the rise of third-world urbanization, and the emergence of scarcity—lead us to think about the future as being radically different from the past. Our own experiences here and abroad persuade us that American cities face problems often more comparable with third-world cities than cities in industrialized nations. This is a paradox of American urban policy. Few other nations would find a popular magazine publishing an article about the "the worst (e.g., British, German, French) city."

Yet in deploring and decrying the state of the American city, we caution against perhaps the most commonplace error in all urban policy debates, the belief that government can do everything at once. Some urban problems represent major tradeoffs — that between exploitation and despoilation, for example — which pose externalities whatever choice is made. Scarcity of fiscal resources and of natural resources will mean that costs and benefits of various policies will have to be more carefully weighed in the future. The prevailing philosophy of "incrementalism" is not very compatible with an economy of scarcity. A policy approach is about choice taking. And choices are neither free nor easy.

We agree, however, with the economist Wilbur Thompson, who once observed that "no nation is so affluent that it can afford to throw away a major city."[10]

Notes

1. Douglas Yates, "The Future of Urban Government," New York Affairs, 2 (1976), 10.
2. William C. Baer, "On the Death of Cities," Public Interest, 45 (Fall 1976), 3–19.
3. Edward C. Banfield, The Unheavenly City Revisited (Boston: Little, Brown, 1974), pp. 1–2.
4. Ibid., p. 10.
5. Ibid., pp. 23–24.
6. New York Times, 5 December 1976, p. 38.
7. Bruce A. Ackerman et al., The Uncertain Search for Environmental Quality (New York: Free Press, 1974).
8. Daniel P. Moynihan, Maximum Feasible Misunderstanding (New York: Free Press, 1969), p. 170.
9. Ira Katznelson, "The Crisis of the Capitalist City: Urban Politics and Social Control," in Willis D. Hawley et al., Theoretical Perspectives on Urban Politics (Englewood Cliffs, N.J.: Prentice-Hall, Inc., 1976), p. 219.
10. Wilbur Thompson, A Preface to Urban Economics (Washington, D.C.: Resources for the Future, 1963), p. 10.

INDEX OF CITIES

GENERAL INDEX